PICK UP YOUR
PARROTS AND MONKEYS ...

PICK UP YOUR PARROTS AND MONKEYS

and fall in facing the boat

Captain J.W. (Penny) Pennington, MC, RA (Ret'd)

CASSELL

To the memory of the soldiers of the British Army,

past, present and future

God bless them all!

And may their country learn to love them.

And dedicated to

my dear wife, Enid,

the light of my life

for all that she endured during the writing

and without whom this book would never have been written.

Penny's story is based on fact and most of the impossible things actually happened. The events narrated are true although some liberties have been taken with the names and in describing the details, as one would expect of any old soldier. Likewise some dates may not have been remembered precisely.

Cassell
Wellington House, 125 Strand, London WC2R 0BB

Copyright © William Pennington 2003

First published 2003

Second impression September 2003

British Library Cataloguing-in-Publication Data
A catalogue record for this book is available from the British Library

ISBN 0-304-36564-5

Printed and bound in Great Britain by Clays Ltd, St Ives plc

CONTENTS

LIST OF ILLUSTRATIONS

All photographs are from the author's archive

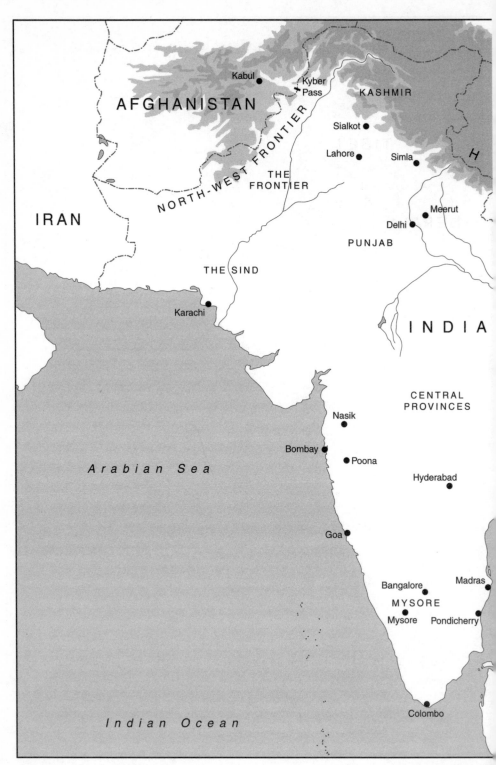

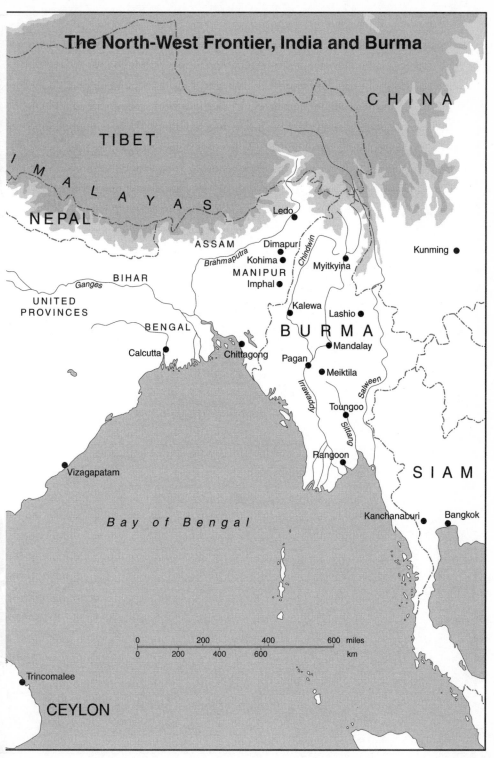

The North-West Frontier, India and Burma

CHINA

TIBET

HIMALAYAS

NEPAL

Ledo

ASSAM
Dimapur
Brahmaputra
Kohima
Chindwin
Myitkyina
Kunming

MANIPUR
Imphal

BIHAR
Ganges

Kalewa
Lashio

UNITED
PROVINCES

BENGAL

BURMA

Calcutta
Chittagong
Pagan
Mandalay

Meiktila

Irrawaddy
Salween

Toungoo

Sittang

Vizagapatam

Rangoon

SIAM

Bay of Bengal

Kanchanaburi
Bangkok

0		200		400		600 miles
0	200	400	600			km

Trincomalee

CEYLON

13

AUTHOR'S NOTE

It was the dream of every British soldier serving in India that he would soon return to England, his homeland. Posted to peacetime India before the Second World War, he could expect to remain there for a period of up to six years, without returning once to his beloved country, as the troops weren't permitted to return home, even if they had the money for their fare – which most of them didn't anyway. During those long years, the troopers would dream of escape from the filth, the decimating heat, the absence of white women, the loneliness and the perpetual uncertainty of life. They wondered if they'd still be alive tomorrow, or buried six feet under, because of the rampant diseases which spread across the land. The soldier's favourite comment was, 'Roll on the boat': he couldn't wait to shake the Indian dust from his feet and be rid of India.

Meanwhile the troopers had to amuse themselves as best they could, and to this end, almost everyone kept a pet – dog, mongoose, parrot, or monkey, for some a snake, or even a tarantula or a scorpion: any living thing which a man could call his own, and which would offer him companionship or entertainment. And it would be his constant companion; wherever he went, the pet went also. And this is the origin of that command: 'Pick up your parrots and monkeys and fall in facing the boat' – the boat being the troop-ship leaving Bombay, bound for old Blighty's shores.

And when the great day came and they tumbled out of the troop-train at Bombay, they would be almost frantic with excitement, waiting for the sergeant-major to cry (oh so loudly, for he too was sailing with them), '*PICK UP YOUR PARROTS AND MONKEYS AND FALL IN FACING THE BOAT!*' And, with a roar from the wildly uproarious troops, they would march up the gangplank and start the three-week voyage back to the land of their dreams.

You are now about to meet one of those British soldiers.

J.W. (Bill) Pennington
VICTORIA, B.C., CANADA, 2003

PREFACE

I had travelled halfway around the world to get here; now I was in the foothills of the Himalayas waiting at Dehra Dun for the train to Kalka, where the broad gauge ends and the mountain railway toy train leaves for Simla. Forty miles, negotiating gradients of one in thirty-three, through one hundred and three tunnels: it's a breathtaking journey, though the many twists and turns leave one likely to suffer from railway sickness. It had been a long, tedious trip from British Columbia to Tokyo, to Taipei, to Hong Kong, to Delhi, for I was no longer young, and fifty years had passed since I was first here. As I boarded the train, I looked back over all those years.

Travelling through the spectacular, unique scenery that is the mountains of Northern India, I arrived three hours later at the popular hill station of Simla and left the train. Strolling to the edge of the plateau I looked to the far distance and was rewarded with a breathtaking sight: to the immediate front and far below the verdant green of the picturesque lower valleys, through which snaked the most brilliant of crystal-clear rivers. Rolling beyond were the endless and ever-increasing mountain ranges, the icy giants in the eternal snows that finally merged into the white mass known as the Roof of the World.

Two hundred miles to the north-west of Simla rises Nanga Parbat at 26,600 feet; a hundred miles north-east of that soars the giant K2 (Godwin Austen), 28,250 feet. East of Simla by one hundred and twenty miles is Nanda Devi, its 25,600 feet making it almost a hill in comparison, and close to the Valley of Flowers – truly a sight to behold when in bloom – tailing away to the south-east, stands Dhaulagiri at 26,800 feet, one hundred and fifty miles short of Kathmandu. The climax of this magnificence is the giant 28,209-foot-high Kanchenjunga, which in turn is peaked by the tallest mountain in the world, Everest, 29,020 feet, in neighbouring Nepal. Strung like pearls as they parade across the vastness of more than fifteen hundred miles, they are punctuated by countless smaller mountains, each spectacular in its own right. I gazed out at the snow plumes, this infinitely arresting arena one of the most beautiful sights on earth.

SET IN THIS vista of solitude and peace and perched precariously eight thousand feet up on the hillside, Simla, with its population of ten thousand souls, had long been a favourite hill station for those who wished to escape the debilitating heat of the scorching plains of the Punjab in India. Such stations – of which there were many, stretching across the foothills of the Himalayan ranges – were a retreat to which the sahibs, the memsahibs and the children of the British Raj would eagerly flock for the summer sojourn. Here, in this paradise setting, they would spend a few short weeks free of the disease, flies, mosquitoes, noise and filth of the teeming Indian cities. It was another world from the furnace-like plains which sapped their energies, and which they had endured for many months. The land here teemed with wildlife, and in the skies flew birds of all description, even the rare and graceful giant eagle. Above all, Simla offered the relief so fervently sought from the confinement and the regimentation of the cantonment – indeed, it became the summer seat of the government, which moved there lock, stock and barrel from May to September.

Far to the south, Ootacamund and Wellington in the Nilgiri Hills – the 'blue mountains' – served the same purpose for the 'gora logs'[1] stationed in that steaming part of India. Not all the troops were fortunate enough to be able to join their families there for those precious summer months: the garrisoning of India required the meagre force of sixty thousand men to be spread as strategically and as widely as possible across the breadth of the land populated by three hundred million natives.

1 Lord. Britishers were usually addressed as 'gora logs' as a mark of respect.

IT HAD NOT changed in all those years; I knew I was home again. And as I stood there looking over the valley, there came the sudden sound of a bugle, its strident tones echoing clear across the hills and valleys. At first I thought it was my imagination, but then I saw, in the far distance, perhaps a mile away, the barracks on the hillside. The sweetest of music, it called for the mounting of the guard; amongst the greenness of the foliage I could see the brilliance of the red and gold colours and the snow-white Indian Army turbans as the men assembled in response, bayonets glinting in the sun. The words of the guard commander were faint; the men moved like robots to his orders and the bugle call. How many times in the past had I participated in just such a scene myself? But as I gazed down, I realized it was almost fifty years since I had last heard the magical sounds of the bustling Indian bazaars, walked amongst the thronging people, explored the jungles to the south, marched on the scorching plains along the Grand Trunk Road, or savoured the tranquillity of the cool mountain ranges of the north.

I had not thought about these things much over the past half-century, but that compelling sound of the bugle, as for so many men, triggered my journey down the memory lane of soldiering.

Had it really been so long? Although I did not feel that different, I had served in His Majesty's Royal Regiment of Artillery for many years. As I watched the blazing sun settling over the towering ice-caps, images came flooding back: the most vivid reminders of those halcyon, sometimes turbulent days of service with the British Raj, service which had carried me around the world in the execution of my duties. The green and mellow pastures of my native homeland were never far from my mind during those uncertain days of war and peace in far distant countries, when I endured extremes of both conditions and climate.

There had been the bitterly cold winter campaign with the British Expeditionary Force on the frontier of France and Belgium where, in 1939, the German Army had launched its devastating attack as part of its planned conquest of the world. That had culminated in the most humiliating defeat of the King's Armies, driven into the English Channel at Dunkirk. Their forlorn and tattered remnants were saved only by the Royal Navy and hundreds of civilian boats sailed by other stout-hearted Englishmen, who navigated their tiny craft – tugs, yachts, ferries and small vessels of all kinds – back and forth over the twenty miles of water to rescue the defeated boys. And boys we mainly were: teenagers, who braved the shelling, the gunfire, the bombing and the strafing by the German Air Force and the gunboats. Many of these courageous sailors gave their lives, but they saved a third of a million British soldiers to fight again.

In contrast there were the scorching plains and leaden skies of India, and a boredom that drove many men to an early grave, self-executed by a toe through the trigger-guard of a rifle. It was often a love/hate relationship with India, where death came quickly, but not always easily. Cholera and other deadly diseases struck like lightning, and you never knew when it would be you: alive and well before breakfast, dead and buried six feet under by supper, the saying went. And there was no leave home to England for the common soldier; he must serve in that country for perhaps six years, with only a week a year to spend in the hills, if he was lucky. The officers, on the other hand, got ten days' local leave and two months' privilege leave each year, when most did go home.

And then there were the steaming jungles of Burma, amongst the most pestilential in the world, where sickness and disease claimed more lives than their brutal and merciless enemy, the Japanese. Many were struck down, indiscriminately, and had to endure the ravages of this jungle warfare – recurrent malaria, dysentery and other jungle ailments – for the rest of their lives. The exotic cities of Mandalay and Rangoon were captured for ever in all their glamour by Rudyard Kipling, but those writings in no way represented the reality of such places to me and my comrades. The glorified verse of 'the paddles chunking from Rangoon to Mandalay' was anything but an experience to be enjoyed, and when the 'sun came up from China 'crost the bay,' it brought with it not the Chinese, but rather, the barbarian sons of Japan who murdered and pillaged their way throughout that fair land. It was of little consolation that Kipling was alive and well in India whilst I was serving there with the Raj: I never saw him – indeed, I had never even heard of the writer in those days.

Returning to England was the fervent wish of most British soldiers on the sub-continent: every man looked forward eagerly to hearing those magical words which would make it a reality: 'Pick up your parrots and monkeys and fall in facing the boat!' In his dreams, every man prayed that one day soon it would be him making that journey home, and it would start at the Gateway to India, the monument in Bombay, where a

Blighty-bound troop-ship would be awaiting. And when that day came, the troop-train steamed into the siding a mere hundred yards from the boat that loomed high above it; as the troops prepared to embark, they would become almost delirious with excitement, laughing and shouting to each other as they awaited those magical words. The solitary figure on the quay, standing there in all his might and glory, would be the sergeant-major, who was also relishing the moment when he shouted, almost screaming, 'Pick up your parrots and monkeys and fall in facing the boat!' Echoing his voice, the men would shout back at the top of their voices, 'Pick up your parrots and monkeys and get fell in facing the boat!'; the phrase could almost be heard the length and breadth of the country. For virtually every soldier in India kept a pet, a dog, snake or mongoose, or the most popular of all, a parrot or monkey. The moment had arrived and within weeks they would be reunited with family and friends, and all that they loved and cherished in dear old England – they could taste the beer already, beer such as they had never found in all those years in India.

That paradise was but a twenty-one-day sail away.

I RECALLED THE ugly, cold barracks of Aldershot and Woolwich; I had visited the latter after returning from Burma and it had not changed one iota. The wind still whistled and howled through its bleakness and the parade squares were, as usual, filled with awkward-looking recruits, and a sergeant-major instructor revealing what the future held for them unless they knuckled down and listened to his exhortations, which, he professed, would make them the finest soldiers in the world. And even in the most bitterly cold weather overcoats were rarely worn; if they were, the collars were never turned up, for that was untidy, unsoldierly, and smacked of weakness. That was a rule inviolate, so the parade was always dressed for the fairest of weather, regardless of reality. And though their uniforms hung like sacks from their backs, in time, the Quartermaster would tell them, even recruits as hopeless as they would fill them out properly. In time, even *they* would look like proper soldiers.

The main parade ground leading to the church looked as long as ever, and the impressive guard room where I had spent many nights on duty whilst training at the Boys' Depot was still very much in use. There was the duty bugler carrying the tea urns to the men on duty – everybody knows that the

British Army lives by tea alone – and the sentry who would march twenty paces in front of the building, all the time cursing the discomfort of the high jacket collar and the heavy boots which pinched him so excruciatingly.

Next to the guard room was that holy of holies, the Officers' Mess, an imposing structure appropriate for the officers, gentlemen in all their finery, who were above reproach in all that they did, and who sat on pedestals so high it hurt one's neck even to glimpse the busbies they wore. I had never before seen the interior of that grand building, but now the time had come, and it was with a moment's hesitation that I entered, walking through the archway that led to the sumptuous mess and lounges. This place was sacrosanct, quite inaccessible to Other Ranks, and even the most senior Warrant Officers entered only with the express permission of the Mess Secretary. But today I was no longer a common boy soldier, but rather, 'one of them' – for now I was a Captain of His Majesty's Royal Artillery, dressed as sartorially as any in my serge uniform and Sam Browne. As I entered a few eyes looked askance at me, an intruder, but this cool reception turned to a hearty welcome when they saw the Burma Star and Military Cross that I wore. 'Please join us, and what may we offer you to drink? A burrah peg[1] or a pink gin?' How the world had changed.

That visit to the barracks brought back so many memories, especially of the magic and pleasure of serving with the horses, no matter how much care and attention they had required. Though the horses were long gone, the atmosphere still seemed to smack of their presence.

IT HAD BEEN a full life, I thought, filled with victory and defeat, despair and elation, happiness, and downright misery at times. It was a life with no regrets, for I would willingly face it all again, especially if it could all be repeated once more at the King of England's expense – though perhaps with purse strings not quite so tight.

My purpose in visiting India this time was to revisit old haunts, to recall in greater detail some of my experiences there. I wanted to savour again the questionable delights of the cantonments and the bazaars, to see those stations on the plains where I had spent several years of my young life, to try my pidgin Urdu amongst the crowded hordes, and to renew my links with the Indian Army.

[1] A large whisky

Whilst in Delhi, I made a start with the latter ambition, having been invited to dinner in the palatial home of an Indian dignitary, where I had dined with the celebrities of the country and rubbed shoulders with senior officers of the military in a style that was once quite foreign to me. The setting oozed wealth and success; I was deeply honoured to be present. It had been a wonderful evening, attended by obsequious waiters – one waiter per guest – dressed in full regalia, including red turbans, white tunics, red sashes and gold shoes. At the end of the evening, my host invited me to take part in events on the morrow, kindly offering transport back to my hotel. As I left the mansion, I saw a Rolls Royce awaiting me, driven by two fierce-looking and long-bearded Sikhs who were garbed as resplendently as the waiters. Waving goodbye to my host and colleagues, I was whisked away in fine style to my hotel for the night: the YMCA. It was not in the most salubrious part of Delhi, but my room there cost a paltry one rupee a night. Neither the driver nor his companion made any comment, though I noted the incredulous look of the former in the rear-view mirror, and when I alighted at the YMCA to their bows, I detected a smile upon their faces. It was probably a first for a Rolls Royce to draw up to the front door of that poor but popular establishment, and most of the guests came out to see who this important person could be.

It was a promising start, and now the way lay open to explore my fancies; and after India, perhaps Burma . . . to live that hell again?

MY MIND WENT back to the night of February 23, 1945.

The worst was yet to come, for we had now arrived at the western bank of the Irrawaddy. Codenamed *Extended Capital*, the idea was to destroy the Japanese Fifteenth Army in a vice. General Bill Slim proposed to trap the Fifteenth Army, isolating them from other Japanese forces further south. There would be four points of attack across the river, with the 19th Indian Division crossing at Singhu, some thirty miles north of Mandalay and storming the Japanese head-on. West of the city and thirty miles distant, the 2nd British Division would cross at Ngazun. About ten miles downstream, the 20th British Division would strike at Myinmu. Finally, a further seventy miles to the south-west, Nyaungu would be taken by the 7th Indian Division.

I had been seconded to the 2nd British Division to provide artillery support for the crossing, which was to take place on February 23. The company of infantry was poised ready for the assault; only the noises of the jungle were to be heard: the cries of animals and the screams of prey. The rumble of the rushing waters muffled any whispered orders. It was hoped that a silent crossing could be achieved against an unprepared enemy. I was to be in the first wave of the crossing.

Though there was an air of tension, there was also a great sense of determination pervading the atmosphere. There was little joking now; one infantryman vainly attempted to put on a show of bravado, quipping that the first pleasure he was looking forward to was deflowering any Japanese prisoners who were taken – or, as he bluntly put it, 'I'll have their knackers for garters and fill their stomachs with their own shit. And then I'll really get down to the fine points.'

But his platoon commander told him sharply, 'Keep your fucking mouth closed or I'll ruin your marriage prospects.' It was too much for joking.

The Padre, or Sky Pilot, as he was more affectionately called, was quietly making his rounds, stopping frequently as he met the groups of men clustered around their boats. 'Lads,' he said, 'we must say a little prayer. Will you join with me, for we shall need our Lord to be with us tonight, especially during the next few hours. We shall need Him to give us the courage and fortitude to meet our enemy, and to slay him for the inhuman beast that he is. We must pray that He will protect us and bring us safely to the end of the battle.' A silence fell, even amongst the most sceptical. The Padre had served with us for a long time and the men were accustomed to him breaking into their conversations to inject a little 'religious propaganda', as Smudger always said. But tonight, well, somehow it seemed a little different. It was quiet now and the cigarettes had long been extinguished, the rifles laid aside and the rasping sound of the bayonet sharpening stopped; the fidgeting ceased. The Padre continued, 'Visit, we beseech you, O Lord, this place and drive from it all the snares of the enemy. Let thy Holy angels dwell herein to preserve us evermore, through Jesus Christ our Lord. Amen. Please say after me. Yea, though I walk through the valley of the shadow of death, I will fear no evil; for Thou art with me: Thy rod and Thy staff shall comfort me . . .'

The reverent mood was broken by a voice from the rear, 'Cor blimey, the silly old bugger. Next thing we know he'll be telling us that in the midst of life we are in death, and that he's on his way to shuffty all these mansions the head man in the sky owns to prepare a place for us.'

There was good reason for us to feel apprehensive. We knew that not all of us would survive; but death had been our constant companion for a long time now, and most had a fatalistic attitude: there would be wounds and the blood would flow and, yes, many would be buried by the banks of the Irrawaddy – a place that would forever be a part of England – with nothing more than the bayonet and a rifle stuck in the ground to mark their graves. Meanwhile, the preparations for the assault continued.

The moon shone on the swirling waters of the Irrawaddy, illuminating the small boats of the passing Burmese which drifted along silently. The night was warm and peaceful, with a cooling breeze which carried their songs of love across the waters to the waiting troops; they appeared to know little of the impending battle. But their serenity was soon transformed as they got caught up in the maelstrom of machine-gun fire which changed that tranquillity into a nightmare. Their world was turned upside down.

And as the British soldiers waited on that northern bank, our thoughts were of far away England, home, and our families and friends. And we were wondering how many more rivers we had to cross – for there was always one more; when, if ever, would it be the Thames, or the Mersey? At first light we would cross one of the most dangerous rivers in the world to attack the Japanese. Many knew it might be the last time they would see the sun rise, on this foreign and God-forsaken land.

In my role of Forward Observation Officer providing artillery support to the Worcester Regiment of the 2nd British Division, my two signallers and I were making last-minute preparations. We would be under surveillance by the Japanese the whole of the way across the water, without protection; it was to be a bloody journey, with the full moon illuminating the scene.

I was dressed like most of the men, in faded, ripped jungle-green battledress. My accoutrements were few, for I needed to travel light. Still, with the rifle which now felt like it was glued to my hands, binoculars, pistol and water-bottle at my waist, I carried enough. Looking across at the infantry huddled in small groups, I could see them caressing their rifles and testing their bayonet blades. They would bear the brunt of the fight when it came; now they were performing the age-old ritual as soldiers have always done, inspecting their weapons. There were Bren guns to strip and clean and grenades to load in pocket pouches. Knives had to be sharpened and weapons loaded. No flags would be carried, for now every man was the flag of the regiment. And the big guns, my guns, were half a mile away, anticipating my cry to fire. There was a wireless silence and it felt like they were very isolated, but they too were ready and waiting. There were no 'last letters' to loved ones being exchanged; that had all been done a long time ago.

It was unusually quiet now. I felt uneasy and wondered . . . It was to be a silent approach – we were praying for the element of surprise – and we were now ready to cross the river. At 02:00 hours the landing craft slipped from the shore beneath a partial moon low on the horizon, which did nothing to diminish the brightness of the Southern Cross.

The Irrawaddy was some two miles wide at that spot, with large sandbanks and shifting shoals, and flowing fast, five or six knots. We knew the Japanese were on the far shore, and they would now be alerted by the sound of the boat engines. All we could do was to hope for the best. The crossing was expected to take some twenty minutes, but during the night, completely unknown to us, the water levels had fallen dramatically: what was to have been a relatively easy crossing proved instead to be an extremely hazardous one, bordering on disaster. As the darkness slowly faded, dissolving the stars which hung like huge lanterns in the clear sky, there were now many more sandbanks visible, upon which several of the boats had foundered. Floating on the surface of the water were the bloated bodies of the Japanese who had died for their Emperor a few days ago several miles upstream, in the fight with the 19th Indian Division. And the smell was vile and overpowering.

A large number of our home-made bamboo boats were being towed, but the tow ropes of some broke and they started drifting helplessly, at the mercy of enemy machine-guns. Many of these were waterlogged, collapsing under the heavy weight they carried, and as they sank in the turgid water, the men could be seen floundering. The water was too deep to stand and the current too strong for a man to swim safely. Those unable to swim at all were the first to drown, and the others quickly fell to the vicious Japanese guns.

I was also under fire, like the rest of our boats. Rifle fire directed at the Japanese was ineffective, and all we could do was to watch in horror, and swear – and pray. I had to ignore the surrounding chaos and concentrate on getting to the far bank. Many of us were filled with despair as we struggled in the moonlit waters, knowing that failure was at hand. In our exposed position in the middle of the river, many of the Worcester infantrymen died, shot like sitting ducks.

I was in the leading wave of the assault, and we could do nothing for those so helplessly stranded. There had been no surprise and all our planned subterfuge had been wasted. Silhouetted under a clear full moon, all we could do was put our trust in God, knowing that the Japanese were waiting for us. And they were, and in full force. The shouts and cries for help from the injured huddled in the boats presented a target the Japanese machine-gunners could hardly miss.

Now it was my turn, and as we reached the shore, bullets ripped through both men and boat, which was rapidly taking on water. But the Japanese were not yet finished, a phosphorus grenade was hurled into our boat; as we scrambled ashore from the quickly sinking vessel, we feared the day was lost.

The sands of the beachhead were soft and difficult to traverse, and being totally exposed to enemy fire, that stretch of hell was soon littered with bodies. But we were too busy with our own problems to worry about that: in our mad rush to escape the burning boat and hail of fire, we had leapt into the slimy water as quickly as possible, but in our desperation to escape the hail of death, we'd left behind the wireless set, without which there was no contact with the guns, and without the guns the battle would be lost. Racing back with hearts in our mouths, we dodged the raking fire, then rushing madly into the water, which was alive with the bursts of bullets, we scrambled into the now drifting boat; though riddled with holes it had stayed afloat just long enough for us to rescue the wireless. Leaping again into the chest-deep water with the vital equipment, and then floundering our way along the sandy beach, we dashed madly back to the comparative safety of the elephant grass. Quickly we established contact with the guns on the northern bank of the river, singing out the gunners' cry: 'Troop target, HE 106, Right ranging—'.

ON BBC RADIO that evening, noting the current events of the war, Winston Churchill, the British Prime Minister, said, 'And today we crossed the Irrawaddy on a bamboo stick and a piece of string.'

chapter one

BLACKPOOL

1920 to 1934

I was born in 1920 in Salford, Lancashire where the cotton mills processed cotton imported from India and returned it as finished garments at a price still affordable to the natives, yet with huge profits for the mill owners. Part of the Greater Manchester area, Salford was typical of the towns and villages that had sprung up around those dark satanic mills during the industrial revolution. It was not a salubrious place in which to live and raise a family. The inhabitants often slaved twelve or more hours a day, seven days a week, in the most appalling working conditions. Those who were able to escape from the tyranny and oppression of the mill owners who ruled their lives did so knowing that any alternative they chose could never be worse than their present existence. My father, recently discharged from his service with the Lancashire Fusiliers after four years fighting the Germans in the Great War (1914–1918), had seen the wholesale slaughter of the battles that raged on the Somme, at Mons and in Delville Wood, where, in a single day, tens of thousands of men had died. He chose not to be one of those who remained.

So we moved to Blackpool on the Fylde coast of Lancashire, famous for its glorious beaches and the playground of millions. The weary and downtrodden mill workers flocked here; for a few days every year this magical place would release them briefly from their lives of misery and sordid living conditions. It was an exciting place for a boy to be raised. There were the pristine beaches where I could dig for cockles at the water's edge, or fish for crabs in the warm summer pools left by the receding tides.

The promenade spanned the seashore for five miles and was punctuated by the North, Central and South piers, which themselves provided endless entertainment with their slot machines, games and amusement arcades, and fishing from the jetties. And stretching from the Central Pier to the Windmill, which still stood though its days of grinding corn were long gone, was the Golden Mile, with its magical mixture of fun fairs, pubs, fish and chip shops, souvenirs, fortune tellers, ice cream, candy floss and all manner of sideshows. These, with the cabaret spots and exhibitions, provided continuous activity for the holidaymakers who descended there in hordes.

A mile or so to the south, and separated by the hotels which catered for the richer visitors, was the Pleasure Beach, known as the Coney Island of Britain, but magnified tenfold. It was the Mecca for all who aspired to endless fun and recreation. There was the Big Dipper, perhaps the tallest, fastest rollercoaster in the world, and not for the faint-hearted. The Indian Theatre revealed the mysteries of the East; there was the Haunted House for the not-so-easily-frightened, and palm readers promised romance, riches and travel to exotic lands.

The merry-go-round, echoing with the shrieks of children, the dodgem cars, the tunnel of love, where every boy took his special girl – or the cave of horror to frighten her into an illicit cuddle – the rifle range, the skittle and bowling alleys, Noah's Ark (the size of a large house, which rocked on its foundation): here were acres of fun-filled entertainment for all ages, a glorious escape from the harsher realities of life.

And everywhere there were restaurants, pubs, cocktail bars and the ubiquitous fish and chip shops, catering for all purses. For winelovers, Yates Wine Lodge was the place to go, so popular that sometimes you could hardly get in; as it was just across from Blackpool Town Hall, it wasn't rare to see the Councillors taking a break there from the rigours of local government.

The chatter of unpolished Lancashire voices rang out clearly; for the few who came from faraway places like London or the South of England, or from the distant Isle of Wight (quite twenty miles over the ocean!), it was indeed a foreign language: 'Eeh lad, whatsta doin with thisen! Don't thee give 'im owt. I've told thee afore, never do out for nowt, and if tha ever does owt for nowt, make sure tha does it for thisen!' Lancashire folk were then, and still are, the salt of the earth, a friendly people, hospitable and kind to one another and to all strangers. Most would give you the shirt off their back if your need was greater.

As many as sixty excursion trains a day arrived into the North Station alone at peak holiday times, and the Central Station was equally busy. In a city whose normal core population of fifty thousand swelled to tenfold that on August Bank Holiday, not everyone found accommodation to their liking; many ended up sleeping under the piers or on the beaches. Those with rooms to rent would advertise thus: 'Attractive and well located, a perfect gem of a place to enjoy your holiday. In the midst of fun and glamour, clean and spacious with extensive sea views.' But the hapless guest might find on arrival, when it was too late, that he had rented a pokey, wretched little room at the back of the gas works which had seen neither mop nor cleaning rag for a very long time. It was certainly located where all the action was, though, for a constant procession of heavy trucks going in and out of the gas works day and night, smelling dreadfully of diesel oil, made sure of that. And it was well situated at midnight when the pubs closed and the drunks went singing down the street. For the extensive sea views, you must walk two blocks to the other side of the gas tanks, when you might be in luck – always providing it was a clear day and not too obscured by the smoke of the never-ending trains passing by.

During the Summer Wakes weeks, the soft golden sands were covered with sunbathers, and so crowded that the jugs of tea sold by the beach stalls needed to be transported with the utmost care whilst negotiating the myriad bodies, beach-chairs and prams. The Punch and Judy shows were magnets to the children, who gathered around eagerly, creating further obstacles to free passage. Closer to the water were the donkey rides, and games of soccer, rounders and other sports. The kids, using Grandad's walking cane, would write messages in the compacted sand at the water's edge like: 'I Love You Grandad, can I have some ice cream, please' or 'Will you ride on a donkey with me, Grandad?' The crystal-clear water beckoned: the men rolling up their trouser legs were an incongruous sight; the more timid satisfied themselves by wading only to the depth of their ankles.

Every autumn, when most of Britain's other resorts had closed down, Blackpool became a blaze of coloured lights, 'The greatest free show on earth', aptly named the 'Illuminations'. Stretching five miles along the entire length of the promenade, it was like a fairyland: millions and millions of electric light bulbs festooned the effigies and ornaments created for the occasion. As well as the visual pleasure, the Blackpool Illuminations also provided diabolical fun for the mischievous, who competed for the greatest score in bursting the bulbs with their catapults. Every evening the crowds swarmed the entire length of the spectacle on foot or by coach, many eating their fish and chips wrapped in the *Blackpool Evening Gazette* – they always tasted better when eaten off a newspaper.

And above it all, dominating the skyline: the Blackpool Tower. Built in the eighteen-nineties, this landmark stood more than five hundred feet tall and when illuminated at night, it was a beacon that could be seen from far and wide. Within the magnificent edifice was the huge, almost legendary ballroom, the scene of many world championship competitions. There was the circus, too, and, for a half-penny, the magnificent big wheel standing a hundred feet high adjacent to the Tower would give you a perspective of the Fylde coast in several distorted views as it rolled you skywards.

In later years the Blackpool Tower became the symbol of my childhood dreams. Whenever I returned home, I would watch eagerly for that first glimpse of it from the train. Within a few minutes of steaming out of Preston, I would peer out of the window, and there it was, etched in the clear blue sky twenty miles away, as if pointing to say, 'Welcome home.'

I WAS A MEDIOCRE student and didn't enjoy school, and although my exam results made me eligible to go to grammar school, my parents elected to send me instead to Palatine Central School. About three miles from home, I cycled there every school day, rain or shine. If the bike was broken – and flat tyres were frequent – then I had to walk; there was no money for the luxury of a bus. Most lunch times I went to my Aunt Alice who lived quite near to the school, a kind and loving person who always made much of me, and for whom I had a deep affection.

I was in a gang: there were six of us, high-spirited, energetic ten-year-olds letting off steam – and getting up to a lot of mischief, just for the fun of it. My friends were the sort I'd expected would become paratroopers or commandoes during the Second World War. We weren't 'bad lots' really; we never ran into trouble with the police, though we sometimes came close to it, so we were always cautious in the company of coppers. To us, some of our escapades felt very wild; popping fireworks through letter boxes, breaking windows in unoccupied houses and, of course, shooting out the electric light bulbs of the Illuminations were sometimes downright dangerous.

Every year, as Bonfire Night approached, we would cart around our effigy of Guy Fawkes, the man reputed to have tried unsuccessfully to blow up the Houses of Parliament. We prepared for November 5 for weeks, gathering dead tree branches, old tyres, wood and cardboard: any debris that would make good fuel and assembling it in my back garden, ready for the big night. Aunt Alice brought the fireworks and provided the delicious home-made parkin, which we ate as the pinwheels, rockets, Roman candles, fire-crackers and other fireworks illuminated the night sky, as bright as the Illuminations. Potatoes were roasted in the embers of the bonfire, and devoured voraciously.

EMPLOYMENT IN Blackpool was erratic because of the seasonal nature of the economy. Crowded in the peak holiday season, deserted in the long winter months, it had the reputation of 'slavery in the summer, starvation in the winter'. Unemployment was very high during those dreary winter months, and well into the spring; not until April would there be any activity on the Pleasure Beach in preparation for the summer season. At the age of thirteen, I had to work part-time at a bakery, evenings and weekends: Dad wasn't working and we were running out of money. I didn't mind; it was a new experience making deliveries on the carrier bike supplied, but it was hard work, and left little time for homework, or play.

During the school holidays I also spent much of my time working, but now and then Dad would take me to the Bloomfield Road football ground to watch the big soccer games. We'd delight in the antics of the famous football star Stanley Matthews, dribbling the ball in rings around his opponents. Spectators came in droves, packed in buses from all over Lancashire; when the huge crowds gathered there raised their thousand or more voices in 'Land of Hope and Glory', in their broad and beautiful accents, it seemed to carry one away to another lofty world. Nearly all the football crowds wore coloured scarves and hats, or emblems appropriate to the team they supported. Although the rivalry was enormous and the competition fierce between the groups, it was always in good humour. There were rarely any fights; everyone seemed to enjoy themselves, and it was wonderful just to be there.

'OUR GRACIE', Gracie Fields, who was beloved by everyone, but especially Lancashire folk, came to Blackpool to make one of her films. I saw her ride past the Tower on her bicycle singing, 'On a bicycle made for two.' And she waved to me!

Those were happy days, but my future was bleak: my lack of higher education and the poverty of my family destined me to a life of manual labour and uncertainty. But fate intervened, and with welcomed consequences for me: I was not to stay in Blackpool much longer now.

IT WAS AN evil hand of fate that changed the people's lives: Germany had reached a ten year non-aggression pact with Poland and the Nazis were in charge of all the German state governments. SS leader Heinrich Himmler had taken control of the secret police and made it an independent organization within the Nazi Party. The middle of that year, 1934, had seen the purge of the 'night of the long knives', an attempt to break the power of the storm troopers, and seventy leading Nazis were executed. And Britain increased the size of the RAF.

Herr Adolf Hitler, the leader of the German Nazi Party, was the principal figure in the talk of war that was everywhere. Germany, contrary to international agreement, was rapidly building up its armed forces, which the majority of world leaders acknowledged cursorily with little more than a wag of the finger as a mark of disapproval.

And the large increase of German 'tourists' to Britain was not at first noted, not until someone realized that the age group of these visitors was substantially lower than usual: now they were younger men of military age, who seemed mostly interested in spending their time along the coastline of England and in the industrial areas, especially those of potential military interest, whilst making copious notes of what they saw. There was no bathing in the warm waters, or lying on the beach sunning themselves like normal tourists, nor were their cameras seen snapping the frolics of the beautiful girls on the yellow sands, in their skimpy swim suits, normally a prime target for young and carefree men. To the shrewd observer it was another indication that Germany was preparing for war and that Britain, like it or not, would not escape. The leaders of the country would have done well to have faced facts at that time.

chapter two

WOOLWICH: THE BOYS' DEPOT

May 1934 to September 1935

One bright Saturday morning in spring, my father took me to the Territorial Drill Hall and introduced me to the Recruiting Sergeant, who, almost immediately, gave me the King's Shilling – as a token of my country's gratitude – which left me rather shocked. My father had talked to me about an army life, but I didn't think we'd come to any conclusion. I had certainly never said outright that I was going to join the army; though I readily agreed that I'd been thinking about it, right enough, I would have preferred to have been the person who told the Recruiting Sergeant I wanted to join up. But the sergeant gave me a lecture, promoting the merits of a military calling to any young man and taking great care to point out that such a golden opportunity was offered to only the fortunate few, and eventually, I agreed. Without further delay, the attestation papers were drawn up and signed. It was May 1934.

The Drill Hall was just across the street from where I worked after school, evenings and weekends, as a delivery boy, my pittance supplementing the meagre family income. Now I had committed myself to the army, though, I was in a state of suppressed excitement. I was anxious to get started, but time passed slowly, as it always does when you are waiting for something to happen. It was September, four months later, that I received my letter of notification saying I had been selected for service, and that I could shortly expect to receive orders concerning my posting to Woolwich.

Though we all knew this was coming, the reality of my departure shocked my parents, and they started preparing for my new life with sadness, seeking comfort from friends and relations. The news spread quickly amongst my large, close-knit family, which had lived for generations in the northern part of Lancashire. Two hundred years before, our ancestor Sir Richard Pennington was the Squire of Lancaster Castle, well known for its torture chambers in the dungeons below. Since Richard's time, stories had abounded of the ghosts who walked the Castle ceaselessly in their futile search for those who had tortured them and put them to death. The bloodstains on the cement floor from the repeated executions by sword and by axe can still be seen. Nobody knows what became of Sir Richard, though – he may well have fallen victim to the highway robbers and other cut-throats who abounded at that time.

My Uncle Amos and Aunt Edith lived there now – not in the Castle, of course – with their only child, Connie. My uncle was the regional manager for the Co-op meat distributors and whenever I visited, I was treated like visiting royalty; I always came away with a very large box of chocolates, and never less than a five pound note slipped into my pocket. I had relatives in Wigan, too, who had a pastry shop; I never went home hungry from Cousin Helen's place either.

Cousin Nancy, and her mother Aunt Emily, lived in a railway house at Gowdall Gate, where they were responsible for the opening and closing of the gates when the trains passed through. Nancy was huge: she ate too much, and was built like an enormous pink jelly, wobbling every step of the way, but a nicer person you would never meet. She loved her fish and chips so much that she'd cycle miles to get them: the nearest chip shop was a good seven miles away. Nancy spent years working for the railway; she knew her job and had a good relationship with her 'customers', but when the red warning lights were flashing and the train was thundering down the track, she was blunt: 'Get off ta ruddy lines, tha damned fool! Tha can hear the train coming can't thee, or are tha deaf as well as gormless? If tha stands there with tha big mouth wide open like the idiot tha is, a train will come an' 'it thee.'

Many of those relations I couldn't get to see came to Blackpool to wish me well in my new career; I tried not to envy Cousin Henry, who turned up on a new motorcycle with a most attractive brunette riding pillion. Must be rich, I thought wistfully. Gathered around me, the older well-wishers gave

35

me plenty of heart-felt advice: 'Come back a General,' or, 'Don't let the bastards get thee down,' while my contemporaries were saying, 'Wish I were coming with you. Can I carry your kit-bag?' or 'Don't forget to save a place for me on the boat.'

I went back to my old school to say goodbye to my friends, those I had adventured with around my home in Kenilworth Gardens; they all looked at me with envious eyes when I told them I was going to London, and then to the end of the world, to see all those faraway places with strange-sounding names. I would be off in a few weeks' time, but I promised I would miss them all, and that I'd write. I told the girls, 'I'll send you rubies from Burma,' and the boys, 'Jade for your cufflinks from India,' but these forced light-hearted comments did little to stop the tears when I finally said goodbye at Blackpool Central Station.

DRESSED IN WELL-WORN and patched shorts with an open-necked shirt and jacket and carrying a small suitcase containing little more than a change of underwear, a tooth brush and several dog-eared copies of my favourite comics, I waved as the train slowly steamed away from the plat-form. My mother was a picture of sorrow, standing there waving a last goodbye; hanging out of the window, I had a final glimpse of my parents as they retreated into the distance. It was a sad parting, but I was glad: the great adventure had begun. I was just fourteen years old and now I was finally on my way at last, there was no sadness or remorse – that would come later, when I was overwhelmed with homesickness, far away from the life I had loved. But now a new chapter was opening, and as I sat alone in the train compartment eating the cheese and tomato sandwiches pre-pared by my mother, watching the familiar outskirts of my home town slide by as the train steamed along, I savoured the moment.

The first part of my journey was some twenty miles, and the sight of the unknown countryside added to my excitement. Already I felt different as I arrived at Preston Station. The weather was miserable, raining heavily, with a cold wind scooping up the tattered newspapers from the gutters: it was verging on a full-blown storm. It took several enquiries to find my way, but as I walked through the forbidding gates of the barracks in the garri-son town of Preston, I started a life which had changed little since the days of Rudyard Kipling.

Ever since I'd signed on the dotted line, I'd been dreaming of being a soldier, to march with the flag to the roll of the drums in far-flung corners of the British Empire, and to see it all at the King's expense, as the recruiting posters advertised. Now I was to do all that, and more. I was to taste the pomp and circumstance of the British Army in times of peace; the loneliness of soldiering in the Indian cantonments; serve with the British Expeditionary Force during the six months' phoney war on the French/Belgium border against the Germans, with our subsequent ignominious defeat by the Blitzkrieg, and our withdrawal to Dunkirk. I would learn the hard way what it was like to fight in the filth and horrors of battle against a ruthless Japanese enemy in the death-ridden, pestilential jungles of Burma, thousands of miles from home, part of a forgotten army, desperate for ammunition and supplies which lay on a dockside in Liverpool whilst the stevedores struck for more money. I would see little of my homeland for many years, because I would always be 'somewhere over there'. Today was the beginning.

THE TRANSFORMATION FROM civilian to soldier was abrupt as I arrived and was challenged by the sentry on duty. I was gripped with exhilaration, and perhaps an element of fear, as I entered the barrack gates and strode into my future. The sights and sounds of the British Army enveloped me instantly. Dominating the parade square were the grey barracks, so typically British Army that I would later recognize them as such wherever I went. There was the ring of steel-tipped boots marching in step, and the exasperated Drill Sergeant's raucous voice reverberating around the square, with his endless tirade of cajoling, pleading and threatening the squad's ineptitude: 'Smarten up, you lily-livered bunch of pansies. Get fell in jeldi[1] or I'll have your guts for garters! You might have broken your mother's heart, but you won't break mine! You're wandering around like a cloud of farts in a thunderstorm. On the double, Quick March! You, Gunner Rear, you 'orrible little man! Swing those bloody arms, you're in the British Army now, not the Girl Guides! Don't be frightened of opening your legs, you've got nothing between them so there's fuck-all to lose. By the time I've finished with you, you'll be sorry you were ever born! And they ask why England should tremble! Thank God we've got the Navy!' Harassed

1 Quickly

37

and exhausted, the men could only respond in mute obedience and pray that this too would soon pass away. It was hard to believe that this scruffy group of ruffians, still dressed in their ragged civilian clothes, would one day adorn some of the finest parade grounds in the world.

But there was no time to stand and gaze at these unfortunate recruits enduring the scathing wrath of the Drill Instructor. Abruptly returned to reality by the loud cry, 'You there, boy!' I realized that I too was on parade as I turned to face the corporal addressing me.

'What's your name, boy?'

'Pennington, sir. Joseph Pennington.'

'Stand to attention when you speak to me, lad! And don't bloody well call me sir. That's for the officers to be called, not the scum like us. Call me corporal!'

Meekly responding, 'Yes, corporal,' I stared in respect at the immaculate soldier confronting me, awaiting further commands.

'Tomorrow, Pennington, you are for the Boys' Depot in Woolwich. Right now go across to the mess on the other side of the square there and get yourself a set of eating irons. Have your supper and then go to the Quartermaster's Store to draw your bedding kit. And don't walk across the parade ground. Go around it, it's hallowed ground, not a bloody highway! You got that bloody lot?'

Feeling very subdued after my first tussle with military authority, I quickly found the mess hall where I ate, drew my bedding as ordered, and then returned to the barrack room. Though I was tired and went to bed early, I slept restlessly before being awakened by the call of the bugle. It was reveille, time for breakfast, and the beginning of a new day.

After the meal, I was given a travel warrant and then hurried back to the station to catch the seven o'clock train to London. I was still dressed as I was when I left home, and still carrying my tatty little suitcase. Arriving at the station and presenting the warrant to the Railroad Transport Officer, I was directed to the platform where my train from the North would shortly arrive. In renewed excitement I realized this was not only a major step in my new life, but I was also about to undertake the longest railway journey I had ever made. Most people in England died in the same place they were born, often without travelling beyond the outskirts of their town or village. Society in those days was not very mobile, and to travel more than fifty miles from your birthplace branded you a wanderer – good for you, King George! And here I was, about to travel two hundred miles to a strange destination: it was a very long way for a lad whose previous travel experience had been confined to a day in Fleetwood, a fishing village seven miles up the coast, and two trips to Lancaster, all of fifty miles away from Blackpool: in my book these qualified as journeys of consequence. Now my heart raced to the shrill sound of the engine's whistle as the express train whizzed through Lancashire and the Midlands counties, pausing briefly at the industrial city of Crewe before hurrying on through the speed-blurred countryside to its final destination. It was only then that the reality struck me: I had left behind all that I loved and cherished.

The first misgivings arose as I began to recall that meeting with the Drill Sergeant at the Blackpool Recruiting Depot, who had offered me a life filled with adventure and glory, in the most exotic corners of the world.

'A life fit for a man,' he had said – even though I was just a boy. 'Join the Army and see the World,' proclaimed the posters. 'Friendship and comradeship, with the finest fighting service in the world! Excellent pay and as much as you can eat!' The sergeant hadn't told me that, as a boy soldier, my daily pay was to be the princely sum of one shilling and tuppence, from which barrack room damages would be levied (even if there were no damages, we had to pay into a general fund: no one was allowed to argue about this). I had also to make an allowance to my parents (if any, the questionnaire said: most enlisted boys were orphans), to buy toothpaste, soap, shoe and Brasso button polish, stamps, writing paper, greeting cards, and any other incidentals which the army cared to mandate. There would be precious little left to squander on personal luxuries, certainly not enough to pay for even the cheapest seats at the cinema. And, to demonstrate his great concern for my welfare, the sergeant had also said: 'That in order to prolong and so take full advantage of the wonderful opportunities which now lay before you, fortunate boy that you are, I am also taking the liberty, with your approval naturally, of changing the attestation forms to a period of nine and three.' At my puzzled look, he had explained, 'That's nine years with the colours and three with the reserves.'

I had wondered what he was talking about; only now, as I speeded towards London at the King's expense, in the luxury of a third-class railway coach (feeling very hungry, as I had not eaten since breakfast at six that morning), did I begin to realize that the nine with the colours described by the sergeant would be the time I had to serve with the flag; only then might I be released from my regiment and returned to civilian status, where I would be placed on the inactive rolls for a further period of three years, during which period I would be subject to recall for any purpose whatsoever. I pondered once more the implications of 'nine and three'. I had a better understanding now, but I was worried about the word 'might' in relation to my discharge at the end of the nine years. There was room for prevarication there by the army; it did not sound so certain now. It meant they could defer my release if they wished, and the same provision was quoted in the section about the Reserves. They had you coming and going, and there was not a thing you could do about it.

I was to find prevarication an appropriate word to describe much of the behaviour exhibited by the military: they had a very evasive attitude towards everything in life and quite often one would find what they *said* they would do quite different to what they actually *did*. So, for the next twelve years, my heart and soul would be owned by the British Army, to do with me as they pleased – and, I repeated to myself, they might not even release me after I'd completed my nine years with the colours. The benevolent Recruiting Sergeant had also failed to reveal that the period I had agreed to serve would not become effective while serving as a boy, and I was classed as such until I reached the age of eighteen. Only then would I muster the rank of Gunner, and make a start on the specified agreement of nine and three. So, being only fourteen now, I could expect to remain in the service of the King for some sixteen years: a lifetime for a boy of that age to contemplate; I hadn't even lived that long!

On the other hand, after that period – which presently seemed a hundred years away – I could count on a pension, perhaps sufficient enough to keep body and soul together. And, if supplemented by begging on the streets, it might be enough to buy a packet of Woodbines, or even the occasional pint – didn't all soldiers, both young and old, love their beer and tobacco? And the Sheilas, of course, mustn't forget them: I would surely want to take girls out. All those pleasures were very much part of the decadent life of the brutal and licentious soldierly, as the British soldier was so often described.

I was to learn later, however, that even these meagre financial rewards would not be forthcoming as soon as I expected: not only did my service fail to start properly until the age of eighteen, but my pensionable service was equally delayed. But I would still be only twenty-seven when the money started to roll in – enough: the future would take care of itself. I decided to let the fates decide; I would savour the moment and smell the roses!

AWAKENED FROM MY reverie as the train entered the approaches to London, I saw my reflection in the carriage window. Returning my gaze was a round, smiling face with a prominent Roman nose and rosy cheeks: a handsome, if somewhat baby-faced boy of fair complexion, capped with short blond hair. I was slender, but with broad – if skinny – shoulders; given the proper food and exercise, I would quickly develop an athletic stature. Quietly spoken, with a Lancashire accent, I was a typical English boy, happy and innocent, though that innocence was destined to recede quickly, given the realities of life with my new 'family'. And the image smiled back at me as I thought with glee: no more school! I'd tired of those endless rounds of English, French, or even woodwork: all those subjects held little interest for me. Like all school children the country over, we made up names for our teachers; Mr Sutton, for example, was known affectionately to all the students as Sister Mutton. And it was such a long and tiring bike ride from home: a good three miles. But that was all finished with now: no more homework, or reprimands for mistakes, or being late for class, or for inattention during algebra lessons, which could warrant a caning from the Headmaster. The expression of relief and pleasure so evident on my reflected face was because my school days were over. Soldiers didn't go to school, did they? You don't need an education to kill someone; why would you? And if you did, it wouldn't be that kind of school anyway . . . as doubt began to subdue the jubilant face, I saw the train was arriving and gathered together my few belongings.

THE TRAIN DREW into Euston Station and then I was swept along the platform by the hurrying passengers, all in search of the exit. Now to face the challenge of completing my journey alone. With some hesitancy, and not a little trepidation, I made my way to the Enquiries Office, where I was told to take the bus to Woolwich Arsenal, and to enquire further upon arriving there. It was early afternoon, a bright and sunny day, when I boarded the Woolwich bus for the hour-long trip through London. I was overwhelmed by this strange, fascinating city, the crossroads of the world and the centre of the British Empire. The whole world seemed to live there, it was so exceedingly crowded, and infinitely busier than even August Bank Holiday at Blackpool. The crowds were thick on the sidewalks; the traffic was so dense, with double-decker buses and taxis causing much congestion, that I began to worry that I would ever make it to Woolwich. In spite of the intense activity and the incessant din of the big city, I still felt a little lonely and I was glad when the bus driver told me I should alight at the next stop.

Still clutching my suitcase, I was lucky enough to see a police constable nearby. Showing him my letter instructing me to report to the Royal Artillery Depot, I stood awkwardly, not knowing quite what more to say.

Having read the letter, the constable said in a fatherly manner, 'What you want is the Boys' Depot, and I can see you are just the ticket for the place. You're on the right road here, lad. It's a long walk, but you'll have to get used to that being in the army, seeing as how they march round a lot, won't you? You can't get lost if you follow this road for about a mile, until you see on the right the high stone wall which surrounds the Depot. That's the place you want, and just inside the iron gates you will see the guard-room. Go and report in there, and give them this letter. And good luck to you in your new life, lad. If I were your age, I'd do the same thing me'self.'

The walk took me about twenty minutes, though the road was uphill and, with my heart once more in my mouth, I entered the forbidding gates. My military career had begun.

WOOLWICH ARSENAL IS a sprawling complex developed on a Roman settlement: a vast area covered with buildings, the originals of which were constructed in the early seventeen hundreds. As the name implies, it was originally the arsenal of the British Army, where guns and projectiles were forged. It was also the birthplace of the Royal Artillery, in the year 1716. Next to the Artillery Barracks is the famous Rotunda Museum, displaying the development of guns, medals and military documents over the centuries. The Boys' Depot was within the confines of the Artillery Barracks, the whole of which is enclosed by the aforementioned, almost impenetrable stone wall.

I was not the only boy presenting myself to the Corporal of the Guard that day: there were nearly thirty of us, all of whom had entered into similar contracts with his Majesty, King George V. In my imagination I wondered how our new lord and master kept abreast with the events in his army. Perhaps at breakfast the King was given a status report of new members who had recently sworn their loyalty to him and were now in one of his barracks awaiting his call. He might even have a list of the names of these newcomers, with all their history. So he would know all about me, I thought, when my birthday was; perhaps he'd even send me a birthday card, or a small present. I'd certainly go to tea with him if he asked, I thought; I wasn't naïve, just fanciful. I reflected that these remote people in high places were not always unapproachable, and it would be nice to talk to His Majesty about his army and find out if there was anything special he would like me to do? I would be very happy to do something for him, I thought, perhaps something by way of the role of Artillery in close quarter fighting. After all, even a King needs a little help at times.

As at Preston, I was instructed to go to the mess hall for a late lunch, where I joined many other boys, all looking as hungry as I was. The army appeared to be very conscious of the need to feed its soldiers, the potential cannon-fodder of the future. The mess was a large, austerely furnished hall capable of holding almost a hundred boys, seated at tables each accommodating sixteen. Hungrily wolfing down bangers and mash followed by treacle pudding – staples on the limited menu for the soldiers of the British Army, wherever they were stationed – I surveyed my new companions, a diverse group whose only similarity was our age and the fact that we were all expressing our excitement in the loudest possible way. Though there were one or two who sat quietly, only toying with their food and clearly unhappy with their new life, for the most part, the exhilaration loosened tongues in pleasure and anticipation of what lay ahead: here we were, ready to serve. Friendships started immediately that day, some of which were to last a lifetime. Amidst the clatter of the cutlery and the loud conversations, it was hard for me to maintain my discussion with my new-found friend sitting next to me. Everyone wanted to talk, and nobody was prepared to listen.

Suddenly, above the noise roared a voice: 'Quiet! Stop talking. Silence, I said!' In a flash all conversation ceased, and all heads turned to the source of the command. Standing just inside the entrance was the imposing figure of Sergeant Lambert, the man who was to be our guide, teacher, counsellor, judge and guru during the next twelve months. He was also to be our disciplinarian, punishing when necessary, shaping our behaviour and character; his ways of doing this would leave their mark for the rest of our lives. As he prepared us for the hardships and disappointments which lay ahead, some would come to hate him, others to idolize him, but above all, under his ever-watchful gaze, he would make us into soldiers fit to serve our King and country. Sergeant Lambert was a man of great importance to us, with a character of unsurpassed strength, in a role no one could play more successfully; doing so repeatedly with each new intake of boys. He looked a stern man, even forbidding, a model of perfection in dress and stature: immaculate and composed, he stood there in the silence whilst being assessed by the boys.

Surprisingly, his first words were more like those of a father than his appearance suggested. 'Today, I welcome you to your new family. As the person in charge of all your activities until you graduate as a qualified trumpeter, I want you to know that I will help you all that I can. You must never hesitate to come to me if you are in trouble of any kind, and I will do my best to put things right for you. I expect you to work hard, and implicitly obey the commands of the non-commissioned officers who will take part in your training. There is to be no swearing or fighting, smoking or drinking, and you are to develop a healthy comradeship with each other. You are to be meticulous in your hygiene, and properly dressed at all times. You must assemble punctually at the appointed times of parade. If you fail to observe what I have said, you can expect to be punished accordingly. You are now to fall in by the marker outside the building, where you will march to the Quartermaster's Store to draw your bedding. Move!'

Quickly, the buzz of conversation resumed as we leapt to our feet and swarmed through the door. Standing outside was the solitary figure of Bombardier Weald, also impeccably dressed, the peaked cap bearing the badge of the Royal Artillery above the strap pulled well down over the eyes, the brass buttons on his khaki tunic shining and the brown belt around his waist highly polished; even his enemies must agree his dress was faultless. The high-necked collar held the grenades, and under the right lapel of the tunic was the blancoed white lanyard. Below the riding breeches he wore puttees, starting at the regulation three inches below the knee-cap and winding down to the ankles, the end seam on the outside. His feet were shod with heavy black boots reflecting a shimmering, mirror-like shine; it was said you could tell your future if you looked hard enough. Standing rigidly to attention, his cane securely under his left armpit like the sergeant, he was the quintessence of uniformed splendour and authority. For the moment, his face was an impenetrable mask as he gazed unseeingly into eternity, in accordance with approved military behaviour.

Suddenly, at the sound of us boys, his expression changed and he commanded, 'Stop the talking and fall in three ranks in front of me. Stand to attention, and take those bloody silly grins off your faces, or I'll have your guts for garters!'

A thin voice from somewhere in the rear rank of the squad piped up: 'The sergeant told us there was to be no swearing, and you just said bloody.'

Quick as a whip the Bombardier responded, 'Who said that?'

Timidly, the miscreant identified himself. 'I did, Bombardier. I just thought it fair that if we can't swear, nobody else should.'

The figure of authority replied, 'Oh, you do, do you? Well, you don't bloody well do as I do, you do as I tell you!! And I don't want any more lip from you. What's your name?'

With a crestfallen face the lad replied, 'Green, Bombardier, Tommy Green.'

Casting his eyes throughout the ranks, the Bombardier said, 'Mr Tommy Green thinks running an army is a partnership affair. Are there any more of you dumbbells who think the same way?' There was not a word from the now subdued assembly. 'Right glad am I to know that, because it means that no one will have to share Tommy Green's punishment of cook-house fatigues for three days for his insolence. But let this be a lesson for all of you. Never answer back your superiors, because next time the pun-ishment may be far worse than that of Master Green's.

'Right. Upon the command, Right turn, Quick March, you will turn to your right and, starting with your left foot, march smartly away.' Acting on the order, we moved off, although more like Fred Karno's Army, famed for its sloppiness in drill movements, than in a smart and soldierly-like manner.

The square looked enormous, certainly as large as a football field.

Totally devoid of trees or vegetation of any kind, the cement was barren and colourless. On one side it was bounded by the barracks in which we would live, a three-storey building with barred windows, depressingly drab in appearance. The second side of the parade ground, facing our accommodation, housed the cook-house and mess hall; the third provided sounding sheds for bugle and trumpet training, and the fourth was the Quartermaster's Store and other administrative buildings. Behind rose the high cement wall with its large, iron-barred gates, physically separating us from the distracting, though inviting, pleasures of the civilians without. The sounding sheds were disused horse stables, corrugated iron roofs open on all sides, like a car port, under which we aspiring musicians could practise bugle and trumpet calls to our hearts' content. These 'Badgie Wallahs' as they were known (derived from the Indian word for musicians), were required to do 'voluntary' practice for one hour every evening except on Sundays. As the sheds were large enough to hold as many as ninety boys at any one time, and there were always three classes in training, each of thirty boys, the noise could be positively deafening – but this also meant a boy could fail dismally in his rendition of a particular call without suffering the embarrassment of his colleagues hearing it and their consequent derision.

Brought to a shuffling halt outside the QM's Store, we filed in and were given four grey blankets, and were then admonished by the QM Sergeant to take great care of the blankets, and anything else we were issued, under the threat of dire consequences. By some strange reasoning, he contrived the penalty to be equivalent to three times the value of a missing item: first, to pay for the lost item, second, the cost of issuing a new one, and third, the cost of replacing the one taken from the Stores. Clever though this was, it didn't wash well with us and we still pondered the matter well into the night. Indeed, many of us were never to resolve the matter in our own minds, and it remained forever a mystery.

Following the bedding issue, the Bombardier bellowed, 'Now, pay attention to me, lads. We will now march across to the barrack rooms, where you will choose your bed and leave your bedding there. As soon as you have done that, you will immediately parade again outside to return to the clothing section of the Quartermaster's Store, and draw your uniforms.'

Responding to the order, we moved off in formation and were dismissed in front of our new home. With a surge we rushed forward to stake claim to the bed each considered most suitable, preferably in a quiet corner of the room, away from the entrance door, and as inconspicuous as possible.

The room had forty iron-framed single beds around the perimeter, each separated by the regulation four feet. The legs were easily detachable, and had the potential for many uses. The mattresses consisted of three separate 'biscuits' filled with hair, providing a concrete-like foundation on which to sleep. A twenty-four-inch bolster, also filled with hair, served as headrest. On the walls above each bed was a metal cabinet to hold toiletries and small personal possessions. Standing at the foot of the bed was a kit-box, some eighteen inches deep, about the same height and width as the bed, to hold clothing and uniforms.

There was electricity for lighting purposes only; heating was provided by the coal-burning stove standing in the centre of the room. Coal was only issued during the winter months; the army, in its typically autocratic way of doing whatever it wishes, whenever it wished, had decreed the winter season to be officially between October and March. However, during those bleak winter months the stove was to prove hopelessly inadequate, and even the issue of a further two blankets to supplement the four already provided did little to alleviate the misery of the harsh English winters, during which snow and bitterly cold gales swept relentlessly through the Depot.

There was only the one door into the crowded room which, in spite of the windows in two of the walls, had a gloomy atmosphere. There were neither curtains nor blinds and, apart from the beds, it was sparsely furnished: two tables with benches adjacent to the stove were the only other things in the room. The floors were of polished wood, without carpets or covering. The whole contributed to a cheerless and dismal setting, fully consistent with the drab exterior appearance of the building, but this was of no concern, as it would have little or no affect on its occupants. In the mad rush to occupy a bed, arguments were inevitable where the choices were disputed, and force equally inevitable to settle the fight. Shouts and laughs mingled with the cries of victory and despair, then the situation resolved itself and eventually we all filed out onto the parade ground as instructed.

It was now late afternoon, and there was still much to do. We were still in civvies, so off we were marched, back to the Quartermaster's block, to draw uniforms and kit – at least then we might start to look like soldiers. Moving along the long counter inside the building, the three old sweats on duty handed out the uniforms and paraphernalia that would magically transform us from urchins to boy soldiers in the Royal Artillery. We were the butt of many ribald remarks and jokes made by the storemen, though fitting the uniforms was a cursory affair at best: most of the boys, not unnaturally, were thin because of the inadequate food they'd had throughout their childhood, when poverty was so endemic. In those days, words like balanced diet, calories and vitamins were as foreign as a ten franc note, and as rare as a ten pound note. So there was little effort to provide clothes that would immediately fit; to begin with, the uniform was invariably on the large side and the storemen were wont to say, 'Don't worry mate. You'll grow into it soon.' The result was that, in most cases, the newly attired boy soldier looked nothing less than slovenly.

Two tunics with tight-fitting collars of the most uncomfortable design, and two pairs of dress slacks and riding breeches completed the dress uniform. The greatcoats (strictly for winter wear and *never* with the collar to be turned up) were draped like so many tents over us ill-clad boys. Even the peaked cap was oversized, because it had to be pulled well down over the eyes of the wearer.

The boots were enormous, and felt impossibly heavy: they were black and ugly, thick with grease. We new soldiers had to labour for hours to eliminate the grease from the leather, and then to prepare the base for a shine truly worthy of the King of England's Army was the order of the day – and the night as well, for we often had to work into the early hours to produce results which would not jeopardize a satisfactory inspection on the morning parade. The word 'bullshit' was synonymous with the British Army; 'bullshit baffles brains' expressed the virtue of overcoming all obstacles with words, as opposed to worthy deeds, and sometimes one had to wonder if it was not the most important factor in preparing a soldier for war. Such an enormous amount of time was devoted to spit and polish that it must surely be of paramount importance for an élite fighting force if it is to reach the pinnacle of perfection.

Amongst the hubbub and excitement, the fitting of the uniforms was finally concluded, and the remainder of the clothing, including socks, vests and pants (all in triplicate to allow for one on, one in the wash and one in reserve) was issued and placed in the dark blue canvas kit-bag we were each given. Next up was the issue of personal items including soap, tooth-brush and paste, hairbrush and comb and, incongruously for most of us, shaving gear. Last of all we collected enamel mugs and plates, knife, fork and spoon (eating irons), a brass button stick and brushes, a variety of badges, and a 'housewife', an indispensable item to repair clothing when necessary. Staggering along with the now heavily laden kit-bag slung over our shoulders, still in high spirits, although the toll of the day's activities was beginning to tell on us, we were then marched back to the barrack room. There we left our kit-bags on the beds and went off to the mess hall for cocoa; supper was not served every night, and this was one of those nights. Most of us were not hungry anyway, so there were few complaints from the tired group of fledgling warriors. As we left to return to quar-ters, the Bombardier told us, in no uncertain terms, that lights out was at ten o'clock, at which time we were to be in bed, with no talking or fooling around. He spelled this out very clearly, stressing the fact that offenders could expect to be severely punished.

AS THE WEEKS and months progressed, we quickly learned that the threat of disciplinary action was not an idle one. Dependent on the infraction of military discipline and the degree of violation, the punishment could range from common fatigues, such as cook-house duty, peeling potatoes and performing other menial chores like scrubbing pots and pans and floors, to those of a more serious nature, including jankers, and no one was immune to the threat of being marched in before the Commanding Officer by the Sergeant-Major. 'Lef' right, Lef' right. Halt! Prisoner, cap off. Sir, Boy Jones, Sir!' There were liberal awards for offenders – extra parades and guard duties, pack drill, CB (confined to barracks); the list was endless. Damage to Government property, invariably classified as wilful or gross carelessness, and never accidental or unintentional, could result in fines resulting in many months of financial hardship. A popular punishment – perhaps for failing to polish the back of a cap badge, or a twisted boot lace on parade – was several evenings of cleaning the gun limber, an ammu-nition cart, old and disused, whose steel-covered shaft was rusting away. The punishment, measured in so many inches, was to return it to its original brilliance by sanding and the application of metal polish, and then burnishing the offending metal with the chain-like metal-pad: demeaning and humiliating work, requiring lots of elbow grease.

And there was always the fear of the Glasshouse: the military detention centre, which soon sapped away one's pride and self-respect. For repeated offences such as insolence, or AWOL (absent without official leave), the culprit would be placed in an isolation cell for extended periods of time, and subjected to the most severe discipline. Movement from one place to another was always done in double-time and accompanied by the harsh swearing of the guard. There were no privileges of any kind, and a prisoner could spend weeks or months without talking to any fellow inmate. The most famous – or infamous – detention centre was at Aldershot, and the brutality practised there was legendary throughout the British Army. The very mention of this notorious place would create fear in many a soldier's heart.

The threat of court-martial was also ever-present, with the possibility of being dishonourably discharged. For some, repeated violations were often intentional, as a means to just that end, though the road to success and the return to civvy street after that would be fraught with suffering.

Jimmy Anderson was a classic example of a boy so thoroughly disenchanted with his new life that he resorted to a most painful method of obtaining his release. It was the common, if erroneous, belief that if a boy failed to qualify as a bugler at the end of the training period, he would receive an honourable discharge, as he was of no further value to the service. In pursuit of that objective, and utilizing one of the easily removed iron bed-legs from his bed, Jimmy was so desperate that he endured hours of agony every evening, tapping away at his front teeth with the bar. The torture he suffered was clearly apparent, and most distressing to the rest of us, who failed to get him to stop. Slowly, the constant abuse worked and the selected tooth – the one against which the mouthpiece of the bugle or trumpet was placed – became loose. Now, with great confidence, Jimmy was able to report that he had toothache, and that he wished to have it examined.

Whilst waiting for the call, he indulged in his flights of fancy: no more school, his mates would welcome him back at home, and he could take up his old life where he'd left off – which was breaking open gas meters in newly vacated houses and spending the proceeds (all in pennies) on luxuries such as cream cakes, chocolates and other delectable items. Gone would be the discipline and the monotonous rigidity of the endless parades and inspections; the six o'clock in the morning reveilles; the mandatory cold showers. And the Pleasure Beach offered inviting opportunities for further gain without need of work (Jimmy came from Poulton, near Blackpool).

But Jimmy's dreams were shattered: the tooth was extracted, creating more pain, and not without a great number of searching questions by the inquisitive dentist as to how the tooth had reached its present parlous condition. His vision of discharge was shattered by the dentist's observation that whilst the loss of the tooth was unfortunate, it would in no way detract from Jimmy's ability to continue his time at the Depot and qualify as a bugler. It simply meant that he must now place the mouthpiece on the other side of his mouth, and he would find the results would be equally as good.

The verdict was a great shock to Jimmy, who had already mentally packed his gear and knew exactly what time train he would catch to return home. It was a very contrite and disillusioned boy who returned to his comrades – to a mixed reception of derision and sympathy.

Jimmy's lack of success in what was considered a surefire way to escape from the Military's vice-like grip was felt by all, bringing many gloomy forecasts of what might lie ahead in the future. Release was clearly unattainable without recourse to the most desperate methods: severe injury, or even desertion. But to be on the run for the rest of your life? Heaven forbid! The ramifications set our heads awhirl, for that was no release: better to bear the present than to leap into a life filled with uncertainty and the constant fear of detection. Perhaps the only acceptable route to civvy street was to pay the one hundred pounds demanded by the Government in release of the obligations made – but who had such wealth, let alone be willing to part with it? Not our parents: they were mostly poor, and in most cases only too glad that someone else had accepted responsibility for the continued support of their children.

We also failed to understand how one or two boys could get so disenchanted after just a few days that they were prepared to even contemplate such a course of action. Discussion amongst us failed to provide the answer, so, short of robbery providing funds for our release (which was favoured by some, but without practicality), the only solution was to put aside the question of discharge and soldier on.

AT TEN O'CLOCK precisely the trumpet call for lights out echoed across the Depot, and we surrendered to sleep: our first day had drained us, both mentally and physically. A few subdued whispers, sprinkled with sobs from more than one source, petered out and soon silence reigned in the darkened barrack room, broken only by snores and the occasional rambling aloud by dreamers. Tomorrow was another day and our training would then begin in earnest, so we needed our sleep that night. For some, though, however tired, this was elusive, for others their dreams were punctuated with nightmares; Jimmy was one of the latter. A lucky few would sleep the sleep of the supremely confident.

'RISE, SOLDIERS, RISE, and put your armour on.' The call of the trumpet was loud and clear as it summoned reveille within the military enclave. Cleaving the silence of the dawn now breaking across the barracks, we were stirred into life, ready to face the challenges of the day. Almost before the last echoes had died away, the door was flung open with a crash and the sergeant hammered against the wall with his cane, crying, 'Rise and shine, beds in line, piss pots on the verandah!' Striding around the room, stripping the blankets off some, prodding and slashing at others with the cane he wielded with great accuracy at the more prominent parts of the unfortunates' bodies, he quickly brought us all to full alertness.

'Wakey, wakey! Dress in your running shorts and shoes and get fell in outside! On the double! You have five minutes to get there.'

Tumbling over ourselves, we hurriedly searched for our clothes, dressed and went out into the cold morning to be greeted by our physical training instructor. The wind was blowing from the north and under grey skies laden with rain, we were led across the square and out through the main gates. Skirting the exterior of the high walls, we followed the road leading to Woolwich Common, a broad expanse of grassland about a mile south of the barracks. The Common was popular with both the civilian population and the military, and on summer evenings especially, young and old congregated there. As we cut across the open country, our pace increased to a steady run, which we maintained for a further two miles – now in the pouring rain – before starting the return to the barracks. Saturated and exhausted, we straggled back under the exhortations of our instructor, who insisted we close up into some semblance of order. Through the iron gates, coming to a halt on the square, the rain mingled with our sweat as we were dismissed with instructions to shower, dress in fatigues, and go to breakfast. It was now seven-thirty in the morning, and we had to parade again at eight-thirty.

Still, showered and dressed, our mood was upbeat as we filed into the dining room, savouring the aroma of bacon and eggs – several sizzling strips of crispy bacon and two golden fried eggs, and as much toast as you wished, with margarine and jam, and mugs of boiling hot tea, liberally laced with sugar and milk. It was a welcome meal for a hungry lot of lads, and if we were lucky, and there was enough for second helpings, we were free to help ourselves. That was to be the generous standard of every breakfast and midday meal while we were at the Depot; the evening meal was a different story: if we were lucky, there would be bread and margarine and, occasionally a bit of cheese or jam or, very rarely cake. Generally, though, if we were hungry in the evenings, we had to provide for ourselves. Those fortunate boys with thoughtful parents regularly received food parcels from home: a variety of cakes, biscuits and tinned foodstuffs, which were much in demand. Comrades who were always hungry were a ready and lucrative market if you wished to share the food with them – the price of sharing meant exorbitant donations from the buyers. Those who were perpetually hungry were allowed to buy on tick until payday.

The breakfast menu included shepherd's pie, sausage and mash, rissoles and mash and liver and onions. Dinner – the midday meal – was varied: stew or meat pies, or roast beef with all the trimmings: roast potatoes and Yorkshire pudding and vegetables. Dessert might be apple dumpling or fruit served with custard; rice pudding or other exotic – to us – selections. The choice and quantity of food might have looked generous, but we were subjected to intense activity and exercise every day, as a result of which we were always hungry. Most of us had 'hollow legs' and anything qualifying as food – and which was digestible – was eagerly devoured. We thrived, and quickly filled our uniforms, as predicted by the Quartermaster.

ASSEMBLED AGAIN AT the appointed hour of 08:30, we were marched to the Sick Room for a short arm inspection by the Medical Officer. As we filed past him, we were ordered, 'Drop your slacks . . . Cough. Next boy!' Although none of us were quite certain of the purpose of this particular inspection, we dutifully obeyed with a wide variety of sounds which the MO accepted as representing a cough. Opinions ranged from, 'I think he's a queer and this is a way of him getting a cheap thrill,' to, 'He's just checking to make sure that you've got all the necessary spare parts to qualify as a male and not a member of the fairer sex masquerading as such.' The latter speculation was the most fervently desired; however, the whole procedure was completed without incident and we departed unscathed, albeit somewhat abashed.

And then once more to the QM's Stores, this time to draw the musical instruments that were to form part of the ritual of our daily lives for the next several years. Not until we attained the dizzy age of eighteen would we be relieved of the responsibility of summoning the rank and file of the regiment to the performance of their duties. There was a specific bugle or trumpet call for each activity – Mount, Charge, Dismount, Fatigues, Fire Alarm, and so on – which the soldiers were required to observe; the call was to be made precisely at the appointed time, and usually with preceding warning calls. For example, if the execution call to parade for stables was at 07:00, then the warning sounds would be blown at 06:45 and 06:55. The trumpet and bugle calls were to become indelibly imprinted in our minds and, for some, would be remembered forever, even until their dying days. There were official words for each tune, too, though the approved versions were often changed or distorted to meet the whims of the player, in the same way that the appropriate calls for specific occasions were sometimes made as a prank – often with serious consequences to the offending trumpeter.

The call 'Dismount' which, played to the words 'Smartly now get down,' gave the order for the mounted troops to dismount from their horses and stand to attention holding the bridles. One poor innocent was dared to play 'Dismount' instead of 'Reveille' outside the married quarters early one morning, which he did, much to the astonishment and disbelief of everyone. The consequent punishment inflicted on the brave lad was commensurate with the bitter anger felt by those who had been so impertinently awakened in that far-away military cantonment.

Bugles and trumpets, which were equipped with gold cords and red tassels, were required at all times to shine with the brilliance of the sun reflected from the gold. The silver and gold instruments were prone to tarnish very quickly from handling, so we spent hours trying to keep the required pristine appearance. The trumpet would normally be slung under the epaulette on the uniform's right shoulder, resting on the back. The bugle would be carried in the right hand, the cord being threaded under the left shoulder epaulette with the tassels resting on the breast pocket. They provided a colourful addendum to the otherwise drab khaki uniform, the severity of which was otherwise ameliorated only by the gleaming gold buttons fastening the tunic, the four pockets and the two epaulettes and the white blancoed single strand lanyard looped under the epaulette of the right shoulder, and the brass buckle of the brown leather belt.

The uniform itself was not the most comfortable dress to wear: the jacket was of heavy cloth which was very warm during the summer and the high-necked collar always seemed to be too tight, and was frequently the cause of irritation to the skin. The riding breeches were less trouble-some, although the puttees, which were bound around the lower part of the leg, starting three fingers' width below the knee cap and finishing over the boot tops, could be most restrictive and bothersome if improperly applied. The boots, tipped and heeled with steel, were heavy and cumbersome but, with diligence, soon acquired the required brilliant shine. The peaked cap with its leather band and brass badge of the Royal Artillery, although also unpleasant to wear on a hot summer's day, completed a very smart and commanding appearance, converting even the most insignificant person to the very model of a soldier.

Once we'd drawn our instruments from the QM's Stores and deposited them in the barrack room, we were allowed a tea break of twenty minutes, and then required to form up on the parade ground for drill. Here we found Sergeant Lambert and Bombardier Weald waiting to put us through two hours of the most rigorous drill imaginable. For some there were blis-ters from the new boots which didn't fit properly, but that was no excuse to be absent from the parades which followed, during which the agony was only compounded. Others became exhausted because of their unfitness, but they too had to continue: there was to be no respite for any of us, for any reason, from the demands of our instructors. We were reviled for mistakes in executing orders and belittled for the slightest reason.

And so, with dragging, sore feet and wet with sweat, we were dismissed to the barracks to collapse on our beds. This was our first taste of what was to become an almost daily ritual for the twelve months we were to be at Woolwich. Few of the boys enjoyed the square-bashing, but the endless drills soon gave us a precision to be proud of, and we learned how to carry out even the most complex manoeuvres. We would be able to take our place in any military ceremony and be worthy of the British Army's reputation for excellence in drill.

But now it was time for the midday meal, and then to parade with our instruments in the sounding sheds bordering the parade ground, where Drum Major Paddy Brogan waited. Paddy, known as the wild Irishman, was an old soldier, and truly a legend. No one knew for sure when he had taken the King's shilling, but it was so long ago that speculation had his enlistment any time from the time of the Indian Mutiny (in 1857!) to the First World War. Old and wrinkled, and with the deep brown tan which comes only from long exposure to the hot Indian sun, he was a kindly and forgiving man, slow to reprimand and gentle in his correction of our many errors. The road to perfection in our calling was long and demanding, but Paddy became our friend and coaxed from us the high standards which were expected of a qualified Artillery Trumpeter.

And the day was not yet over. Within the hour, I found that we were to be subjected to school, and it was with great dismay that we were marched off to the schoolhouse. Our teacher, who more resembled a pugilist than a man of learning, was also a disciplinarian who demanded strict obedience and attention during class hours. He readily wielded a cane on any offender, for the slightest of reasons; three strokes on the hand was the punishment for any unfortunate enough to catch his eye. Not unexpectedly, few of us found great pleasure in the schoolroom: for most, it represented boredom, and a return to something we had naïvely thought we were finished with once we'd joined up. Worse, we were to find that schooling was to persist not only at the Depot, but also throughout our service. Essentially, the topics were english, geography, history and mathematics. The emphasis would be on the British Empire for geography and history, and mathematics, algebra and logarithms were studied as they applied to gunnery. We also did map reading, and some elementary techniques in survey work, including the calculation of bearings and ranges for artillery targets, utilizing logarithms and the slide rule. At this stage, we acquired only the more rudimentary aspects of gunnery; the more advanced knowledge of that science would be acquired later in our careers. We had lessons every day except at weekends, and rarely for less than two hours. Homework and examinations were also part of the process, just as they were in civvy street, with educational certificates awarded to those who completed the examinations successfully, in the order of Third, Second and First class, and the highest award of Special class, though few of us were to attain the latter after completing the Depot training.

When we were posted to a regiment, not only would we continue to attend school, but if we were serving overseas, then we had to learn the language of that country too: if the regiment were to serve in India, then it would be mandatory to study Urdu, probably from an Indian munshi[1].

SO THE PATTERN of our daily routine was set: it started with a three to five mile run across the Common, followed by drill on the square, physical training, map reading, and the schooling curriculum, punctuated by meal times, medical and kit inspections. Fully occupied during the daylight and evening hours, there was little time to get into trouble, but many of us managed to do so somehow, for a wide variety of reasons.

Exposure to the role of horses in the artillery and learning to ride and to care for the animals would follow in a few weeks' time. It was a busy schedule, and we would be hard pressed to maintain the pace successfully. And we were not allowed to leave the confines of the barracks for the first three months of service. Closeted completely in a world dedicated purely to the art of soldiering, with nothing more than a glimpse of the outside world through the barracks gates or whilst struggling across the Common, all we could do was anticipate the pleasures of renewed acquaintance with the cinema and the other aspects of our former life, which we now treasured so much.

The evenings, however, were devoted to entertainment in the form of attending or taking part in sports activities of all kinds: soccer, hockey, boxing and more. Boys who showed promise would provide demonstrations

1 Teacher of languages

to the regiments who were stationed nearby. Whenever any major boxing championships were held, they would be supplemented by a three-bout session by the boys. These boys were supposed to provide a demonstration of their art, not to make any effort to win by harming the opponent, but this didn't always work and the fight would sometimes take place in earnest. This happened to me one night in the barracks of a field artillery unit. Both boys entered the ring and, at the command of the referee, 'Shake hands and come out fighting,' we did so. Anxious to display the noble art of boxing, my opponent and I fought not to win or hurt, spending the first round only tapping each other lightly. This shadow boxing was not what the audience of about two hundred soldier fans wanted; starting to shout and boo us, they demanded reality and blood. We took this to heart and, in a clinch, I whispered, 'Let's do it', and we went to work in no uncertain fashion. Within seconds my opponent was down on the canvas from one on the chin and out of the fight, to the cheers and the roars of approval of the onlookers. The tumultuous applause signified that we had done the right thing; our reward, which was the main reason for taking part in the exhibition, was a steak and chip supper that evening in the regiment's mess hall. We both agreed it had been worthwhile, and adequate compensation for any damage sustained: when we returned to the barracks it was with full stomachs, and no ill feeling on the part of my opponent.

THE DAYS PASSED quickly and, almost without realizing it, we progressed from our original awkward clumsiness to a more matured and polished group of boys. There were other personalities at the Depot who influenced our lives, like the riding and gymnasium instructors. Of officers, we saw few, and only one made casual contact with us, a young Second Lieutenant, and we didn't think much of him. On the rare occasions he addressed us, he came over as arrogant and conceited. Reserved in manner, he appeared to be indifferent to our wellbeing, and uninterested in us as individuals. A figure of supreme authority, we were in awe of him; his attitude and aloofness typified the enormous gap which, by and large, existed between the officers and other ranks of the British Army, although there were exceptions, as we were to find later in some regiments. Most officers were unapproachable, and appeared more preoccupied with polo and the like, spending little time carrying out their duties with the men, leaving the day-to-day routines to the warrant and non-commissioned officers.

The end of the first three months was a milestone for us: we were not only allowed out of the barracks, but also given a week's leave and a travel warrant to return home to our parents. It was a happy assembly of boys who packed kit-bags and collected pay packets that Saturday morning. I walked down the hill to the Woolwich railway station to connect with the Fylde Coast Express at Euston Station, which would take me to Blackpool, stopping only at Crewe and Preston. Dressed in my uniform, which I did indeed now fill, as promised all those weeks ago by the Quartermaster, and complete with spurs and stick and a new name – I'd become Penny to my colleagues early on, and Penny I would remain for the rest of my life – it was with some pride that I set off.

Once home, my parents showed me off, giving friends and neighbours every opportunity to admire their soldier son. But my old school mates and friends were different; their attitude towards me had changed – or was it me who had altered? We appeared to have little in common now, and I found it difficult to reminisce with any pleasure about our previous escapades. I felt rather sad about this, and began to look forward to returning to my new friends, with whom I now identified more closely. So when the day came to return to the Depot, it was with some eagerness that I boarded the train at Central Station; any misty eyes evaporated quickly as the train left the station.

HORSES ARE REMARKABLE animals, as we were soon to discover. They can smell fear, and always know when a rider is frightened. Blind forward, and seeing with each eye separately, their vision can encompass 340 degrees. They have the herd instinct and don't like to be alone; they are protective of each other and whilst grazing, one will act as lookout. They see easier in the dark than humans, and need little sleep, when they do, it's usually on their feet. Their ears move independently and they can filter out sounds at higher frequencies. As they work well together, horses are particularly suited to use as a gun team: their powerful shoulder muscles mean they can reach speeds of over forty miles an hour.

But they need to be fed four times a day, watered and groomed, and they must be shod frequently: horses need a great deal of attention. And they live to an average of twenty-five years. Though still a common sight on the streets at that time, pulling cabs, charabancs, rag-and-bone carts, milk carts and for sundry other purposes, our association with horses had been only casual at best. This was about to change, and our lives were to become interwoven in a love-hate relationship.

An intimate introduction was made in the riding school soon after our return to the Depot. It wasn't hard to find, as the pungent stench was like a beacon, readily smelled two or three hundred yards away. It was located in the adjacent men's barracks, as were the stables, and approached by the cobbled alleys. First order of the day was to familiarize ourselves and make friends inside the huge riding ring, which was done by holding the bridle and walking the horse around the sawdust-covered ring, all the while making conversation to assure the horse of our friendly intentions. Most of the horses were fairly docile, but a few were excited at meeting their new riders. Suddenly, one of the animals broke free, causing a general stampede which ended only when they were all recaptured and led individually back to the stables. This was a bad start, but we returned the following morning to try again, this time rather more successfully.

It was with some trepidation that we started the next lesson: mounting the animals. The first step was to set the stirrups to the proper length, done by facing the saddle whilst standing holding the stirrup iron under the armpit and adjusting the stirrup leather to the length of the arm. This ensured the approved riding position for the mounted branches of the British Army: it fell between the long cowboy style, where the legs were fully extended and designed for the comfort of the rider whilst in the saddle for long periods of time – more commonly known as the 'ankle and arsehole grip' – and the jockey position, where the stirrups were so shortened that the rider's knees almost touched the chin. We were taught that our knees had to grip the saddle, with heels forced down and toes pointing up. This was not at all comfortable at first; it would take time to harden the leg muscles and to get used to the position. On the order 'Mount', the rider was to gather the reins in the left hand, place the left foot in the iron, grab the saddle horn by the left hand and hoist himself into the saddle: not a very complex procedure, but several of us added a further step by continuing the momentum and sliding off the other side of the saddle. When the laughter and shouts of derision had subsided and order was restored, the next step was to achieve a military riding position, with the hands firmly holding the reins, palms up and resting on the horn. Sitting erect, chin in and chest out, completed the picture.

Given the order 'Walk', we were supposed to take up the slack on the reins and, squeezing our knees and gently prodding our heels, lead the horse forward. At this stage spurs were not worn, nor would they be until we were substantially more advanced.

The order 'Trot' was given, and the horses responded without further guidance – as they actually did to most of the commands, having heard them so often. All we had to do now was to stay on, which most of us managed, albeit in various ungainly positions like sitting off the saddle and astride the mane, with the head between the horse's ears. Several of the riders found themselves lying in the sawdust, wondering what happened. With great shame they spat out the sawdust, dusted themselves down and remounted, taking great care this time to hold their knees securely against the saddle before resuming the trot.

At the end of the hour's practice the horses were led back to the stable to huge sighs of relief from us all.

The same exercise was repeated again the next day, and we got rather more competent as the lessons went on – riding was a lot of fun, although in the early days the aches and pains we accumulated caused a great deal of discomfort. Then the day came when we had to ride bareback, with just a blanket strapped on the horse, no bridle, but a piece of rope through the horse's mouth. Going over the jumps like that was no easy task and for most of us, measuring our lengths on the ground was pretty common. There wasn't much to hang on to, so 'picking a chip' (falling off) was as easy as eating apple pie. But most of us graduated to being sophisticated horsemen; by the end of the training we had become quite accustomed to such sarcastic remarks, 'Who the hell told you to dismount?' after falling off, or 'Grip the saddle tighter with your bloody knees. You've got sweet Fanny Adam between your legs to harm!'

Apart from leading the horses back to the stables after lessons, we took little part in caring for the animals; this chore would come when we were posted to the regiment.

ON SUNDAY THERE was always church parade, and for this we would assemble in all our finery on the square adjacent to the barrack room. From there we would march to the long ceremonial parade ground which fronted the Artillery barracks complex, and fall in on the right of the men who were there for the same purpose. Quite three or four hundred yards long and almost as wide, the square was bordered on three sides by the Church, the Guard Room, and the Museum respectively. To the left of the Guard Room, separated by the main archway entrance to the barracks, lay the Officers' quarters and Mess. The several hundred soldiers parading there would march off to the music of the band which preceded them and, watched by the crowds of civilians who always came, rain or shine, to enjoy the spectacle, proceed to the Church, which was one of the original buildings of the Artillery barracks. Undamaged for more than two hundred years, it was to be almost destroyed by German air raids during the Second World War.

AFTER SEVERAL MONTHS of training, we became sufficiently capable of both drilling and playing our instruments at the same time, so we got to lead the parade. The ritual was always the same: the units would assemble within the barracks – tallest on the right, smallest on the left – where the most searching inspection would take place. Imperfections in dress would be noted, and the offender reprimanded there and then. A twisted bootlace, a cap worn at an angle, or the need of a haircut would bring instant wrath: charges of being improperly dressed would be issued and the culprit warned of his impending punishment. The units would then march through the archway onto the square to the sounds of the many orders given by those in charge. Then we'd march to the far end of the parade ground, halt and properly dress ready for the ceremony. The order would be: the mace-bearer, we boys with the drums and the buglers, playing our stirring music as we moved off, followed by the men. Regardless of the weather, in snow or rain, the heat of summer or the wildest gale, we would be there, enduring whatever the elements chose to throw at us. On a fine summer day the spectators would throng from far and wide, and it was truly a colourful occasion enjoyed by all. To the stentorian voice of the Regimental Sergeant-Major, the march along the parade ground to the church would begin. Sometimes, if the bystanders were lucky, the Royal

Artillery band would be present, playing such martial tunes as 'Talavera', a famous battle in the history of the British Army, and other equally rousing compositions. The exhibition would last the better part of an hour and, to the applause of all who were gathered, the parade would come to a final halt in front of the church where the troops would file into the pews.

At the end of the service, and after a brief ceremony on the square again, the parade would dismiss and disperse to the barracks. We would throw ourselves on our beds to relax after the three hours of activities. And then the rest of the day was now ours to do with almost entirely as we pleased. First was dinner, roast beef and Yorkshire pudding, if we were lucky. A few would write letters home, or sleep for the afternoon, but most of us would go for a walk on the common, or into the town of Woolwich, although there was precious little to do or see there as all the shops were closed for the day. Of course, there were those who would devote their time to poodle faking (looking for the girls), but rarely did they find them – with all the troops that were stationed in Woolwich, the competition was so fierce as to make it a worthless journey. While we were still new boys, still in our probationary three months, Sunday afternoons meant utter boredom as we were still confined to the barracks and options were limited to sleeping, reading, card games, wandering around the barracks, or sports, so most of us elected to play soccer. Bad weather would severely limit our choices, and if the rain was really heavy it would be a pretty dismal day.

By the end of Sunday, we had to prepare ourselves for the new round of Monday's parades and training. This meant inspections, and inspections meant a great deal of spit and polish, which was usually done during the evening. Those whose boots had not yet reached a gloss in which one's face could be reflected must spend the time 'boning and bliffing' in search of that questionable objective.

The following day our training would start again, the endless ritual with which many became bored. The drills became more rigorous, the homework for school and the examinations more complex, and the riding instruction more demanding, as we progressed to riding bareback – no easy task at the gallop and over the jumps with only a rope through the horse's mouth to act as a rein, and not without its casualties, as many were to find.

Hardly a day went by without the early morning run across the common, and the bugle practice in the sheds was ever-present. Physical training for an hour a day, with adequate food and all the outdoor activity, slowly contributed to changing our bodies from the unhealthy condition most of us were in when we entered the Depot. We were rapidly becoming a product of the British Army in every sense: more mature, and with a greater measure of self-esteem. Our habits, responding to the strict discipline thrust upon us, improved enormously; we became a cohesive band of comrades. And our characters were being formed. Those who failed to measure up were discharged from the service, much to the sorrow of those friends they had made during those few short months, to return home or from whence they came.

Even the worst of those of us who remained could be proud of our achievements. There were two awards of distinction: one was the issue of a silver bugle to replace the brass one, in recognition of the highest standard of overall performance in every aspect of training; the other recognized the athletic competence in gymnastics, for which a blue gym vest was awarded. I was lucky enough to be awarded both – I was to become known as 'Suicide Pennington' for some of my gym exploits in officer training – and, more importantly, I won the added – and rather more important – distinction of a posting to the crack regiment, the Royal Horse Artillery; there would be only four postings to this élite segment of the Artillery.

FOR ALL THE hard work we put in, the year went by in a flash, or so it felt, and now the passing-out rituals were upon us. After all the pomp and ceremony performed in celebration of the occasion, and the goodbyes to those who had played a part in our mustering as fully fledged buglers, we were granted a final period of leave before joining our appointed regiments. We would take many memories with us: the friendships we'd developed, the fun we'd had – and we *had* had fun – and the jokes we had played, like making French beds for the unsuspecting, with the top sheet doubled back like an envelope and so blocking all attempts to get in the bed, or stuffing a rag in someone's bugle so that his face would turn red by his thwarted efforts to sound a call, or, even worse, loosening the girth strap, resulting in an inelegant dismount of the would-be rider. Of course, many of these larks had resulted in a trip to the Sergeant-Major's office and the curt command, 'Remove your trousers and lie across the chair,' whereupon six of the best were inflicted on the bare bottom of the offender. I would long remember the indignity of my own visit there after being caught smoking after lights out.

That year was truly an experience of a lifetime, and at the end it was, in many ways, a gloomy, sad parting for the twenty-eight of us (only two had been discharged as being unsuitable in the end). We had become a tightly knit group to survive the ups and downs of the rigorous training. Few of us would meet again, but we would hear of the successes achieved by so many of our friends, who were to gain rank of high distinction, or who would win medals for valour. We were about to be posted to regiments all over the world; I was destined for India, but my first post was to a battery of Royal Horse Artillery presently stationed in Wales. That last day brought promises from each of the lads to keep in touch, which few of us ever did, but we all wished each other – in rough soldier slang – to keep our peckers up, and *nil desperandum*.

And so we went our various ways to serve our King and country, to acquire further territories for his Majesty, King George V, and to defend the greatest Empire the world has ever known. And some might add, 'and to peacefully annex those lands which seem to be desirable, occupied or otherwise, by force if necessary. And to convert the heathens to Christianity.'

chapter three

NEWPORT: C BATTERY, ROYAL HORSE ARTILLERY

September 1935 to December 1935

The prevailing weather when I arrived at Newport in South Wales in September, 1935, was simply terrible – hardly surprising, for it had the reputation of being a cold, bleak outpost during the winter; there were some who were adamant that it rivalled Cherrapunji in Assam, reputed to be the wettest place in the world. The rain was falling in sheets, and it was a sorry figure that walked into the barracks and presented himself at the Guard Room. Totally saturated, I was taken inside by the friendly sergeant on duty.

'Here's someone who looks like a duck out of water. Come on in, lad. Sit yourself down, we'll soon have you right, ' said the jovial sergeant in charge of the guard. 'You look in a right mess and we wouldn't want you to go sick on the first day of joining us. Not bloody likely. This calls for medical treatment, I can see that. Here, Jack,' he said to his second-in-command of the guard, 'Get some of that medicine out that we keep for emergencies and give the boy a shot of it. You can write it in the Report book that when . . .What did you say your name was, Badgie?'

With a shiver, I gave my name, wondering what this treatment was going to be.

'When Trumpeter Pennington reported for duty he was seen to be in dire circumstances and desperately in need of medical attention. In the circumstances I deemed it necessary to provide him with such medicine as is kept in the Guard Room for such a crisis and to relieve his plight,' the sergeant continued.

To my enormous astonishment, the medicine proved to be a large bottle of rum, and I was even more amazed to hear the sergeant say, 'Here you are, Trumpeter, warm the cockles of your heart,' whereupon a large tot of rum was poured in a mug and handed to me. I took a quick swig and was then divested of my drenched overcoat and uniform which were clinging uncomfortably to my body. Placed in front of the roaring coal stove, I proceeded to dry out, a mug of boiling hot tea now replacing the rum. The sergeant greeted me again, making me feel at home. 'On be'alf of the rigiment, me and my friends wot is here on duty, greet and welcome you to our midst. And you can 'ave one more short one for this celebration and to make up for the failing of the wever. Jack, don't neglect our new-found musician. Just a small one this time though, only three inches!'

This was a warm welcome indeed, and one that I was to find time and time again throughout my service. To most of us who served in peacetime the regiment was Home, and whilst the discipline was strict and unwavering, it truly fashioned itself on the concept of family life: that of sharing the good times and the bad times, of comradeship, supporting and protecting each other at all levels, regardless of rank. We learned always to see the bright side of things, and to face together the vicissitudes of life as soldiers around the world have done since the beginning of time.

My new regiment was 'C' Battery, Royal Horse Artillery, which was to be my temporary home for a few weeks before being posted to my permanent unit overseas. The barracks, a conglomeration on the slopes overlooking the town of Newport, were like all British Army barracks in Britain, identical, faceless, cold and austere. The sights and sounds were the same: the stables, with their overpowering stench, the clatter of hooves on cobblestones, the drills on the barrack square and the accompanying screaming of orders by irate instructors. You could be in any military barracks in Britain and never know the difference; in a way, that was comforting. For me, though, there was one significant difference now: I was surrounded by men, and only men. They were everywhere: in the barracks, on the square, the mess room, the canteen and around the town, hardened soldiers, most of whom had served for long periods in remote parts of the Empire, seeing and enduring often deplorable conditions. Rough and tough, many of them could say as Kipling put so well: 'I've taken my fun where I've found it; I've rogued an' I've ranged in my time, I'd 'ad my pickin' o' sweethearts'[1]. Adversity had been their constant companion; they had seen the best and the worst that humanity could offer. Vice and deviations from the path of virtue had very much been a part of their lives; certainly many had done those things which they ought not to have done. And I had now live with these men, a frightening thought for me and the other boys in the early teens who, until recently, had lived, slept, and eaten together in the same surroundings for the past year.

Several hundreds of my new comrades occupied the artillery barracks, with only two boys. We rarely saw each other, living in separate barrack rooms, each of which accommodated some fifty men. Inevitably, the rooms were heated – as and when the regulation coal issue was permitted – by a coal-burning stove. The kit-storage was displayed on metal shelving on the wall above the head of the bed, where the sword was also hung, with the clothing box at the foot of the bed: the standard layout of a British Army barrack room.

We boys would have little contact with those of our own age; that was the norm for much of our service. I missed the companionship I had enjoyed at the Depot; this was a different world, a lonely world, and I would find it difficult to become part of, or even to penetrate without shared interests and activities. Alienated from my contemporaries throughout my youthful years, I never really experienced the joys of transition from boy to manhood, as my old school friends would at home. Always in the presence of men – we were absolutely forbidden to fraternize with the girls in town, even if we'd had the time – we boys grew up quickly and learned about life too quickly, without experiencing the normal stages of innocence. We developed habits which, in civilian life, we might not have picked up until years later: we were soon swearing like troopers, smoking and gambling like troopers, and learning the cunning and tricks necessary to survive in a military environment. We would become self-sufficient and independent; wanting to and capable of doing things our own way. The character I formed over the next four years or so reflected my

1 'The Ladies' by Rudyard Kipling

attitude and behaviour for the rest of my life, and it was modelled entirely on soldiering. Destined to be a true product of the British Army, I developed a sense of independence which would serve me well in later years.

BUT HERE IN my first real posting, I had changes to my uniform that, though minor in detail, were significant in practice. The Royal Horse Artillery had the prestigious honour of being 'the right of the line', which was echoed by the words of the trumpet call which was heard throughout the day: 'The Royal Horse Artillery, the pride of the army. The first on the field and the last to retire.' The single strand lanyard, previously worn on the right shoulder, now changed to a plaited lanyard threaded under the epaulette of the left shoulder. The gun wheel on the cap badge was raised and would rotate, whereas before it had been a fixture. The buttons of the tunic were no longer flat, but rounded like a ball; hence the men of the Horse Artillery being scornfully known to the other artillery units as, 'Those ball-buttoned bastards!' – but then, not everyone could belong to such a prestigious club. And puttees were discarded in favour of black knee-length jack-boots, which really distinguished us from those who were obliged to wear the common puttee with riding breeches. I was really excited at these changes, and proud that I was to serve with such an élite branch of the Gunners. The right of the line: that was the privilege of the Royal Horse Artillery; if the entire British Army were to parade ceremoniously and in order of precedence, units of the Horse Artillery would be on the right flank of the formation – much to the chagrin of all the other regiments. (At one time, I was the senior trumpeter in A Battery of the First Regiment Royal Horse Artillery, which would place me on the extreme right of the British Army.) A further signal recognition of the Royal Horse Artillery's high eminence was that we had the honour of firing the first rounds of Allied artillery gunfire at the beginning of both the First and Second World Wars.

In the beginning, British gun trains were manned by civilians who, with their own oxen, were rented by the army. This was not a very satisfactory arrangement, for they were not subject to military discipline and the speed of the train was always dictated by their current attitudes. Accordingly, their speculative services were dispensed with and the Government formed the Driver Corps: regular soldiers who took over the responsibility for the gun trains and who were later to become known as the Corps of Artillery Drivers. The Corps usually formed up on the right of the infantry so they could bring the guns into action satisfactorily, and that became the accepted position. Originally, only two members of the gun team were mounted and the other gunners were on foot, so the process of coming into action was still very slow. However, in 1793, certain units mounting every member of the crew were formed and the process speeded up considerably: thus the Royal Horse Artillery came into existence, and from that centuries-long habit of forming up on the right of the infantry, we truly earned our title: The Right of the Line.

The word *Ubique* (everywhere) on the cap and collar badges signified that wherever the battles raged, in the deserts, the jungle, the plains or the mountains, the guns were there, offering our mighty power in support of the infantrymen; thus our *Ubique* designation:

> There is a word you often see, prnounce it as you may —
> 'You bike', 'you bykwee', 'ubbikwe' – alludin' to R.A.
> It serves, 'Orse, Field, an' Garrison as motto for a crest;
> An' when you've found out all it means, I'll tell you 'alf the rest.[1]

In virtually every war more soldiers have been killed by artillery gunfire than any other weapon, and its devastating effect on those at the receiving end of the bombardment is, at the very least, totally demoralizing. A high proportion of casualties in modern warfare is attributed to shell shock. The Royal Artillery Regiment had played a part in almost every battle; it could be seen everywhere, living up its motto: *Quo Fas Et Gloria Ducunt*: Where Right and Honour Lead. Its list of battle honours is long and impressive.

At Warburg, in 1760, a British battery opened fire at point-blank range on a French cavalry unit whilst crossing a river and tore it to pieces. At the battle of Minden in 1759, ten artillery guns, by coming into action quickly, intercepted a superior French cavalry charge directed against an already tattered British force. Again at extremely short range, they opened fire, regardless of the heavy fire they themselves were under, and broke the French ranks, thereby saving the beleaguered British regiments. And on another occasion they so harassed an overwhelming enemy force

1 'Ubique *Royal Artillery*' by Rudyard Kipling

of ten thousand against a British unit one fifth of its size that they caused it to unconditionally surrender.

The artillery played a key role in the battle of Louisbourg in 1758 for the British capture of Québec: in the fight of the Heights of Abraham, the steep cliffs made it impossible for more than one gun to take part in the assault against the French, but that single gun had such a considerable effect on the formidable French troops that it determined the outcome of the battle.

In the Crimean War, soon after the disastrous retreat at Balaclava in 1854, a more bitter battle, between the British and Russians, took place at Inkerman. In spite of the crushing odds, with the Russians mustering fifty thousand, the relatively small force of the British did not give in and it was the guns again that turned the tide: the Russian attack failed dismally, suffering enormous casualties. There were many individual moments of valour, like the British Gun Sergeant A. Henry, who personally fought off many of the Russians and guarded his gun against all-comers before he was bayoneted to death; for this he was awarded the Victoria Cross, a medal which had just been struck for bravery. But it was the accurate and devastating fire of the 18-pounder guns which eventually defeated the Russians. Galloping into action on their flanks, the guns were brought to bear with such precision, racking the Russian line with shot and cutting wide swathes of destruction through their demoralized ranks, that they were forced to withdraw.

Stories of the guns and the bravery and heroism of the men who served them runs like a thread through the history of the British Army. I was proud to join their ranks.

IN ADDITION TO all the other equipment, I was issued with a rifle and, above all things the most important to me, a sword, which reached from the ground almost to my chest! Not as heavy as the 303 rifle, which weighed nine pounds with its bayonet attached, it was nevertheless a cumbersome object for a young lad standing less than five feet high. It was standard equipment for all gunners, man or boy, to be carried during ceremonial parades or whilst on active duty; fortunately for me, the occasions were few but, when it was required, it was a severe impediment to mounting or riding, or, for that matter, performing drills of any kind.

Within two days of my arrival at the barracks, once I had drawn all my equipment and completed the necessary documentation and was considered to have settled in, I was assigned to regimental duties and training. These were onerous, and the same routine was always followed, every day of the week, every week of the month; this ritual of employment was typical of the British Army peacetime activities and you could gamble – and win – that whatever was going on in Newport was also happening in Aldershot, Bulford, Catterick, London or anywhere else in the country.

Reveille was early, usually at six in the morning, so the duty trumpeter must be up before that time to sound the call. Often, though, the boy would have just fallen out of bed and was still asleep placing the trumpet to his lips, resulting many times in flat notes and a deeply embarrassed lad returning to his bed. The awakened troops must prepare for the day, and the stable detail must assemble in the horse lines to muck out and wash down, a dirty, smelly, and unpleasant job, which few relished. Rough exercise followed, and by six-thirty the steel-shod hooves would be heard ringing on the cobblestones of the Newport streets outside the barracks. There could be as many as thirty or forty horses being exercised at the same time, half mounted, with the riders leading a second horse by the reins. On a cold morning the horses were often frisky and difficult to control; breakaways were not uncommon and many a man lost his seat whilst trying to keep his two nettlesome mounts together.

The Riding Sergeant showed great consideration for me, as I had joined the regiment with so little experience. It was a bit of a shock to find I was pressed into this duty so quickly, and it was with some anxiety that I mounted up to take part in the rough exercise for the first time. I needn't have worried, though, for the sergeant had made sure that the horses I was to be responsible for were of a relatively docile disposition, and not given to excitable behaviour as a rule. And of course, it was raining heavily, as it frequently does in Newport during those November days. The men who'd been stationed there for some time expected it and were accustomed to it, but it wasn't a good start for me. I had lived with the wild and driving winter gales in Blackpool when the rain fell endlessly, and without mercy. I had even enjoyed walking along the seafront, being soaked by the giant waves formed by the violent winds and flung across the breakwater. But there I hadn't had to exercise horses on the promenade, and at such an early hour, on an empty stomach! Newport became synonymous to me with rain; I had yet to encounter the monsoons that awaited me in distant lands.

There were few other souls on the streets at that time of the day; just labourers going to work early in the half light and boys delivering news-papers, with maybe a horse-drawn milk cart on rounds, a postman plodding from door to door, or the coalman delivering his wares to those who could afford them, already blackened by the dust of his trade. It was far too early to hear the cries of the rag-and-bone man; only later would his dejected-looking pony and the rickety cart trundle along the streets collecting old junk of any kind in exchange for a balloon or a small paper flag. 'Union Jack, for the children to play with,' was his cry; he had precious few toys to give away. There were few cars about, and other than the occasional bus, there was not much noise or movement to alarm the horses.

There was little protection for either man or beast from the driving rain, which now fell almost torrentially, creating pools on the roads and filling the clogged gutters. The storm-darkened sky and the constant down-pour reduced visibility to a few yards and it was largely habit which guided the horses along the appointed route, with little or no direction from the riders. Wearing only a peaked cap and a groundsheet over our uniforms, we were saturated in minutes. And as we rode along the dreary streets lined with the rows of identical stone houses, none of which had gardens, no flowers or trees of any kind, cheek by jowl in a colourless setting with their front doors opening onto the pavements, we sought to isolate our-selves from the depressing monotony; knowing that tomorrow and the next day we must endure the same routine. Our spirits lifted and the pace of the horses increased as we drew near to the barrack gates; we were all hungry and seeking refuge from the elements. For the men, however, returning to the barracks did not mean instant relief and time to dry out and relax: the horses always came first and only when they were unsaddled, dried down, watered and fed and bedded down were we riders free to address our own needs. It was almost eight o'clock before these chores were finished and then we were able to hurry to the dining room where, hopefully, breakfast was still being served. And if it wasn't, then we were out of luck.

Whilst in the stables tending to the horses the men, in spite of the discomfort and anxiety to get the job finished before the food was gone, exhibited patience and acceptance of the duties by singing songs which had long been associated with the Gunners. One of these, most appropriate to the moment, and sung with gusto was, 'I'll be there . . . '

Oh! You ought to see the drivers on a Friday night,
Rifting out the harness in the pale moonlight,
For there's going to be an inspection in the morning,
In the little harness room across the square.

I'll be there, I'll be there,
In the little harness room across the square.
When we're filing out for water, I'll be kissin'
The Colonel's daughter,
In the little harness room across the square.

There were other verses with far more descriptive suggestions better kept to ourselves, so these were sung very quietly, as it would not do for the sergeant-major, or the officers, to hear the blasphemous content directed at their persons; the reprisals were too severe to be contemplated.

I WAS FASCINATED with the guns and in my spare moments would visit the gun sheds adjacent to the stables. Painted grey, with the burnished steel of the breech gleaming brilliantly in the light, the oak solid wheels banded with steel, they were an impressive sight. Emblazoned on the barrels was the Royal cipher: the Colours of the Royal Regiment of Artillery. In battle, for the foot regiments to lose the standard was a shameful thing and to be avoided at all costs. To the gunner, the loss of a gun with its precious cipher to the enemy was therefore to lose the regiment colours. This was an act of disgrace and the fear of every gunner, who would willingly sacrifice his life and die fighting to prevent so unspeakable a loss. At my first close inspection, I stood almost in adoration, longing for the day I would be part of the gun team and hear its voice roar with authority myself. Not the most modern of weapons, a 13-pounder (soon to be replaced by the 18-pounder and 25-pounder), was still an ordnance well loved by all artillerymen; it had proved its worth many times on the field of battle. But I was not yet to sit by the breach behind the steel shield as number two of the gun team, awaiting the order to fire, not even during gun drill. But while I waited, I continued to be enraptured by the sight of these guns, and accorded them the reverence they commanded.

Being a transient, I never quite became accustomed to the regiment: I was with it, but not of it. The men appeared friendly and considerate, although I sensed their reservation whilst talking to me. Perhaps this was natural enough; if they were an intrusion in my life, then certainly I was in theirs. I was always treated with respect and courtesy, but had to accept the foul language which flowed so naturally from them. It was a boisterous atmosphere in which to live, a typical soldiers' barracks, especially on Friday night when our pockets were replenished by payday. The carousing continued through Saturday, or until the money ran out. Gambling groups played twenty-one, or shoot, or poker whilst strictly forbidden drinking parties were held around them.

At times these parties became wild and frightening for me, like one evening when, after drinking too much, one of the gunners leapt on his bed, drew his sword from its scabbard and waved it dangerously in the air. Those who were more sober could not at first decide if he was playing a game of intimidation in fun, or if he was really in earnest to cause damage or even injury to those around him. As he lunged forward with the blade, a violent expression on his face, it rapidly became clear this was no pretence, and that the man really had gone berserk. Quickly three of his colleagues flung him to the ground, wresting the sword free and casting it aside. The place was in an uproar now, and many of the troops had run from the building to escape the fracas. Those who remained came forward to help, bringing with them the water-filled fire buckets positioned around the room, all except one of which were promptly poured over the apparently madman, who was then brought to his knees and had his head stuck firmly in the remaining water-filled bucket.

After three successive dunkings he had sobered sufficiently to be released, although he was still watched closely by those around him. Gradually he calmed down, becoming quite rational and very subdued as he lay quietly on his bed. After awhile the incident was considered closed, and the activities of Friday night resumed their light-hearted manner. I never really understood what had gone on. Was the behaviour of the man feigned, or was it real? High jinks or drugs? Surely not drugs; they were not in style in those days; could have been the beer, but the man didn't drink any more than the others, and they didn't go into hysterics even after one over the eight. He had served eight years in India and Aden, the latter station being particularly desolate, but nobody really cared to speculate on the truth, or even talked about it after the incident was over, and I was left forever wondering what had really happened that night. But I withdrew a little more into my shell because of it.

RIDING EXERCISES CONTINUED, but this time I was in the big league, with more advanced activities awaiting. Most of this took place in the riding school – not so different to that at the Depot; it just seemed smaller now because the moveable fences over which the jumps would take place were scattered around it. As the days progressed, these became higher and higher, and the spills were more frequent. Often wearing full equipment with sword and rifle, trumpet slung over the back and holding the bugle in my right hand resting on my knee, I found it hard going and within minutes was sweating heavily. But there was no respite, and the Sergeant Riding Instructor always kept us hard at it for the full hour. Sometimes the whole battery would parade mounted on the barrack square, again in full dress regalia, performing complicated manoeuvres in preparation for ceremonial occasions – and this was done regardless of the weather conditions. Parades could go on for hours, but they were always scheduled as the last event of the day so that after supper the men were free to relax for the evening.

We were allowed out of the barracks both during the day and the evening until ten o'clock; if you wanted to stay out later, a special pass was required, and these were issued only in unusual circumstances. I rarely went out in the evening; on the few weekends I did walk into the town, I found it dull, with nothing for a boy to do. I was invariably penniless anyway; the shops and restaurants were too expensive and so of little interest. The rain discouraged exploring further afield. I preferred to spend what little money I had in the barrack canteen, where char and wads' were cheap, or in the library where I could sit quietly and read to my heart's content, or watch the town: the windows overlooked Newport about a mile away in the valley and the ever-changing activities down there entertained me, especially the railway station. I had a fine view of it and the trains that

1 Tea and cakes

entered and departed every few minutes and I would sit there speculating on their destinations, wondering which, if any, would be going to Lancashire, perhaps even to Blackpool. And as they steamed out of the station, their shrill whistles echoed across the valley, as if calling me to say, 'We are always here when you want us.' A contact with the outside world, a lifeline to home, it provided some comfort in my loneliness.

ONE MORNING I was told to report to the office, where I was met by the Battery Sergeant-Major. My posting overseas had arrived. Although no surprise to him, I was a little taken aback by the speed with which this was to happen: I would be aboard a troop-ship sailing to India within the month; I was off to E Battery, Royal Horse Artillery. I was granted embarkation leave for two weeks, and was free to go wherever I wished during that period, but I must then return to Newport and report back for duty at the barracks on December 12, 1935. I was to return my rifle and sword to the Quartermaster's Store at once, then present myself to the Medical Inspection Room for vaccination and inoculation.

I had to sign a statement saying that I accepted this posting to India without coercion of any kind, and that my decision was entirely voluntary. It was a further requirement that I was to remain in that distant land at the pleasure of his Majesty's Government. With my head in a whirl, completely consumed with the excitement of soon sailing to the mysterious Far East, I signed the document without demur. The interview with the Sergeant-Major concluded with a handshake and congratulations for being so fortunate to get posted to such an illustrious regiment, with a final comment, 'Don't let the wogs get you down. Keep away from the *kala bibis* (black women) in the bazaars, and keep your topee on at all times. Remember, there are only two occasions when a soldier must remove his head-dress – in church, or before your Commanding Officer on a charge.'

I understood *some* of the bits about the wogs – the wily oriental gentlemen – and the black women, having listened to the ramblings of old soldiers who had served in India and been fortunate enough to have returned to dear old Blighty more or less intact and unblemished. But I'd also heard plenty of tales about British soldiers who were not so fortunate, returning home scarred in body and mind from their contact with the Indian women and the rigours of the climate. I wasn't even really sure what a wog looked like; there were few in England, so opportunities to see them were rare. Those I had seen at the Indian Theatre at the Pleasure Beach: they were black, so they must be wogs – but perhaps that was just make-up. Well, I would soon find out.

But I wasn't so sure what the Sergeant-Major meant about the topees. A stern-looking man, he had a wrinkled face burned almost black by exposure to the hot Indian sun and looked ravaged himself by the hardships he had endured for so many years; perhaps he also had served too long in remote Indian stations.

After returning my equipment to the QM's Stores as instructed, I went to the MI Room and was given the inoculations and vaccinations required to fight a variety of diseases and sicknesses to which all British servicemen might be exposed when serving abroad. These were the first of the many injections to which I would be subjected throughout the years ahead, and soon my arms would be pitted by scars marking the faraway places I'd been. Back in the barrack room, the men grinned as they ragged me about my session with the medical orderly, asking which part of my bum had suffered with the inoculation, and how deep had the bayonet penetrated. In response, I grimaced as I sat down on the tender side by mistake, involuntarily exclaiming, 'Ouch!', which adequately replied to their taunts and brought even louder laughter from the questionable sympathizers. But I had neither time nor inclination to join in the discussion concerning my rear end; it was all getting a bit too personal anyway. I had to start my leave in the morning, so after a quick supper, I packed my kit-bag for those two weeks of freedom.

Early to bed, I slept poorly, worrying about missing the train in the morning: must not forget the rail pass, or my pay for the period whilst away. Would my bugle and trumpet be safe in the locked box at the foot of my bed, and what about any letters or parcels that might arrive during my absence – especially if Aunt Alice sent me her usual treat of cake or parkin? The morning came soon enough, and happily, none of my forebodings proved true. With two weeks' pay in my pocket – ten shillings, the largest amount of money I had ever carried – I felt rich. That was the residue of sixteen shillings and eightpence minus the allowance to my mother and other stoppages. I was off to Blackpool, the only place I had friends and family, and with money in hand, I'd be able to have a grand time. Maybe I would see Peggy, a girl I had known at school – I had never dated her, but now, perhaps I would take her to the flicks, and even buy her an ice cream at the interval when the ushers came round. With such largess in my pocket, all things were possible.

Down at the station in good time and looking every inch the proper soldier in my khaki uniform, finally complete with shining steel spurs and swagger stick, I boarded the train after twice checking it was the right one, and that it really did go to Blackpool – but no, I would have to change at Preston, where I would join the Fylde Coast Express after a twenty-minute wait. Exactly on time, the express steamed into the station and I boarded to find all the third class seats were taken. It didn't bother me: I stood in the corridor so that I could watch for the Tower, but as it came into view, I felt rather indifferent, perhaps even a little blasé. I was now part of a new family, and wherever I went in the future, it would be with the Gunners, not the family in Blackpool. There was just a tinge of remorse at the thought that I would probably not see my parents again for several years, maybe even ever again, for they were not young any more and might even die while I was away. And what about me? The old soldiers said death and burial came quickly in India: you could be alive and well at breakfast time, sick by noon and buried by sundown.

I quickly cast aside that depressing thought as the train drew into the familiar station and I saw my father waiting, obviously pleased to see me. There was not just a handshake, but a firm and welcoming embrace, to express his love and affection. My father wanted to carry the kit-bag, perhaps not so much to relieve me of the task, but rather to once again experience the days when he too was in uniform and living out of a kit-bag. Then it was onto the number thirteen bus and a fifteen-minute ride home, where Mum had the red carpet out and a cup of tea ready. After a long-lasting hug, I was made to sit down in front of the coal fire: it was indeed a special day; the luxury of a fire in the grate was a rare one in light of Dad's unemployment. Glancing around the living room, I saw that my mother's housekeeping hadn't changed: *a place for everything and everything in its place*, reflecting her heartfelt belief that cleanliness came next to godliness. And supper was ready, with a big helping of one of my favourite meals, rabbit pie – there was a small cup in the middle to hold up the pastry – with mashed potatoes and green beans. That was followed by a trifle, the likes of which only my mother or perhaps Aunt Alice could make. Washed down by several cups of tea, it was a banquet compared to what I was eating in the army.

Nothing would do now but that I must tell them all about being a soldier. Dad had a knowing look on his face as I told of the quiet and sedate life I was living: no drinking beer for me, or smoking, and certainly no chasing the girls in Newport. Statements that obviously pleased Mum were met with Dad's comments written on his face, a broad grin which spoke volumes: if that was how a soldier lived now, things had certainly changed since his days. But then, most soldiers were adept at lying whilst keeping a straight and innocent face, weren't they? Without that ability, they would certainly never survive the life they had chosen.

I unpacked my few belongings in the bedroom where I had slept for so many years. My bed was so old that it had a distinct concave curvature in the middle – but nothing could be so unforgivingly uncomfortable as the three rock-like biscuits that passed as mattresses on a British military bed. Anyway, right now there were more important things to do: first, I must visit Aunt Alice, then my old best friend, and then . . .

MY EMBARKATION LEAVE was not a great success. Most of my friends were otherwise occupied whenever I called upon them: perhaps next time; right now they had more important things on the go, and it was unlikely they would be free for the next week or so. I tried the Tower and the Winter Gardens, which were always popular meeting places in the past, but there were no familiar or welcoming faces. It was a different world, and not one that I was particularly enjoying, so I spent much of my time wandering around the deserted Pleasure Beach, where the now-silent sideshows and amusements were a pathetic picture of desolation, contrasting sharply with the gaiety of the summer months. As I meandered along, I reminisced about my school days, and of the endless fun I had always had on these same entertainments which were now so derelict. There were no tourists in December, and few of the residents of Blackpool cared to amuse themselves with outdoor activities during the winter months: they stayed home, away from the gales which swept down from the north, bringing destruction to property and possessions, and even injury or death to those foolish enough to challenge the wrath of the devastating weather.

I was one of the few who revelled in the huge waves cascading along the beaches. The ruthless and intense violence was just my cup of tea: I enjoyed myself immensely as I clung to my cap with one hand, with the other firmly locked to the iron rail which bordered the sea front. Of necessity it was a short adventure: it was not long before I reluctantly acknowledged defeat by the raging storm. Retreating some fifty yards to the far side of the promenade, I found sufficient refuge to watch the damage being wrought as the waves came crashing down on the tramcar lines spanning the length of the promenade. Walking towards the South Pier, wet to the marrow and with the wind tearing at my clothes and threatening to strip them entirely from my body, I knew I would always remember the harsh face of Blackpool's winter, compared with the benign panorama it presented during the summer months.

AS THE TRAIN left the station it was déjà vu, an almost exact reproduction of the last parting. A soldier's life is always liberally punctuated with, 'Hello and goodbye,' and, 'See you next time?' Barely out of sight of my parents, my mind was already racing ahead: I was off to see the world, and at the King's expense. Back again in the Newport barracks, and the Saturday night's revels in full swing, I joined with the troops in the barrack room who were singing as they gambled and drank the night away. The object of the song at that particular moment was the riding instructor – not necessarily the riding instructor of C Battery, but of all riding instructors, wherever we were:

> *What's he want to wear his spurs for,*
> *What's he want to wear his spurs for,*
> *What's he want to wear his spurs for*
> *When he couldn't ride a Piccadilly pros …*
>
> *I'd been in the saddle for hours and hours,*
> *I'd stuck it as long as I could*
> *I stuck, I stuck it,*
> *At last I said fuck it,*
> *My arsehole is not made of wood …*
>
> *What's he want to wear his spurs for …*

This was followed by other songs demonstrating our innocence; my vocabulary was again improved as I listened to the ribald remarks which accompanied the singing. It was a common saying that if ever the troops were silent and morose, it indicated low morale, and that trouble was brewing. That was not the case this night as our songs and laughter echoed throughout the barracks, and no one thought to reprimand us. All was well in the ranks that day. It was my fervent hope, as I looked more closely at the men, that my prospective new friends in faraway India would offer the same companionship. I was beginning to feel sorry to leave these men, and they would always be in my mind whenever I thought of the Royal Horse Artillery.

But tomorrow it was to the boat.

MY WAR WAS getting closer. Germany repudiated the disarmaments clause of the Versailles Treaty and introduced conscription. Though Britain and Germany agreed that German naval vessels would not exceed one third of the British fleet in number, Germany spoke with forked tongue, and their construction of U-boats was increased dramatically. Now war was inevitable.

chapter four

HMT NEURALIA:
LIVERPOOL TO BOMBAY

December 1935 to January 1936

On the day of my departure from Newport, I was pleased to find I was not to make the journey to India alone, though I was the only trumpeter in the group of five gunners and two junior NCOs. We were all pleased to be escaping from the humdrum life of peacetime soldiering in England. This was the great moment we'd all looked forward to for weeks: for a while at least there would be no more square bashing or rough exercise, no more guard duties, or kit inspections or mucking out the stables. Our kit-bags were heavier than usual, as we were also carrying our KD (khaki drill) tropical uniforms which had been issued a few days before. Dressed in FSMO (field service marching order), including overcoats, with our topees (sun helmets) slung over our shoulders, we were an incongruous sight on that unusually warm day. No onlooker could doubt we were destined for the tropics, and many of the spectators were quick to shout, 'Good luck, Tommy!' or, 'Come back safe, lads,' as they waved goodbye to the departing train.

We arrived in Liverpool and many more troops boarded the train. We soldiers were in separate coaches from the civilians; soon there were several hundreds of us crammed into the third-class compartments.

There were sad scenes at some of the stations as families waved farewell to their menfolk. With tears in their eyes, mothers clung to children as the families' sole providers left, all doubtless wondering if and when they would see their husbands and fathers again: life for most of them would degenerate into loneliness and financial hardship. Whilst the men would have the comradeship offered by their new family, the regiment, and would be assured of food, clothing and medical attention where necessary, this was rarely the case for those who stayed behind, who would return to homes ill equipped to sustain them through the cold winters that lay ahead. As well as the struggle to survive without adequate food to eat or coal to burn, there would be little contact with the army, far away on the other side of the world.

The British government didn't have a good reputation when it came to dealing responsibly or kindly with soldiers or their dependants. For some unknown reason, the Government preferred to turn a blind eye both to the paltry welfare provided and to the shocking conditions under which the soldier and his family laboured. The politicians were sincere enough on the platform, but their compassion was expressed in idle rhetoric, without a single shred of substance. 'It's Tommy this and Tommy that, an' "Tommy, go away." But it's "Thank you, Mister Atkins," when the band begins to play.'[1] Although I was still a boy, I would come to understand this myself all too soon, and be quick to look askance at those with ready praise for the wonderful things the Government did for the Armed Forces.

LIVERPOOL WAS A mighty port, one of the busiest in Britain, from which ships plied constantly around the globe, carrying passengers and goods to and from every corner of the world. A prosperous harbour, it played a major role in the affairs of the Empire in peace and war. None of us had any idea of the great hardships its people would suffer in later years, during the bombing in the Second World War, or as the port's decline because of changing markets and new methods of transport brought great poverty to its inhabitants. (And, quite unknown to me at that time, Liverpool was also home to the girl who was to become my bride. She was six years old, going on seven, and her name was Enid.)

The ship awaiting our contingent was HMT *Neuralia*. Silhouetted against the dawn sky heralding the beginning of the new day – for we had travelled through the night – she was an impressive sight. Surrounded by vessels of all kinds, passenger liners, freighters, warships, and even a

1 'Tommy', from *Barrack Room Ballads* by Rudyard Kipling

sprinkling of tall-masted sailing ships, it became a kaleidoscope of colour as the sun slowly dissipated the darkness. His Majesty's bands were already present on the quay, resplendent in scarlet and gold-trimmed jackets and black trousers with the plume-tipped Busby helmets, in sharp contrast with the drab khaki uniforms of those of us who were about to board. Playing martial tunes proclaiming the might and glory of the British Empire, with instruments gleaming in the now-risen sun, they marched the length of the quay adjacent to the troop-ship with all the pomp and circumstance that the British Army does so well. It was a stirring spectacle to our band of soldiers who had just arrived weary and unshaven after the discomfort of the train journey. But our ablutions must wait until we were aboard; our greater need now was food, and it was a heart-warming sight to see that, at the far end of the sheds where the train had arrived, breakfast was being served.

'Fall in facing the boat!' The order rang loud and clear as the band marched off to provide room for the troops to assemble. The markers were in place and, in compliance with the order and struggling with our kit-bags, we formed up in threes facing the boat. Even then, there were those in the ranks who fervently wished that they were listening to the order, 'Pick up your parrots and monkeys and fall in facing the boat!', coming home to Blighty, rather than leaving her shores again. They dreamed about those magical words while they were serving in foreign stations they hated, longing to return to England. For many, their lives were totally consumed by that need, their minds permanently back in England, however far from home their bodies were.

But now, we were leaving: 'Right turn. Forward march. Left wheel. Single file as you march up the gang plank!' And, as we trod for the last time on the soil of England, some paused in the middle of the gangway that bridged the gap between ship and shore to look once more at the country of our birth, and with the wistful thought that, perhaps one day . . .

Once aboard, we were escorted to the decks where we would spend the three weeks that it would take to reach our final destination. Instructed to leave our kit below, we were informed, over the ship's loud-hailer, that she would be sailing very shortly and if anyone wished to go on to the main deck for the departure, they might do so now. As expected, there was a rush to claim a prime place on the rails of the top deck, and, after a great deal of pushing and shouting in the mad rush, I was lucky enough to be one of those who did so. The dockside far below was still a seething mass of activity in preparation for the departure.

Last-minute consultations between the ship's officers and the dock officials culminated in the removal of the gangway. And as the hawsers were cast off, severing the ship from the dock, the hundreds who still lined the shore broke into rousing cheers to the sound of the band as it played 'Rule Britannia'. Echoed on board by the troops and accompanied by the sirens of the *Neuralia* and a dozen other vessels at anchor in the bay, the farewells could be heard miles away. As the propellers turned and the ship slowly moved away from its berth, with the band now playing 'Auld Lang Syne', those on the ship and on the shore became more emotional, creating memories which would be indelibly imprinted on many minds for ever. There was a renewed outcry from all who were present – an outburst of compassion and despair for most, of hope for others. Though I, and many of the troops aboard, were elated at the prospects that lay ahead, there were, however, those who would rather have stayed in England's green and pleasant land, where conditions were visibly improving and the great depression they had struggled through during the last few years was about to end. Prosperity was imminent, bringing with it rewards beyond our wildest dreams; the good times would roll again, that was, according to the predictions of our country's leaders.

As the clamour of the goodbyes faded away and the coastline receded, the *Neuralia* gathered speed under the direction of the pilot, who would see us through the hazards of the local currents to open waters, after which he would board his launch to return home. The fanfare of the royal send-off was over: another batch of troops had been dispatched as reinforcements to the outposts of the Empire. Now the cold winds blowing off the sea beneath the darkening clouds brought reality back to those of us who lingered by the rails, quickly persuading us to seek refuge below.

THE *NEURALIA* WAS not an old vessel, compared to other British troop-carriers. Built with her sister ship, the *Nevada*, in the year 1912, she had a displacement of 9,000 tons and a capability of fifteen knots. She had also gained the reputation of providing her own bad weather in even the calmest of seas; in a gale it was impossible for even the most mature sailor to withstand seasickness. Still in use as a troop-transport in the late fifties, she had played various roles during her life, from hospital ship to passenger vessel plying the route between England and the Far East. Primitive by modern standards, she nonetheless did sterling service, though few of the soldiers who sailed aboard her were quick to expound on the delights and comfort of having done so.

Returning to the living quarters two decks below, I saw for the first time the conditions there and realized that this journey would not, by any stretch of imagination, be roses all the way. The inadequacy of the living and sleeping space allocated to the group with whom I was travelling was clearly apparent. By day it served as an eating area; the tables and benches were each designed to accommodate sixteen men, squashed together with arms touching. We would also spend our free time there. By night, the tables would be collapsed and stored so that hammocks could now be slung in the same space. And, somewhere in all this, we had to find space to store our kit-bags and other possessions. It was clear that chaos would erupt if we didn't take great care: tempers could flare so easily in that confined, hot and oppressive little space. At mealtimes, two men from each table had to go up to the galley on the deck above to collect the food. Carrying it back down the almost vertical and already slippery steps, which daily became worse, was a hazardous proceeding; a false step was likely to empty a container of stew, or other food, long before it reached the mess tables. Unfortunate, too, was the person who stood below to receive the unexpected gift; the first time it happened, laughter and sympathy were offered by the audience, but the second time brought wrath on the careless offender.

Slinging a hammock wasn't an easy task; occupying it was another matter entirely, requiring skill and determination, and frustration was the order of the day as we made our first attempts. It reminded us of those early days of riding instruction, when the order to mount was executed in a similar manner, and resulted in the rider sliding so ungracefully off the other side of the saddle.

I, like many others at that first meal, found myself wondering how the officers were quartered, and if they were also eating from mess-tins, after going to the galley to collect their food. Past experience brought the quick answer: certainly not, they would be eating in a first-class dining room, with a choice of the most sumptuous dishes from a menu as long as your arm, and served by an ever-attentive waiter. 'Today, we recommend the roast beef served with roast potatoes and asparagus tips . . . a little more red wine, sir?' Nothing but the best for our officers. Perhaps I would not have been so envious had I known that one day I too would get a chance to experience the same luxuries – but that was a long time in the future. Meanwhile, for supper it was bangers and mash with treacle pudding to follow, and the pudding so heavy you couldn't give it away!

Few of us slept well that night, unaccustomed to the hammocks which swayed constantly and the persistent groans and creaks of the ship, so we passed the long night smoking and chatting in low voices of the pleasures of sailing on a troop-ship. Others were reacting to the turmoil of the day, locked in nightmare; their cries added to the already impossible conditions of our new barrack room. We were all thankful when the call came for our morning physical exercise on the top decks and the luxury of a hot shower and a clean shave in the ablution area. Then bacon and eggs for breakfast – both of which were so cold and greasy as to be quite inedible, which brought a deluge of curses on the cooks and anyone else even remotely involved in the preparation and delivery of the food. There must have been a lot of ears burning, including those of the officer on duty who had failed to visit the mess decks. Had he done so, and asked the customary question, 'Are there any complaints?'– never expecting for a moment that there would be, for to complain often led to reprisals for the individual foolish enough to do so – he would this time have met with the most candid complaints, articulated by everyone at the table, and ejaculated in such eloquent profanity as only a soldier can.

After the meal we were informed, over the public address system, that there were to be no parades for the remainder of the day, which was greeted with cheers throughout the ship. As if by magic, gambling games sprang up in every corner of the boat: on the main deck it was housey-housey, the most popular pastime of all for the troops; and, where money changed hands, the only legal gambling game allowed. By the nature of the game, one couldn't lose too much money, yet if you were lucky, and there were a lot of players, the pay-out could be well worth winning. The decks rang to the sound of, 'Eyes down, look in,' as the caller pulled the numbers: 'The first number is number eleven, legs eleven,' followed by, 'Kelly's eye, number one; Dinky do, number two; Two and six, half a crown; One and six, pick up sticks; Number four, knock on the door; one and three, unlucky for some. Is anybody sweating?' And so went the numbers, with everyone 'getting a sweat on' as they neared the final number which would make them a winner. And suddenly the call, 'House!', by that lucky person, to the accompaniment of 'You lucky bastard!' or 'Yes, I know that cunt. If he fell down the toilet he'd come up with a box of fucking choco- lates!' And then it was off to the canteen for the winner and his muckers to 'swill a few gills' in celebration.

As well as housey-housey, which was allowed, there were card games everywhere, mostly operated by members of the ship's crew. Secreted away in the most secluded areas, and guarded by a network of lookouts to give warning of any approaching authority, they operated Pontoon, Shoot and Find the Lady, amongst others. However, the game which attracted the heaviest gamblers was Crown and Anchor, with a maximum wager set high enough by the operator to please everyone. It was a 'roll the dice' game; a plastic sheet about two feet square was balanced on any conven- ient stand – a capstan was ideal. It was divided into four squares, each containing the symbol of a crown, an anchor, a king or a queen. You placed your money on the symbol of your choice and, when all the players had done so, the dice – which have crown, anchor, king and queen symbols on the faces instead of number dots – were thrown. If the faces on the dice matched your bet, then you were a winner; it could be a single or multiple pay-out, according to the symbols shown by the dice. If you'd placed your bet on the crown and the rolled dice displayed two crowns, then you got double your money.

It was a simple, fast-moving game requiring neither skill nor experi- ence; it was entirely a matter of luck. Some tried to predict what the next roll would show, encouraged by the operator's comments (when the last throw had resulted in three anchors, 'Where there's three, there's one!'), only to find they could have done better by closing their eyes and placing their coins by chance. It was a fascinating game and it was possible to win a lot of money if you knew when to stop, but not many did, and few ended up with a profit.

If the lookout gave a warning cry, then the board and money were hastily removed and the players would engage in innocent conversation until the danger was over. And within seconds of the all clear, the game resumed with the players' money replaced as if it had never been disturbed. The operator was invariably the winner at the end of every session; Kipling was so right when he wrote, 'If you can make one heap of all your winnings And risk it on one turn of pitch and toss . . . you'll be a Man, my son."[1] They were all men, and they all lost.

Returning to other activities, they did so unabashed; there would be another payday soon, and then they'd show 'em: 'Next time we'll get it all back from those bloody conniving sailors, and then some, the bastards!' There wasn't much else to spend our money on: cigarettes and a few rationed pints of flat beer. There was no canteen heavily stocked with exotic foods and drinks other than tea and buns, more commonly known as 'wads'. There were essentials like soap or razor blades, toothpaste and the like, but little else in the way of luxury goods – let alone anything of interest to soldiers – so was it any wonder we went back to the games and the gambling again and again?

The time passed pleasantly enough; inspections and parades were few, allowing plenty of time to write home to wives, mothers or girlfriends. Soon we were well into the Bay of Biscay, which had a fearsome reputation for angry seas and the consequent miseries of seasickness. Those who had sailed off the coast of France between Brest and Cape Finisterre maintained that if you could endure that voyage and reach the coast of Portugal without ailment, then you were home free, and it would be plain sailing thereafter. How wrong they were this time: the Bay behaved in a kind and gentle manner, with a calmness that surprised everyone, but the worst was yet to come.

This happened off the coast of Spain where, entering the Straits of Gibraltar, the ship was met by high seas which became almost mountainous as Gibraltar came into view. Dominating the blackness of the stormy sky, the Rock was an impressive sight. Rising sharply from the sea and towering above all else, the western face was studded with white and pink buildings amidst the greenery, whilst the barren eastern face, upon which the residents relied for the collection and storage of the rain to meet all their water needs, fell away with unbelievable steepness.

1 'If—'

Anchored in the waters below were a mixture of ships, predominantly those of the British Navy. It was a commanding sight for those fit enough to see and enjoy the spectacle, but there were few inclined to take advantage of the pleasure. The rough seas were already claiming many victims, who sought nothing more than to be alone in their suffering. Violently sick and oblivious to the world about them, they cared for no one. As they retched agonizingly, they prayed for deliverance, or even death, as an escape from their torment, which only increased as the winds and the waves became more powerful. The ablutions and the deck areas were crowded with these poor souls, the floors reeking like open sewers and becoming ever more treacherous to negotiate as they were inundated with vomit and other bodily fluids.

At the beginning of the ordeal I appeared to be immune to the pitching and tossing of the boat, and I revelled in clinging on at the very front of the prow, thoroughly enjoying myself as I was almost swept away by the heavy spray. The storms on the Blackpool promenade were never like this! But my pleasure was short-lived, and before long I too succumbed.

For three days the raging seas pounded the ship mercilessly, without respite. When the waves finally subsided, we were a sorry sight to see: bodies lay everywhere, men who were too weak to rise, or oblivious of either need or desire to do so. Covered with the vile slime, many of them had lain there for those three ghastly days without help. Not once during that period was an officer seen on the upper or lower men's decks to see how their men were faring. Perhaps they too were suffering like we were. But their absence did little to endear them to their men.

Soon after the coast of Morocco, visible on the starboard side of the vessel, had faded into the distance, order was restored: the decks were washed down, the kitchens functioned again and appetites returned. Normal activities resumed. And now the Mediterranean smiled upon us. The surrounding waters changed to a sparkling blue, reflecting the clear skies which now prevailed; the sun was high in the sky and the troops basked in its welcome warmth. Life was worth living again, and better days were ahead for us all.

Skirting the northern shores of Africa, Algeria and Libya were now just a smudge on the horizon. The *Neuralia* was well into the three-week journey to India and the weather became noticeably warmer. The order was given for tropical gear to be worn: a comical sight at first, the short sleeves of the khaki shirts and the even shorter shorts revealed an odd assortment of skinny legs, knobbly knees and bony ankles, all a deathly white through lack of exposure to the sun. Even those of us who had bathed on the English beaches at the height of the summer failed to show the slightest touch of tan. The spectacle provided a great deal of amusement, a welcome diversion from the monotony of shipboard routine.

AT LAST PORT Said came into view: the first opportunity to stretch our legs ashore after those long and lethargic days. Even before the ship had docked, it was surrounded by bum boats (the term originally used to describe a river Thames scavenger's boat) and the boats' occupants offered for sale a wide variety of fruits and trinkets. The bum boat wallahs would throw a rope to the buyer standing at the rails of the deck above and, with the goods placed in the basket attached to the end of the rope, the offering would then be hoisted aboard. Payment was by reverse procedure. Sometimes the payment was not made promptly enough, and the angry bum boat men would express their opinions of the British Army in general with such charming expletives as, 'You bastard, you fuck me up, you no pay me, I piss on you! Allah piss on you! God damn all soldiers!' Having had their fun, the object of the tirade would then laughingly throw the money into the boat and peace would be restored, as would the winning smiles on the faces of the bum boat wallahs.

And the best was yet to come. As soon as the ship docked, we were allowed ashore, where we could board buses to places of interest. Although we'd been warned of the rampant venereal disease awaiting those who failed to deny themselves the pleasure of the local women, the red light districts in the souk proved more popular than haggling in the bazaars for souvenirs or riding camels across the desert. Many of those who chose the female delights got their just desserts quickly enough, and came away with their own souvenirs: a nasty dose as predicted.

It was the first experience of the East for me and my new friends, who – luckily for me – were a good-living group, more interested in viewing the local sights than sampling them, so we confined ourselves to the more innocuous pleasures of wandering through the crowded and colourful streets, which rang with the constant babble of the natives. None of the local concoctions for us – brews reputed to cause instant blindness, or some other incurable malady. We'd been warned of the many dangers that abounded, so we kept together as a group. Even so, it would have been tempting providence to enter certain areas, which were out of bounds to all ranks. Swordsticks, one of the first things we soldiers bought on landing, would have been of little help if we were attacked by a mob in those dark and filthy warrens, as so often occurred. Even the well-armed Military Police patrols were cautious in those parts of the city; if they caught you there, you were likely to spend the rest of the voyage in irons. The general feeling of all us first-time abroad men was that if Egypt was any reflection of what we might see in India, we were not impressed with what the future held for us.

However, if one looked beyond the squalor of the immediate environs, the landscape presented a picture of beauty as it merged with the shimmering seas of the Mediterranean, marred only by the coaling procedure taking place aboard the *Neuralia*. A cloud of coal dust hung above the ship, coating its crew, decks and equipment with black, and the natives toiling endlessly up the gangways, carrying coal bags on their backs, were an archaic, sorry sight. Yet few felt any sympathy for the labourers, even though they would be paid a pittance for all the pain and suffering they endured: they were, after all, only wogs, and such menial tasks were expected of them without complaint. It was for the British to rule, and to say what the natives must do. The white man's law was all-powerful here: life east of Suez was cheap, so it was said, and the slaves now fuelling the troop-ship were as good as being over that line, and shouldn't expect better.

The labourers went on toiling late into the evening, but the cleansing of the ship was completed only just in time to greet the rising sun. Almost immediately the anchor was raised and the ship entered the Suez Canal, perhaps the most interesting part of the journey for everyone. The changing landscape was one many of us had never seen before. Since biblical times, man had sought a means of connecting the Mediterranean with the Red Sea; their many attempts always failed to produce more than a short and incomplete passage. Even Napoleon Bonaparte tried, but the link didn't become reality until the skills of a French engineer, Ferdinand De Lessops, were applied, after gaining the approval of the Egyptian government; the project was finally completed in 1869. The Canal was almost a hundred miles in length from Port Said to the Red Sea and, in parts, so narrow that a bare few inches would separate the hull of the boat from the concrete sides of the canal.

Every inch of the rails on the decks was occupied by the troops in our efforts to see the much-vaunted link to India, which meant British ships no longer needed to circumnavigate the Cape of Good Hope, the southern-most point of Africa, a route that was several thousand miles longer. We marvelled when, to move safely and without damaging the ship's hull, the engines were stopped and the ship was pulled forward by coolies on the banks of the canal. There would be as many as twenty or thirty of them heaving on the heavy ropes attached to the vessel. The slow progress was marked by the chanting of the coolies, dark figures standing in sharp relief against the background of the golden sand dunes, rivulets of sweat stream-ing down their bodies in the glare of the sun. It was hard to believe this wasn't a scene from a Hollywood movie, but reality.

At the time of my passage through the Canal, Mussolini had thrown the might of the Italian Army against the people of Ethiopia, an obscure war occasioned by his belief that the Ethiopians posed a threat to the adjacent Italian possession of Somalia, because of their recent purchase of weapons. On board the *Neuralia*, word went round that an Italian troop-ship return-ing from Djibouti, where they had been fighting this questionable war against the ill-equipped and poverty-stricken Ethiopians, was also in the Suez Canal, and about to pass us. Orders were given that under no cir-cumstances was anyone to behave in an improper manner towards the Italian soldiers, and that no incidents of any kind would be tolerated. The order fell on deaf ears as we hurried away to make our preparations for the occasion. Britain had long considered the invasion of Ethiopia by the eyeties was an unworthy and even barbarous act, and that Haile Selassie was innocent of the accusation: now was both the time and opportunity to show that feeling.

As the Italian troop-ship, whose soldiers lined the rails in anticipa-tion of seeing their British counterparts, passed the stationary *Neuralia* at the entrance of the Great Bitter Lake – so close that you could reach out and touch it – a fusillade of objects was hurled at them like shots from a blunderbuss. A wide variety of ammunition including eggs, tomatoes, rotten fruit and bags of soup, pepper, or tomato sauce – which burst apart upon impact – was directed at them; more damaging were the mess tins, knives and forks and other solid objects, which caused injury to the Italian soldiers on the receiving end. Almost anything to hand was thrown. This bombardment, together with the cat-calls made by the British, left the unprepared and now insulted Italians in a state of shock and anger, but any reprisals they had in mind were too late: the ships had drawn apart and the moment was past.

The most unpleasant part of the voyage was now upon us: the Red Sea and the approach to the Indian Ocean, not far from the Equator. Hot and humid under the clear sky – the temperature in the middle 30 degrees Celsius – without even the slightest breeze to ameliorate our acute discomfort, many of us elected to sleep on the upper decks in search of relief. But the competition was strong and a man was very fortunate to find a place there; if you were lucky enough to do so, you had to be awake bright and early to avoid a dousing with cold water, for the decks were hosed down soon after four in the morning. Listless in the sultry climate, we could do little to escape the oppressive conditions which we had to endure for the next few days; at least there were no parades or lectures during that time. Djibouti was followed by Aden, a barren landscape in soaring temperatures, and so untenable as to be designated as a two-years-only stint of duty for those unfortunate British soldiers who must be stationed in the most depressing isolation there. And then we passed the equally colourless and uninhabitable rock of the island of Socotra, standing lonely on the starboard side, and we entered the Indian Ocean at last, where the abundant flying fishes frolicked in the warm waters and the dolphins played tag with the bows of the ship as it steamed on towards its destination.

It was about that time that I lost my small satchel, which contained all my wealth, almost three shillings. Try as I might, I failed to find it. Seeing my despondent face, my friends asked me why the expression of gloom, and when I told them, their immediate reaction was a whip-round with their topees. They handed over the collected sum, more than ten times my loss, and I was almost overcome with tears of gratitude. I couldn't thank them enough for their generosity. Those rough, foul-mouth soldiers looked like angels to me, and I learned never to judge a man by appearance or language. You had to strip away the often-assumed bravado during their daily activities before you got down to their true nature. But the satchel was never found, and I was sure it had not fallen overboard, so . . .

THE DISTANCE FROM Aden to Bombay was some two thousand miles and, depending on the vagaries of the weather, was now just a handful of days away. We wouldn't see land again until we arrived; the only way we knew it was there was by the flashing lights of the beacons warning off the ships in the area. Those last few days we sailed over a vastness of water, unbroken by land or other vessels, apart from one ship travelling in the opposite direction. Too far away to hail by voice, signal lamps flickered messages back and forward: she was another troop-ship from India, heading full speed to Blighty. Everyone's attention was caught; those on the homeward-bound troop-ship were likely to be a happier lot than us heading east. And those returning home would already be savouring the taste of old English ale, a pleasure they had foregone for many years, and the charms of the English lassies were doubtless setting their heads in a whirl. For the eastbound soldiers, our thoughts centred on the Indian beer, wondering if it compared well with the nectar we were accustomed to. And the same applied to our thoughts about the Indian women, what would they be like? The opinions we had already formed were not very encouraging, though we'd been told the Anglo-Indian girls were not too bad; at least they spoke English and wore civilized clothing like the girls at home. Seems like the thoughts on both ships were much the same, no matter which direction they were travelling.

Well, we travelled in hope, and tomorrow was Christmas Day, a day to celebrate, no matter where we were. But it was a strange Christmas here in the tropics, a setting so totally different from the English countryside clothed in a mantle of snow, with the trees bowing under its weight. Here there were no church bells ringing out the message of peace and goodwill to all men, no cheerful crowds parading the streets shouting, 'Merry Christmas,' or children trying out their new sledges, no snowball fights, or carols sung along with Salvation Army bands. It was a day when all English people counted their blessings as families and friends exchanged gifts before sitting down to enjoy a traditionally huge meal, of goose, or chicken, or turkey, with all the trimmings, over which Mother had slaved all day. And after the bird, the Christmas pudding and the trifle, it was off to the pub for a pint or two; though Mother would be more inclined to have a gin and lime, or perhaps a shandy, or even a Pimm's Number One cup, just the one, seeing as it's Christmas.

On board the *Neuralia* that Christmas there was a quietness, all day and into the evening; the men sat silently as we listened to the BBC on the wireless, for once not hiding our sadness as we thought of wives, mothers and sweethearts. Forgotten for a while were the card games, the tombola, the crowns and anchors: our thoughts were several thousand miles away, in another part of the hemisphere entirely. A soldier's life was not always a happy one, and the sacrifices for serving your country were often very great.

I FOUND THE nights almost idyllic at this time as the ship forged ahead through the phosphorous waves of the Indian waters. When I began to read Kipling, much later on, I understood how views like this must have been of great inspiration to him in his writings of the East. The stillness of the placid waters gave one a sense of isolation, and blended with the heavens in an almost magical union. It was easy to imagine that I had left the world that once I knew and was embarking on a journey to a distant planet, where I would find happiness, and the fulfilment of all my dreams: a world of peace where wars and hatred had never been known. Seeing this vision and reflecting upon it, I, for all my youth, began to understand that there was infinitely more to life than I had ever thought. I think I started to mature during that moment. I was astonished at the myriad stars the sky held. My science teacher once asked how many stars we thought we could see in the English sky on a clear night. My reply, echoed by my classmates was, millions, of course. We were all surprised when our teacher told us only about three thousand could be seen by the naked eye. Now, gazing around me, I could easily believe that there were a hundred times that number visible in these tropical heavens. The sky was ablaze, the stars so close that I could almost reach up and touch them. Searching for the constellations that I knew, I thought how different these skies were to those at home. For the first time in my life I saw the Southern Cross, though it was not quite what I expected, as two of its arms looked a little askew, giving it a lopsided appearance. The brightness of the stars was undiminished by the glow of the moon which was now rising; it really was possible to read a book by their light. It was with a deep reluctance that I turned away from the glory of the night sky to rejoin my comrades, for I would need the sleep. Tomorrow would bring an end to the journey which had taken me halfway around the world.

THE LAST DAY was all preparation for disembarkation, and the beginning of my new life with the British Army in India: the jewel in the crown of the Empire. Awake very early that morning, I realized at once that the throb of the engines and the movement of the ship had ceased. Hurrying to the deck above I saw that the ship was, in fact, anchored in the waters off Bombay; the lights of the city offering a brilliant, mute welcome to the new arrivals. The reception was everything I had expected of the mysterious East: the first light of day brought into focus the teaming masses of dark-skinned people on the waterfront, with their multicoloured turbans; the babble of foreign tongues, though some distance from us, could be clearly heard above the other noises of the busy harbour.

The rising sun now highlighted the city and the land beyond it, and I caught my first sight of the country which was to be my home for several years. And above all else, I could scent the unique and all-pervading smell of the place, which reached far out into the ocean. It was hard to analyse, for it was blended from the sweet fragrances of the faraway northern valleys of the Himalayas, where the profusion of flowers covered the land with exotic blossoms. Their perfume was carried by the winds to the sweltering plains below, and on to the distant parts of that great sub-continent, gathering in the more odorous smells of a people who mostly lived in poverty, whose way of life cared not to – or could not – recognize even the most elementary rudiments of sanitation. The mighty rivers, polluted and stinking from the refuse of humanity, contributed to the smells that perfumed even the far coasts of the land. The lifestyle and habits of the four hundred million inhabitants of India permeated the exquisite fragrance emanating from the cool mountain ranges, reducing it to little more than an offensive odour, at least for those of us newly arrived from a more civilized country.

As the lights on the shores faded in the rosy dawn, the substance of the city came into view, dominated by the Gateway to India, the huge structure which had seen the arrival of countless British soldiers. The *Neuralia* was guided to the landing dock by the gentle nudges of the ever-attentive tugs; as the ship was secured and the gangway placed in position, the clamour ashore become more intense and alive with activity. Most of those on the quay were dark-skinned, in sharp contrast to the few pale faces I could see, and in even sharper contrast to those aboard the ship, which, as well as us soldiers, included wives and children who had come to India to join their husbands and fathers, and officers returning from leave to rejoin their regiments. And there were a number of potentially 'returned empties', of whom I would learn more about in later days; these were the girls who had optimistically come to India in the hope of finding a husband, either in the British military or the civil service. The unsuccessful spinsters were, rather cruelly, dubbed 'returned empties' as they went back to England unbetrothed and unwed. And every ship carried a sprinkling of British civil servants who came on behalf of the King Emperor, to guide and direct the people of the land in accordance with his wishes.

Aboard the ship we troops were assembling, glad that the journey was over. I was full of excitement as I dragged my kit-bag to the landing deck, wearing my Wolseley helmet, to protect me from the blazing sun which, even at nine in the morning, was casting its brilliance and heat everywhere. (The Wolseley was a sun helmet made of a stronger material than a Pith helmet, to protect the head, used mostly on ceremonial occasions.)

And, as we took our first step on the gangway, we were already bathed in sweat and feeling the discomfort we would come to know so well. The stentorian voices of those in command, both aboard and ashore, were clearly heard above the bedlam of noises, as were the martial tunes being played by the Royal Artillery band as it marched the length of the docks with its measured tread. Beyond the activities alongside the ship stood the troop-train, black smoke rising from the funnel. Its drabness was punctuated only by the flashes of colourful headwear and the dress of the bandsmen.

My walk down the gangway added but a few more steps to the countless thousands which had been made by the soldiers of the British Empire since 1857 and the days of the East India Company. I was to join the garrison of some sixty thousand who were presently stationed in India to keep order in the country, and to provide protection from potential invaders –

especially from the Russians in the north-western sector, where there was always a potential threat of invasion through Afghanistan; and where the British forces were already engaged in constant battle with the Pathan tribes on the North-West Frontier. I would also be part of that campaign in later days. But how long was I to stay in India, I wondered, the normal six years that British troops could expect to serve; or was there going to be more to my life there?

I WAS TOO immature then to analyse the activities that would eventually lead to world-wide conflict in 1939. It meant nothing to me then that a man named Adolf Hitler already had an iron grip on the German nation and, in defiance of international agreements arising from the First World War, had been rearming that country's fighting services on an enormous scale during the last three years. Germany was rapidly becoming the world's mightiest military power, and the writing was clearly on the wall for all who cared to see. The next year, Hitler's forces would reoccupy the Rhineland. In 1938 they would occupy the Sudetenland, and invade Poland in a Blitzkrieg war the following year, throwing the world into a state of utter chaos and bringing death, destruction and misery to untold millions of people. During those early years of danger, Britain and other major powers had done little to prepare for the consequences, turning a blind eye to the shining beacons heralding disaster. They would pay dearly for that *laissez faire* attitude.

In London, Paris and Washington, life went on as usual; people were carefree and prosperous. I knew nothing of world affairs, so, as I placed my first step on the soil of India, the 'Jewel in the Crown' of the British Empire, it was with a light heart and a head full of expectations of the adventures which lay ahead in this enigmatic land.

chapter five

INDIA: MEERUT

January 1936 to February 1936

Few things had changed in India since the Raj had come to stay; and this certainly applied to the troop-trains which bustled constantly to every corner of the country. Built in the early eighteen hundreds, and showing their age badly, they could hardly be described as deluxe accommodation – they could never pretend to be even the faintest shadow of the Oriental Express, which was later to earn the reputation of being the most luxurious train in the world. These wagons were compartmentalized to hold units of six soldiers, arranged in tiers of three; the upper bunk was the most eagerly sought and always grabbed first by the more seasoned soldiers. It was a very crowded arrangement, with six men and their equipment living within the confines of some fifty square feet for up to several days at a time. What with the smoke from the permanently burning cigarettes and the filth of the engine fumes, it was difficult sometimes even to breathe, let alone to eat and sleep there. But somehow we adapted to the cramped conditions and even found room to gamble and cavort as only soldiers can. I, generously, was given a top bunk and so would be able to live in relative peace, able to look down on the activities below, and out at the passing landscape. The windows were designed to prevent entry by the natives, to provide ventilation, and to screen out the ubiquitous mosquitoes and other insects.

For what seemed forever the train stood there while we were boarded. It looked to me like the coaches were devouring everything in sight. Once on board, we all tried to make ourselves as comfortable as possible until, at last, with a whistle and great fanfare, the troop-train departed on its long journey to the Meerut Cantonment, some six hundred miles away to the north-east. As we passed through the suburbs of Bombay, I saw the most indescribable scenes of poverty: the natives lived cheek by jowl in ramshackle hovels which served as home. Made from tarpaulin, corrugated iron, grass and even cardboard, these flimsy shelters did little to protect the inhabitants from the searing heat or the monsoon rains which pelted them mercilessly. Thrown together, literally, by the side of the railway lines, these makeshift homes were incredibly dangerous, especially to the naked children whose playground was constantly bisected by the trains. The polluted water, harbouring dysentery and cholera, had to be carried from often-distant wells, and there was never enough to eat for anyone; the enlarged spleens were evidence of the malnutrition that abounded.

Not even the most elementary hygiene was practised. Open sewers were everywhere, as was disease: in rubbish tips, in public places, and always along the railway tracks. There was no medical service for these unfortunates, no hospitals or doctors – indeed, no one appeared to care whether they lived or died; and die they did, by the hundreds every day. Hospitals and physicians were for the rich.

Few, if any, of these destitute people worked: most had neither trade nor occupation, and the city was full of labourers searching fruitlessly for even the most menial tasks. To eat, they must rummage for scraps in the disgusting tips filled by those who were only slightly better off, or beg from the passing troop and passenger trains. For us soldiers new to the country it was a heartrending scene and we responded generously. But this picture of despair and misery was one to which we had to become accustomed, as it was to be a familiar sight – a microcosm of India – wherever we went in this teeming country. By comparison, the poorest white man in England would live amongst these people in absolute luxury, wanting for nothing.

And the soldier, though in the midst of relative plenty, would always be unhappy because of the loneliness and isolation imposed on him in this foreign land, separated from his homeland and loved ones by six thousand miles, an insurmountable distance for one of the rank and file, who had neither money nor approval to realize his dream of going home.

THE FIRST TWENTY miles by train from Bombay is northerly along the inlet to the town of Thana. Built in 1853, it is the first section of India's vast railway system. Thana is a relatively nice place; 'acquired' as an early Portuguese settlement, it had many fine mansions. In the thirteenth century Marco Polo described it as 'a great kingdom, lying towards the West, where there is much traffic and many ships'. Recaptured by the Mahrattas a few years later, it was subsequently occupied by the British after a three-day siege. Our route would pass through Kalyan and head north to Nasik and beyond, parallelling the Trunk Road. It would be a circuitous journey to Meerut, stopping at various staging camps en route for troops would detrain for onward posting to other parts of the country. Deolali, a hill resort a hundred miles or so from Bombay, was the first stage. It was an agreeable place to serve, and well known throughout the British Army in India as the place to acquire the 'Deolali Tap' – that is, to go stark raving mad, crazy, berserk, demented or simply puggled[1], faked or otherwise. It was the dream and design of many a soldier to get there, as it was often the prelude to being diagnosed as 'mental', and thus becoming eligible to catch the next boat home.

It was not a pleasant journey, for as the train slowly made its way into the mofussil[2] and the sun reached its zenith, the temperature in the coaches became unbearable. There was no air conditioning, ice or even fans, and we stripped down to the skin, underpants and all, in a desperate effort to relieve the discomfort of the heat. The drinking water, believed to be sterile although stale to the taste, was almost hot enough to brew tea. There was no ice available, nor were there showers. The toilets were an abomination: nothing more than holes in the floor of the carriage. Swarming with flies, they were filthy and few cared to use them. By night, the stench from the toilets and the suffocating odours of the occupants crammed together became even worse. The mosquitoes, gaining access from heaven knows where, droned incessantly in their millions as they fed upon the exposed white bodies, adding yet another measure of discomfort. And then, in the gloom, the cockroaches made their unwelcome appearance, especially in the toilet areas, where they marched across the floor in serried ranks. Sickening to walk upon, they were nevertheless ruthlessly crushed by the disgusted troops, with or without our boots on.

1 Drunk   2 Hinterland, in the sticks

When dawn came it illuminated our haggard faces; we were glad to see the light of day again after a night of horror. We had awakened to an unexpected silence: the troop-train had stopped at a remote station where breakfast would be served, somewhere north of Deolali.

Dressing quickly, we emptied on to the platform, mess tins and mugs at the ready as we lined up to receive our first meal in twenty-four hours. In the cool of the early morning light and back in the coaches, we eagerly devoured the porridge and bacon and eggs, washed down with heavily sweetened and scalding hot tea: life was worth living again! Even then, the ubiquitous beggars were at the windows pleading for the scraps, fighting amongst themselves as they scrambled for even the tiniest morsel. As the kitchens on the platform were dismantled and the train resumed its journey, there remained not a shred of evidence that barely minutes before several hundred of his Majesty's fighting men were eating a meal there in that outlandish part of his Empire. The beggars had returned to the villages and fields, awaiting the distant sound of the next approaching troop-train, when perhaps they too would eat again.

A train journey across India was always tedious and lengthy. The trains seldom travelled faster than thirty miles an hour, and any ride was invariably punctuated with frequent stops, all of which appeared to be in the wilderness, remote from any signs of life; this was especially so during the nights. And as the first rays of the sun alighted on the stationary train and heralded the new day, the barrenness of the landscape was slowly magnified and then brought into sharp focus, creating a deeper sense of isolation and remoteness. Even at that early hour the peasants were working in the paddy fields, or drawing water from the village well, guiding the bullock-drawn carts slowly along the tracks, leaving plumes of dust as they crossed the arid land, or perhaps carrying sugar cane or firewood to the nearby villages. No traffic, no industry; even the pye dogs in the villages just across the tracks were still: there was a great, almost eerie silence, broken only by the sound of the escaping steam from the engine and the sporadic cries of the few natives at the station, which now seemed to be a world apart. Above, the sky was a blaze of changing colours being washed by the brush of the rising sun – now cloudless and empty, except for the vultures soaring above in constant search for prey, scavenging for the killings of the night or, at worst, the crumbs of the hyenas' feasts.

Beyond the confines of the troop-train, another day of struggle for man and beast was about to begin. The peasants would work until sundown, pausing only briefly at midday for a chapatti or something similar before continuing their monotonous tasks in the continual fight to find sustenance for the family. The bullocks started their endless circling of the wells, drawing water to feed the fields through the myriad irrigation channels so laboriously dug.

For us, our boredom was broken only by the interminable stops for food, water or repairs to the engine, which was always in trouble. What else was there to do except gamble, swear, fight, or curse the military powers who so indifferently ordered us to the miseries of an Indian train journey? Why the hell would England, or anyone for that matter, want to own this God-forsaken land, where squalor was a way of life? Give it back to the Indians, was the most often quoted phrase of the Pongo (slang for soldier, it means ape in Latin), whose one and constant thought was to be back in England, away from these ignorant black bastards, these fucking wogs (wily oriental gentlemen), with their disgusting habits and filthy ways.

No one listened, except for the Indians themselves, who would have been equally glad to see the back of the white man and his cruel despotism. They cried that the British East India Company, and later the British Raj, had already ruled too long; now, after almost three hundred years, it was time for them to go. And a Hindu named Mahatma Gandhi, returning to his homeland from South Africa, had taken up the torch, spreading his fiery crusade for independence to every corner of the sub-continent. His words were seized on eagerly, and echoed by all who heard them, and the cause strengthened as his message was passed on by his devoted followers. We British soldiers might perhaps realize *our* freedom sooner than we expected.

The British soldiers reacted to Gandhi in a derisive manner, of course, as only soldiers can. There was a beer issue on the train that evening and the teetotallers were quick to swap their three bottles of Murree beer for the Indian cigarettes, vile though they were. The entire train was soon engulfed in song as the beer began to flow, and Gandhi was the object:

There was a young man called Gandhi,
Who went to a pub for a shandy,
He lifted his cloth

To wipe off the froth,
And the barmaid said, 'Coo that's handy.'

There was a young man called Gandhi,
Who went to a pub for a shandy,
When he lifted his cloth
To wipe off the froth,
The barmaid said, 'Wow, what a dandy.'

There were to be no attacks by the dacoits on this journey, although these armed robbers were always in the background, waiting silently with their ponies for the opportunity to strike, their prime objective being the theft of the weapons carried by the troops. It was standard practice for two men in every compartment to be detailed as guards, with the responsibility of alerting their comrades to any suspicious situation. These men were fully armed and ready, with a round up the spout, and authorized to fire without further permission in the event of an attack. All British troops carried side-arms and rifles, unloaded, whilst travelling by train across India.

At one of the stops, I strolled to the head of the train with a couple of friends to talk to the engine drivers; we were all surprised to find how well they spoke English, albeit with a lilting singsong tone. They were both Anglo-Indians, the result of liaisons between English soldiers and Indian women. There were many of these half-castes in India; it wasn't uncommon to find a half-caste woman married to a white soldier, although this was very much frowned upon by the sahibs: it was considered bad taste, that one had almost gone native. The Anglo-Indians were unfortunate people, betwixt and between, being neither Indian nor English. Looked down upon by both races, though they considered themselves British by birth, they were not accepted by either the British or the Indians. They didn't mix with the Indians, whom they considered to be in a class far below them; they referred to them as wogs. They were given to such comments as, 'I'll be glad to go back home and away from these black heathens, it is so long since I am visiting there.' Home was England, a country they had never seen, and where they would be unlikely to be accepted by the English even in the rare event they did get there. Because of the condescending attitude of the British community in India towards them, they not unnaturally suffered from an inferiority complex.

Nevertheless, for the main part, they were the only social contact for the white-women-deprived soldiers; they were usually the only female partners available at the dance clubs, and were so few as to be in great demand. They were mostly darkish-skinned, though some were of a fair complexion, and they dressed in European style, affecting many of the ways of the English and doing what they could to fit in better – 'Two shades whiter in seven days,' proclaimed the advertisers of skin lotion. They tried so hard to be equal, and it was so very sad that they never quite succeeded. They were, however, accorded the majority of the Government-controlled jobs and virtually ran the railway system, communications, offices and other vital civil positions. These Eurasians were known variously as *chee-chees, half and half, half chats, fifteen annas' worth,* and by many other derogatory appellations. The snooty English had much to be ashamed of in their treatment of Anglo-Indians.

The two Anglo-Indian engine drivers had many questions for us: which part of England did we come from? Would it be a good place for them to live when they went back there? It would be so wonderful to live entirely with their own kind, surrounded only by pale faces, unmarred by colour – in the civilized atmosphere which was their right and inheritance. And would they have any problems with the money? They had used the Indian currency all their lives – the rupees, annas and pice – and they knew full well there were four pice to the anna, which was a sixteenth part of a rupee, but English pounds, shillings and pence were altogether something else. But they were quick to demonstrate their knowledge of the matter by telling us that it took thirteen rupees and eight annas to buy an English pound note. No, it would come easily to them; it would be as natural for them as would their adoption of the European way of life. Nor would there be any difficulty with their English-born counterparts. Some Anglo-Indians tried to assume the arrogance of the Englishman when talking to an inferior; the Anglo-Indian stationmaster, for example, was usually an imperious man who was a god unto himself as he mimicked what he thought was the manner of an Englishman. Perhaps like many stationmasters in the United Kingdom, his arrogant manner with the lowly natives made it abundantly clear that he was Lord God on high and that his instructions were to be obeyed implicitly. And how do you know whether or not you are true blood or a chee-chee, apart from the lilting tongue and the brownish complexion? The first time I heard that they did not have half moons on their fingernails, where the pukka sahibs do, I was quick to look at my own nails, just to make sure.

That day I was offered a special treat: one of the train drivers had suggested I travel with them on the footplate when they left the station. I thought this was a great idea, and the sergeant with me at once approached the officer in charge of the train, who readily agreed. Clambering onto the footplate, I was invited to occupy the number one driver's seat from which, under strict supervision, I would control the progress of the engine. This time it was me who sounded the warning whistle that the train was about to depart. Normally there was a crew of two, or possibly three, men and the two armed guards on the footplate, but this time there would be three more: me, the sergeant and another soldier from my compartment. There was hardly room to move as we crowded in there, and the coaling procedure was a tricky affair with so many bodies in the way of the shovelling of the coal. Within seconds of leaving the station we were all saturated with sweat, as the rising sun combined its intense, growing heat with that of the glowing coals in the furnace. The temperature soared well above the one hundred degree mark and the coal dust turned to a black mud on our faces. And the noise was deafening, what with the clatter of the pistons and the escaping steam and the stoking, liberally magnified by my repetitive use of the whistle. Though the gauge registered a mere thirty miles an hour, it felt like the train was rolling along at twice that speed, and the few trees and buildings in the wastes of the landscape were gone in a flash. There was only one emergency to deal with, and that was a heavily laden bullock cart stuck on the railway lines, the driver having fallen asleep – a common occurrence in India. Fortunately the train was stopped easily, but the guard had to dismount to awaken the driver and clear the way. It was great fun for me at least: I was, after all, still just a fifteen-year-old enjoying his first experience as an engine driver! And it certainly compensated for not being able to smoke or join in the revelry of the beer-drinking with the rest of the lads; they were very protective of my innocence then. For me, it ended all too soon, and when the time came, I was sorry to leave the controls. I would always remember the brass plate in the cab, on which was the legend *Built in Manchester 1901*, though the others were more than happy to return to the relative quiet and coolness of the coach.

EVERYONE WAS GLAD when we finally reached Meerut, some thirty-eight miles beyond Delhi, where the train stopped briefly to deliver a detachment – including me – for posting to the British Army in India Headquarters. Tired, dirty and dishevelled, bored and lethargic after those days on the train with little or no exercise, it felt good to be able to stand upright and walk more than a couple of paces without bumping into something. And the opportunity to shower and change into clean clothing was very welcome. Transport was waiting for us and after a short drive through the narrow streets congested with the local Indian population, we were deposited at our new quarters, which were about a mile from the station. The site had long been a military cantonment, its historical days of British occupation going back to the seventeen hundreds. Clean and spacious, it was, for all practical purposes, isolated from the native quarters in the south of the city, which had a population of some two hundred thousand. In true British Army style its design and setting were fashioned almost identically to the barracks at Aldershot, and exemplified the saying that, wherever the British Army goes, it takes Aldershot with it; whatever the surroundings may be, the outside world is not allowed to encroach. It must remain pure and unsullied, reflecting all the beauty of the old country. Consequently, the abrupt change from the culture shock of Indian society and its way of life to an atmosphere and disposition more reflective of our homeland, was very pleasant indeed, although the smells and heat of India within the cantonment were ever-present, and nor could it help being tinged by the presence of the Indian Other Ranks (IORs) and the Indian servants, more commonly known as the wallahs.

To the north lay the open maidan[1], a vast stretch of open land as far as the eye could see, with barely a stick or a stone upon its surface. About a hundred miles beyond the horizon, and invisible to those who devoutly wished they were there, lay the foothills of the Himalayas, behind which towered the mighty snow-covered peaks separating India from Tibet and China. Even on a cool winter's day in Meerut, the difference in temperature between the cantonment and those lofty peaks could be as much as 120 degrees Fahrenheit. And in summer, all eyes would turn wistfully to those distant and unseen mountains, vainly seeking their solitude and coolness.

Meerut is a large city and cantonment in the United Provinces of

1 Exercise ground or parade ground

northern India, where the infamous Indian Mutiny started in May 1857, an insurrection long in the making, the quest of ultimate victory leading once more to Indian independence. Ever since the arrival of the Honourable East India Company there had been resentment on the part of the natives, perhaps not an uncommon feeling for a population who sensed that they were to become subservient to the newcomers from over the oceans. On the other hand the Company, and later Queen Victoria, the Queen Emperor, had, through the years of their occupation, undoubtedly introduced changes considered beneficial – at least by the British – to the natives, and for the prosperity of the country as a whole. They had built a wide network of railways across the country, constructed countless bridges, vastly improved the roads, and so communications, for the benefit of all; they had formed the basis of a democratic society, established and enforced law and order, and outlawed thuggery and the barbarous practice of suttee, whereby custom dictated that the wife of a man who died must be immolated with him upon the same funeral pyre.

To the outsider, it might appear that the British were successfully planting the seeds of the civilized western world, but this was not the opinion of those whose lives were being changed without their prior consultation and approval, who believed that the British had no right to alter customs which had endured for centuries. There was a continuous annexation of land and possessions, often without payment, and taxes and tolls were ever-increasing. Huge profits were being derived by the John Company, who were shipping the fruits of Indian labour to the western world (with the rewards to the Indians a mere pittance), whilst the daily lives of the downtrodden showed no sign of improvement.

Of extreme concern to all native religions was the belief that both the military and the British civilian intruders were vigorously promoting the Christian faith amongst the Indians, who were considered nothing better than heathens; this interference with their beliefs and religious practices was totally unacceptable to the Indians. These efforts to convert the Indians to Christianity were also supplemented by the large groups of English missionaries who were aggressively evangelizing in their mission to convert these savages to the Christian way of life, especially in the northern areas of the country. The Commanding Officers of at least two famous Indian regiments were also, openly, active in this respect, and many British Army officers were engaged in converting their troops to Christianity, so the missionaries were not alone in their quest.

When the sowars[1] had enlisted in the service of the Company, they were given to understand they would not be required to sail across the oceans, but now it was ruled that they must do so in order to fight in other countries on behalf of the Raj. That meant they had to cross the 'Kala Pani' (the Black Water), which would endanger their faith. And so the seeds of defeat were firmly planted in those early days by the invaders themselves, and nourished later by their own acts of greed and selfish indifference.

IN JUNE 1757, Clive of India, with a meagre force of British soldiers, defeated a far superior army of Indians at the Battle of Plassey, to the north of Calcutta, thereby, in a single act, gaining control of the whole of Bengal in the north-east sector of the country for the Honourable East India Company. It was said at the time of the battle that British rule in India would last for another hundred years before being expelled from the land – a prophecy which was to prove remarkably inaccurate.

If I had been more aware of the history of that place, and the terrible events that happened some eighty years before, I might easily have imagined the events that took place there some eighty years ago as I stood outside my new barracks. Little had changed since then; if I had been present and a witness to the uprising, I would not have been able to detect any difference in the geography and physical layout of the cantonment which now lay before me. The site of such violence and horror, when the triumphant cries of the mutineers mingled with the despair of the besieged Britishers, was today peaceful, and it was difficult to believe that it could ever have been otherwise. Looking to my right was the artillery park where, in 1857, the Horse Artillery ordnance of four 6-pounder guns had stood, replaced now with six modern 18-pounders. To the right of the gun park were the horse lines, today the calm scene of the routine stables activity: almost identical to what I'd left behind, apart from the sight of the horses now being groomed not by troopers, but by the Indian syces[2].

It was believed that the catalyst for the uprising in Meerut was the introduction of the newly issued Lee-Enfield rifle, which was replacing the heavy Old Bess smooth bore musket after long service in the British

1 Native horse soldier   2 Horse grooms

Army. Because of the tight fit in the barrel of the new rifle, the cartridges first required to be well greased; although the native troops had long been accustomed to biting the cartridges with their teeth in preparation for loading the old musket, they had heard rumours that the new grease used on the ammunition would be pig and cow fat. To the Mohammedans the fat of the pig is despised as being unclean, and for the Hindu, the cow is holy. Thus the grease was both repulsive and unacceptable to either religion, and the cause of great alarm, as they believed their faith would be lost should they touch the unclean cartridges. Most of the native troops had been assured by their commanding officers that the rumours about the origins of the grease were untrue; that it was not derived from either of the animals. If they wished, they were quite at liberty to use instead the same oils to lubricate the cartridges that they used in the daily preparation of their food. They were also told that it was no longer necessary to bite the new cartridges, as these could now be readily torn open with their fingers. So there was no risk of contamination. But the sepoys' declined to believe their officers, listening instead to the rumourmongers amongst their ranks.

Also igniting the flame for the mutiny, in the distant city of Barrackpore near Calcutta, was a sepoy named Mangel Pandy, a name that was destined to become synonymous with future mutineers in the British Army. In a drunken frenzy, armed with his musket and sword, he incited his regiment to rise up against the Raj. In the course of doing so, he shot and wounded a British officer, the Adjutant of the regiment, who was saved from further injury only by the intervention of his Sergeant-Major Hewson. Pandy was subsequently court-martialled and sentenced to death; being hanged within hours of the sentence in the presence of his regiment, which was then ignominiously disbanded, under the watchful eye of the British regiment summoned to attend the scene. This, then, was the prelude to the revolution which brought about the rape, the burning and the brutal massacring of women and children in their hundreds while the bitter fighting that spread across northern India culminated in the execution of hundreds of sepoys for their dastardly actions.

This event occurred two days before the native 3rd Indian Light Cavalry Regiment, parading on the barrack square at Meerut for rifle drill, refused

---

1 Native soldiers

to carry out the loading procedure when ordered to do so by the Commanding Officer. After repeatedly refusing orders to execute the command, eighty-five of them were placed under close arrest and interned in the hospital, the only building capable of holding such a large number of prisoners. Only five of the regiment had obeyed the order to load their rifles. At the following courts-martial on the barrack square, they were sentenced to periods of hard labour, some up to ten years, to be served in the desolate Andaman Islands in the Bay of Bengal. They would lose any pensions to which they might otherwise have been entitled – and most of them were soldiers who had served many years in the service of the Raj, and thus forfeited substantial reward.

At the conclusion of the courts-martial they were clapped in irons, pleading on their knees for leniency; with tears in their eyes, they were stripped of their rank and medals before being marched away under heavy guard. Unwisely, an Indian regiment had been chosen as the escort, and they themselves would mutiny the next day. The night that followed – usually silent throughout the hours of darkness – was filled with the noises and sounds of the restless native soldiers as they gathered outside their quarters, planning further acts of insurrection. Buildings were set afire and sporadic rifle fire could be heard around the cantonment. There were rumours and whispers of impending disaster for the British, but any of these which reached the white sahibs fell upon deaf ears. To them it was unbelievable that the mutinous acts of the Indian regiments would continue after some two hundred years of faithful service under the British flag. There was hardly a single white officer of any native regiment through-out the whole of India who questioned the Indian soldiers' loyalty to the Raj, and they were prepared to stake their lives on this belief. But the swords were being sharpened, and many of them subsequently did forfeit their lives for that erroneous assumption. The centuries of festering resent-ment against the British was about to climax; the Indian Army was ripe for revenge. And for days now, stories had also been heard by the British officers about the mysterious chapatis – small loaves of white bread – that were said to be passing from village to village throughout the northern provinces, as the signal heralding the imminence of the rebellion.

The following morning, Sunday the tenth of May, was so typically hot and humid that the garrison church parade was deferred until six o'clock that evening, when it would be cooler. Shortly before that time, and in spite of the apparent unrest, the troops had assembled carrying only their side-arms, their rifles remaining in the barrack rooms and the ammunition in the powder magazine as instructed. Early that evening several officers were warned that further action was planned by the sowars and the sepoys; just before the appointed hour of the church parade, the service was cancelled, because natives troops had attacked the prison and released the prisoners. The guard of the 20th Native Regiment had made no attempt to prevent this, and idly stood by as the prisoners streamed out. In a flash they were joined by hundreds more, who were now intent on murder and, having broken into the magazine, stripping it of powder and shot, they surged out across the cantonment.

Strangely enough, although the noise and the firing had been going on for an hour or so and the native lines were aglow with fires, no British troops were yet alerted or sent into action to quell the riots. When the alarm was finally given, both military and civilian residences were blazing and the situation was well out of control. Indecision by the military leaders at both local and senior levels contributed to the success of the now wild and demented behaviour of the mutineers.

Unbelievably, it was not until the following morning, Monday, that any decisive action was taken, and even then it was an uncoordinated affair of piecemeal action by the British troops. Pillaging was now rife, all the horses had been released from the stables and the cantonment was in a state of chaos. The three native units stationed there – two foot regiments and one cavalry regiment – were now on the rampage, and the English force of some two thousand strong, consisting of the 6th Dragoon Guards, a battalion of the 60th Queens Rifles and two batteries of artillery, appeared to be powerless to quell the rioting. The rebels were in complete control, many of them setting off to Delhi, some forty miles to the south-west, to join their comrades who were already forcing the surrender of that city. Unlike Meerut, Delhi's peacetime garrison consisted entirely of native troops and the mutineers' control of the capital was therefore easily assured.

Meanwhile, in Meerut, the killing of the British residents in the civil lines and the plundering of their property by the sepoys intensified. They appeared to have a free licence to conduct their murderous activities.

The lack of a concerted offensive action by the British was blamed solely on the incompetence of Major General Hewitt, the commandant of the Meerut and Delhi Garrisons, who failed so miserably to appreciate the situation and take remedial action before it was too late. His lack of decisive action, in spite of the positive recommendations by his subordinates which would quickly have contained the uprising, was to be the subject of the most severe criticism, with the conclusion that he alone was responsible for the flames of the mutiny which spread across the length and breadth of the sub-continent. His delay in alerting the Delhi command of the Meerut fracas, and his failure to dispatch troops there, led to the engulfment of that city and the massacres of English women and children that followed at Cawnpore and other garrison towns.

When the relief force, of a few hundred men and guns, was dispatched to Delhi, it was too late. Had it reached the city stronghold, it would have faced an impossible task, for the capital was now garrisoned by thirty thousand renegade Indian Army troops, and more were expected as the uprising gathered momentum. But the pitifully small band of British soldiers faced grave dangers before it ever reached that city. They were harried and mauled by the professional thieves, the Goojars, who were well armed, highly mobile and inclined to commando tactics. By striking hard and quickly, they soon weakened and eventually decimated the British. Small groups of rebels also on their way to Delhi added to the dangers faced by the white soldiers. The forty-mile journey to Delhi was fraught with danger, and on top of the natives, there was the river to cross. The future looked very bleak indeed for them.

History would point the finger of blame very strongly at Hewitt, and his lack of responsible action for the most atrocious acts of evil which were carried out by both the natives and the British. The sowars raped and disembowelled pregnant women, decapitated children before their mothers' eyes, and tortured husbands whilst the wives cried out for mercy. There were massacres in Jhansi, Meerut, Cawnpore, Delhi and other cities across northern India, where men, women and children were first tortured before being hacked to death by the tulwars[1] of the sowars. For five days the British survivors at Cawnpore had resisted, without food or water, before finally surrendering. At Jhansi the garrison was at bay for five days before being wiped out in a cruel orgy of bloodlust. In the Johan Bagh, sixty-six

[1] Swords

British were killed, and similar incidents took place elsewhere in those cities. It is said that Rani Lakshmibai was responsible for the outrage, although she professed to be sympathetic with the British.

In retribution, the English executed the offenders by firing them from the muzzles of the guns, the victims tied to the barrels of the 18-pounder horse artillery cannons and blasted to eternity by the revenging gunners. They also publicly hanged the sowars, the Indian cavalrymen, indiscriminately leaving the bodies to swing and decay along the length of the Grand Trunk Road as a reflection of their anger. The state of mutiny, which lasted for several months, would forever divide the blacks and the whites of India, the memories lingering of the hatred and brutality of that period of turmoil; that gulf would never be bridged. Yet it is also true that during that time of great upheaval, there were many isolated acts of mercy by individuals on both sides, and courage was everywhere abundant. The Victoria Cross was awarded to several British soldiers, and boy buglers were singled out on several occasions for their bravery in the most appalling conditions.

Of all the atrocities, the unspeakable acts committed by the Indians in Cawnpore, and the deception which became known as the Massacre at the Boats, remained particularly etched in British memory. The ruler, Nana Sahib, who was believed to be friendly towards the British government, had in fact assumed the leadership of the mutineers and was the great deceiver. Having promised the release and safe passage by boat for the beleaguered garrison of Cawnpore – consisting of several hundred men, women and children – if they laid down their arms and surrendered, he recanted as the disarmed gathering was led to the banks of the Ganges River. As they waded into the water, defenceless, and clambered into the boats without weapons, the sepoys, at the direction of the treacherous Nana Sahib, opened fire at short range, cutting them down in a murderous hail of fire. Most of the poor wretches died there and then, and the few survivors managed to travel but a short distance downstream before they too were caught and put to death by the sword. Many others who had remained behind, mostly women and children, were later killed in a mad orgy of butchering by the natives, and their dismembered bodies were flung down a well which was filled to the very top with the limbs and torsos of the victims.

The later discovery of the corpses and the severed heads and body parts of these innocents put new resolve into the hearts of the British soldiers, who pursued the wanton and merciless dispatch of any sepoy who fell into their hands even more vigorously. In retribution for the women and children who were butchered by the Indians, the enraged British troops swept across the country avenging their murdered compatriots. Their cruelty was more than equal to that of the sowars who had slaughtered so freely.

The Cawnpore massacre took place at Sati Chaura at the edge of the cantonment, and close by is a memorial Church which was consecrated in 1875. On the Church walls are inscribed the names of those who died on that day of June 27, 1857. The memorial to the victims, originally sited at the well, now rests in the Memorial Gardens of the Church.

CONTINUING TO SEARCH the landscape, shaded from the sun by the verandah of the barracks, I could see the parade ground to the left where the mutineers had assembled in defiance of their officers' orders to return to their quarters. Beyond the square stood the church of St John's, virtually unchanged since it first stood as silent witness to the strife which prevailed on that hot and humid Sunday morning in May of 1857. Yet, sitting in the pews of that graceful and serene old church, as I would do so often during the coming Sundays, there was no indication that my comrades of eighty years before had ever occupied these very same seats; the only visible sign of the church's past association with the military was the display of the regimental colours of regiments long gone, faded and rotted by exposure over the many years, like those in St John's church in Woolwich, and the stained glass windows and memorial plaques to those who had given their lives in the service of the Raj. There was little else to mark the events which ultimately brought about the end of the Empire, except on Sundays, when the troops marched down to the church to the sounds of the massed bands, parading in full spectacle along the Mall in all the pomp and splendour the British Army does so well. Dressed immaculately in khaki drill uniforms, with buttons and bayonets flashing, it made both British civilians and off-duty soldiers lining the route feel pride in their country.

Even in my days, a legacy of the Mutiny remained: we carried weapons as we marched into the church; the rifles and side-arms were loaded and each man had a bandolier of fifty rounds of 303 ammunition. The weapons were lodged at the back of the pews and invariably the sermon would be liberally punctuated by their rattling as bored soldiers expressed their desire for the service to be over. As with most of the cantonments in India, it seemed that time had stood still, and the British soldier remained the supreme master of the land.

The Mall – there was always a road bearing that name to be found in any town the British settled (another little touch of England to remind one of true civilization) – was the prime artery of the encampment, running from east to the west, giving ready access to all the facilities in the European settlement. Originally occupying the area adjacent to the artillery barracks, and to the north of the Mall, was the élite British Cavalry Regiment, the 17/21 Lancers, with the skull and cross-bones as the focus of their cap-badge. More famously known as the *Death or Glory Boys*, the regiment had a decidedly superior attitude towards the other horse units in the camp – or anywhere else in India, for that matter – although they in turn were snubbed by the Royal Horse Artillery Batteries. The Lancers, like my new Battery, had seen service in India for many years and were highly skilled. They would present glittering displays whilst on parade, with a perfection envied by all, and in a performance that was second to none. They were also a very tough bunch of troopers.

As I watched them on parade one day in their full dress uniforms, the colours a brilliant mixture of reds and yellows and the black bearskins pulled over the eyes, the pennants flying, the sun glinting on the tips of the lances, the harness jingling and, in the lead, the colour standard flapping gently in the breeze, I was impressed by their fierce and militant appearance. With their heads erect and their impassive expressions, they would be a fearsome body to face as an enemy.

There was a rumour that another mounted regiment in the area had vented its wrath on a nearby Indian village as a reprisal for the beating of two of its members, who were accused of raping a woman there. They saddled up en masse, armed with sword and lance, and torched the village. The punishment subsequently meted out to the participants of the raid, a lengthy term of imprisonment, was an example of the severity the British Army is capable of inflicting on its own if they decide to take the law into their own hands.

But the time was now, I had just arrived in this strange, faraway country and yet knew little or nothing about either the cavalry raid or the Indian Mutiny. Below where I stood was the Aboo Canal, which bisected the cantonment in half. North of the canal was devoted almost entirely to the British forces; the barracks, housing for both the military and civilians, public offices, the library, church, powder magazine and all the rest of the related facilities. On the south side of the canal lay the Sudder bazaar, which the troops were allowed to frequent; it was not permissible for us to go into the native bazaars or villages outside the confines of the camp. To be caught out of bounds could result in severe punishment, and the suspension of what few privileges we normally enjoyed. The military authorities turned a blind eye on the bazaars in the cantonments, as opposed to giving them formal blessing, but they were considered safe enough for the British soldier to visit, provided he behaved himself and did not incite trouble. Of course, everyone knows that British troops are usually the model of perfection as far as their behaviour is concerned, and it's always the other party that prompts the fight. It was rare for a man to go there alone, though; usually we would visit only in the company of several of our friends.

The crowded back alleys of the bazaar were an open invitation to pickpockets and smash and grab thieves, and fraught with danger, requiring only a spark to set the place ablaze. It was prudent therefore to be constantly on the alert and prepared for any eventuality. It was also common for British soldiers to carry a swordstick, in spite of regulations to the contrary. Usually the three-foot-long black imitation leather cover housed a thirty-inch blade. Readily obtainable in the bazaar, at nominal cost, the troops found them useful weapons when faced with trouble. Another popular weapon of defence was a hockey stick with a steel fitting on the blade; it also was a very effective comforter – purely in self defence, of course. It always surprised me that, given the number of Military Police who patrolled the bazaar, so few of the troops were charged with carrying the forbidden weapons.

Also to the south, but unseen from my vantage point, were the native lines with their supporting services, the transport areas and the racecourse. A grey, sprawling place void of colour, the cantonment offered the bare necessities of life. There was a library, a canteen, a cinema (though none of the pictures shown were of a current issue, they were all likely to be many years old), and the Ladies' Temperance League. Located in an English Elizabethan-style house, and surrounded by flower gardens, it offered tea, cakes and light snacks to the British soldiers in a setting representative of a tea house in Cheltenham or Brighton. With its décor and atmosphere redolent of its English counterparts, it reminded the lonely troopers of that other life they had left, and which awaited their return one day. The dear old ladies who ran the place were very attentive to their wards, deeply intent on persuading them of the merits of abstinence. But few of the men listened to their cajoling, preferring the debauchery of the rowdy canteens in the evenings, and the swilling of beer, which always appeared to be available in unlimited quantities. The consumption was governed only by the availability of rupees to purchase it. But the ladies were sincere in their efforts to provide, through friendly conversation, a brief escape from the rigid and sterile existence of life in the camp. Often spoken of flippantly, though always in good humour, their presence and attention would long be remembered as an oasis of care, especially by newcomers to Meerut.

'COME ON, YOU idle lot, get your kit and move into the barrack rooms,' cried the bombardier who had escorted us to the unit. 'Follow me,' he ordered, and in we went. It was a large single-floored building with extremely high ceilings, the interior of which was separated by arches into four components. Very spacious, it was designed to provide the maximum air circulation and exposure to the outside areas. On both sides of the sleeping quarters were wide verandahs that appeared to have no purpose other than adding to the spaciousness of the building, and a barrier between the occupants and the activities of the outside world. There were twenty beds on each side of the rooms in each of the four parts of the building, all set apart by the regulation six feet between beds. These were inevitably constructed of iron, Aldershot style, and equipped with the three hard biscuit-blocks which served as mattresses, accompanied by the bolster-like pillows. There were two folded blankets at the foot of the bed, and, of course, the lockable storage box for personal items. No pictures or other forms of decoration were evident on the plain, colourless cement walls. The setting was purely military, without even the remotest suggestion that another lifestyle existed; it was cold and sterile.

Most of the men compensated for this by pasting photos on the inside of the overhead cupboard doors, generally of family or girlfriends who, though continually in their minds, were always an impossible distance away. And in the true soldiers' style, there were inevitably pictures of naked ladies, displaying all their charms in the most provocative manner. These, however, were but wishful thinking; the reality lay in a liaison with a brown-skinned Indian girl, deep in the depths of the Sudder bazaar's red light district, with none of the ecstasy displayed by the fair, voluptuous beauties in the pictures. Such liaisons with the natives were generally unsavoury affairs, accomplished in haste, and without foreplay or afterplay: straight on the job, followed by a hasty exit and a mind mingled with fear of the possible consequences and guilt of the moment.

Many of the beds were already occupied by members of the regiment; we new boys were not placed together, but interspersed amongst the other residents. There was no choice: we were detailed as to which bed we were to have. Dumping kit-bags on the ground, we threw ourselves on our beds, thankful that the long, tiring journey of seven thousand miles, with its endless movement and disruption, had at last come to an end. To sleep in comfort again would be bliss after those miserable days crammed like sardines in that medieval troop-train, with its primitive facilities and the filth of the thousands of soldiers, English and Indian, who had travelled on it for the past fifty years or more without it ever having been cleaned. And now the train would stand somewhere on a deserted railway siding in the blistering heat of the days and the freezing coldness of the nights before being pressed into service once again to torment another batch of inexperienced squaddies. They too would be exposed to all the unpleasantness I had suffered: their bodies constant prey to the ever-present insects and the repulsive cockroaches which roamed and thrived abundantly.

The calls of 'Char wallah, boat garum, char hie, Sahibs,' and 'Sweetmeats, Sahib,' brought to life those who were on the verge of sleep, and directed their gaze to the verandah. There squatted the Indian tea vendor with his urn of scalding hot tea – 'very hot', as his cry of 'boat garum' denoted – and his opened tin boxes displaying a mixture of cakes and buns and sweetmeats for the ever hungry sahibs.

That vendor was not the only one; there were others stationed along the verandahs, and they were always assured of a thriving business, not least because the constantly cash-strapped troops were not required to pay at the moment of purchase, but allowed to pay on tick, settling up with the chah wallah on payday. There were no chits for any transaction and the chah wallah was never seen to write anything down, but the payment requested on the due date was rarely questioned. I was one of the first eager buyers joining the line up with my drinking mug, then sitting down on the steps of the building with a few of the other new boys to discuss our next movements. This decision was made for us by the arrival of the Troop Sergeant who, after introducing himself and welcoming us to the regiment, proposed to take us on a tour of the immediate surroundings of the regimental area.

Finishing our tea and wads, we made first for the horse lines where the animals had just returned from exercise on the adjacent maidan. Although it was late afternoon, the sun was still high in the sky, with the blistering heat relentlessly beating down. I and my colleagues, who had yet to become accustomed to the hot Indian sun, left the shade of the building with great reluctance, instantly being struck by the heat which bounced off the cement pavement like a heavy blow to the body: 'Mad dogs and Englishmen' indeed! As we walked across the square and paused at the gun sheds, the sergeant told us the origins of the artillery, and its role in the past providing close support to the foot regiments during battle. It was unusual these days for the guns to be placed in front of the infantry; they'd normally be in action several hundred yards to the rear (although there were many occasions when a section of guns would be detached from the main Battery and placed within the forward troops area to provide open fire on enemy strong points which otherwise could not be shelled), the artillery still kept its honourable position *the right of the line, the first on the field and the last to retire*, as I had learned all those months ago in England. The sergeant, a veteran of twenty years' service with the guns, was a true student of the Royal Regiment's history, and his intense interest and understanding of his subject was inspiring.

Here in the horse lines, the unsaddling and rubbing down of the horses was being completed, but it was a very different scene to that in Newport just a few weeks before, where we men were responsible for mucking out and bedding down the animals. Here, the syces were responsible for this work, and other menial chores. A central walkway ran the length of the enclosed stables, with rows of horses on both sides, facing each other, separated by a low barrier. There were several stables, each of which accommodated twenty-five horses and at the end of each, there was a storage area for equipment. Now, the horses were being dried down preparatory to watering. We were told that though the Indian syces were doing the work, that didn't mean that the British gunners would be entirely exempt from stable duties: grooming duties would be shared with the syces, and though they would do the mucking out and hosing down, which required little or no experience, the end responsibility for the wellbeing of the horses would rest with us. At that time there were some two hundred horses in the stables, including several polo ponies belonging to officers of the regiment, which were also attended by the syces and other ranks detailed for the duty. The sergeant cut short our visit as the afternoon was drawing to a close and the supper hour was fast approaching.

As our group returned to the barrack room, the trumpet sounded mealtime. When the new contingent entered the building in the company of the older members, we were surprised to find that it consisted of several bright and pleasant rooms – quite out of character for a military facility, for it was not sterile in appearance, but was much more homely, with curtains at the windows and pictures on the walls. The paintings, although portraying military scenes, brought life and colour into an otherwise drab environment. The tables, which were the regulation six feet long and seated six, were decidedly British Army issue, but were pleasingly covered with white tablecloths, set with crockery, cutlery and the other trappings which made for a complete and attractive dining room table. It was a pleasant – and unexpected – atmosphere in which to dine, even if the temperature did hover at a constant 100 degrees Fahrenheit. There was no table service, of course, but a convenient selection bar where the food was provided in large quantities, sufficient enough to satisfy even the most voracious soldierly appetite.

After the meal, it was back to the barrack room to prepare for the activities of the evening. This meant different things to different people; in my case I chose to go for a stroll around the cantonment in the company of two of my colleagues. It was a lovely evening, with the quick twilight so typical of the tropics. The sun had dipped beyond the horizon, leaving in its place a welcome coolness and tranquillity, which cleansed the body and soul of the hectic activities in the unbearable heat of the day. Though clearly still a military cantonment, as we walked the spacious and uncluttered roads in the soft night air, it was a different place from that at which we had arrived just a few hours before. A light breeze prevailed, rustling the leaves of the trees, and in the stillness of the evening we could hear horses and dogs, and the laughter of the troops in the camp, and, in the near distance, the sounds of music and drums in the bazaar. On the maidan, several officers played a scratch game of polo, the click of the ball resounding loudly when it was struck. To the immediate right, a game of soccer was underway, watched by a large audience from the barracks who were in great spirits, encouraging the players to get the man if they couldn't get the ball! And in the far distance came the echo of the tukto bird, with its incessant and monotonous cry of, 'Tukyu, tukyu, tukyu tukyu', endlessly throughout the night, for miles around, and without pause.

Suddenly, the stillness of the moment was broken by the strident command: 'Halt, who goes there?' And in the absence of a response from the startled walkers, the repetition of 'Halt, who goes there?' Still nonplussed by the startling cry of the sentry and again failing to reply, we were cautioned once more, 'Halt, or I'll fire.' Then sounded the ominous click of a rifle bolt as a cartridge was rammed into the breech. This caught our attention at once, and together we shouted, 'Friends'. It was a smiling guard who ordered us to advance to be recognized; we were all feeling rather foolish for not having acted upon the first command. The guard warned us that other guards were patrolling the cantonment, cautioning us to be alert and more responsive next time: it wouldn't be the first time in the cantonment that a sentry had fired without giving a second opportunity to obey. He jokingly told us about the hapless sentry who, after challenging in the approved manner and failing to receive a satisfactory answer, did fire his rifle at what he thought was a figure stealthily passing by on the other side of a hedge. The shot hit home right enough, but, to his dismay, the roar of a large injured beast was heard. What he had fired at was the hump of a wandering water buffalo, and it was a very embarrassed soldier who paraded before his commanding officer the next morning to face the buffalo's irate owner, who was seeking compensation. Not unnaturally, the soldier was promptly and forever dubbed Buffalo Bill by his comrades.

We accepted the lesson and, as we walked on to the perimeter of the cantonment, the sounds and noises subsided into a quiet that was both restful and rewarding. The heat of the day was entirely gone; the sun was well below the horizon, offering hardly a vestige of light other than a few streaks of crimson and gold, appearing as scars in a changing sky. And, as if to confirm the magical setting which had appeared, the strong fragrance of the frangipani and other flowers which grew in such abundance nearby drifted down to envelop me and my friends in their intoxicating perfume. In the far distance could still be seen the smoke and the fires lit by the natives in preparation for their evening meal. The tranquillity which surrounded us was in direct contrast to our initial impression: that India was a noisy, ghastly and inhospitable land with a merciless climate, unworthy of the Englishman. It was with light hearts that we walked through the glowing soft lights of the camp back to the bungalow, and back to reality.

THERE WERE TEN of us who had arrived with the new draft to join the famous 'E' Battery, which was now to be our family for the next few years. Our new comrades had turned out in large numbers to welcome us: men who looked so mature, bronzed, lean and fit in comparison to us pale-faced and white-kneed youths who had just arrived. There was Dodger Green, a burly giant with red hair and a constant smile on his face, with many years' service as a sergeant in the regiment, and a man to respect because of his size and energy. Smudger Smith, a lance-bombardier, was a theatrical type with an engaging manner, always a ready wit and never despondent, he was a classy dresser in his civvies, adopting black shirt, white tie and black titfer, like a present-day American gangster. Jim Revel was a gunner, another strong man who could banter with the best, and was able to recite endlessly the filthiest jokes and stories one could imagine; he had a vocabulary of swear words the envy of all. Chalky White, another gunner always ready to take on the world, had an inquisitive mind and a fount of knowledge readily available to all seeking information on just about any subject – especially women and beer. Bombardier Woods, nick-named Lackery (Urdu for wood) was another happy-go-lucky philosopher who would give you the shirt off his back. Taffy Jones, a gun team driver, was a Welshman with a perpetual song on his lips, his 'yakky dars, no stars' and other Welshisms clearly proclaimed his birthplace as the Rhondda Valley – you could almost see and smell the coal dust from the pits. And there was Norman Collins, an ex-gun sergeant recently reduced in rank to bombardier for drunkenness, though soon to be reinstated. Whilst all these men were to become friends, it was Norman who was to be closest, the one I would turn to most. A one-time Badgie[1] himself, he became my guardian, counsellor and mentor for the next few years as, under his watchful eye, I matured to manhood beneath the hot Indian sun. Norman held several medals for his boxing prowess, excelled at all kinds of sports, was fearless and forthright in all his activities; though somewhat reserved, he was like the proverbial rock of Gibraltar. He had a forceful personality, but was respected by all who knew him, and I thrived under the protection and guidance of this new-found friend.

FOR NOW, IT was almost ten o'clock and most of the men were winding down their activities. Reveille would be at six in the morning and it had been a tiring day. The punkah, the Indian version of a fan, a light framework covered with cloth and suspended from the ceiling and worked by pulling a cord, was circulating the air around the room, but the atmosphere was heavy with the heat of the day, and the men wore only the minimum of clothing. Taffy encouraged the punkah wallah to further efforts. With an, 'Atcha[2] Sahib' the native worked his toe, which was tied to the cord, a little faster and increased the motion of the punkah slightly before resuming his former speed, then lapsing once more into sleep. The result was negligible. One of my barrack mates, Dodger, had the most to say about the matter: 'The fucking things are overrated. Wouldn't cool my arse darn in an 'undred years. Why, it's the best way I know to pissing well burn to death. All you 'ave to do is sit under one of them. Might work in the shithouse though, keep the flies down a bit. Could improve the Eskimos' lot when they're cuddling up for the long winter's spell, and nothing to do outside of shagging all the time. What about you, Taffy, I reckon you could use one to 'elp you when you've got the 'orn on. Which is all the time from wot I can see! The only people to get any value from them bleeding punkahs is the wallah wot works it, and he's asleep 'arf the time. Give me a good woman any day to keep me cool.'

1 Trumpeter, from the Hindustani Baja Wallah or music man   2 OK

Taffy put in his four annas' worth too. 'The only farting people who think they're any good are them back 'ome in Wales, 'cos they don't know what the 'ell 'ot weaver is like. It's always cold enough there to freeze your goolies off, and if it does warm up in the summer the papers are full of it. You can just see the 'eadlines: "People are gasping for breath in this oven-like temperature we have all over Great Britain. It's 72 degrees again today and no relief in sight. Millions rush down to the sea to escape the unbearably hot weather. A new record of 80 degrees is set in Upper Minchinhampton, the highest in nearly fifty years!"' And he went on, 'Now them's the people wot should be using the punkahs. They can take the fucking wogs with them too – I'll even put up a few chips to do that. And I'll get the missus to go out on the batter a bit more often, then she can chip in like.'

It felt like I had to learn how to sleep all over again: first there was the hammock on the ship, then the cramped confines of the troop-train bunk. Now I had to learn the ropes of sleeping inside the mosquito net which was strung around the four iron uprights at the corners of the bed. The trick was to enter the bed so quickly that the mosquitoes didn't get in at the same time. The speed at which they moved was uncanny and I soon found out you'd be very lucky indeed to reach the safety of the net alone. Having done so, it was important to tuck the net in securely. All around me was the constant drone of mosquitoes in their countless millions, the pitch loud and penetrating. Once successfully inside, and having checked to make sure I really was alone, I sat there gazing mistily through the netting at the activities around me. Men everywhere were performing the same ritual, preparing for sleep, but only a few were actually under the sheets. Most lay naked on top, though some wore shorts or a wet towel across the stomach, the towel being dampened repeatedly throughout the night.

In front of my bed was the gun rack for storing the rifles under lock and key, firmly bolted to the cement floor. About ten feet long, there were several such racks in the bungalows, providing a measure of safety from the ever-marauding loose wallahs¹. Well versed in the art of their chosen profession, they were adept at acquiring virtually anything they wished, regardless of precautions taken. In accordance with the policy adopted subsequent

¹ Thieves

to the Mutiny, it was the continued practice to safeguard the rifles in this manner. Stored at central points throughout the bungalows, they gave ready access in the event of an emergency, but there was still a good measure of security – not that that was really any great advantage, as the bolts and ammunition were kept separately in the Guard Room as a further safety measure! Both rifles and bolts were of priceless value to the thieves, who found a ready market for them, especially on the North-West Frontier where conflict was raging between the Pathan tribesmen and the British.

But the bolts were of special interest: the Indian gunsmiths had no difficulty manufacturing the 303 rifle, but couldn't do the bolt, thus making it a coveted acquisition. If a soldier lost a bolt, or the whole rifle, it was a most serious crime, reflected in the harsh punishment meted out: a serious term of imprisonment. The loose wallahs were not just interested in armament and it was a careless man who failed to secure his watch and other valuable items at all times. They usually chose the darkness of the night to make their forays. Silently, their bodies smeared with cooking oil, they would steal into the dimly lit area taking whatever they could find, then they were gone in a trice. It was said they could steal the very blanket upon which you lay, and you would never know it had gone until the sun rose. One story going round was that one morning the lads woke up to find not only had the rifles gone, but so had the gun rack, retaining bolts and all, and never a sound was heard – and the author was prepared to swear on a stack of Bibles a mile high it was true.

I had heard such stories whilst in England, but like all new recruits I was sceptical; as I lay there surrounded by all things Indian, they sounded much more plausible now. I fell asleep to the droning of the mosquitoes, with dreams of tangling with the loose wallahs who were stealing my trumpet; the punkah wallah offering me a turn with my toe on the cord, and shooting a tiger which turned out to be a local pie dog, all jumbled with other events of the day.

REVEILLE CAME ALL too quickly, but as I wasn't the duty trumpeter that day, I was able to enjoy the luxury of lying abed until the waking call aroused us all. The mosquito net at first confused me, and it took a moment to orient myself. In spite of the weird dreams, I had slept well, undisturbed by mosquitoes, though twice during the night I'd been awakened briefly by the sounds of vainly clapping hands trying to kill mosquitoes which had penetrated someone's net, and by the mournful cry of some poor devil having a nightmare. Heaven knows being a soldier in India was reason enough to suffer nightmares, they were commonplace. And just before dawn, the 'napees' – the barbers – moved from bed to bed shaving the faces of those still sleeping, who awoke to a cleanly shaven chin without having felt the lathering of the soap, or the open razor sliding across their neck. Beware the napee who caused the slightest nick to the skin in the process, Hell would be his reward!

The bearers brought us mugs of the sergeant-major's legendary tea, scalding hot, with an excess of sugar, and strong as molasses; the proverbial spoon would have no trouble standing upright in these mugs. The char wallahs opened for business on the verandah at an early hour too; indeed, some of them remained there throughout the night.

The room was transformed from the peace of the night to the helter-skelter of preparations for the day: first, to the ablutions adjacent to the sleeping quarters, where long rows of communal showers and sinks were already alive with the men, laughing and joking through their toiletry tasks. Hungry, I hurried through the process of washing and cleaning my teeth, having to fight for space at the wash trough, and thankful for the boundless supply of hot water. (Hot water supplies had always been severely limited in England.) Having raced back to my bedside and dressed in khaki drill shirt and shorts, I walked across the gravel square, but as I approached the dining hall, I was met by the unusual sight of numerous vendor wallahs who had established themselves around the entrance. They served a wide selection of foodstuffs, designed to supplement or replace the military menu, which was liable to be limited in its offering. The vendors were doing a brisk business. There was the dood (milk) wallah, the mukkin (butter) wallah, the roti (bread) wallah, the char wallah, the bacon wallah, the undah (egg) wallah – done anyway you chose, fried, boiled, scrambled, or as you wished. And there was the Bombay Oyster, no matter how bad a night you had suffered: the raw egg in vinegar laced with salt and pepper was guaranteed to put lead in your pencil.

I didn't relish the porridge on the menu for breakfast, so I chose to patronize the outdoor cooks, ordering bacon and doe (two) undah rumble tumble. Whilst this was prepared over the smoking coal-fired grill, I chatted with the cook who bantered with me, saying that a chota babba (young boy) like me should not be so far away from home, and asking me what I was doing in India with the other white sahibs. The conversation was limited, the Indian having little English and I knowing not a single word of Urdu; it was accomplished more by gesture than by word. As the food was handed to me, it was clear that the man had something important to say, because of his gesticulations and finger-pointing to the sky. Turning away with the plate of food in my hand, I was taken aback by the swooping of a kite hawk, poised for an attack on my bacon and eggs – but swift though it was, my even swifter evasive action foiled the bird's attempt, and I quickly sought the refuge of the dining room. My near escape was enjoyed immensely by my comrades, who had all learned that lesson long ago.

Also searching for scraps of food were the ever-present black-feathered mynah birds, constantly cawing and making themselves a nuisance to those who chose to eat out in the open air. There are three species of these beautiful birds: the Lesser Indian Hill Mynah, the Greater Indian Hill Mynah and the Java Hill Mynah; slightly smaller than the Java, the Greater Indian Hill bird is almost twelve inches long with a powerful, deep orange-red bill, thick legs and yellow skin patches on the head: a handsome bird, but not averse to attacking anyone who gets in its way.

It was seven o'clock in the morning and the sun was already casting its powerful rays over the cantonment. Breakfast over and feeling good about life, and in company with the sergeant in charge of my section, I was taken back to the horse lines, to be introduced to the two horses which were to be my responsibility to care for, and to ride on all mounted occasions. The first was named Dolly Grey, and she was a real softy, without a shred of harm in her; no fits of temper or contrariness, she was always forgiving and obedient. Under fourteen hands and with a dumpy girth, her silky coat was almost white: she was a beautiful creature in all respects. She was a pleasure to ride, constantly docile and willing, not given to demonstrations, no matter how long or arduous the journey. I was lucky indeed to have such a fine friend allotted, for many of the horses were of bad temperament and often disliked by their riders. The second horse was one used only for playing polo, owned by one of the regimental officers, and was the absolute antithesis of Dolly: the same height, though slight of build, Henry was jet black, a sensitive animal, but mean-natured, always ready to object in the strongest terms to whatever the rider wished. Quick to snap at the unwary admirer, Henry was not a popular animal, especially with the syces who had to groom the beast, as they'd been bitten more than once. I never really understood why the horse had been given to me as a mount, except that it was small in stature and unsuitable for a heavy rider.

I was told to saddle up immediately and cement my relationship with Dolly. Together with others who were similarly celebrating their newfound acquaintances, we were to take part in the regimental parade on the maidan, in the order of 'A' to 'F'. 'A' gun would be on the right, with others formed in the same order to the left. On the right again of the guns would be the Battery reconnaissance and headquarter units. On the extreme left flank was the service unit. Five mounted officers would be positioned in front of the assembly, the Commanding Officer being to the front and in the middle of them. Adjacent to, and on the right of the reconnaissance group, were the two Battery trumpeters, prominently mounted on their white horses (apart from these two, all the other horses of the regiment were of a chestnut brown). Each gun team was drawn by British soldiers, one for each pair of the six horses. The Gun Sergeants, one from each of the gun crews of six men, were immediately in front of the guns they served. Following the rear of each gun was the ammunition limber, served again by six men, but in this case by Indian Other Ranks. At this stage, a most detailed inspection was carried out by each section commander, for thirty minutes, after which the commanders reported to the Battery Sergeant-Major. Bringing the assembly to attention, the Sergeant-Major in turn reported to the Adjutant that the Battery was all present and correct, then, standing the parade at ease, marched back to his position. The Battery was once more brought to attention at the command of the Adjutant who duly reported to the Commanding Officer that the Battery was ready for inspection.

By this time we were reduced almost to despair, our endurance wilting, having been at attention for almost two long and painful hours on the blazing maidan, targeted by the merciless sun, now at its meridian. Sweating heavily and feeling highly uncomfortable in the tight-fitting full dress uniform of breeches and jackboots, the exposure was beginning to take its toll. The Wolseley helmet was unbearably heavy, as it was made not only to offer shelter from the sun, but also to provide protection to the head in the event of a fall, which is why it was used on all mounted occasions. Now it felt like an excruciating band of iron around the forehead, with the chinstrap cutting uncomfortably at the neck. The pith helmet, our preferred headdress, was made of lighter material and design, incorporating banana leaves; it was less troublesome, but was used only when dismounted. Our faces were turning a vivid red and we didn't think we could go on much longer. It was no surprise when one member of a British gun crew fell to the ground, fainting from heat exhaustion, but no one else moved, and not a sound was heard. The patience of the troops was now almost beyond control, and the man would lie there until the regiment moved off. In the midst of the inspection we dared not even flinch, and were unable to wipe away the sweat dripping down an itchy nose or to brush away the countless flies from the mouth. The torture was agonizing beyond compare.

Ignoring the prostrate figure, the Commanding Officer continued his rounds at a leisurely pace, his indifferent behaviour towards our obvious deep discomfort making it all the more unbearable – some would add, unforgivable – on the part of the Commanding Officer. The slightest movement would bring the wrath of the Sergeant-Major down on the offender, so the suffering must continue, and relief must wait a while for the collapsed man. Now the horses were fidgeting too, impatiently pawing the ground, saliva dripping from their mouths. At last the inspection was over and the Commanding Officer returned to his position at the saluting stand for the march past. An audible sigh of relief came clearly as we swung into the salute and then into the gun lines.

Now well past midday, few felt the need for food; the urge was to strip off our uniforms, take a cold shower, and seek the comfort of sleep under the mosquito net. Ice was not available in the barracks and for a cold drink of water it was necessary to resort to the chatties hung in the trees outside. The bearers had to keep these earthenware bowls filled; by the process of evaporation, they provided ice-cold water. In the same way, beer wrapped with straw in Hessian sacks was made cold and palatable. Awaiting us back at the barrack room were servants ready to assist in the removal of uniforms and jackboots; the latter was accomplished by the servant bending down with his back to the sahib, grasping the boot between his legs and pulling, whilst the sahib pushed with his other boot on the servant's backside. This did not always work, as it invariably pushed the servant forward, causing him to fall flat on his face, much to the amusement of all except the bearer. Boots off, clean clothes were laid out on the bed, ready for master to dress, but most of us simply fell on our beds and slept until suppertime. Others lay there sweltering with but a towel across their stomach, searching for an escape from the torturous realities of the day. A few wrote letters home, or read, and the card addicts started the inevitable game of brag, gambling with the last of their payday money. What else other than charpoy-bashing was there to do on a hot Indian afternoon when it was too early to go drinking, or exploring the bazaar, and so far away from the pleasures of England. There was little to occupy our minds, other than to talk about 'back when'.

I rested on my bed, listlessly watching the geckos clinging to the walls stalking their prey, moving only in short bursts of lightning speed until, once within range, they shot out those long tongues like a shot from a gun to capture the unwary flies, then lay motionless waiting for the next meal to arrive. You had to be pretty desperate to consider that to be a worthwhile pastime; most of those who could not sleep were thinking about women, or rather, the lack of them. I had already discovered that the greater majority of the troops were obsessed with women; white women especially were a great void in the lives of these servants of the King Emperor. Though eternal, the quest for female companionship was always evasive and frustrating: in dreams they would experience all manner of erotic sexual acts, repeated time and time again, only to dissipate with the coming of the dawn.

There was a great risk of picking up VD from the local girls, as there was with prostitutes everywhere. A widespread affliction in the army, its incidence was unbelievably high in the Meerut Cantonment, where almost half the men were infected. In many parts of the country it was even higher, sometimes reaching the appalling figure of almost seventy per cent. In England it was about twenty per cent, in the German Army less than eight per cent, whilst in the French Army fewer than five per cent suffered. The worst incidence on record is that of a British infantry regiment in Chakartra, a hill station in the Himalayas, where more than eighty per cent of the troops in the regiment were found to be unfit for duty.

Even the most restrictive precautions observed by the military had done little over the years to minimize VD. They tried establishing regimental brothels in garrisons across the country, with the most stringent medical inspections, but though successful at first, the military had later to bow to the loud disapproval and intense pressure exerted by the Women's Temperance Association, churches, politicians and other campaigning groups back in England. Nothing would do except the immediate abolition of these red light centres, which was discouraging for both the men and the commanding officers: the latter reeled under the heavy blow of having their men incapable of carrying out their duties; the former, the misery, pain, shame and despair of contracting the hated diseases.

Lord Kitchener, Commander in Chief of the British Army of the India of the 1900s, could not understand the sexual desires of the British soldier, and believed that these could be curtailed by keeping the men fully occupied. But his creativeness in establishing an award for the regiments with the lowest sick rate, and the army's own determination to establish supervised brothels, did reduce incidence considerably.

For us, the only acceptable alternative was masturbation, which was the chosen option in preference to visiting the bazaars, particularly for the longer-serving soldiers, whose behaviour was clearly adversely affected by the absence of women.

Homosexuality was the other approach, but not a popular one. True, it was practised in the army, and wherever else men banded together in the absence of women, and it was no less so in the barrack rooms where I lived. It was a common arrangement for men to team up as pairs, sharing everything including money, and all aspects of their lives other than sexual activities. They might go to a brothel together, but that was all there was to it: it was almost like a marriage, but without the sexual overtones. Homosexuality, on the other hand, was a discreet affair, like the two men who were known to be gay in my barrack room: they kept very much to themselves, publicly displaying no affection for each other and always conducting their pleasures in privacy. Darby and Joan, as they were known, were very reserved in their relationship, and the attitude of the majority of the troops appeared to be one of acceptance. There was little discussion of the matter, and never was there any open indication of disapproval from the men.

There were other factors too: the harsh life to which we were subjected, the prolonged absence of family and relatives, and the fact that we soldiers were serving a country whose leaders and people were neither interested nor cared about the conditions overseas we had to endure. For those who were interested, analysis of the death rolls would have spoken volumes of the privations and suffering of those who committed suicide by either the toe on the trigger of the rifle, or hanging themselves, or by more violent means: falling victim to alcoholism and drinking oneself into oblivion, or being committed to institutions for the insane, were ever-present threats.

This was a life where unhappiness and discontent flourished, and the disappointments and futility of daily existence could drive even the most gentle of men to injure or even murder their comrades. Tempers were on a dangerously short fuse, and quick to ignite. There were fights, over cheating at gambling, or a trivial remark made in innocence and interpreted as a personal affront. It took a strong, disciplined man to withstand the social privations and vicissitudes of the lonely military life in the tropics; I fervently hoped that I would not fall prey to these temptations and dangers, and manage to avoid damage to both body and mind.

IT WAS NOW about six in the evening; the barrack rooms began to show signs of life. The parades were over and the syces would have taken care of the horses and the stable chores for the day. The evening was ours, to do with as we wished, just as it always had been in that setting unchanged since the men of the garrison had striven to put down the Great Indian Mutiny of 1857. The central gun racks were there, the concrete floors, the punkahs, even the geckos crawling on the walls were the same. It had been a hectic day and I was feeling a little the worse for wear, jaded by my first exposure to the demands of service with the British Raj. Perhaps a long, sound sleep would put me right: tomorrow was another day.

I integrated very quickly with the men of the Battery, helped by my quick and evasive repartee when asked questions to which I really didn't know the answer. I rarely saw any of the officers of the Battery, except when on formal parades, most of which were held only in the presence of the non-commissioned officers. The officers were almost an enigma: known to be present but rarely seen in flesh and blood; their days were totally occupied with polo, pig-sticking and tent-pegging. Every season before the monsoons broke, their talk was of nothing other than the Kadir Cup, a garrison pig-sticking and dangerous sporting event in which the officers of the Battery excelled. In the evenings, it was always tea dances or dinner parties, the grand ball, or the continual entertainment of guest nights in the mess. And there was the perpetual merry-go-round of fishing, hunting, shooting, trekking and climbing in the Himalayas.

The officers were not denied the pleasures of returning home; they were granted several months' leave every two years to travel wherever they wished. Most went to England, travelling in luxury on the mail boat from Bombay to London for the short fourteen-day journey. Many had the opportunity of shipboard romance with the wives of the men who must remain in India, fleeting affairs, soon forgotten by both parties. Returning to India via the United States or Australia, they would visit a while, being entertained by their military counterparts, comparing notes on their different lifestyles. They appeared to be fully devoted to the search for pleasure and self-satisfaction; no wonder it was necessary to have an independent source of income in order to support that extravagant life style; military pay alone would never have sufficed. Unapproachable, they were detached in any contact or dealings with the rank and file. Certainly they looked impressive, in exquisitely tailored uniforms with highly polished leather Sam Brownes, slapping their glossy riding boots with leather riding crops to the sound of jingling silver spurs.

There was one officer who spoke to me, enquiring – with what sounded like genuine concern – how I was getting along, serving with the Battery, and if I was happy being in India. At first I was horribly tongue-tied, answering hesitantly 'it was all right'. After a few more searching questions, the officer advised me that if I was unhappy being there, it was possible that I could be sent home to England. Then I was more positive, telling the officer that I would rather stay and continue to serve with the Battery. It was a brief conversation, but now I felt that someone in authority was interested in my welfare. Another officer, and one I was to grow to admire, was the Major who commanded the Battery, and whose horse-holder I was to be. He was a much warmer individual, treating me almost as an equal, not in the least like a common soldier. He always had a kind word and, whilst out in the field on exercises for the day, would give me a bar of chocolate that he had thoughtfully brought along.

The officers as a group were by no means disliked by all the troops, although their indifferent attitude towards the men hurt some of them. They were looked up to, but the general feeling of the troops was that a more humane and personal relationship was deserved. The officers, by virtue of serving in an illustrious regiment, were seen as persons of consequence, of wealth or social status. Breeding was of the utmost importance in the opinion of the Officers' Selection Board, who believed it imperative that the individual came from a good aristocratic background, with ties preferably linked to royalty. Good schooling at one of the better known establishments was important as only a person of education of the required quality could be 'the right type' to command men, in either war or peace. Nor must money be found wanting, for it was essential an officer could entertain in the grand style and live in a manner befitting the honour of serving in such a famous unit.

From the beginning, officers only became such by buying their commission, a practice that was discontinued not so many years ago, in the eighteen hundreds. The prestige and the glamour of the rank was the attraction, but, once having achieved that honour, many officers were content, thereafter serving little or no time with their chosen regiment. Their absence and lack of interest brought no cries of concern, though the impact on the efficiency to the unit might well have been questioned; the higher the number of such officers in a regiment, the lower the performance could be expected. Of course, once in, they could then purchase still higher ranks, and it was not uncommon at that time to find wealthy, blue-blooded gentlemen of a tender age, sometimes as young as sixteen or seventeen, in positions of high command.

Promotion from the ranks to commissioned officer was extremely rare, except during times of war, and such recognition was limited to the senior ranks of the Warrant Officers who had already made their mark in the service. The exceptions to this were Quartermasters, who were usually Subalterns, or perhaps Captains, being acknowledged by brother officers because of specialized knowledge of supplies. They could expect to reach only the lower ranks, usually not progressing beyond Captain. These rankers, as they were known, rarely felt comfortable in the presence of their brother officers; their common upbringing, the lack of an Oxford accent, or experience in the more cultured aspects of life – not to mention the lack of money – they were often rejected.

But for all their supposed resentment, the troops would never talk derogatorily of their officers in the presence of strangers. In a way, it was a reverse snobbery that caused them to uphold their esteem.

HERE IN MEERUT there was little square bashing, although inspections on the parade grounds and in the barrack rooms were frequent. An emphasis was placed on training with horses and guns, which I enjoyed, able to ride Dolly Grey the way I wanted. Galloping and performing figures of eights and other manoeuvres to my heart's content, we would race across the maidan, getting along famously. The maidan, a large open area of wasteland, was of hardened mud and clay, with a scattering of weeds and crab grass, ideal for horse riding and used by all the mounted regiments. It was so large that it was not uncommon to see three or four different units practising there at the same time. Dolly was very responsive, she was a solid horse to ride and I never had a moment's uneasiness: it was like sitting on solid bedrock, yet cushioned by the softness of down.

But there were moments when the dangers of horse riding were brought cruelly to mind: once, during a mounted regimental exercise, I saw the terrible sight of a rider being dragged to his death by his horse. His foot had caught in the stirrup as the animal reared and causing him to fall. The panicking horse, racing madly along the maidan, was pulling the unfortunate rider into the far distance at breakneck speed, the man screaming for help and his body bouncing wildly as it careened over the rocks and unevenness of the ground. Others chased after the runaway, also galloping at top speed, but it was too late. When they finally caught the animal and released the man, he had many broken bones. He had lost much of his clothing – even a boot had been stripped from his foot. Worse still, his scalp had literally been torn off as he had been dragged over the ground; the dreadful ordeal had lasted several minutes and it was too late for him: he was beyond help, and his ending must have been hideously painful. His body was a horrifying sight, and his comrades made haste to cover and remove him, for the vultures were already circling and the sun was high. He would be buried within the hour, in accordance again with the saying in the East: 'Alive and well at the break of day, and buried by sundown.' He was a bombardier, one of the longer-serving members of the Battery and due to go home soon. He was popular with his comrades and an experienced horseman. There was a girl awaiting him in Devon. I, like everyone else, was shocked. It was a salutary lesson for me about the frailty of human life, particularly in India.

IT WAS NOT all play for me. School was to start again, after all those wonderful weeks away from the classroom. For two or three hours a day, I was to sit in the small school building with several other boys from nearby regiments, all equally disenchanted with the prospect of studying. English, maths, military history and map-reading were again the subjects, but of a more advanced nature. These would continue as part of my daily ritual for all my service as a boy soldier. To these was added lessons with the munshi – the teacher – learning Urdu, the language used by the British and the Indians in their daily lives. This was fun, not least listening to the delightful singsong of the munshi's voice when he was speaking in English. All Indians spoke this way; it was believed to have evolved from their contact with the early Welsh missionaries who spoke naturally with a lilting accent.

But there were many compensations for enduring the more boring topics. There was little organized physical training, but sports abounded. Most evenings when the oppressive atmosphere declined, there would be a soccer game to watch or play, or hockey on the cement-like hard ground. The pitch for the latter was made with muttee, a mud-like concoction that made for a fast-moving, at times dangerous game. There were several tennis courts well used by those crazy Englishmen, even during the heat of the day. The cantonment was well provided with playing fields, a great source of enjoyment that lent meaning to the saying that the battles of the English were won on the playing fields. Boxing was a very popular event, with lots of talent amongst the thousands of soldiers in the cantonment, but my own interest had waned; it was far safer just to watch. And, when the games ended, there was always the canteen where you could sit and fraternize whilst drinking a bottle of the cold Murree beer. Brewed in the foothills of the Himalayas, it was the nearest to the taste of proper English beer. And the char and khana wallahs were always brewing up and preparing their tasty foodstuffs for the hungry.

And almost every man had a pet of some sort, a dog or mongoose or parrot or monkey; some had snakes or even spiders: anything on which to bestow a bit of love and attention. I didn't keep anything exotic, for Dolly Grey was my real love, but I did share a bulldog with Norman, my friend and mentor, which was the terror of the regiment. It had been given to us by one of the officers who was going home, the nasty polo pony Henry's owner; he knew we would take good care of Towser, as he wasn't able to take him back to England. Towser would eat anything he could lay his paws on, which created no end of trouble for us – one day he went into the Officers' Mess and stole a dinner; there was a tremendous ruckus about that and it was only because the wretched hound had been owned by an officer that we were able to keep him.

And poor Towser really wasn't very bright: he was trotting along one day, minding his own business and not watching where he was going, when he ran into a post and knocked himself out. It didn't seem to make much difference to him when he came round, though. (Fortunately, he didn't have to be destroyed when the regiment eventually left, as Norman stayed on in India and was able to keep him.)

My turns as duty trumpeter, which alternated weekly with my counterpart, were not all that demanding, but it did mean some restrictions on my movements, as I had to be at the appointed place and time to make the calls. The occasions I or the other trumpeter, John Thompson, failed to execute these duties in a satisfactory manner were few, but liable to draw the anger of the Battery Sergeant-Major when they did occur. We'd be called into his office and given a stern dressing-down, and the strong hint that any further occurrences might result in being transferred to a common royal artillery unit, which meant both I and my confrère would be careful not to offend again. I had been surprised to find that my partner was an Anglo-Indian – a chee-chee – in the belief that only the best were posted to the *right of the line* regiments, but it turned out that this particular boy had received the highest passing grade at the Indian Boys' Depot in Mhow, and was thus accorded the signal honour of joining the Battery. Unfortunately, John Thompson was a surly individual, obviously with a chip on his shoulder and resenting the fact that he was a half-caste. We didn't see much of each other.

In discussion later on the topic, I wondered about the origin of the term Anglo-Indian, and whether it applied only to half-castes. The learned Norman Collins, who had served many years in the country, settled the argument, saying he believed it was first applied to those Britishers who were long-time residents of India, but more recently it denoted those who were of mixed blood.

The relationship between the soldiers and the natives was not exactly one to be desired; the former constantly criticized the work of the latter for their lack of perfection and seeming inability to perform even the simplest of tasks. The native workers were denigrated at every opportunity, and quite often thrashed, physically and mentally, for any apparent insolence. The natives in turn responded with silence. The same wide gulf separated the Indian and the British soldiers, and it was difficult to bridge. We were worlds apart in so many respects, and made little effort to understand one another, or to make conversation, rarely even stopping to pass the time of the day as a friendly gesture. The British showed little interest in Indian customs or religions, or indeed, in any of their activities. East is East and West is West, and never the twain shall meet, except in friction and with indifference: this was not a very happy state of affairs and the result was confrontation and lack of understanding.

In the case of the Indian Other Ranks it was a peculiar situation. Being responsible for the gun limbers, the British gun teams were dependent upon them for the supply of ammunition, without which the guns were useless. Both played an essential role; they needed to be a united entity. In battle, this relationship of the British Other Ranks looking down with such obvious contempt on their dark-skinned fellow drivers could scarcely contribute to fostering the cohesive comradeship required to fight the enemy, rather than each other. But it had always been like that, and little effort was made to improve the relationship; it wasn't likely to change in my lifetime. Perhaps if the troops had been less inclined to refer to them as wogs, black bastards or 'kala niggers', amongst similar demeaning expressions, it might have helped. As ambassadors of England they were by no means messengers of love and affection. In retrospect, the troops were the bastards who needed to smarten up; even now, the natives think of them in turn as 'those unmitigated white bastards'. Like their officers, they were arrogant and had nothing but contempt for the Indians.

Further, as if to emphasize their differences with the natives, the British continued to show their indifference in manner and superiority in strength. It was customary on or close to the anniversary of the 1857 Mutiny for British troops, with the guns of the artillery, to parade through the towns and villages showing the flag, as a demonstration of the power capable of meeting any further disturbances against the King Emperor. The British soldiers were always glad when the ceremony through the crowded and silent city was over, knowing full well that the natives were likely to retaliate with violence, with their swords and knives. The mounted men felt very vulnerable; they could be swallowed up in this unwelcoming place and overwhelmed so easily. During the rebellion, the British forces had numbered only some fifty thousand in India, and were responsible for the security of the three presidencies of Bengal, Bombay, and Madras. (The East India Company first landed in the latter in 1639.) Now, whilst there were about the same number of troops in the country, the population had grown enormously and the areas to control were considerably larger. The British had good reason to be uneasy.

AND WE HAD good reason to be uneasy at home too. Europe and the Middle-East were unsettled. In March 1936 Germany occupied the Rhineland. In May, hot on the heels of the departure of Emperor Haile Selassie, Italian troops marched into Abyssinia; on May 9 the country was annexed. It would later be used as a springboard for the Italians to attack British frontier posts. In July the Spanish Civil War started.

chapter six

INDIA: DELHI

February 1936 to April 1937

The most splendid and imposing exhibition was the annual Durbar at Delhi, held in the spring before the hot weather arrived. The Battery would leave Meerut in grand style, in full marching order, for the two-day journey, travelling along part of the old Trunk Road which had echoed to the countless footsteps of marching British soldiers down the ages. The roads were narrow and crowded and the dust rose like the smoke from a factory chimney; it was a long and tedious journey of almost forty miles.

The two-mile-long column, comprising a train of horses and guns and related equipment, and the men dressed in field service marching order, was capable of remaining in the field for an indefinite period of time. As well as the fighting arm, there was all the apparatus required to service it: water wagons, field kitchens and water supply units, tents for sleeping and eating, the medical unit (of limited resources), fodder for the horses and farriers to replace lost shoes. There were spare horses to replace sick or injured animals, syces, bearers, khansamas[1] for the cooking, napees, the sweepers and all manner of servants. The followers more than doubled the length of the military train; the Battery on the move clogged the road as it moved slowly along its route. When not on a war footing, regiments received an allowance for the hire of animals when undertaking moves of some distance, in order to transport what otherwise might be described as unnecessary goods and equipment. This journey qualified, so I had the experience of travelling with five elephants,

[1] House servants

twelve camels and several bullocks. The elephants were fun, and I got a huge treat when I was lifted off the ground by the animal's trunk and then firmly deposited on its back. The camels were not popular as they were surly and unfriendly, and more than one gunner got bitten, which was pretty serious as camels are noted as disease-carriers. Soldiering with camels was certainly not a popular pastime. The bullocks didn't interest us troopers at all.

We were to leave the cantonment at Meerut in the early hours, to make the most of the cool air before the sun rose, so the compounds were alive with activity by three in the morning. Preparations had started several days before the departure date, now only the last-minute arrangements were required. At the three o'clock reveille, we awakened in darkness and ate a hasty breakfast before final preparations were completed. Interspersed by the shouting and cursing of the troopers as they worked in the gloom, order was eventually salvaged from the apparent chaos that reigned.

The roads in India were marked with stones every mile along the verges, indicating the distance to the nearest city. To us, the miles seemed to pass so slowly as the column moved sluggishly on its way. The speed at which we travelled was depressingly slow, averaging no more than three miles an hour: the train would move at a walking pace for fifty minutes, then halt for a ten-minute rest break for the animals, and for the men to smoke and talk, and curse the increasing heat of the day. Nostrils and throats clogged with the prickling dust, eyes were reddened by the blinding grit as we marched to the sound of the gun caissons and the limbers rattling as they bounced on the rutted surface of the road. We were already tired, weary and saddle-sore, though but a scant few miles had been covered. Still, we managed a song, one that was sung by our forebears a hundred years ago, and the words were much the same now as then:

We are the Horse Artillery
We are the RHA
We don't have to march like the infantry
Ride like the cavalry
We are the Horse Artillery

We are the Horse Artillery
We are the RHA

We don't have to 'enge' with the Engineers,
March like the infantry
We are the Horse Artillery

We are the Horse Artillery
We are the RHA
We don't have to ...

And so on – and this was encouraged, for discipline was not as strict as it was in earlier days, when such a song might have been viewed as insubordination and punished by the lash. The officers and the warrant officers now approved of this and could relax in the knowledge that the men were in good heart. We would be amongst the last British soldiers to make this march to the Durbar; by the turn of the next half century, there would be no white sahibs left on the soil of India and only the boots of the Indian sepoys and sowars' would be left to tread this famous road.

Midday, and the sun high above, we were only twenty miles nearer our destination, though we'd been in the saddle for six hours. Our water bottles were nearly empty, and the remains tasted tepid and foul. We had still another hour or so's march to face, by which time we would be about halfway there. Tomorrow would be the same again.

Arriving at the pre-determined bivouac, reconnoitred earlier and prepared by the advance party, we were greeted by the welcoming sight of the camp already established, the areas marked out and the tents erected. The field kitchen was ready and a meal being prepared. There was renewed life and activity in the column as we entered the temporary campsite, our laughter and jokes returning. Shouts for the attendance of syces and servants rang loud in the air, but they'd travelled at the very rear of the train and were still straggling in. Scared of dismissal if they weren't quick to attend their masters, they hurriedly responded. Settled in and stripping off heavy clothing and equipment, we couldn't relax until the horses had been attended to and bridled to retaining ropes hung between the trees.

The chores finished, and the passing afternoon turning to the cool of the evening, we sat around the wood fires, telling soldiers' stories. In the half light, the magic returned as the stars began to appear in the clear sky. The scent of the burning wood, with the low chatter of the voices echoing quietly throughout the camp, contributed to the sense of escape and the pleasure of being in this open stretch of land that was home for the night.

For me, it was a new experience and, in spite of the rigid discipline and the constraints imposed by the narrowness of the British Army's outlook, I was truly enjoying soldiering in India. I knew then that when the time came to leave the country, though I'd be happy for many reasons, the memories of this evening, and of similar experiences, would be those I would always cherish, rather than the burning heat of the sun, or the bitter cold of nights sleeping on the hard and unforgiving ground, or even the filth and the dirt, or all the many trials and tribulations that constantly beset those serving here. And when I was long gone, back in my home-land thousands of miles and another world away, it would be these moments of joy I would describe to my children.

Tight security was arranged around the camp, strengthened as the evening surrendered to the darkness by the night guards with their rifles and fixed bayonets, who were strategically placed around the perimeter. A central Guard Room was established too. No one was allowed in the area of the troops' sleeping quarters, and after ten o'clock the servants were relegated to their own area near the horse lines. Passwords were given only to the trusted few who might have occasion to leave the confines of the camp. Intruders would receive an unwelcome reception; this could well be the night when the second warning to halt and be identified would not be given by the guard. We could all sleep peacefully this night, at least.

DELHI WAS THE capital of India, and at that time, the seat of the British Sirkar, the government, and the headquarters for all the forces under the Raj: both the British and Indian Armies. The original seat of the Sirkar had been Calcutta, but it had been moved to Delhi for various reasons, not the least of which was the proximity of Simla and other hill stations, offering the attraction of refuge in the cool mountain ranges during the summer months. Delhi was one of the most populated cities in the world; though dotted with the golden spires and domes of the temples covered with the most intricate carvings, and set on the plains of the United Provinces by the banks of the Jumna River, it was a teaming and unlovely city. The Battery had again made an early start and crossed the Bailey bridge over the river soon after midday. As the rattle of the gun wheels and the hooves rang out on the steel structure, there was a moment of concern: recoiling violently in fear of the noise, a horse had galloped forward out of control, brushing aside vain efforts to catch it. Its rider, now on the ground and being trampled by the oncoming horses, was plucked to safety from the wheels of a gun carriage in the nick of time. Riding at the head of the column alongside the Major, I was struck by the runaway horse, but luckily, I was able to keep my seat. Dolly Grey was thrown against the metal railings of the bridge, which startled her, but both she and I were unharmed, the fracas was brought under control, and the march continued.

From the elevated bridge over the Jumna, quite a half-mile wide, we could see the massive and sprawling conglomeration that was Delhi. Situated by the Aravalli Hills (better known as the Delhi Ridge, the desperate scene of the siege during the Mutiny,) and the Yamuna River, the city has been raped and destroyed many times since it was first founded in the Mahabbarat period. About 100 BC it was rebuilt by Rajah Dilli, who gave the city its modern name. The original city, Shahjianbad, as it was then known, was reconstructed on its present site by the Moghul Emperor Shah Jahan. Sacked and pillaged by the ravaging hordes of the Moghuls from the North, it was rebuilt at least seven times.

On the death of its last true Emperor, it was controlled by the Marathas until Lord Lake and the British Army took control. Shah Alam, the Emperor at the time, was placed under the protection of the Raj by Lord Lake, but, though retaining the title of Emperor, he had been denuded of all power by the British. Lord Lake administered the city in the name of the Emperor, which effectively fell within British jurisdiction.

Delhi was a remarkable city, a combination of the old and the new. Old Delhi, in essence unchanged from what it must have been and looked like a thousand years ago, was honeycombed with twisting, narrow streets and dark alleys, many of which were unnamed. It was a veritable maze, where few white sahibs dared – or were stupid enough – to venture alone. The teeming, bustling area of the Chandi Chauk bazaar, the main commercial centre of the old city, has grown over the years in a hodge-podge fashion with little or no semblance of order in its layout. It has evolved to look rather like a jigsaw puzzle in the early stages of its assembly, each component unaware of its place or purpose, and clearly it is bursting at the seams trying to accommodate the enormous numbers of people who are crammed into a space woefully inadequate for the purpose. It is perhaps the most densely populated area in the country, a typical Indian city scene, but on the macro scale, surpassing even Calcutta which became known as the cesspool of India.

The streets were barely ten feet wide at best, without sidewalks, and were clogged night and day with all manner of conveyances, from tongas to put-put rickshaws, from hand-carts to buses which apparently had God's approval to do just as they pleased, crowding the ever-narrowing passageways. Also competing for access through this mass of congested traffic were the animals: the elephants and the camels, the hallowed cows and the pigs, and other livestock being taken to the market. There was an all-pervasive stench of urine and cow dung, mixed with bad fruit and rotting meat. The mangy mongrel dogs ferreted for any scraps of food they could find, constantly under foot and causing further obstruction.

For the regiment to force its way through this almost impenetrable wall of resistance was a daunting task. Open sewers abounded and the ditches running down the centre of the roads were clogged with refuse; the smells from them were also foul. There was an abundance of vermin, including rats, openly scurrying around. Yet, for all this, it was a fascinating place, and alive with commercial and industrial activity. Merchants selling jewellery, gold and precious stones, silks and handwoven rugs and carpets and materials of every kind were cheek by jowl with others offering every conceivable personal service. It was like any bazaar in the larger cities, but on a far grander scale.

Adjacent to this kaleidoscope of colour and filth was New Delhi, providing a contrast in beauty and symmetry. Spacious and orderly and with the most modern structures, it was planned by the celebrated architect Sir Edwin Lutyens, and built in the nineteen-twenties under the jurisdiction of the British. With roads wide and straight, the edifices handsome, and the setting one of orderliness and geometric harmony, New Delhi was a paradise compared to other Indian cities, and it was where the wealthy civilian and military sahibs resided whenever possible. There was also a housing area specifically for Indians holding high office in the government departments, though placed at a discreet distance from the residences of the élite. Indians below approved rank were not permitted to reside in those residential sectors.

From the bridge now could be seen the mixture of decrepit hovels and shanties where the common people lived, in the most unsanitary and crowded conditions. I could clearly distinguish the primitive shelters of the bustees[1] thrown up by the sides of the teeming streets. They were much the same as those I had seen on the fringes of Bombay, but now magnified a hundredfold: an unpleasant sight, even from the distance of the bridge, where the smells were yet to be suffered. Approaching closer to the city, the worst of our imaginations became reality, and soon we were in the turmoil.

Forcing our way through the great multitude of people in the ever-narrowing streets was a daunting task; the natives began harassing us and throwing stones and soon the horse drivers were using their riding crops on the heads of those who were crushing closer and closer. The gunners were dismounted and they too were hammering away at the mob, which appeared to be becoming angrier. Striking out ruthlessly with their rifle butts, the gunners cleared the way, leaving the bodies of the beaten strewn on the streets. Whilst striking out freely against all who hindered our progress, amidst the screams of the injured, could be heard the lashing tongues of the Tommies: 'Out of the way, you black bastards or I'll maro you jeldi[2],' or 'Tum boselica wallah[3]'. Gradually, by sheer dint of force and determined effort we broke free, regaining our seats as the mêlée subsided and the column moved forward. The locals had now ceased to follow or impede and the situation had eased. As we crossed the city and reached the western side, the maelstrom of traffic subsided, giving way to the wide roads leading to the fort and allowing the Battery to regain some semblance of order. We thought it significant that the Indian Other Ranks had not been molested during the incident, nor had they in turn assisted the British troops in fending off the crowd. We could draw only one conclusion.

The streets were still crowded, the cement pavements broken and in disrepair and littered with bodies which bore the yellow faces and skins consistent with the signs of malaria. These were the homeless who lived on the streets, and the sick and the dying awaiting the charnel houses. Covered with festering sores, or open wounds spurting with blood were victims of leprosy, often in the advanced stages of deformity. The stumps of their arms and legs a mass of oozing pus, they lay in silence. Beggars were

1 Slum area   2 Kill you quickly   3 A very bad expression!

everywhere, asking alms from those who were themselves on the edge of starvation. The children constantly pestered the column, pleading for baksheesh, never accepting no for an answer. It was a scene of bedlam, and a real shock to those of us unaccustomed to the sight of such abject misery and poverty, me included. And there were piles of faeces, lying wherever the natives' spirits' bowels were moved. Revel's only comment on the dreadful scene was to say, with a thick Irish brogue, 'Now I know why they call it the turd world!'

We were relieved to arrive at the maidan next to the exhibition grounds and the magnificent fort, there to spend the night and recoup for the following day's activities and parades.

THE DELHI FORT was an imposing citadel, a magnificent bastion standing alone in its glory. It had a perimeter of more than a mile, and though the high walls surrounding it were long gone, with only a few broken stones remaining, it gave an overwhelming impression of strength and permanence. Built by the Shah Jahan Mohammed in the seventeenth century, the golden walls were tinged with deep reds and yellows that had blended together through the years of exposure to the sun. It was truly an architectural masterpiece, dominating the landscape with its glowing colour and high-turreted walls. It was well named as the Red Fort.

To the south, about four hundred paces away, was the Chandi Chauk Sudder bazaar, a sprawling metropolis in itself. It was lined with gold and silver merchants offering the rarest and most beautiful precious stones: rubies from the Mogaung mines of Central Burma, diamonds and jade fashioned into the most stunning ornaments fit for a queen. Outside the myriad shops sat vendors selling everything imaginable, from sweetmeats to kitchen implements, brass and fruit, gold and silver. You could buy anything there: a shave, a haircut or a massage, and the nautch girls would entertain you whilst you waited. It was no wonder the Chauk was known as the richest street in the world.

Between the great gates of the Fort and this enormous bazaar lay the Jammu Musjid, the Mosque of Assembly, an impressive building of monumental proportions and design, prominently set within sparkling approaches. Pure white and garnished with gold, it dazzled in the bright sunshine. Architecturally, it was the perfect companion to the Red Fort, complementary not only by design but also by purpose. It was the most outstanding shrine in the country, the Mecca of the Sikh religion.

In the grounds of the fort, there were now more pale faces to be seen than there were dark, for the white sahibs had arrived in force. Contingents from every branch of the military from across the country had gathered there for the celebration of the Durbar. The British foot soldiers, the cavalry and the gunners, all bedecked in their finery, were present in impressive numbers. Standing with them were the representatives of the Indian Army, also displaying their splendour and magnificence. Legendary cavalry regiments – Hodgsons Horse, Probyns Horse, the Bengal Lancers, the Poona Horse and others – were to the forefront. Originally militia units or bands commissioned by the princes and rajahs for their own protection, they had now sworn allegiance to the Crown. India did indeed shine like the jewel in the crown of Empire that day. It was to be another unforgettable memory for me.

A great multitude of natives had gathered, jostling and pushing for a clear view of the spectacle about to commence. A noisy mob with its high-pitched babble, they were anxious to catch a glimpse of those supreme beings who controlled so much of their lives. Try as they might, they were pushed back by the police using their six-feet-long steel-pointed lathis with great effect, but still they pressed forward, striking those who resisted and trampling those who had fallen.

Set against the massive structure of the fort was the dais where the celebrated persons of honour would watch the march past. The Viceroy of India, as the representative of the King Emperor of India, and the most prestigious person in the land, was prominently on view, his wife at his side, the first lady of the Indian Empire. Present also were the most senior members of the Indian Civil Service, the so-called twice-born, because of the enormous power they wielded and the importance in which they held themselves. Members of the English ruling class, they had the highest social standing in the hierarchy of the country, with precedence over all other British classes. Snooty and patronizing, as were the King's commissioned officers, yet they deigned to mix or speak with the so called 'box wallahs', the derogatory term for those English civilians in India employed in commerce and non-government occupations. Many were in very senior positions; some as owners or general managers of large and wealthy organizations, with hundreds of workers under their control, and with great financial responsibility. These outcasts in the strange society dictated by the twice-born autocrats, lived and consorted only with their own kind. India was not alone in its practice of class distinction, though theirs related to caste. The British, however, were the recognized leaders in the art of dividing people.

The regiments began to assemble as commanded by the bugles sounding across the gathering. With the drums rolling and to the fanfare of trumpets, they marched onto the ceremonial grounds in front of the fort to spontaneous applause, even from the natives. Following the cavalry came the foot soldiers, led by the Scottish Regiment, the Ladies from Hell, who had journeyed down from the North-West Frontier to play their part in the pageantry now in progress. Led by the pipers, playing nostalgic melodies of the Highlands, it was not difficult to imagine the lochs and dales of that fine land; I closed my eyes and imagined those friendly mountains rising above the blue and pristine waters, the hills in the early morning mist, with the sheep in the valleys, and the shepherds and sheep dogs. Kilts swinging and in perfect unity, they would tear many a heart that day. For a Scotsman, there could be no finer sight, and as the band started to play 'I belong to Glasgow', even the Sassenachs' eyes were blurred, and the ladies in the audience were unashamedly wiping away their tears.

No group of soldiers marched with greater pride than did those Highlanders, their bright tartan colours and swinging sporrans catching the eye. Speaking later with some of them, I learnt that the Frontier was the permanent home of the regiment, a place of open warfare with the Pathans, and a posting not eagerly sought. The native servants there, with their long exposure to the Scots, spoke not with the usual English singsong accent, but with a Scottish burr; it was highly amusing to hear them repeating, 'Hock away wid ye, ye dirrty black barstarrds!'

Following close behind were the Khyber Rifles, an Indian regiment, also stationed on the frontier and a legend in the armies of the Raj. They marched at double-quick time, exceeding even the rapid pace of the Kings' Own Yorkshire Light Infantry, who were themselves noted for their speed in movement. Capable of marching thirty miles a day in FSMO – field service marching order – with few stops other than to eat, they would be ready with loaded rifles to fight any enemy who awaited them. The drill and precision of the battalion marching there were a delight to watch.

Then came those magnificent fighting men from the north, the irrepressible Gurkhas, with their slant eyes and wide smiles. Short in stature but huge in courage, they feared nothing and were justly acclaimed as the finest soldiers in the British Army. Friendly to the extreme with those British soldiers who had fought alongside them in so many campaigns, they were the devils of death to an enemy. Treated with respect and goodwill, they were the only coloured soldiers to be accepted as true comrades by the British soldier. To them the word defeat had no meaning; they would continue to fight where they stood to the bitter end. Their kukris were vicious instruments in their expert hands, and they were often prone to use those weapons in place of rifles. But they were also a light-hearted people. They too had served long under the British Raj; the Gurkha was the untarnished model of all the attributes required by a fighting man, one who would overcome all obstacles in the pursuit of victory. So entranced were they with the noble profession of soldiering that in the evenings or moments of leisure, and in spite of the shimmering heat, they could be seen on the barrack square wearing off duty attire, drilling in groups, marching with their rifles, thoroughly enjoying themselves, while other soldiers would be enjoying a game of soccer or rugby in the adjacent space. They were remarkable men, salt of the earth.

And so the long ceremonial procession continued as regiment after regiment marched past the Viceroy, the cavalry lances dipping, the swords of the officers extended in deference to the Viceroy, and thus to the King. There were more than a thousand men parading in the dusty arena, and the participants were becoming exhausted from the heat. But the spectacle was not yet over; in the relative silence, as the last regiment moved beyond the saluting base, the rattle and grinding of gun wheels on gravel became louder.

There was a hush from the crowd, for they knew what was about to happen. Suddenly entering the arena at a gallop was the Battery of the Royal Horse Artillery. The red and yellow of their uniforms caught the eye as they thundered past the main stands, the drivers furiously lashing the horses. Riding like very devils from hell, they created a storm of dust as they swerved into action. Falling from their mounts as the bugle call brought them to a frontal crash action, the guns were rapidly unlimbered and formed in line in preparation to receive fire orders. The ammunition limbers were positioned by the sides of the guns, the gunners taking up their allotted places and the horses, lathered in sweat, ridden away at breakneck speed. Now rang out the orders for the guns to engage an imaginary enemy with open sights, with the distance and bearing of the target being given. Quickly following was the command for independent gunfire. The number two man of the team set the elevation to the required range of the gun by the hand wheel, in this case virtually zero, whilst number four opened the breech ready to receive the ammunition. Quickly the round was rammed in the breech and closed with a slam and locked, almost trapping the server's fingers. Many a man had suffered such injury by not removing his hand quickly enough. The gun ready to fire, the crew took up kneeling positions. Raising their right arm to signal readiness to engage the target, the number ones, the sergeants, waited for the order. Because it was an engagement over open sights with the enemy presumed to be immediately to the front, that order was given without all six guns being ready at the same time. Explosions crashed out and, although not using live ammunition, the debris of the charge flew from the muzzles with great force, scattering the surrounding area with the acrid tang of the propellant and affecting the eyes of those close by. From the time the Battery had made its appearance to the moment of the first round being fired was less than two minutes. To the shouts of approval of the thrilled spectators, the horses reappeared, the guns and the ammunition limbered up, and they galloped away. It was a demonstration of perfection and precision by the well-drilled gunners, in keeping with the high standards expected of the Horse Artillery.

As a final demonstration, the gunners performed a musical drive, executing the most complex manoeuvres. At a dashing pace, it required great accuracy of timing and judgment of movement in order to avoid collision. Criss-crossing the arena as the guns wound through each other in a figure of eight, it was imperative that they get it right; the interval between the guns and limbers crossing was measured in fractions of seconds. Failure would be disastrous to man and beast. My role here was to signal the various actions by sounding my bugle, indicating what the next manoeuvre was to be. Though I was terrified of making a mistake, I concentrated hard: my father and mother would have been so proud of me at that moment.

On the area in front of the fort, huge marquees had been erected, one being designated for the Viceroy and his close friends, the most senior of the civil service, the generals and a host of Indian princes and their ladies who were still being wooed by the Sirkar, and revelling in the honour and recognition being accorded them. Those socialites of a lower order who were ostracized from that illustrious group gathered further downstream in the evening, gossiping and sipping a pink gin, burrah peg or wine. The ladies exchanging their critical views of dress and behaviour of the very senior mem-sahibs at the saluting base.

My friends and I listened to the continuing music of the regimental bands, whilst drinking warm and tasteless Indian beer in front of our bivouacs or tea from the ubiquitous char wallahs, watching the stream of people going by. Not for us the Viceroy's lavish dinner party for more than a hundred of the most exalted guests, hosted at his expensive and elegant mansion; no, we would feast on bangers and mash, followed by caramel custard pudding, if we were lucky enough to find an English-style restaurant open. Those soldiers who did stay for supper were dismayed to find stew being served up, ladled into the GS issue mess tins, lukewarm and tasteless. However, our servants, as usual, did their best for their soldier-sahibs, performing their miracles in the most difficult surroundings, making the lads as comfortable as possible while they prepared to visit the famous Chandi Chauk.

Strolling past my tent, clinging to the arms of their officer husbands, the ladies looked ravishing to our hungry eyes. One in particular, a sultry blonde with a gorgeous figure, a most seductive sight, caught the eye of Dodger Green, who was vocal in his approval: 'Cor, look at them tits. What wouldn't I give fer just a short time with that smashin' bit of stuff, and me on the job 'aving a go at her jeldi, stuffin' it in!'

Lackery laughed as he told his chum, 'No chance, me old cock sparrow, in a pig's eye will she see you as the man of her dreams, and the salvation of her starving sex life. Your cock wouldn't be big enough for a shrunken mouse!'

Undismayed, Dodger retorted, 'I knows she would, if I could just get my hands on her for just a few minutes. She'd have the ride of a lifetime!'

Lackery, anxious to move, simply said, 'Come on you dirty old bugger, you're nothing better than a bleedin' deprived sexual maniac. Pull yer finger out and let's get moving to where the real goods are.' The red light district in the Chauk was calling him away – so that delightful confection never did have the pleasure of shacking up with Dodger, which was probably just as well for him: she would have worn him out in no time.

We finally made our way to the Chandi Chauk and as I wandered with my friends past a jeweller's shop, we were accosted: 'Hello Sahib. My shop you are coming to? You are my first customer of the day and will bring me very good luck. For you, I will give a very good deal. You are wanting watch? This very good one and I am giving you wholesale. I am asking twenty rupees only, Sahib. I am losing money, but for you it is my present.'

I decided to try my hand at bargaining, offering five rupees. The response was quick: 'Oh! Sahib of the most high, I have wife and many children. They must eat. But because you very good and honest man I want you to be happy. I am taking only ten rupees.'

'Get knotted. You're nothing but a fucking black rogue and the son of a Calcutta whore,' I said, demonstrating my advancing knowledge of soldiers' language.

'Seven rupees, and that's it.' Falling over himself, the vendor pushed the watch on me, blessing me for having taken pity on his family, with the wish that Allah would smile upon me always. I, smiling to myself, was quite satisfied, not knowing that in later days, when I understood the art of bazaar bargaining a bit better, I could have got the watch for five rupees after all.

We were now in the depths of the Chauk, where the swarming crowds vied for a position of advantage. This cosmopolitan metropolis of natives was a heterogeneous mixture of nationalities, from far and wide beyond the borders of India: Burma, Siam, Vietnam and from the Middle East, each person searching for this fabulous 'richest street in the world – Chandi Chauk'. From within the country were the vocal Bengalis of the east, the darker-skinned Tamils of the south, fierce Pathans from the Frontier, the militant Balutchis from the west, the Sikhs from the Punjab, and the men from the Khyber wearing baggy pantaloons and carrying shotguns. They were all babbling and shouting in a hundred different tongues and dialects, dressed in a wide variety of costumes representing their particular part of the country. On the crowded sidewalks the people haggled for the goods, gesticulating excessively as they drove bargains. Men, sitting on the cement playing Mah-Jong or Find the Lady, were repeatedly struck by the sandals of careless passers-by. Others, walking blissfully hand in hand, had the air of lovers. Sikhs – 'There is a boy across the river, with a bottom like a peach, but alas I have no boat'[1] – with aquiline noses and long flowing beards, swords at the waist and long curved knives in the belts, moved in clusters through the filth of the gutters; most carried black umbrellas, an incongruous sight as the rain would not be seen for several weeks. Perhaps they used them as a sun shield, I wondered, though I had never actually seen one open. Was it part of the Sikh dress code?

The saris of the women, reflecting all the colours of the rainbow, were in marked contrast to the drab costumes of the men, who wore the white thin cotton dhoti or the longhy, cool and comfortable to wear. Some of the women were heavily veiled, only their dark and sultry eyes visible, reflecting their religious code; others carried a child on the hips, with another soon to see the light of day and place further demands on an already over-burdened society that was sick and dying from lack of nourishment. Others balanced chatties of water on their heads, looking serene as they glided gracefully through the multitude. And around all, the crows above in the cloudless sky and hopping along the streets kept up a perpetual squawk.

The throng became thicker as we went deeper into the warren in search of the dancing girls, constantly assaulted by the vile smells of unwashed humanity and animals. The sacred cows were oblivious and unconcerned as they fed off the roadside stalls, ignoring the admonitions of the stall keepers, moving on only as they wished, and fouling the streets wherever they went. The crowds were entertained both by the penetrating music on the radios and the exhortations of the vendors on every stall selling their wares. The Indian music was dissonant, the cacophony pitilessly overwhelming.

You could buy almost anything from the enterprising Indians, goods or services. Ears were being cleaned out, the cotton wool forgotten left one wondering if the instrument being used by the self-styled doctor – he was probably a sweeper moonlighting – would penetrate the brain while he was poking about in the ear; or get yourself an enema right there and then on the sidewalk (the filth of the streets was not measurably worsened by earlier administrations of the treatment), or have a bothersome

1 From a Sikh poem

tooth pulled. An X-ray machine (as old as Methuselah) was set up on the sidewalk, for any purpose you wished, diagnostic or just the thrill of seeing your own innards. Step this way for open-air exhibitions, free for all to see and enjoy.

The most popular of the sideshows was the practice of dentistry in the open street; the crowd loved every minute of it, being both attentive and critical of each move by the patient or 'physician'. Seeing that a 'show' was about to begin, we lads decided to stop by to see what was going on and pushed our way to the front. The prospective client was seated in a chair out on the sidewalk, unhappily awaiting his call, the crowds surging around, almost swamping him. He was diminutive, aged about fifty, perhaps a little diffident, and by no means a happy man. He wore a sad expression as he sat on the chair, in some discomfort. The alleged 'dentist' was the antithesis: he looked like a born pugilist; he could easily have been taken for a professional wrestler. Aggressive and tall, he carried his thirty-odd years well on his muscled frame. Clearly relishing the task that lay ahead, he approached the nervous patient, talking soothingly to put him at ease, but receiving only very subdued responses. After a few words of encouragement, the practitioner displayed the instruments he intended to use: a screwdriver, a hammer, a pair of pliers and a bucket. All looked very substantial and capable of doing almost any job – certainly the job the dentist had in mind.

Seeing alarm on his client's face, he made the encouraging remark, 'Not to worry. I am having much luck with these. I am doing good job. You see!' At the outset he informed the people there were to be no interruptions: 'You are keeping quiet so I am concentrating on matter at hand.' (He really meant the tooth in the mouth!) It was a tricky job and he wanted to do it justice. The crowd smirked. With a few more words of comfort to the patient, who was becoming increasingly nervous, the dentist said: 'Let's get started.'

Theatrically, he at once set upon the unfortunate victim, who was by now almost paralysed at the thought of what might happen to him, but he quickly found the offending tooth. So began the struggle, which lasted for quite thirty minutes or longer. And the worst was yet to come.

'I've seen worse wrestling matches than this, but not as much blood,' said Chalky. 'He'd do a lot better if he put 'is 'and up the poor bugger's arse and pulled him inside out. His teeth would be out in the open then, and he could use 'is 'ammer much easier-like.'

The patient was by now in an awful mess, absolutely hysterical, frothing at the mouth, crying out that he couldn't take it any more, and please make it stop now, while he was still alive.

Surprisingly, it didn't take all that much longer, in spite of the dentist's continued bungling, with time off to think about his next move. He was very indecisive, often repeating himself. The tension continued to mount, and was finally broken by his shout, 'I am getting it! I am getting it!'

The swollen crowd was enjoying the drama immensely and, at the patient's screams, gave forth a great roar of approval. In the excitement their cheers were long and loud, and punctuated with ribald remarks. Encouraged by what he thought was a vote of confidence, the dentist made a supreme effort, and the molar was finally extracted. The patient was beyond caring, though, having fainted a few minutes before as the blood flowed copiously from his mouth.

At the moment of victory, the dentist flourished the tooth high in the air for all to see, his symbol of triumph. The audience was ecstatic that the play had finished happily, renewing their faith and confidence in the dentist's ability. He acknowledged their due approbation with a gracious bow. The victim, once again conscious, but brutally mauled, paid his two rupees and miserably slunk away to the gibes of the crowd. With the scene ended, the multitude strolled off down the street, still enthusing about the show.

As for their delirious enjoyment at the show, I couldn't help thinking they were born too late: they reminded me of the crowds witnessing the guillotine executions of the aristocrats during the French Revolution. They could not have reached a higher state of frenzied excitement; no thought had been given to an anaesthetic to ease the pain of the poor wretch of a patient, not even a shot of puggled pawnee[1]. And surely the self-professed dentist could have found something more in keeping with his profession than a pair of pliers; the loose wallahs' bazaar could provide almost anything, after all. The dentist, meanwhile, was already butchering his next victim.

'Cruel bastards, aren't they,' commented Dodger. 'Why fart around with a toothpick? Should have used a sledgehammer, it would've been

1 Alcohol

quicker, and a lot easier on the poor bugger! Well, I suppose that's what life's like for 'alf the people in the world. Nobody gives a monkey's fuck. It weren't like this in my 'ome town, I can tell thee, the pits was bad enough, but it made up for it if tha'd had a piece of grumble and grunt[1] waiting for you. Makes yer think, dunnit, mate. Bet 'im with the lost tooth bangs the hell out of 'is missus tonight.'

Dodger's words of wisdom; having watched the crude and callous treatment of the poor wretch who lost his tooth, I was inclined to agree with his belief that the Indians were nothing more than heathens, or, as Revel preferred to say, 'Ignorant lot of bastards, but what can you expect from them living in a country like this? Mind you, the women were always a good screw, you just had to be careful they were not poxed up, and that the bloody great Pathan husband wasn't around when you were on the job. He'd cut your goolies off jeldi, no two ways about it.'

THE SETTING SUN in the cloudless sky created a spectrum of colours in the evening dust so wonderful that mere man would be quite incapable of reproducing it. Above, it was a paradisiacal ending to the day, but as you turned your eyes to the tawdry landscape the bubble burst, shattering any illusions you might have. This was no Garden of Eden we were soldiering in. Feeling pretty disgusted with what we had just seen, we walked up the street in search of other attractions. Over the vast area of several acres, clothing was prominent; it looked to us like every resident of Delhi was present. Everything imaginable was there to be bought; apparel in profusion of every imaginable type, from top hats to brassieres, evening dress outfits, wedding dresses, hunting jackets, military overcoats, even a Busby. There were military uniforms enough to dress a regiment, parkas, swimming suits and masses of other things; the selection was endless – and, surprisingly, mostly of British origin. Much of the stuff appeared to have suffered many previous owners; we conjectured that a lot of it was probably stolen. Norman wondered which Quartermaster's Stores had been raided. There were slippers, shoes and chaplis[2] galore, virtually all junk like the clothing, and mixed with all this rubbish was more rubbish: pogo sticks, bald tyres, wrecked bicycles, vehicles, motor scooters, cooking utensils and other worthless items, all well used and worn, and all

1 A loose woman   2 Sandals

of questionable value. But the natives still haggled enthusiastically, no matter how tattered the article.

Everything in India is recycled over and over again, passing through the hands of many people before being finally rejected, and even then . . . Of great interest to us were several French letters, each 'guaranteed' to be in superb condition, having been used only a few times, and with great care. The vendor claimed they were irrefutably the best available at any price; two or three men were already haggling for them. Lackery thought that was terrible; even he never used the same one more than twice! It was about the biggest junkyard in the world, or certainly in the eastern hemisphere.

The medicine man was present on the other side of the compound, with his snake oil and aphrodisiacs, enough to 'satisfy the wildest desires of any sexually-deprived woman – or male – to hound you constantly, never letting you go.' He was a likely source of fun, thought Chalky, walking up to him asking what it could do for a man, getting a hard-on. The medicine man replied, 'Is guaranteed putting lead in your pencil and getting it up.' Not satisfied with his answer, Chalky wanted to know how he could make that guarantee. 'I am eighty-two years old, and good example. Wife tired of me wanting it, so go to neighbour every day for jig-jig, but sometime she get tired too. So I am taking goat. Is liking very much!'

That brought the laughs, and even more with Revel's question: 'Do you drink it or put on your dick, and how many times a day? Before or after supper – the medicine, not the woman?'

The medicine man answered, 'Both, and whenever you can!'

Jim answered, 'We can do all that now, we can't even get the women. What else can it do for a man?' With a twinkle in his eye the medicine man responded, 'Oh, Burrah Sahib, is getting rid of pox and Delhi-belly very quickly, I am telling you, man. You go see my sister in place called House of Pleasure. She many girls. She is giving you good time.'

After more bantering, Norman thought we should move on. 'He doesn't look as if he could shag any old biddy himself, even if she sat on it. Bet he's not had a stand-on in years, but you never know. Let's get to hell out of here before he screws us!'

Further on a pack of iniquitous moneylenders were willing to consider a loan at a mere twenty per cent a month, compounded. Once you borrowed from them you were captive for life, for it was impossible to pay off the principal. Rather, it increased, and the original sum progressively doubled in short order. The fat stomachs and the sly expressions were eloquent testimony of their success.

And there were others who tried to take your money with the most plausible stories: professing to be graduates of Poona University, which they had probably never seen, with degrees in Public Service; smooth and evasive, they could easily mesmerize you. There were grass skirts too, modelled courtesy of the girls at Madam Jeejeeboy House of Pleasure (a popular spot!) just up the road – admission one rupee. 'Girls extra, but no charge for getting boils on John Thomas.' Fortune tellers promised: 'My price one rupee for telling all lies. Two rupees telling half true with few lies. Three rupees telling all truth, and ten per cent discount at Madam Jeejeeboy's place. (You are having good time there! Also my sister's place!)'

Further on were Eskimo tents, guaranteed suitable for the hot weather, but not in rain, snow or ice. Electronics and watches made in Japan, Britain, Greenland or the USA, and all guaranteed to fail within thirty minutes of the purchase – and no refund. Food of all kinds, from the far reaches of the world: tinned delicacies from Harrods, no less, prepared in 1914, or kippers from Norway (they died swimming here); chocolates from Switzerland, open and melting with the heat, tinned salmon from the west coast of Canada, packed in 1921, and jars of pickled eels from Bangkok, looking forlorn and inedible. The display of meats, standing uncovered in the sun, had a decidedly unhealthy colour. Tinged with green bordering on grey, the ever-changing blanket of gluttonous flies was a mute testimony to its unwholesomeness. Not even ever-hungry boy-soldiers would be tempted.

The local liquor was altogether something else. It made varnish remover taste like a most palatable dish of ice cream, and it packed a punch calculated to deprive you of all desire to live. Distilled from the toddy tree and fermented overnight, it cost just four annas a gallon. Potent and vile, similar to drinking hydrochloric acid, a few spoonfuls would do you in. It was so devastating you would drink it only once, and that was enough if you had any respect for your brain; the memory would linger always, as would the regret at having swallowed that vitriolic puggled pawnee – mad water, as it was known. A highly visible example of its effects was close to the stall that sold it: lying around, in various conditions, were the emaciated bodies of those natives who persisted in drinking the poison. It was unlikely they would walk again. They might even be dead by morning.

Accosted by every vendor in the bazaar, we comrades bought nothing, not even the souvenir key chain emblazoned with the name *Delhi*, proclaiming its source of origin, and inside stamped, *Made in Manchester*. Anything you were looking for, be it wine, women or song, or a dose, it was all there in good measure at the Chandi Chauk, and I wouldn't have missed it for all the tea in Darjeeling. And if you tired of the normal bazaar attractions, there was the loose wallahs' bazaar to explore, half a mile further on, a promising place to buy back anything you or your mates had lost or had stolen; if not your own stuff, you'd certainly find *something* once owned by a British soldier. I was astonished at the wide range of more unusual goods on view: there was a profusion of prostheses: arms, legs, teeth and other false body parts, a pickled brain, a selection of scalping knives and surgical instruments, a homemade gibbet, bayonets, binoculars, military boots, stethoscopes, a periscope (heaven knows where they stole that!), a wide variety of military equipment and, funnily enough, a set of thieves' tools (talk about chickens coming home to roost!). There was a gruesome-looking object, suspiciously resembling a scalp, but none of us were prepared to hazard a guess at its past.

Scattered in the confusion on the table, with the hawkers of other stalls trying to attract the attention of the rich white sahibs, and almost obscured by the miscellaneous junk, were numerous military medals. Gathering these together, my eye was caught by one in particular. Closer inspection revealed it to be a genuine Chillan wallah[1] campaign medal, which caught my attention immediately. Though my knowledge of military history was skimpy, I did know a little of this campaign, and was well aware of the significance of the medal, which commemorated the famous battle, in February 1849, between the British and the Sikhs who had revolted in the Punjab. The Sikhs had fought valiantly, but were defeated after inflicting great casualties on the British. The British soldiers paid a high price for the annexation of that territory to the Raj. I called Norman over, who confirmed what I'd thought; he also told me it would be worth at least six months' pay. The haggling between the loose wallah and me began, the former obviously unaware of the value of the medal, the latter

1 An old soldier of the Chillan campaign

not too aggressive on the price. I knew I must have that medal at all costs. It was almost a deal between gentlemen, and I got it at a good price; with congratulations all round, we decided we'd had enough. Except for the medal, no one had bought anything, and we decided to call it a day for the sightseeing.

REGULATIONS PLACED THE red light district of the Chauk out of bounds, but tacitly the Military Police didn't enforce the rules. It was a common rumour that the Provost Marshal himself was a frequent visitor to the place, and it was suggested that he was also having his palm crossed with silver for closing his eyes. We assumed he was gorging himself on all the tasty tidbits he fancied. It was also noticed that many of the Provost Marshal's friends were allowed to join at the feasting table; all getting their thrills buckfree. Anxious to keep on the right side of the law, Madame let him do as he wished, to keep him happy.

There had been considerable doubt that I would see the red light district this evening, in spite of the bantering that had taken place earlier, and the promises that I would 'get fixed up tonight'. We'd got as far as the outskirts when the news was broken to me that, on second thought, it wasn't such a good idea that I should go to these places of ill repute. I was dismayed, but despite my imploring, the answer was a firm refusal from Norman Collins. I was far too young for such capers; I must wait awhile. Bitterly disappointed, I begged to at least be allowed to go into one of the brothels, promising that was all I wanted to do, and I wouldn't even *look* at the girls. Norman, with a wry look, finally agreed, and, whooping in ecstasy, I quickly forged ahead lest he should change his mind. Arriving in the brothel area, the pimps were coming from all directions offering their ladies: 'I have very good white girl. She is waiting to see you. Very cheap for master. You are coming, running, jumping quickly, jeldi! Is very good jig. She is nurse. You like fat girl, thin girl? I have Anglo-Indian girl if you like better. Or good Brahmin girl – high caste. Come from good family. You stay long time and having good jig-jig. I am taking you there in tonga. You are coming Sahib?'

The street we walked along ran through a slum lined with rows of hovels, where the ladies of the night beckoned from the doorways and the windows, openly displaying their charms and attractions. Leisurely moving along now, the band assessing the merits of one place over another, my companions elected to enter a relatively salubrious-looking dwelling (compared with the surrounding shacks). It was aptly named the House of Pleasure – memories of the medicine man made us grin. Greeted at the door by the Madame of the establishment, we were shown to a sumptuously furnished room, lavish and well appointed, and in great contrast to the decrepit appearance of the exterior. Seated with great courtesy by this lady, in the sickly and overpowering scent of the room, we were offered tea.

Gracefully declining this, Revel, in his inimitable and charming manner said, 'Bring on the fucking bibis.'

Not discouraged by this haughty demand, the Madame clapped her hands, which brought a bevy of girls into the room, all wearing next to nothing, and requiring little imagination to assess their desirability. As she introduced each girl by name, the girl stripped off the last few stitches she wore, which brought expressions of approval from all but me. I was too mesmerized by the sight to make any comments, not believing it was happening to me, but my older friends were carefully appraising the merits of the girls.

'You are liking one? That one very good fuck. You have very good jig-jig,' the Madame promised of each girl.

In due course, Revel decided, 'I'll take that one. Come on luv, let's be having you, see if I can educate you in the noble art.'

Madame, having agreed on the price of two chips, or rupees, for a short time, gave a smile of approval, taking the hands of the couple and leading them to the privacy of a small room which contained just a charpoy and table, the only necessities for making love. They were then left to their own devices.

This scenario was quickly repeated twice, leaving me, Norman and two others to drink tea and speculate on the ecstasy being enjoyed in those rooms. There was an embarrassing silence as we sat there, none caring to break the spell or truncate vicarious pleasures. Satisfied, and with beaming smiles, the lovers returned to the parlour to meet the questioning looks of their friends, but little was said and they kept their experiences to themselves as we walked back into the alleys. I was astonished that it was all so easy and civilized. Quickly consummated, in a pleasant manner, the girls were obviously enjoying the proceedings, even if they were not chosen. Their enquiring expressions asked, 'What about you?'

Taffy commented, 'Not so different from buying a pound of beef, eh lad, is it?'

I thought, next time, that's for me!

THE BROTHEL ESCAPADE over, we wandered deeper into the Chauk, fully alert to the strange-looking characters lounging about. How different the place looked at night. Gone were the women with their pretty saris, the laughs of the playing children, the dogs and the birds, and the carefree gaiety of the daytime when one could walk in safety without fear of molestation. The sweet fragrance of the jasmine had been replaced by the pungent odour of cooking oil, a poor substitute. The kerosine lamps and the guttering candles burning in the earth-built muttee huts added their flavour to that of the cooking ghee, producing a rather sickly smell.

Peeping through a window, we caught a glimpse of the life of an Indian family. Crowded, a group of six or seven were occupying an area large enough for only two or three. Roughly furnished, there was tatty matting on the floor where the babies lay covered with threadbare blankets. Though there was hardly enough room to breathe, they looked comfortable and light-hearted, talking animatedly and smiling as they recounted the day's events. Mother was handing the sweetmeats around whilst playing with the children, fussing with Grandad, or trying on the new sari brought home by her loving husband. They were happy and contented, and the men looked pleased the labours of the day were ended. However small the place, there was room to sit and talk, a charcoal stove on which to prepare the meals and charpoys to sleep upon, and that was enough.

Mother was cooking the late supper, the spicy odours drifting through the open door tantalizing my nostrils. I had never tasted Indian food, cooked the Indian way; it smelled good. I had expected something different to what I saw; apart from the setting, they are not so different from us, I mused. With a start I realized that I was not simply looking through the window, but intruding on a family gathering. Feeling somewhat guilty about invading their privacy I quickly withdrew. They probably didn't even know I was there, and had they done so, might perhaps have taken exception to my inquisitiveness. And I was rather sorry about that.

Moving deeper into the murky depths, there was a great silence, the quickening gloom broken only by the dimmest of lights, showing a party of old men sitting on their haunches; talking quietly, with the acrid smoke of their foul-smelling beadies' permeating the atmosphere. The shadows held only the silent watchers, shrinking further into the blackness at the approach of footsteps. The shrill scream of a woman echoed through the night, being raped or butchered; it mingled with the howls of mongrel dogs, too distant to investigate. And the thieves were there, waiting for the unwary, ready to pounce. Norman called a halt. It was far enough and only trouble lay ahead in the depths of those burrows. Weary now, we hailed two tongas – a horse-drawn, two-wheeled cart for four – to return to the camp, threatening the drivers with all kinds of punishment if they didn't race. The result was a dead heat, lathered ponies, and a few more annas to the tonga wallahs.

Our night on the town was ended. I was teased mercilessly for having ventured into the brothel and failing to lose my virginity while others were enjoying themselves: a fruitless journey, but plenty to think about on a sleepless night!

THE EXTRAVAGANZA WAS ended and it was time to return home to Meerut, with the hot season to look forward to. It was close to the end of February, and the climate would change soon. On the plains the hot weather would arrive in earnest and, before the end of March, the temperatures would climb into the hundreds; temperatures exceeding 140 degrees Fahrenheit were not uncommon. The heat brought the promise of prickly heat and its attendant discomforts. Striking mostly under the armpits and in the crotch, the pain was as if a thousand red ants were feeding; the torture drove the poor victim to distraction: the more you scratched, the worse the aggravation, and even the slightest touch of clothing was agonizing. Liberal and constant dusting with body powder over the wide areas of inflammation provided only meagre relief. There was no quick fix. You lived with it.

With the increased humidity, a great lethargy would descend upon the whole land, even the natives themselves failing to shake off the languor that affected all God's creatures. The dust devils were everywhere, their funnels of particles and debris creating a haze as they danced across the plains reaching for the sky, covering the villages and cantonments with a

1 Cigarettes

fine powder. Eyes would smart from the stinging dust; it penetrated clothing and felt like abrasive sandpaper on the skin. I had yet to experience this heat, which would beat down relentlessly like blow after blow from a hammer when it reached its zenith in July. I had been in India only a few weeks, and had missed most of the delightful weather of the winter months of October to February, a period when life took on a more zestful meaning.

We travelled back by the same route. The long and tedious journey was not uneventful, for at the halfway staging camp I was injured. Dolly Grey was off-colour and so not able to carry me, so I had to ride Henry the polo pony, which had been taken to Delhi so that his owner could play a chukka or two with other polo enthusiasts. Early on the morning of departure from the camp, the horses had been saddled and the order given to mount. Henry the polo pony, resentful at the prospect of carrying me, refused to respond to my instructions to walk, as indicated by the pressure of the knees and the tightening of the reins. I pulled sharply on the reins in reprimand; the stubborn animal got a jerk to the mouth and reared violently. Falling backwards, turning a complete somersault, the horse fell to the ground, trapping me under its back, and then rolled on to me. It was a frightening thing to happen; my reaction was to shout long and hard, but the words wouldn't come. The horse then rolled over me again, doing so twice more before regaining its feet. I lay flat on my back wondering what had happened and if Judgment Day was approaching, unaware that men were running from all directions to my aid. It was not the rocks underneath that felt so hard and unforgiving: my trumpet, slung over my back, and the real casualty, was flattened as if by a steamroller. Beyond help, the trumpet would never again play another call; it was relegated to becoming another souvenir for me. Helped to my feet, I was carried to one side to assess the damage and to gather my composure. I was able to sit up, but I was in some pain and it was clear that I was in no condition to ride that day.

Were the ammunition limbers to become my means of transport, rough and exposed, travelling through the heat and the dust? There were no doctors, nurses or hospitals in this lonely landscape, only the poor villages, the walls of the muttee huts plastered with cow dung drying in the sun to be burned as fuel, and the festering gutters a source of disease.

There would be no cures there. Delhi or the cantonment, the nearest places where medical attention could be obtained, were both an impossible distance away. Any medical help here would be by the kindly, though inexperienced hands of my comrades. Major Percival and other officers were quickly on the scene, concerned that I was hurt. The horse was led away and the Major's car brought forward. I would continue the journey by wheels, and not by hooves. Nothing more than badly shaken, I sat in the luxury of the back seat, the Major sitting next to the driver. It was with a smug expression that I looked out of the window passing the column, the troops giving me a rousing cheer, which I acknowledged with a graceful gesture befitting royalty.

Travelling in style and comfort, I would be back in Meerut long before my colleagues. I looked forward to the home comforts of the cantonment: hot showers, a comfortable bed and escape from the noises of Delhi, maybe even a chance to write home.

Whilst in Delhi, several friends had asked if I would speak to Major Percival about opening the swimming pool this year. They knew I was close to him; they weren't at ease talking with him like I was, and were reluctant to raise the issue themselves. So I dutifully asked if the pool could be opened earlier than usual, and he promised that as soon as we returned to the station it would be cleaned and opened. It didn't normally open until March because of the threat of snakes, which abounded at this time of the year. Sure enough, when I went to look at the pool the following day, there they were. The pool was located close to the outdoor ablutions, which had the same problem from time to time. Surrounding the grass of the pool were shrubs and undergrowth, which made perfect hiding places for the snakes. The pool was left uncovered during the winter months; although drained at the time of closure, it now held a few inches of water, debris and snakes. The natives cleaning the pool were adept at removing them, grasping the reptiles behind their heads, and throwing them to their helpers on the side. Then, held down with a forked stick until secured, they were picked up and stuffed in a Hessian bag. Because snakes were worshipped by some religions, they weren't killed, but were later released in the fields outside the cantonments.

Drained and refilled with clean water, the pool was ready for use, but constant watch would be required: it was still the snake season. Contrary to the old soldiers' tales, the cantonment was not infested with cobras or kraits, which were dangerous and to be feared, but of a relatively harmless type whose bite would be nothing more than an unpleasantly painful experience. There were shouts of congratulations from the men arriving home that afternoon to the pool sparkling invitingly in the afternoon sun, happy to see that I had worked the miracle. I didn't bother to disabuse them of the notion that I'd been rather brave to ask my officer for anything.

The Battery's chances of enjoying its pleasures early were quickly dispelled, however. Riots had broken out in the streets of Meerut, and the troops were called out to help the civil power to subdue the protestors. With the cavalry, the gunners marched on foot into the town to find hordes of natives in battle, the Hindus fighting the Mohammedans. This was by no means an unusual affair, these religious and longstanding conflicts were a way of life in India. It took very little to trigger the violence, and chaos and brutal savagery usually erupted. When the troops arrived, a full-scale riot was in progress and the scene was one of utter turmoil, with hundreds of natives embroiled in the disturbance. Swords, knives, stakes, iron rods or any weapon which came to hand were being used in the killing and maiming; a not-unfamiliar scene to most of the troops. The congested street was covered in blood; discarded sandals and clothing littered the ground. And there were a hundred British soldiers tasked with quelling this ruthless mob of several thousands.

They followed a well-practised drill: there were strict written directions which must be followed in providing aid to the civil power. There was to be no firing of weapons except on the specific order of the locally authorized Civil Commissioner, although the Commissioners generally conceded that the use of force must be strong to be effective. First, the troops advanced to within fifty yards of the crowd as a force of intimidation, with warnings given over the loud-speakers that they were to disperse, or the police and the soldiers would take action. Being so excited, and swept beyond the point of no return, the natives ignored the order, which really served only to increase the violence. Quickly now, both the troops and the police forming a solid mass, they advanced into the crowd flaying them with their rifles and lathis[1]. Where resistance was heavy and no progress

[1] Sticks, steel tipped, used by the police and about six feet long

made, the troops resorted to the bayonet, effective only on the nearest rioters; those in the middle of the swarming mass were completely unaware of the damage being inflicted.

The angry mêlée continued, the throng wreaking further injuries on itself. It was clear to the officers and the Commission's representative that they must resort to firearms. Jumping on the platform in front of him, the civil representative declared the Riot Act twice in quick succession, in accordance with the rules set down. From his standpoint overlooking the horde, he identified two individuals whom he considered to be the ring-leaders. Calling to the officer in charge of the riot squad, and pointing to these two men, he instructed him to open fire and kill them. The officer, naming two of his troops, in turn ordered them to load their rifles and, having identified the targets, open fire. The soldiers having taken sight and fired, both of the men dropped dead. When firing on such occasions the soldier must use maximum force, always to kill, never to wound. The rifle shots had their expected results, and with their leaders dead the crowd dissolved in an instant, disappearing into the warrens of the densely populated slum area.

Soon the only remaining Indians were the two shot men, dead and harmless, unable to 'Fuck a pig in a fog', as Jim Revel so charmingly put it. 'Shove the bastards in the back of the truck. They don't know their arses from their elbows now,' Revel continued, the usual life and soul of the party.

Both shot in the heart, Chalky White said to Dodger Green, one of the marksmen, 'You never could have done that on the rifle butts. You couldn't even have hit the bloody fat arse of the sergeant-major. You must be fucking pissed! Did yer hit the one you were lookin' at, or were you aimin' at 'is fucking cock? Fucking lucky shot anyway. I wonder what their women are like, they'll need some fucking company now to keep them warm. What say we find out where they are, and give 'em something to remember us by. Like a good fucking. Feel up to it, mucker?'

The bodies were taken away, and it's doubtful if either Chalky or Dodger had their way. Back in the cantonment there was a great deal more jesting taking place, and it was a long time before Dodger lived down the name: 'Master cock shot who was all goolies[1].' Word of the killings spread

1 Urdu for balls

rapidly around the city and peace was restored for a while. But this wasn't the last time we were called out in Meerut in aid to the civil power: as the temperature increased, so did the violence of the riots.

THE WEEKS PASSED, filled with the repetitive sequence of individual, section, and Battery training. We had gun drill, exercises using maps with a one-inch scale to select targets of an imaginary nature, the range and bearing of the target computed from the coordinates of the gun position and the target, the angle of sight determined by a comparison of the contours showing the elevation of the land. Speed was of the essence in placing the guns in action, so this was practised over and over again. Many hours were spent mastering the complexities of the heliograph, a device to communicate over long distances using Morse code. Two mirrors mounted on a tripod were manipulated to align the rays of the sun in the required direction. With the keys of the instrument, a message might be transmitted in the form of Morse code through the reflection of the sun's rays. Great distances could be spanned and it was a prime means of communication in my day. Difficult to learn, it took considerable expertise to become proficient. The kit and harness inspections were endless, though not as demanding here as in England as the bearers and syces took the brunt of the work.

There was Church parade every Sunday without fail, 'Fall in in two ranks, Church of England on the right, Presbyterians, heathens, and odds and sods on the left.' The afternoons and weekends were free time, to play sports, swim, write letters home or to the girlfriend, gamble, dream or carouse. The options were endless, but few were rewarding; the likeliest choice was carousing. Always in style when the money allowed, it became a regular pastime for most. I was allowed to attend these drinking parties as a welcome onlooker, but I was not allowed to be a participant, in spite of repeated pleas. The banter and singing could be heard through the cantonment; many nights the bawdy songs of some twenty squaddies echoed throughout the cantonment. The songs would go on for hours, some melancholy, others ribald or humorous, all an escape:

I love a lassie,
A bloody great Madrasi,
She's as black as the ace of fucking spades,

She's got hairs on her belly
Like the palms that grow at Delhi,
Nelly, my big fat girl.

Six long years you loved my daughter,
Now you go to Blighty, Sahib.
May the boat that takes you over
Sink to the bottom of the pawnee, Sahib
     Or if you prefer,
Atora cheeny tora chah.
Bombay bibbi boat atcha
May the boat that takes you over
Sink to the bottom of the pawnee, Sahib.

Hukum hie Sir Walter Raleigh,
Hum hie Sir Zider Zee.
Queenie Vitoria very good man.

There were also the melodies reflecting their despondency, like 'I'm only a girl in a gilded cage, a beautiful sight to see'. This group activity nurtured the comradeship and sense of belonging, which we all needed, but soon enough we would have to separate for a while, for the coming of the hot weather would see the lucky few departing for the hills while the rest of us remained on the cantonment. Those fortunate people would miss the monsoons, which were still a few weeks away; the rest of us must wait patiently, cursing the stifling heat and the dense humidity of the air.

The first warning sign of the approach of the monsoons was a profound stillness over the land, broken only by the whispering of the gentle breeze, which slowly became stronger, gathering strength and heralding the violence and fury about to descend. The dust of the ground was scooped up, blowing freely through the cantonment. With the sudden ending of the winds, the temperature would drop sharply. To the flashing of lightning and powerful claps of the thunder, a sprinkling of raindrops would fall. Black or white, strong or weak: as if at a signal, they would meet the impending deluge with glee, forgetting all else, no matter its importance. Joyfully, without regard to dress, hurrying outdoors to greet the rain and breathe the cooling air, people would stand with faces turned upwards to the sky. Some of the troops would strip to the skin, exposing themselves entirely to gain the greatest possible relief from the impending downpour. The sky now became ominously black and threatening, the clouds scudding swiftly across its reaches.

The rain would start to fall, lightly at first then quickly, with a gathering intensity. Soon merciless in its torrential force, it would overwhelm all beneath it, so powerful as to sting the body, an exquisite mixture of pain and pleasure. Deep cracks would appear in the burning ground from which would emerge a myriad insects in their endless columns, their wings open ready for flight. The sound of the heavy rain battering all below was deafening, and a neighbour's voice would be lost in the cacophony of the downpour on the rooftops of the barracks and the metal corrugated covers of the village shanties. Only the high-pitched shrieks of the children could be heard over the monsoon.

Soon the diversion of gambolling in the cloudburst would be over, the deliriously happy people returning to their shelters to dry, and prepare for the long weeks of the rain they must now endure. The brief spell of ineffable relief which came with the first hours of the monsoon soon turned to dislike as the rain hampered all movement, preventing outdoor games and sports of any kind. The Battery's normal activities must continue: outdoor parades, patrolling of the cantonment, the guards wearing clammy, hot rubber ground sheets, duties with the horses and as riders. Even crossing the open ground to reach the dining room or walking to the bazaar was affected. The rain fell ceaselessly and there was no escape. It was not long before we were yearning for the winter weather to return, but that was three or four months away and duty must be done.

Very few men escaped the rigours of the life by desertion; any attempt was doomed to failure. Desertion was a daunting task fraught with danger, leading to conditions worse than those they now faced. In Britain it was easy to blend into the life of your own people as a civilian; to do so in India was a different matter. There were no hiding places for a strange white man. Unable to go anywhere without arousing suspicion, reports of his presence would invariably reach the ears of the police. There were the few who tried to jump ship at Bombay or Karachi, or who attempted the near-impossible journey by foot across the western deserts to the Middle East, but few made it safely. There were always reports, or rather, rumours, of white men living in the villages, having gone native. Such sightings were rarely true, for it was an alternative lifestyle that would be rejected by all except the most desperate man. In the eyes of white men, going native was to descend to the depth of contemptibility.

AT HOME GEORGE V, the King Emperor, had died; the throne was now occupied by the former Prince of Wales. Within a year of his coronation, Edward VIII's position as head of the country was placed in jeopardy by his love for Wallis Simpson, an American twice divorced. He abdicated after reigning for only ten months, later marrying the woman for whose love he gave up the throne and the empire. Meanwhile the Government was still at loggerheads with Germany as she continued her build-up of armaments, contrary to the Versailles Treaty. The clouds of war grew closer and in February of 1937, as Hitler's forces entered the Rhineland, Britain still appeared apathetic about Germany's territorial ambitions.

The people of Britain continued their merry-making, indifferent to the Sword of Damocles hanging over their heads. There was no concern for war. 'If and when the chips are down, we'll be there,' was the popular feeling. The events of the next two years would have a profound effect on my life.

There were no newspapers reporting current events. After the fourteen-day fast steamboat journey to the Indian ports was the overland journey of several days, so when the paper arrived in the hands of the reader it was always stale news. We troops rarely saw a newspaper; none were available in the canteen and there was no garrison newsletter. The library did stock them, but most of the men didn't read much and had no other cause to go there. The wireless spoke only fleetingly about international affairs, and anyway, these were of no interest to us. We knew little about what was going on in England, or the rest of the world, for that matter. The most reliable news came from the new drafts, and that was mostly about the state of the women and beer back home. We lived in a cocoon, isolated from the outside world.

chapter seven

INDIA: THE HILL STATIONS

April 1937 to December 1938

The khuds¹ were calling. April was here and the annual migration was about to begin. Vaccinations for the troops were brought up to date: typhoid, cholera, small pox, and antidotes for snake bites and rabies. I needed most of these and my arms and rear end soon felt much the worse for wear. We had to dig out our cold weather kit: greatcoat, heavier underclothing and a cloth sidecap, none of which ever saw the light of day on the plains. Forty of us were taken to the Meerut railway station by bus, where we were greeted by a seething mass of natives clogging the place, and by the transients who made it their home. Every station in India has a residential population, a village in itself, so to speak. The tenants of these settlements were accepted and allowed to stay. Where else might they go? If they did leave, the waiting list was long and others would hastily move in. The 'legitimate' passengers never complained, very few of them bought travelling tickets and didn't wish to jeopardize themselves. It was a shocking and sorrowful place to live.

The day started early, the first train at five o'clock disgorging its rowdy passengers. There was no choice but to wake up. Personal privileges first, then several buckets of water over the head, and the teeth cleaned vigorously with a twig. Breakfast if they were lucky (the fires smelled and contributed to the squalor of the place). They filled jugs and buckets of the purified water from the train, lining up at the edge of the platform to be the first to board. They lived by begging from the passengers; the children excelled

1 Hills

176

at it, like the boy with the bloated spleen imploring, 'Please Sahib, one anna you are giving. Me no father, no mother, no sister, no brother, me poor little bugger.' Or the pretty young girl in a ragged dress who shyly touched your arm, appealing silently with her big, brown eyes, just waiting, hard to ignore.

The practice of chewing betel nut, the nut of the areca palm with the lime of the betel vine, often taken with tobacco as a mild stimulant, is widespread across the country and fouls all the public areas, streets and sidewalks. The station platforms particularly are defiled by betel nut, the repugnant habit of virtually every Indian, men, women and children alike. Their teeth and mouths crimson with the stain, spitting where they will, the ground is thickly covered with the ugly stains. It was conspicuously so in the stationmaster's office, where it was easy to deduce that his spitting in the direction of the spittoon from the chair behind the desk had to be a major occupation for him. His aim was not to be commended, given the grouping of the offending stains which concentrated at the centre; very little appeared to have hit the target.

Railway stations in India are always a scene of continuous activity, and this one was no exception. Rows of food stalls made of crude push-carts, with tattered canvas or cardboard roofs, had vendors selling chapattis and dal, dood wallahs offering milk, and peddlers of all kinds vying for custom. The sign at the water fountain proclaimed, 'For Brahmins only', laden generously as it was with dysentery and the makings of cholera.

It was dawn, and on the railway tracks the natives bent as if praying, not in isolation or craving privacy, uncaring of those who saw their activity. But it was only the men – one never saw a woman in that posture. What was their secret? I wondered. Jim Revel knew the answer to that. 'They bake it and blow it out in dust.' The man was a mine of information, he always had an answer to every question: 'And it's the same if they want a piss,' he continued, 'they boil it and blow it out in steam!' Was there anything he didn't know?

The troops cleared the platform of the natives waiting for the Kalka Mail train to arrive. There would be separate coaches for the military and Indian passengers. With the arrival of the train, the turmoil reached a crescendo as the Indians shouted even louder, the din becoming more thunderous by the moment, and the jostling began. Boarding was enough to try the patience of a saint. The natives converged on the doors of every carriage, including the military coaches. With bedding rolls, chickens, pigs, dogs, birdcages with squawking occupants, a variety of fresh food and vegetables, and their yelling kids, any effort to board was demanding. They clogged the entrances, forced their way through the windows and, when there was no room left, clung to every niche on the outside of the carriages. In desperation, the roof offered the final solution – that was not as dangerous as one might think, as the train rarely exceeded twenty miles an hour; it was certainly cooler, if a little dusty. For the natives inside, it must have been untenable, packed like sardines with no hope for improvement. The Asian-style toilet, just a hole in the floor, was completely inadequate for the volume of passengers, not that the jammed toilets mattered: if they were occupied the Indians pissed anywhere, so it was no problem – except for the women. The floors were littered with their rubbish, the food remnants were devoured by rats and cockroaches crawled across the faces of those who slept. It was not a journey to cherish.

This time I knew what I was facing. Brooking no nonsense, we elbowed our way through the crowd, blaspheming in pidgin Urdu at the natives, thrusting aside the beggars without sympathy. Threatening to 'Knock the shit out of them,' or 'Kick him in the goolies,' we troops finally occupied our seats, our first priority to get the cards going. Some played Shoot or Twenty-one, the more sophisticated, Bridge, for most of the journey to Dehra Dun, some two hundred miles away. At Delhi the heavily laden train disgorged the natives who were going to the markets, then trundled on with numerous stops at the most outlandish stations with unpronounceable names, and often in the open country. I listened to the clickety-clack of the wheels, stifling in the muggy atmosphere if the windows were closed, or victim to the coal dust and smoke of the engine if opened, for the twelve-hour journey.

On the hot dry plains the lands were parched by the blistering sun. The peasants slothfully laboured in the paddy fields, the women drawing water from the wells to irrigate the crops. Village life centred around these wells, a place to gossip for the women, and for the old men to smoke in the shade of the trees. The temperature that day would reach 125 degrees Fahrenheit. At the stops we would dismount – except for the group irrevocably committed to gambling – to stretch our legs and restore the circulation in our numbed backsides. Standing at the side of the track I saw a railway worker banging the carriage wheels with a hammer, and curiously asked him, 'Kia hukum hie?' (What are you doing?) Pausing in his onerous task, the man replied, 'Nay malum Sahib, railway hukum hie.' (I don't know, sir, it's by order of the railway.) With an understanding smile, I boarded the train as the imperious whistle signalled imminent departure. Gradually as the train forged on, the countryside became more fertile, the valleys and hills dotted with cattle grazing on the sparse grass. Approaching the mountains, the rivers and streams were clearer and it was noticeably cooler – not that a sweater was needed, but it was decidedly crisper.

Dehra Dun is more than two thousand feet above sea level, and a pleasant town by Indian standards. Its military connections started in 1922 with the opening of the Royal Military College, offering training for boys wishing to join the army, which later became the Indian Military Academy, turning out many fine Indian officers, and played a major role in filling the ranks of the army for the Second World War. The lush surroundings, heavily forested, had flowers, fruit, and rhododendrons growing in great profusion. It was also the gateway to excellent hunting and fishing. We would spend the night there, sleeping in the coaches now stationary in the railway sidings. It was a splendid evening and most of the men sat around outside smoking and yarning, savouring the thoughts of the cool climate which we would now start to enjoy in the hills – and, like soldiers the world over, wondering what the beer was like. They were always called the hills, never the mountains; perhaps it sounded more friendly to describe them as such, and, if you were a Scotsman or a Welshman, they brought back the memories of your own hills now so far away. Only the snow-covered peaks in the distance were referred to as the mountains.

It is remarkable how one's attitude to life can change for the better, merely at the thought of living in a tolerable climate. We all slept well that night, in spite of the lateness of the hour and the beggars continuing to press their demands for backsheesh. After midnight a calm settled over the land. Only the howling and the presence of the jackals broke the silence; as they crept closer, bold now in their search for food, their eyes became magnified as they were reflected in the dim lights of the carriages and by the small camp fires which ran the length of the train. It was an eerie feeling to sit outside on that warm and placid Indian evening with only the penetrating eyes of the jackals for company. Efforts to entice the creatures closer by the offer of food failed; the wary animals knew just how close they could go without compromising their own safety. Having failed in their quest, they disappeared without ceremony, as quickly and as silently as they had arrived. Only then did we feel sufficiently comfortable to lay aside the weapons that had been held so closely.

Awakening in the morning, it was so refreshing to stand in the cool morning air, already casting off the lethargy of yesterday. In the background the snow-covered giants soared to infinity, the valleys falling away into the distance as they stretched out to embrace the plains. After breakfast the kit-bags and other heavy gear were thrown into the backs of the military trucks which would travel ahead, meeting up with us later. Today we would hike the first ten of the twenty miles to the hill station of Sabathu, so, after a very satisfying breakfast of crispy bacon and fried eggs, we were on our way, with a decidedly holiday spirit prevailing. Splitting into small groups with my group leading, the first leg of the journey started at eight o'clock on that delightful morning. The sun was still low in the sky and ahead were the magnificent snow-covered mountains, bathed in a red glow.

It was a dramatic picture with the hills rising precipitously from Dehra Dun, a transformation to a captivating world far from the dreariness of the lowlands. Beyond was the much coveted hill station of Sabathu, promising the reward of vitality and renewed vigour to the weary. The journey was to be treated as a hike rather than a march, and so we adopted a very loose formation when we moved off. It was believed that by walking to Sabathu the men would gradually become accustomed to the changing elevation; normally, if one completed the transition from a few hundred feet level down on the plain to six thousand feet in the hills in a matter of a few hours, it would be necessary to do light duties only for a week or so to become acclimatized to the change. Observing this rule was important and to neglect it could cause dizziness and a prolonged period of adjustment. This was common practice, whichever hill station one was going to – but only for the men, not the women and children. The troops were lightly dressed and equipped, wearing short-sleeved shirts, shorts, stockings and heavy boots, carrying only a rifle, water-bottle and haversack rations for the midday meal. A bandolier of fifty rounds of SAA 303 was carried by each man, though without the proverbial one up the spout. The truck would meet us that evening at the campsite.

This would be my first time in the khuds, as it was for several others who had also been in India for only a few months. Unlike me, however, they wouldn't do this again for quite some time. Classed as a boy, I would be sent to the hills every year for the hot summer months, usually June through August, so I and the other boys and the married families would miss the crucifying heat of the plains.

And it was about here on the outskirts of Dehra that I saw a roughly made sign that typified the difference between the hills and the plains. It consisted of two signs really, both of which were about five feet high, each containing an inscription and an arrow scratched in the broken wood. Though roughly made by the hands of a labourer, the moving eloquence of the words said it all: the sign pointing to the north read, 'Those cool mountain ranges where a man may rest peacefully and be caressed by the fragrance of the flowers that grow so profusely in that land of solitude, far from the madding crowd. A place where the Gods live and where all are welcomed.' And pointing to the south, the scribe made it clear this would not be his way, 'For yonder lies the scorching plains, where the heat compares with the devil's anvil and the dust rises like the smoke from the factory chimneys, and a languor persists across the vast wastes of the land, and the peasants labour long into the night so their children may eat.' The sign looked as though it had been there for years. How many other soldiers of the King had stood there over the years of the Raj saying, 'How bloody true that is.'

Once into the march and away from Dehra Dun, the roads held little traffic and we could walk with ease, though, as we marched further along and the roads became steeper, turning every bend was an adventure. There were unexpected and frequent landslides at the most unlikely places, and if the road was blocked, we had to climb over the huge rocks and rubble, taking great care not to slip and hurtle over the side to the depths below. An impetuous step would be disastrous; the drop to the river or valley below was often precipitous, falling hundreds of feet, and a man's chance of surviving was not encouraging.

There was little traffic, buses and bullock-carts being the chief hazards.

The bus drivers, when travelling down to the plains, would turn off the ignition and coast along on the brakes to conserve petrol. Not the best-cared-for vehicles at any time, the brakes repeatedly failed under these conditions, the brake shoes burning out with the impossible task demanded of them. And if the bus should go over the unprotected side of the road, as they often did, nothing and no one could survive the drop of several thousand feet.

I wondered how these buses could be in such an awful mess and continue to receive the same punishment day in and day out, and still survive. None of them could be described as a complete vehicle, perhaps a fender missing here and there, doors and windows which had been ripped out and gone missing, the tread of the tyres so worn as to be almost bald. No self-respecting driver, certainly if he was a Sikh, would consider discarding tyres whilst there was a discernable shred of wear yet to be spun out of them. Very few of the drivers appeared inclined to maintain their vehicles, let alone preserve the original appearance. So, if the engine hood had blown off one night, and was gone forever, it would serve only to be of help in the future when it wouldn't have to be removed to get to the engine.

Some drivers tried to rectify their errors, and it was always preferable to have them laugh *with* you, as opposed to against you, and they would go to great lengths to do this. 'For example,' said the man at my elbow, 'the big fellow standing by the multicoloured truck. That's his own vehicle and he's feeling a bit bad about it right now. Last night he was trying to pull some fellow's vehicle out of the mud, to help him out, like, and in doing so he tore off the entire front bumper of his own car. You or I might have gone ghazi about that and smashed up a few other cars to make us feel better. Not him though, he just went round to the knacker's yard, ripped off another back bumper which was conveniently lying around and installed it right over the top of his own back bumper. So now he's got a truck without a bumper at the front, but with two bumpers at the back. He's different! Some guys will do anything for a laugh! Now he's loadin' up with dried wall turds, or pretty patties as the ladies like to call them, to sell at the local bazaar to compensate for his loused up bumper, you know.

'We call it "a service to the public,"' the man went on to say. And if once in a while things did go wrong, they were always ready to help out: as in, 'No madame, it isn't my fault he was in the middle of the road pissing.

He's not dead anyway, so for two broken legs I can only offer you two chips two rupees (twenty cents US, or one shilling and sixpence pounds sterling). Bring him back tonight if you want, and I'll reconsider. Right now I'm busy, so buck jow[1]!' As they say, East of Suez life is cheap. I felt sure the man was hallucinating, and he was the one who had gone ghazi[2].

Vehicle horns never seemed to go wrong; they were one of the few things in India that could be relied upon never to fail. It is generally acknowledged around the world that the intelligent use of these devices form an essential part of good and safe driving. In India it is believed that driving a car without a horn flies in contradiction of what good driving is all about. It is also preferable to have a decided difference in the tones of the two horns, which must be harmonized in such a manner as to provoke the worst headache that man can suffer. The Indians are extremely skilled in achieving that goal effortlessly, and certainly with great verve. With only one horn blaring in monotonous misery, a man is only half a man. With two, it is done in style, and the hornblowers are assured of approving looks from all. And if, on the rare occasion they fail to provide the expected disharmony, they will smilingly compensate for this by leaning on the horns long enough to provide an intensity of volume instead. Those accursed electronic horns blasted incessantly like a pestilence across the country. And on the tailgates of the trucks and windows of the taxis, there were painted in huge letters: 'Honk, and I'll help you pass. Keep trying, maybe next time I am helping.'

Travelling anywhere, by any means, in India is a nerve-racking affair which should be undertaken only if there is no alternative. The wary traveller should always be aware that using Indian buses presents its own unique problems, not the least of which is that goats or other livestock being brought on the journey are usually tied on the roof. Neither the roofs nor the animals are usually leakproof, so if you are seated below . . .

With both roads and vehicles in such an awful state of disrepair, I couldn't understand how *anyone* could travel and survive: there were grave markers the entire length of the mountain roads, so many, and couched in such derisive terms – 'This popular place to do it! Why not you? You are liking to try?' – that I wondered if they had been placed there as a warning or as a joke. Perhaps the officials were aware of the hopelessness of their

1 Go away!   2 Mad, fanatic

task to reduce the accident toll, so why not be cheerful whilst doing so?

The bullock-carts, like all bullock-carts in India, moved along like juggernauts, the animal oblivious to the outside world, plodding along neither knowing nor caring where they were going. And all bullock-cart drivers would invariably be asleep, and so have little or no control over the actions of their bovine juggernauts.

Those mountain roads were not the safest to travel; what few metalled sections there were had, like the gravelled parts, deteriorated and were badly in need of repair. There were no rails along the sides, so it was the easiest thing in the world just to step over the edge and plunge into eternity: a sheer drop ended on the rocks in the valley below. A bus would skid to the side of the road where, for a moment, it would hang precariously before plunging to the depths and exploding, engulfing the screaming passengers in flames. Even without the brakes functioning properly, the drivers took great delight in negotiating the sharpest of turns with the maximum speed. We saw just such an accident that day, caused by the driver of a passenger bus braking to avoid collision with a bullock-cart and skidding when the brakes didn't work properly. The bus slammed into the rocky cliffside, ricocheting to the open edge of the road, then toppling over the edge as if to plunge to the valley far below. By an act of God it fell no further than twenty feet before becoming lodged on a ledge, where it teetered ominously.

I was close by, so, with my friends, we clambered down to help, but before we could reach them the vehicle went up in a mass of flames. It was too late for those inside the bus, including the driver. Three or four had been flung clear during the plunge and lay on the side of the cliff. Two of the passengers' bodies were mangled and were clearly dead, and the others were in bad shape, with broken limbs and other severe injuries. Ambulances and professional medical care of any kind were just not available, and there was little we could do other than carry the injured back up the hill to the road. After about an hour another bus arrived and the few survivors, the dead and the injured, were placed on board for the two hours' journey down to Dehra.

The drivers of the buses appeared to be indifferent to the pleas of the scared passengers, who must have been in a permanent state of terror, and ever anxious to take advantage of any stop to relieve themselves, voluntarily and not accidentally – judging by the state of the bus floors, it must often have been too late. The suspense of needing to urinate in fear and being unable must have been most demoralizing, but the drivers found this great fun. They were a breed unto themselves.

Some of the routes through to the hill stations were so narrow and dangerous that two-way traffic was not always allowed. At specific times, say during the mornings, the road would be designated for down traffic only, and the reverse during the afternoons. Perhaps the incidence of traffic accidents was lowered in this way, but it was generally unpopular as the total volume of traffic was substantially reduced. The subsequent disruption to the lives of everyone was so bad that eventually only in extreme circumstances was the one-way system in force.

There were dacoits in these hills, as indeed there were everywhere in India and, as a matter of routine, we took exceptional precautions not to be caught by surprise. Being a small group, though carrying a significant proportion of automatic weapons, my party would be particularly susceptible to a surprise attack. The minimum approved size for such columns when moving through mountainous country was equivalent to that of an infantry platoon, but there were few occasions when a commander would not have wished for several times more. When the robbers came, they would do so in great numbers, moving swiftly in a carefully planned attack which was conducted in a very noisy manner with much shouting and screaming and rifle-fire, to create the utmost confusion. These attacks were an almost daily occurrence, leaving a trail of dead and wounded as a legacy. Points were established well ahead of my group – our actual leader was Sergeant Dodger Green. I thoroughly approved of this classic infantry style of patrolling with points well forward on the march. We were lucky enough not to fall prey to the dacoits on this occasion, so from that viewpoint it was a successful journey.

By late morning the roads grew busier, with a noticeable increase in pedestrian traffic. The family groups always seemed to be on the move in India, taking with them all the paraphernalia of a household, every member contributing to the task. The fulcrum of the moving party was quite often the bullock, pulling a cart so heavily laden there was scarcely an inch of space left. Perched on top, and always looking as if they were about to fall off, were the children and the animals. The other members of the family walked single file in the rear, the women a regulation three paces behind the men. Families on the move were a way of life in India, always searching for something better, a place where they could work and earn sufficient money to raise their children's standard of living to something better than that of their own current poverty level. That was the dream of millions living in that inhospitable land, and the competition in the search for Shangri La was so heavy that it truly was an impossible dream. Their needs were simple; all they asked for were the basic necessities to sustain life.

One family I saw already had five children, with another obviously on the way; the family elders, grandparents, perhaps, rode atop the cart, and countless relatives followed them. Like all those who were seeking a better life, they had taken the realities of their lives, hateful as they were, and mixed them thoroughly with the dreams of the future they were going to on this beautiful day, and that was why they were singing with hearts that were full.

It was a busy route for pedestrians too, who marched endlessly in singe file, the women still following three paces behind, hugging the cliff side of the road. They were invariably laden with goods: fruits or nuts or a variety of other foodstuffs, animals for the butcher's block, anything that was grist for the ever-churning mills of the markets on the plains below. India was always on the move.

Climbing higher, the raging torrents of the rivers in the valleys below sparkled in the brilliant sunshine. They were still pristine here, but they would soon lose their purity as they swept on towards the plains, being polluted by the increasing numbers of people who lined their banks. Within fifty miles of where I now stood, the waters would be brown, and awash with the garbage and detritus of millions. The rivers provided not just drinking water, but washing water too: for doing the dhobi (laundry), and for bathing themselves and the animals, which would urinate and defecate as they wished. At the extremities of the now beautiful rivers and streams, the waters would be totally unfit for drinking or for the preparation of food, and the natives who lived along the banks must resort to the use of wells for their needs. The rape was complete.

Progressing onwards, our merry band was soon marching through the increasingly steep and rugged mountains now surrounding us; the snow-covered peaks gleaming in the bright sunlight. Amidst the great silence, broken only by the roaring of the rivers, and the sounds of the birds – eagles and vultures – soaring overhead, we could see the plains stretching away for fifty miles or more, before the distant view was obscured by the haze of the civilization which occupied its vastness. The factory chimneys belched their pollution of gritty black smoke far and wide across the land. In the nearer villages, in the dusk of the evening, could be seen the smoke from the fires upon which the evening meals were being prepared, rising for a few hundred feet before, remarkably, veering sharply to a horizontal line parallel to the ground, stretching in the direction of the prevailing air currents. This phenomenon was a common sight across the northern provinces during the summer months.

In that panorama of an Indian sunset the tiny ant-like figures of the natives could be seen walking across the paddy fields where they had toiled for twelve hours or more, now returning to finish the household chores. Across the valley we could see the flickering lights as the solid lines of the houses succumbed to the darkness. This scene slowly dissolved in the Indian haze, heralding the fall of night, and soon we were clothed in gloom as the shadows crept across the mountainsides – but not before we were rewarded with the magnificent sight of the highest peaks in the colossal mountain ranges of the Himalayas. I was inspired by the way the mountains seemed to soar into the very sky and beyond, glistening white with the sheen of the ice covering the lower areas, and then the naked granite. Beyond the seventeen thousand feet level the snow is perpetual, though towards the very top the incline of the slopes is too sheer for the snow to remain.

There was Nanda Devi in its majesty at 25,600 feet, leading the parade across the north of India where, far to the east, Everest at 29,020 feet was the crowning glory of the highest peaks in the world. The summits wore plumes of silver and pink snow as the last rays of the sun gave its colour to the mountains. Although some thirty miles distant from us, the major peaks stood like bright beacons dominating the sky, reducing their surrounding companions to mere satellites, though few were less that fifteen thousand feet. As my group stood in the half light enjoying the spectacle, we recognized an entirely different India from that which we constantly denigrated so vocally. Now we might be more inclined to open our eyes a little more to seek for the hidden beauty and treasures which must abound in such a fabulous country. Our love/hate relationship with India and the Indians needed to be evaluated more carefully.

We had marched twenty miles and were beginning to feel weary after the long uphill climb; we were glad to finally reach the staging post where we were to spend the night. Our feet were blistered and our small packs had cut deeply into our shoulders. None of us had dared to remove our boots at the hourly ten-minute halts, because that would have meant even greater agony trying to get them back on. In spite of the cooler atmosphere, our tunics were soaked with sweat and hung limp and uncomfortable.

The truck which preceded us had already set up the field kitchen and the evening meal was ready for the hungry troops. Upon arrival we were greeted with cheers and the most ribald of remarks from those lucky few who'd made the journey by truck; the most welcome greeting of all was the sight of the beer bottles standing on the table, so cold and icy the glass glistened with moisture. The bottles had spent the day immersed in the water-filled chatties hanging from the nearby trees. Walking into the camp, we piled our rifles, lit cigarettes and made for that nectar, recounting in high humour the events of the day. Ask any man who has marched twenty miles through mountain passes: he'll tell you exactly what an icy cold bottle of Murree beer does for a soldier! For supper it would be McConachies stew with hard tack biscuits (calculated to break even the strongest of teeth!), washed down by another ice-cold beer, and perhaps yet another, for not all of us were beer drinkers, which meant more for those who were. And, inevitably, the gambling sessions began.

The camp was in a beautiful valley and three of us strolled across to the fast-flowing stream, where we sat on the rocks and dangled our bare, blistered feet in the cold water. It was a peaceful setting, the silence broken only by the gurgling of the rippling water and our laughter as we chatted. It was becoming dark now and with some reluctance we left the healing waters to prepare for sleep. The stars were beginning to show in the cloudless sky and the now-familiar figures of Orion and other constellations glittered with great intensity. The Southern Cross was there, its arm pointing in the direction of the southern pole. Though some claimed only three thousand stars could be seen with the naked eye, my view as I gazed above put the lie to that statement. They were countless in that vast canopy, and the pulsating stars – the dying stars – punctuated the universe like beacons, their ochre glows contrasting sharply with the blue diamonds scattered so thickly in the heavens. Even as I watched, I was rewarded with the magnificent sight of a meteor streaking across the sky almost directly overhead, with a great brilliance that slowly faded to a glimmer as it was lost amongst the twinkling lights. As I gloried in the heavens, I knew there was no sight more marvellous than that of an Indian sky at night.

There wasn't any great preparation for kipping down for the night: we spread groundsheets on the rough ground, having carefully first removed the larger stones and making the surface as smooth as possible. Within minutes of removing boots and donning Jerseys –the first time many of us had worn them – and covering ourselves with blankets, we were fast asleep, though some, oddly enough, missed the sounds and smells of the horses, the rattling and jingling of the harness which were so much part of their lives.

We awoke cold to a sparkling new day. Though there were a few aches and pains from the hard mattress, and the stones which had escaped notice earlier, most had slept well. The crisp air certainly put an edge on the appetite, but 'Chota hazri' – little breakfast – of burgoo¹ laced with sugar, followed by bacon and eggs with lashings of char, set us up for the day. It was early and the sun was just appearing over the snow peaks in the east, casting shadows on the valleys. The only sounds were those of the kitchen utensils as the pans clanged against each other, and the laughter at Dodger's smutty jokes, and the occasional sound of a dislodged rock gathering others as it hurtled down the mountainside to become an avalanche with the speed and noise of an express train. Even the sound of a rushing stream just a few yards away was diminished, and it was too early for the raucous noises of birds scavenging for their breakfast. We were anxiously awaiting the sun's first warm rays, rubbing our hands together to keep them warm.

We would remember this particular campsite, though not for its beauty and tranquillity. We'd all heard that the scorpion was reputed to commit suicide when faced with impending death, and Taffy Jones decided to test it out when he saw one crawling near the wheels of a truck. Taking a large sheet of newspaper, he laid it on the ground and with a twig he flicked the scorpion onto it. When the scorpion was in the centre of the paper,

1 Porridge

Taffy struck a match and lit the four corners. As the flame spread towards the scorpion, and its demise appeared inevitable, its tail could be seen slowly moving over its back, and within a second it had plunged the sting into its own body. It writhed in contortions as the flames slowly consumed it. I wasn't so sure that Taffy actually enjoyed seeing the scorpion die in such a manner, but it entertained the troops, who gaily continued their preparations to strike camp.

The second and last day of the march started immediately after breakfast; the truck loaded with all the paraphernalia set off and soon we were swinging our way once more along the narrow roads clinging to the increasingly mountainous countryside. The landscape was now changing again as the mosaic-like terracing of the hillsides gave way to thicker forestry and vegetation. There were far fewer native farmers tilling the soil on the steep slopes, or women breaking their backs to plant rice in this inhospitable place. As we marched, we sang the Gunners' favourite song – though, strictly speaking, only the mountain gunners held that prerogative, not all gunners at large. Those mountain gunners used mules to carry their guns and ammunition and all the other equipment required by a mountain artilleryman: it was a gruelling life, travelling where no roads or even tracks existed, carrying the dismantled (and dearly loved) 3.7 howitzers over the roughest of terrains. These men were a breed unto themselves: hardy, courageous and determined, who revelled in the challenge of an arduous job. One day far in the future, I would be a mountain gunner, singing to the tune of the Eton Boating Song,

Smokin' my pipe on the mountings, sniffin' the mornin' cool,
I walks in my old brown gaiters along o' my old brown mule,
With seventy gunners be'ind me, an' never a beggar forgets
It's only the pick of the Army that handles the dear little pets—'Tss! 'Tss!
For you all loves the screw-guns – the screw-guns they all love you!
So when we call round with a few guns, o' course you will know what to do –
hoo! hoo!
Jes' send in your Chief an' surrender – it's worse if you fights or you runs:
You can go where you please, you can skid up the trees, but you don't get
away from the guns![1]

---

[1] 'Screw-Guns', *Barrack Room Ballads* by Rudyard Kipling

As we strode along, I thought how different this was to the life in the cantonments, where the bleak whitewashed barracks reflected the blinding dazzling sun as you approached them. The intense heat created a haze so strong that across the maidan on the horizon the most peculiar images would dance, constantly changing: one moment a huge ship sailing through the undulating waters of the ocean, and the next – and I was prepared to swear that it was true, though I wouldn't put any money on it – became a replica of the Blackpool Tower. These illusions were a constant source of diversion as one sat on the bungalow verandah, the sun blazing down, on a lazy afternoon. And without warning they would vanish at the drop of a hat, and then there was little else to do other than to go inside and join the others charpoy-bashing[1], where at least there was a measure of coolness. Now, here in the hills, instead of scorching the eyes out, the sun's glare was diminished; the natives in the valleys certainly appeared to be going about their tasks with more energy than their counterparts below.

The hill station we were headed for didn't have the same notoriety as Simla or Darjeeling; Simla's reputation for poodle-faking – chasing women – was like a beacon; so many illicit relationships happened there that even the men in the ranks knew the scandals. Eight out of ten of the white population there (or in any hill station) were women who had left their husbands on the plains for up to three months, and that was a long time for anyone to give up sex. The young officers going to the hills knew this, and were only too happy to oblige the desperate ladies. The ratio of women to men was one to ten at least, so the competition was pretty fierce, but those lucky women who had the appropriate attractions were blessed with a constant change of partners as the officers stayed for only ten to fourteen days before returning to their units on the plains. The prime topic of gossip was the identification of the unfaithful, though few husbands were ever informed of the behaviour of the errant spouse. They must have wondered though; everyone knew about what went on in the hills. Unfortunately for those officers who had to remain on the plains during the summer, it was an inverse ratio, so they had little opportunity to misbehave themselves in return.

For us, with our thoughts turned to our own hill paradise, we whiled away the hours in time-honoured fashion:

1 Sleeping

I don't want to join the army,
I don't want to go to war.
I'd rather hang around
Piccadilly Underground,
Living on the earnings of a Holborn lady
I don't want to join the army
I don't want to go to war

I'd rather stay in England,
In Merry, Merry England,
And roger all the pretty girls away.

I don't want to join the army
I don't want ...

Then a smattering of:

She had those dark and dreamy eyes,
And a whiz bang up her jacksy.
She was one of the early birds ...
One of the old Brigade.

And that old favourite:

A troop-ship was leaving Bombay
Bound for old Blighty's shores,
Heavily laden with time-expired men
Bound for the land they adore.

There's many a poor bloke out there
Merrily soldiering on.
But you'll get no promotion that side of the ocean
So cheer up my lads, bless 'em all.

Bless 'em all, bless 'em all,
The long and the short and the tall ...

So we sang on the last few miles to Sabathu, not exactly the land we adored, but infinitely better than the plains we'd just left. As we approached the outskirts of the town that evening, Dusty, seeing we were flagging,

ABOVE LEFT & RIGHT
William Pennington,
aged fourteen, a new
recruit at Woolwich
Barracks and aged fifteen, a
qualified Trumpeter.

CENTRE Penny, aged fifteen, in
Royal Horse Artillery uniform.

BELOW Gym team, Boys' Depot,
Woolwich, 1935. Penny is third
from left in the front row.

ABOVE Boy graduates at Woolwich Barracks, 1935. Penny (*front right*) is holding the silver bugle he had been awarded.

LEFT Penny (*right*) and his mentor, Sergeant Norman, in 1936.

BELOW E Battery, Royal Horse Artillery, Meerut, India, April 1936. Penny is at the extreme left of the picture on Dolly Grey.

TOP LEFT Penny in camp in India in 1936, mounted on Dolly Grey.

TOP RIGHT One of our 25-pounder guns.

ABOVE Crossing the river Jumna with the guns – travelling to Delhi for the Durbar.

ABOVE Delhi Fort.

RIGHT On a troop-train to the Himalayan hill station.

BELOW A halt for tiffin during the march to the Himalayan hill station.

ABOVE Just arrived at camp for the night – char time.

LEFT The road to the hills. We marched every mile – all 150 of them, at twenty miles a day.

BELOW The rest station at Saniya, 3,400 feet above sea level.

LEFT Barracks in a
Himalayan hill station.

ABOVE Friends forever. RIGHT Some pets were cleverer than others.

ABOVE Elephant on its way to a
ceremony.

RIGHT A snake charmer.

RIGHT A pre-war image of the P&O luxury liner *Stratheden*, which as a troop-ship carried Penny from Glasgow back to India during the Second World War.

ABOVE E Battery Royal Horse Artillery on church parade in 1937.

BELOW Penny (marked by an 'x' on his topee) photographed with his troop, Bangalore, 1942.

ABOVE Penny – a full-blown Captain – 1943.

RIGHT Penny in southern India.

BELOW Officers of the 134 Medium Regiment RA, in India after the Burma Campaign, 1945. Penny is front left.

shouted, 'Come on lads, let's have some of your favourite marching songs, Colonel Bogey for a start.'

Taking him up, we responded with that famous military air:

Bollocks, was all the band could play,
Bollocks, a million miles away ...

Followed by:

Ta ra ra bum di-ay
I heard the parson say,
Turn all your bums this way
Turn all your bums this way ...
Ta ra ra bum di-ay ...

And once again, one of the old favourites, which we sang ad nauseam:

I love a lassie,
A bloody great Madrasi,
She's as black as the ace of fucking spades,
She's got hairs on her belly
Like the palms that grow at Delhi,
Nelly, my big black girl.

After all, no one ever accused soldiers of having taste!

Arriving at the bazaar that evening which, like all bazaars in the East, was crowded with natives, we saw a sprinkling of Green Howard infantry soldiers, not as individuals, but in groups of three or more – all carrying swordsticks, of course, even though it was rare for an Indian, either singly or in groups, to attack a white sahib: they all knew the severe penalties which would be inflicted if they did. Few Indians dared to face the fury of an English soldier's wrath; although he was usually not downright unkind, he could exhibit the most brutal behaviour. Still, this was India, and one never knew ... The men in Green stood at mock attention at the sight of the new arrivals marching in (straggling would be more appropriate), greeting us royally as we received the salute.

'Come on, you bloody lazy horse gunners. What took you so long? The only time you're the first on the field and the last to retire is when you're jumping in bed with a tart!' they shouted.

We gunners replied with the appropriate double finger salute and the greeting, 'Up you from Wigan.' It was all done in good humour. We were pleased to have arrived.

A few of the natives also came to greet us, especially the shopkeepers who thronged around me and my friends, pressing upon us a variety of goods for sale: 'Very good photos, Sahib. You are sending to your bibi in Blighty,' and, more persuasive for some, 'I got nice girl, Sahib. Good French girls', although that was unlikely, 'give you very good jig-jig. And clean as whistle, Sahib. Very cheap for long time.' The tattoo wallah offered to cover our skins for a pittance with anything from *I Love You* to the regimental badge, *Death before Dishonour*, a scorpion or a voluptuous woman in a provocative pose.

I had to smile at this last, for Dusty sported the best tattoo story I'd ever seen, the ultimate in tattoos. It occupied the whole of his back, stretching from his shoulders to his bum, showing a hunting scene in the fields of Kent with the mounted hunters and the pack in full pursuit of the fox, which was just disappearing up his rectum. Only the tail of the fox was visible, the animal having been put to the ground by the dog pack which was now excitedly at the scene of departure. It was a fascinating picture, imprinted on his skin in such vivid detail you could almost see the despair of the hunters and the dogs as the fox sought refuge in such an unassailable place. It was invariably the focal point of conversations whenever Dusty removed his shirt; any uncomplimentary remarks rolled off Dusty like water from a duck's back. The artist considered it a masterpiece and few disagreed with him. Not amused at the possibility of being the proud possessor of an equally famous tattoo himself, Dodger thrust them aside, shouting, 'Get knackered, you black bastards. I'll kick your fucking goolies in if you don't get out of the way jeldi! Mut bolo, chub arow¹!'

The army in its wisdom had decreed that upon arriving at a hill station, all personnel must remain inactive for a seven-day acclimatization period, during which time no strenuous activities were to take place, no sports, hiking, hill-climbing or exercise of any kind. Naturally, when my group reached Sabathu, we were given the same instructions, despite the fact that we were supposed to have become acclimatized during our six-thousand-feet two-day march. But military regulations must be observed,

1 Don't speak, shut up!

so we spent that first week mostly charpoy-bashing and gambling.

The cantonment was nothing more then a half dozen bungalows well isolated from any native dwellings. It was obviously considered a safer place than Meerut, for the buildings stood alone, with no Guard Room and no wire fencing. It wasn't even military in appearance; maybe the army intended to make a break from the constant military atmosphere which surrounded the troops on the plains and at the frontier stations like Razmak or the Khyber Pass. In those places you lived behind barbed wire all the time, except when out on patrol taming the renegade tribesmen, and you carried more than swordsticks at all times.

It was a tranquil setting on a lightly wooded spur with excellent views to the valley below, and the rising snow-covered peaks to the north, which dazzled in the bright warm sunshine; a silence pervaded the area and the air smelt fresh and fragrant. It was a heavenly relief from the rowdy cantonments and the stench of the bazaars we'd just left a few days ago. We quickly made ourselves comfortable in our new quarters; the various monkeys and parrots which had been brought along fastened to the mosquito-net posts. Mosquitoes appeared to breed anywhere in India, not just on the plains. And we'd have to take good care of the pets here too, for the ubiquitous jackals would be around as soon as darkness fell.

A few nights after arriving an officers' ball was arranged and I was asked if I'd like to act as a waiter. Of course I was pleased to do so, for it meant I'd see something of the good life officers were reputed to enjoy. It was a lovely setting, and a warm and sultry evening – almost reminiscent of an English dance. It was a most elegant party. The women looked just delectable to the female-starved men, me included: they were dressed exquisitely and all looked so charming and delightful that for a moment I wished that I too was an officer, able to meet and live with such glamorous creatures – not to mention all the other privileges they enjoyed.

At least one of the ladies was a little interested in me: by this time I was a fine-looking teenager, my face tanned by the sun, which highlighted my odd-coloured eyes, one blue, the other brown, which many found intriguing. She engaged me in conversation which had little to do with ordering wine: she wanted to know my name, where I was born and what I most liked to do. Her questioning was becoming quite personal when her husband walked up and the moment was lost; after taking a last, lingering look at her, I went about my duties. She was old enough to be my mother, but I thought she was very attractive, and more importantly, she had spoken to me – the first time I'd spoken more than a few words to a white woman since coming to India. But I never saw her again, which was a pity because I was growing up with no white women in my life. However, the tips – and the times I 'forgot' to return the change – also made the evening worthwhile.

Returning to the bungalow I found a drinking party going in full swing, with Dodger holding court: he had the most incredible library of songs, and there was always something new. I was just in time to hear his rendition of a song he swore blind he'd composed:

She was poor but she was honest,
It's the poor what gets the blame.
It's the same the whole world over,
Ain't it all a bleeding shame.

We were only playing leap frog,
We were only playing leap frog,
We were only playing leap frog,
'Til he whipped it up his gonga pouch!

It was fairly mild compared to the usual gutter rubbish; at the drop of a hat he'd produce these relatively innocuous songs that he always claimed were quite suitable for entertainment at a mothers' gathering after church. Where he got the inspiration, heaven knows, but there was an endless flow of them and they went down well with the lads. And he had the voice too; you could hear his Geordie accent three bungalows away! He was a generous, mild and God-fearing man despite his appearance, from which one might think him nothing more than an ignorant, brash brute.

The songs were halted suddenly by a loud shout of, 'Look out,' and we all turned our heads in time to see a krait, a deadly rock snake, wriggling along the blanket on the bed just a few inches from Taffy's bare legs. Two things happened simultaneously: Taffy, face white with alarm, leaped from his bed like a scalded cat, and Norman snatched a towel and threw it over the venomous snake. The krait was called the 'two minute killer', for that was what it was: to be bitten by one meant death within two minutes, for there was no treatment which could neutralize the venom in time.

We all peered up at the open rafters of the roof above, for that was where the snake had come from, anticipating the worst, but we were lucky: kraits are rare serpents, usually found, as the name indicates, in the rocks. Taking hold of its tail Norman smashed its head against the wall and, walking out of the door, threw it in the bushes. After some animated talk, activities resumed.

It was good to be away from the slothful life of the cantonments and feel some joie de vivre again. Though the evenings were chilly, there was a sweet fragrance in the breeze so dissimilar to that of the plains, and the air was crystal-clear, unlike the smog that clogged the plains. The sky was bluer and even the cottonwool clouds looked whiter and cleaner, as though they'd just been washed. And at night the stars sparkled brighter, and there were so many more of them.

Across the valleys in the far distance could be seen the brilliant lights of the Maharaja of Patiala's summer residence, shining like a beacon in an otherwise darkly enshrouded countryside. Said to be the richest man in India, if not the world, it was reputed that he was weighed every year and the same measurement was accorded to him in gold from the taxation of the surrounding village folk. The Maharaja enjoyed the luxury of a power plant to generate electricity, whilst the natives lived in the same gloom they had always lived in.

Discipline was very relaxed here; we didn't have to wear a topee all the time – a welcome relief, for they were the cause of many a headache because the tight-fitting brims created an oven-like atmosphere on the head. On the plains the topee was mandatory and, whilst not the same as the loss of a rifle, the failure to do so, even in the midday sun, brought severe punishment – a soldier could be court-martialled if he was caught not wearing it in daylight hours.

I, like most of the men, didn't think the officers were really concerned about our wellbeing; they left that to the senior non-commissioned officers. In less tropical climes, many men had the rather peculiar habit of wearing their peak caps whilst in bed. Here in India they wore their topees in bed. I had to smile when I first saw this; I recalled what I'd been told so long ago, by the Battery Sergeant-Major in Newport: there were only two occasions when a soldier must remove his hat, in front of the Commanding Officer on a charge, or in church. And how about in bed with a woman, I wondered; you'd have more pressing matters to distract you, so perhaps it was permissible to leave your hat on. Admittedly, topees were removed when going to sleep. There was also the rumour that it was possible to get heatstroke even when wearing one's topee, for the rays of the blinding sun could be reflected from the concrete and so strike under the helmet – fact or fiction, I wondered.

THE STAY IN the hills was a wonderful interlude in the life of a young soldier, but all too soon it was time to return to the scorching plains of Meerut, and then, in the winter of 1938, on to Sialkot, where the regiment had been posted. It was a change of scenery – and a change of pace – but the most likely reason for our move was the growing discontent in the north-west, where the violence was worsening. The city of Lahore, famous for the Mosque of Wazir Khan, Shalimar Gardens and the Lahore Fort, was fifty miles away. It was also the major Sikh centre. In nearby Jammu, the Fakir of Ipi, a holy man, and therefore well respected, was using his tremendous influence to incite riots.

As with Meerut, Sialkot was the image of Aldershot, except that now the regiment was surrounded with barbed wire to keep the hooligans out. It was closer to the Himalayas than Meerut and we could see the gleaming snow-covered peaks to the north, even though they were more than eighty miles away. In the very far distance to the north-west was Nanga Parbat, at 26,600 feet one of the giants. They were a strange but welcome contrast to the scorching plains of the United Provinces they overlooked. Though so far away, they offered a vicarious relief to we men who stifled all day in the leaden heat.

Sialkot was definitely a popular station: the evenings were cooler, although at supper time the temperature was often still in the mid-nineties. The summer days were painfully hot, but the setting sun would see the temperature plunge as much as thirty degrees. To shiver was a pleasure one rarely enjoyed. During the day, only those who must left the confines of the bungalow, and those who stayed ordered a constant procession of cold drinks from the bearer. It was a ritual.

In the long oppressive afternoons the troops cursed as we lay on our charpoys in great discomfort, the sweat literally pouring off us. Outside, the blinding blue sky stretched to eternity, and we knew that tomorrow and the next day and the next would be the same. We did nothing other than stare at the blankness of the walls, the monotony relieved only by the tuk-toos spearing flies and mosquitoes. And the evening was always several hours away and meanwhile the white man's burden must be borne. There were the khuds to look forward to, with their enervating coolness, and within ten miles of the cantonment there was good fishing for the Indian char which abounded in the canals and rivers.

FOR THREE YEARS the ever-changing seasons marched by, the torrential rains arriving with unfailing punctuality. While my departure from India was imminent, I didn't then know I would one day return to this country – and the monsoons. I would once again be one of those who looked forward so passionately to the arrival of the monsoons until one evening a slight breeze would ruffle the leaves on the trees, and perhaps a few leaves would fall; there was a wet breeze, and you knew it was coming, bringing with it the magic of life. Then the dark clouds would fill the sky, and the rains would start. The first few drops would be as large as an English half crown, pelting down with such force that it hurt the skin; a dozen drops would fill a teapot. It was only a warning, for then the full fury of the monsoon would strike with the speed of the lightning which now flashed across the sky, ruthlessly, mercilessly sweeping all before it. It came with the roar of an express train entering a long dark tunnel, and for up to ten weeks the rains would fall endlessly, to be followed by ten months without a single drop falling.

Now the barren ground, brick-hardened by the cruel sun, would put forth a profusion of flowers and from the countless fissures there would emerge a host of insects, and lines of ants marching in search of food. The rains would flood the land and the nullahs¹ and the rivers would be filled. The water swept all before it: penetrating and saturating everything, the dampness turned boots a virulent green if they were left uncovered at night. Yet in spite of the downpour, which brought only temporary relief, the period from June to August remained unpleasantly hot. There would be intervals, very short intervals, when the rain ceased for a while and

1 Ravines

the sun blazed again, bringing the torture of prickly heat. Only at the end of the monsoon could you experience the exquisite pleasure of going to bed with a blanket on a November day, or, in December, eating turkey and all the trimmings followed by Christmas pudding in a relatively cool atmosphere of 80 degrees Fahrenheit. The winter months would extend to January, during which time individual training, followed by regimental and brigade exercises, would take place. All too soon the hot weather would return and . . .

It was not long after moving to Sialkot I met with a fortune teller. Walking across the burning pavements from the bungalow to the adjacent washrooms, I heard a voice say, 'Sahib, I am telling your fortune if you are wanting.' Looking around, I saw, in a very inconspicuous place under a papal tree, this wizened old man squatting with a chatty. A very learned-looking Indian with an aesthetic face, who appeared to be as old as Methuselah, was talking away to himself in a language that was decidedly not Urdu, or any Indian dialect I recognized. Seeing he'd caught my attention, he continued, 'I am telling the truth in everything I will see in your future and I am not wanting much money. For you Sahib, I am doing very cheap because I believe I can bring you much happiness.'

Sceptically, but attracted by the apparent sincerity of the fortuneteller, who had already cast a kind of spell around me, I replied, 'Old man, I will listen to you, for you seem to be different from those fortune tellers that I have seen before.'

The old man was already working himself into a trance, babbling what sounded like a lot of mumbo-jumbo; as he spoke, he waved his hands gracefully and with great delicacy over the bowl of water which sat between his crossed legs. His hands were close to the chatty, but touching neither it nor the water. I had been standing some distance away, but now I felt compelled to sit alongside him. As I sat there studying the Indian's gnarled face, which now had an almost ethereal appearance, I looked down to see the water rippling slightly. After a few moments, as the man raised his voice, uttering words now quite incomprehensible, the ripple became more violent and, as his voice reached a crescendo, the water splashed over the side of the chatty. His hands were still clear of the water.

There was a silence whilst the old man appeared to be in a daze. Suddenly, looking up at me, he said, 'Sahib, the waters tell me that you will be going home to England soon. Perhaps within a few weeks, but I cannot know for sure. Beyond that I can see only that everything will be mixed up and that your life will change. I am hoping this is good news for you, Sahib, and if you are not liking, then you are giving me no money. But it is only four annas.' I was nonplussed by this forecast, for whilst I fervently wanted to believe it, I knew it could not be possible; I'd been in India only half the required time, so to be told that I was to go home soon was an impossibility. Throwing my coin at the fortune teller's feet, I walked away, thinking he was just another Indian charlatan depicting a good future for a few annas. But when I went to sleep that night, I wondered: the man had seemed so different to the others I'd come across.

IT WAS IN Sialkot that I saw a massive stampede of horses. I was sitting outside the bungalow on the verandah before supper, just after the animals were returning from watering about a hundred yards from the horse lines, when I heard the tremendous sound of hooves ringing on the road. Looking up curiously, I saw about a hundred horses racing by in total disorder, followed sharply by a group of cavalrymen. The horses had broken loose when returning to the lines, and the commotion they caused had aroused the regiment's horses. The whole thing had turned into a real nightmare; for each horse that stumbled, a dozen others went crashing to the ground, and soon the roadway was a heaving mass of bodies. It was an almost hopeless task to recover the situation; capturing the runaways was a long haul. Sadly, we had to destroy a number of the beasts, and it was an unpleasant duty indeed for many of the horses' regular riders, who had to take part in the killing.

But this incident was immeasurably less painful than the day we had to shoot our Battery horses, a day most of us would remember for the rest of our lives. With mechanization looming, and because we would be going home soon, the horses were longer needed to draw the guns into battle. Nor were they needed for the ammunition trailers, reconnaissance party, the Colonel of the Regiment and his officers, the NCOs or the men, not even for me and my fellow bugler. Never again would I sit astride Dolly Grey summoning the Battery to trot, to canter or to gallop with my bugle calls, nor would I show off her paces to the onlookers. It was an end of an era, for the horses were to be disposed of, and it was distressingly painful to learn that many of them were to be put to death.

I was told I would be present at the slaughter that was to take place. Not all the horses were to be shot; a few had been transferred to other regiments which would continue to be horse-drawn for a while. Others would follow later. For the men who regularly rode those horses, saying goodbye to an old and faithful companion who had served for so many years was a hard enough task, but it didn't compare to the heart-wrenching for the men who had to act as assistants to the executioner.

The slaughter was to take place on the maidan, and it began with little ceremony. The carrion eaters were already gathering, sensing in their uncanny way that a great feast awaited them. The vultures were circling endlessly with hardly a tremor of their wings, growing ever closer as the moments passed. There were almost a hundred horses to be killed over the next few days, and it was to be done with a device rather like the flintlock of a gun. Placed on the forehead of the beast at a point between the eyes, whilst the horse was steadied by its rider, the trigger was pulled and an iron rod would shoot forward to penetrate the skull. It was said to be an instant and painless death; but it was a death etched in the riders' memory for ever, a truly bitter memory. As the first horse writhed on the ground in the last throes of death, the vultures became bolder and soon were sitting within a few feet of the scene. By the time the executioner had dispatched two or three horses, the vultures were tearing deep inside the carcasses of the animals. The crows were there too, swarming around the dead beasts, and the jackals were waiting and watching, to be sure they would get their share. And there were the hardbitten warriors, tears rolling down their faces, with looks of anguish and despair as they witnessed the loss of dear friends. These men were often referred to as the brutal and uncaring dregs of the slums, ruffians incapable of love and concern; their critics should have seen them then to know the compassion of which they were capable.

The slaughter continued to the noon hour, in a silence broken only by the cawing of the crows and the flapping of the vultures' wings and the occasional scream of the jackals as they fought amongst themselves for the abundant delicacies. With the sun high overhead, a halt was called to the killing, and we tired and saddened men drifted away from the grim, heartrending scene, pausing only to look over our shoulders, as if drawn by a magnet to the unimaginably hateful exhibition. Only the carrion would remain to gorge themselves, the vultures already so sated they could not take flight, no matter how long the take-off they attempted before falling helplessly to the ground. In the cool of the evening another chapter would take place, when the animals of the night assembled for their own gory feast.

And once more we soldiers must carry out this dreadful duty, volunteers all, for we would trust no stranger to carry out the grisly executions. It was little wonder that so many men drank themselves insensible that night.

By the grace of God, Dolly Grey, whom I'd loved for so long, was not to be included in the massacre: she was to be posted to Skinner's Horse, an élite Indian regiment who would do well by her. Originally James Skinner had served as an officer for the Maharaja of Scindia, and later as a captain in the British Army in India. His regiment came to be highly regarded as a well-trained and well-disciplined unit, both fearless and forceful in battle: the Rajputs were natural soldiers, and the British welcomed them to their service. James's father was a Scotsman, a colonel with the British Army in India, his mother an Indian and a Rajput. He was therefore an Anglo-Indian – a chee-chee, or blackie-whitee, or any of the many, mostly derogative, appellations given to those of mixed blood, that is, the Eurasians. The Colonel wanted James to speak English as his first language, much to the chagrin of his mother, who was so ashamed of this that she committed suicide, for she was a devout Moslem.

James made an envious reputation for himself, soon realizing his dream of becoming a commissioned officer of the King Emperor. The deserted remnants of a Rajput cavalry force which had opposed the Maharaja of Scindia, a friend of the British, said they were willing to fight for the Raj providing they were placed under Skinner's command; their previous allegiance to the French was forgiven them. In naming James Skinner as their new Commanding Officer, the British Army's Lord Lake said that the new regiment should be named, 'Skinner's Horse' and the uniform of yellow riding breeches and red turban would be retained, and remained so throughout the regiment's service with the Indian Army.

Though Skinner's Horse would soon have to forsake their beloved horses for the monstrous iron tanks which were to be the future of war, right now it was a prestigious posting for Dolly. As the day to part with Dolly drew closer, I thought also of Henry, the polo pony I occasionally rode, not by the nickname I'd given it, but rather by its number, 141. It was then that I realized how much I cared for Dolly, and what she meant to me: she was the only one who had shared my youth, as we'd ridden the Indian plains together. I believed we had a very special relationship; she'd given me love, something that was absent in my life in this faraway country. She was no cypher in my mind, not just an animal, but my Dolly, a loving creature.

So whilst the tears fell from troops gathered on the maidan, so they fell also from my eyes as I watched the butchery of our beloved horses, doubly hurting from their deaths and from the impending loss of Dolly. Truly this was the end of a chapter in my life; I wondered what would become of Dolly, for it wouldn't be long before Skinner's Horse would be faced with the same heart-rending decisions. I little realized then that there would one day be a link between me and Dolly's new regiment, in Burma, fighting the Japanese, when I would provide artillery support for Skinner's Horse whilst attached to them as a Forward Observation Officer.

THE NEXT DAY another batch of horses was prepared for shipment to other units of both the British and the Indian Army. Whilst loading them into the railway boxcars, I received what I later called 'the last kick': as I walked a fine-looking chestnut stallion up the loading ramp, he lashed out with both hind legs. Standing immediately behind, I received the full force of the thrust in my chest, with such force that I was sent flying. As I lay writhing in agony on the cement platform, there was an immediate rush to help me; quickly bundled into one of the regimental staff cars, I was driven to the cantonment hospital. The injuries weren't serious, much to my relief, for I was afraid that I would miss the boat train, which was to leave the following day. Whenever I was asked how I felt, my instant reply was that I was just fine and that my chest had never felt better, so deep was my desire to 'pick up my parrots and monkeys'; I would indeed 'fall in facing the boat' with the rest of my regiment. Fortunately, I really was unharmed except for a few aches and bruises, so I was able to rejoin my comrades, pick up my kit-bag and at last board the troop-train which would carry us all to the long-awaited ship. We would barely even notice the sordid conditions on the clackety old train: we were going home.

It was whilst travelling in the troop-train across India, anticipating the glories of returning to the land of my birth, that I started thinking of the memories I'd carry home. I'd remember the Grand Trunk Road; the very name conjures up all that is India to the British Army. Filled with romance, victory and defeat, love and hate, the name runs like a thread through the history of the country. It links all the major cities from Calcutta in the east and Peshawar to the west and beyond; to the passes with magical names: the Khyber, Bolan, Landi Kotal, Razmak and Bannu. In the summer the intervening fifteen hundred miles of burning hot plains – the *doabs* – was mostly treeless and arid land, where nothing more than small shrubs and cactus grew, notably in the Punjab. To the extreme north-west lay the Frontier Province where many a British soldier had lost his life at the hands of the Pathans or Afridimen, by bullet, or a knife in the back, or tortured to death, I thought bitterly.

Branching off this major highway between these two extremes, and from the Punjab and the United Provinces, lay the numerous hill stations where the white man sought relief from the crippling heat. And this was the main artery to the multitude of British cantonments which stretched from the Himalayas to the southern most tip of the sub-continent, and across the twenty-mile stretch of water to Ceylon, which was a prized posting. In the early summer mornings the dust would rise from the ruts worn deep by the bullock-carts, but out in the country there would still be a sweetness in the air before the heat brought the sordid smells of the day. The camels, the elephants and the peasants trudging to work, their eyes still filled with sleep, another day of monotony to be faced as they toiled in the fields or at the well until darkness fell. To the Englishman, the Grand Trunk Road epitomized all that was India.

I mused that one day I might say to some civilian, 'If you are ever "in the sunny climes of Inja" and walk along the Grand Trunk Road in Northern India, think of the British soldier as he served there in the days of the Raj. If you try hard enough, you may hear the thumps of those same boots, and the whinnying of the horses and the jingle of the harness of the artillery train as they ride past, or even the sound of the bugle calling, "There goes 'march at ease' so now light your fags". And as you march along with them, look more closely and you will see behind the deep tan of the cruel Indian sun the innocence of young British faces just like you and me. With a little imagination you will hear the lilting voices from Wales or

Scotland, or Ireland, or the Cockney from Bow Bells or the Geordie from Newcastle, or the Lancashire accents of Northern England. If the wind is right you can listen to the kettledrums as they beat out the pace . . . Stomp, Stomp, Stomp, Stomp, Stomp, Stomp, Stomp . . . And as you fall into step with them and sweat in the broiling heat of this alien country, perhaps you will sense the loneliness which exists beneath their banter.' I would tell him to look carefully at those youthful faces, and perhaps he would see my own, as we went about our task of serving in the jewel in the crown of His Majesty the King, and he would see that they too were deserving of the affection of the British people.

I knew that for all the apparent brashness of those who served in the British Army, there was a bravado that helped them to keep that stiff upper lip in spite of all their trials and tribulations. I speculated that the onlooker should be ready for his own reaction, though, for the experience might touch his heart, because he would see that the troopers were men just like the rest of them, and not the much-maligned brutal and licentious soldiery, as those at home are often inclined to call us. Kipling described it so well: 'For we aren't no thin red 'eroes, nor we aren't no blackguards too.'[1] I thought that a civilian might then find it not too difficult to identify with them and offer his salute, or even say, 'Good morning Mister Atkins, and how are you today?' For that is what the multitudes will say, 'When the drums begin to roll.' Rudyard Kipling had a deep understanding of the relationship that existed between the British public and the soldiers of the King. Sadly and tragically, it was so true.

I believed that apart from the bitter memories a few of my colleagues would carry away, there were many of us who would remember their time in India with extreme happiness – and we all, without exception, would remember the unfailing comradeship which had been formed over the last few years; it would serve us well in the years that lay ahead. We were going home, but we were not to be disbanded; rather, we would be more securely glued together with that bond which soldiers of every army foster. Though not all memories of soldiering in the land of 'Ind' would be happy ones – for example, the loss of the horses was indelibly imprinted on our minds – we would be leaving part of ourselves behind, for, all unknowing, our attachment to that 'much hated' country was deeper than we had

1 'Tommy', *Barrack Room Ballads*

realized. It didn't take much thought to recognize that the Indians were not so different from our own people; we might even recall the few instances where, when spoken to on even terms, the Indians had demonstrated equal intelligence and understanding: they were under-privileged, yes, but still human beings who were not all pagans.

I was convinced that none of us would forget the blood-red skies at sunset seen through the shimmering haze, the aquamarine lakes shining like glass in the Himalayas, or the mountain peaks outlined in glistening gold at sunrise, with the highlighted rims of the snow slowly turning to bronze, then fascinatingly glowing through the spectrum of the rainbow before finally reaching a firm white, deeply etched in the clear blue sky. The ever-changing countryside, with the sharp contrast of the lush greenery of the south separated by the hills of the Deccan from the hot and arid plains of the north and the deserts to the west; the spectacle of the northern peaks soaring in the silence of the mountains which were known as the Roof Of The World; the steep slopes falling away to the deep gorges and the roaring torrents below where, if you fell, you would be carried away like a matchstick: all these sights would linger in the mind.

And so, instead of gambling, I spent most of my time on the train contemplating the love/hate relationship with India that I and most of my comrades would retain, possibly for ever.

FINALLY THE DAY arrived. As we tumbled out of the troop-train in Bombay, the sergeant-major, with a huge grin on his face – he knew what was expected of him – shouted, almost screamed those words we all held so dearly, and had waited so long to hear: *'Pick up your parrots and monkeys and fall in facing the boat.'* A roar of laughter broke out from the wildly excited assembly: our dream, our dearest wish had come true. It was goodbye to the life we had endured so miserably (many, anyway), and on our way home to the land we loved so dearly. It was the end of the filth, the decimating heat, the uncertainty of wondering if tomorrow you would still be alive or six feet under. This time, even knowing that stifling hot journey across the Indian Ocean, then the Red Sea, lay ahead, we were undaunted by the thought. Those would be the last days before the final escape from the East. If the boat had to circle a few times as it entered the Red Sea – and troop-ships invariably did so, to induce cool air into the bowels where the smells were so rank that you could cut the atmosphere with the proverbial knife – and so lose a few precious hours, who cared: we were going back to the delights of Blighty. And no longer would the boots of these soldiers march along the Grand Trunk Road, creating clouds of dust and saturated with sweat. Those days were ended; the *gora logs* were homeward bound.

But there was a great sadness as well as happiness in the air, I thought. Many of the men had known and lived with Anglo-Indian girls for so long, perhaps for years, that it was a soul-tearing parting. They were not married, and therefore were not allowed to take the girls back to England. And if the men felt bad about it, think of the girls who stood on that quayside, distraught and in tears, knowing they would never again see the men they loved and upon whom they had come to depend. It was a sad parting, especially for the girls, who were the butt of many jokes and unkind words. The men were at least returning to their homeland, and could look forward to seeing parents, family and friends, folks they might not have seen for several years. And for those who were fathers, their sons and daughters would not be the babies they left all those years ago. There would be some difficult reunions; some would be greeted with happiness, some as strangers. The tears were flowing on both the ship and the shore as the vessel edged away from the dock, then cheers rang loud and streamers were thrown both down from the ship's rails and up from the quay, and the balloons released. India was gone.

IT WOULD TAKE three weeks to sail by troop-ship from Bombay to Southampton, this time aboard the *Nevada*, sister ship to the *Neuralia*. A hundred years ago it took four months for a troop-ship to sail from England to India, with conditions even more primitive than now. Then, there were seven toilets to a thousand men. The forty officers fared better with three toilets between them.

The atmosphere onboard the *Nevada* was unquestionably upbeat, for we were going home, and though the activities of the day were monotonously similar to those on the outbound journey to India, this time they were filled with delectable anticipation. For the officers it would be a quicker and more pleasant journey, for they could travel by the mail-boat. Many would leave the boat at Suez, go overland to Alexandria, taking another ship there to Marseilles, and go on to Calais by train; from there it was a short hop to Dover. We common troopers faced that long, hot and uncomfortable trip. At Port Said the traditional ceremony took place of throwing our topees overboard. If yours sank, then you would never again have to soldier in the East; if it floated . . . well, that's how the story went, but my topee did sink, even though in a few years' time I'd be back.

Blessed was the day we reached Gibraltar, for now we could expect a more civilized weather pattern – the howling winds and torrential rains and the dampness which is England.

It was a Sunday when the ship steamed into the idyllic setting of Southampton Harbour, a sunny day; it was also a day which made a mockery of the return of the happy and excited troops. Most of us had been away soldiering on the Indian sub-continent for several years, having converged on Bombay to join the troop-ship, and this moment was one of great expectation: the dream of walking down the gangplank to the land of our birth. It was not to be, however, for this was Sunday, and on Sunday in Dear Old England the normal activities of daily life were abandoned for a day of prayer – or, more likely, a day in bed until it was time to go down to the pub for a few pints and a game of darts. The docks were closed and the ship was unable to berth; we had to wait until Monday to disembark. The long wait was vividly etched in my mind: I watched the pleasure boats that came out to see the troop-ship newly arrived from India, filled with men desperate for all the pleasures Blighty had to offer. As the boats circled the ship, some were filled with beautiful girls – all white girls were beautiful to us – who waved and shouted, 'Why don't you jump overboard and come ashore with us!' Alas, though tempting, it was not possible, so for almost twenty-four hours all we could do was stand at the rails of the boat and watch the parade of spectators waving to us lonely soldiers. The hours were agonizing as we thought of the pleasures so close, yet so far away at that moment. As the darkness fell, so we became increasingly bitter at the apparent indifference of those responsible for the delay.

At four in the morning the loudhailers rang loudly through the ship: 'Rise and Shine, beds in line, piss-pots on the verandah. Prepare to disembark.' The moment was here at last. A hurried breakfast and muster on deck saw the ship alongside the quay with the gangplank in place. And in spite of the early hour, they were there waiting: the families, the wives and the girlfriends, all those who had come to welcome us home: a sight to gladden anyone's heart. Here was Blighty at long last, and the waiting was ended. There would be reunions, and pubs, and the taste of real English beer, so wonderful after all those years of the swill we'd endured in India.

When I walked down on to English soil, there was no one there waiting for me. I was not dismayed. I too was home and a bright future lay ahead.

WHILE I'D BEEN half a continent away, things had been moving on in the Old World. Adolf Hitler, now Chancellor of Germany, had forced political union with Austria, the land of his birth. In May he had announced his programme for expanding Germany: 'It is my unalterable will to smash Czechoslovakia by military action in the near future.' A number of threats followed and on September 15 the British Prime Minister, Neville Chamberlain, made his first aeroplane journey, to meet Hitler in his mountain eerie in the Bavarian Alps, where Hitler agreed to defer violent action for the time being. A week later the two men met again, and Hitler upped his demands. On September 26 he made another verbal attack on Czechoslovakia. The next day the Royal Navy was mobilized. The day after that, the German Army followed suit. On September 28 representatives of four major powers – Chamberlain for Britain, the French Prime Minister Deladier, Mussolini and Hitler – met in Munich, where Hitler bullied the west into signing the Munich Agreement and handing over the Sudetenland – the German-speaking frontier areas of Czechoslovakia.

And Chamberlain returned home having signed an agreement with Hitler that in future Britain and Germany would consult over any difficulties that arose between their two countries. On his arrival back in London, Chamberlain revived one of Disraeli's great lines when he announced to a worried country that he had 'brought peace with honour'.

But it was an uneasy peace that was not to last much longer.

chapter eight

ALDERSHOT

January 1939 to September 1939

England showed her indifference towards the Battery in her usual manner, receiving those who had guarded her Empire in the East for all those long years as if they had never been away. On that Monday morning at least the weather offered a welcome home, for there were only a few clouds in an otherwise perfectly blue sky. We had been feeling very bitter about the authorities' lack of action which had delayed our disembarkation, but now, with the sun shining on us and the gangplanks in place, all was forgiven. Looking down at the shore, everything looked so clean and tidy, compared to the ports we'd stopped at on the way – and there was not a wily oriental gentleman in sight. A huge crowd had gathered on the dockside waiting for the two thousand troops, and as the first footsteps rang on the gangway and the first soldier appeared, they pressed forward eagerly, welcoming home their husbands, sons and fathers. Rising over the confusion and babble could be heard solitary voices: 'There he is, it's our Jack. It is 'im, isn't it, Gertie?' And the exultant response, 'Yes, it's our lad all right, our lad, bless 'im. Don't 'e look thin? Welcome home, Jack, luv!' The cry was taken up by others as they identified their loved ones, and there was an outpouring of love and affection.

But there were no bands or other official signs of welcome, and the only streamers and decorations were those provided by the welcoming families. Once again Kipling was right when he wrote, 'It's Tommy this and Tommy that and Tommy go away . . . We serve no red-coats here.' Britain was always keen to send her soldiers off in grand style, with bands and a great palaver, but she was reluctant to welcome them back with any kind of ceremony.

But I thought the troops had been given a wonderful reception, for I too had basked in the aura of loving welcome, and was as excited as everyone else. As the men marched down on to the quay, ranks were broken and in an almost hysterical scene, reunions with family and friends were made. Children, their faces red and rosy, were grown almost beyond recognition; our faces, by comparison, were gaunt and withered by the merciless Indian sun, our bodies emaciated from lack of proper nourishment, for the food in India had had no real substance. But however toilworn, every man's face wore an expression of deep happiness. We were home.

It could not have been a happier day for those who had waited so long and so patiently. The troop-trains were waiting and, bless them, so were the Ladies' Voluntary Organizations, the Temperance Society well to the fore. They too had stood patiently on the quay for several hours, waiting their chance to offer tea, sandwiches and cakes to the returning heroes. Alas, there was no beer, but that would follow soon! In a most unusual deviation from normal practice, those men whose families awaited them at Southampton were given immediate leave, paid and issued rail passes to their homes, and allowed to depart at once.

The remainder of the contingent was not so fortunate: we had to board the troop-train bound for Aldershot, unable to disembark until it reached its destination. There was great dismay about this because, for some, their dreams of England had always been synonymous with beer; they were desperate to get to the nearest pub and satisfy their years-long craving for good English bitter, but it was not yet to be. Troops-trains are notoriously slow, and it was positively heart-breaking to be trapped for so many hours inside those coaches when a public house seemed to come into view every few hundred yards every time we passed through a town or village. All they could do, and did, was to shout loudly whenever the train stopped, in the hope that some good Samaritan would come to their rescue with a glass or two of England's best – and that actually did happen on one occasion, when an elderly gentleman (who must have been an ex-soldier), brought over six bottles of that amber nectar when the train stopped near a village with the local pub prominently in view. That man would be praised for the rest of his life.

Equally dismaying was the sight of all the beautiful girls, so many of them, and all inaccessible. There was great dissension, and we prayed for that interminable journey to end soon.

I, OF COURSE, was going home to Blackpool for my leave. My parents, naturally, were delighted to see me. I had almost reached my eighteenth birthday; they were astounded and happy at how well I'd grown. And for those relatives who were unable to come to Blackpool, now I had enough money to go to see them. I revelled in the accolades heaped upon me and enjoyed being back home immensely. I had brought presents for my mother and father; although they were very inexpensive – chocolates, tins of fruit and other such things which were becoming scarce in England – they went down a storm with my family. And of course, no soldier left the East without his share of the ubiquitous Indian brassware which was then a real rarity in England.

But I didn't get the same reception from my old school friends: once again I found I was a stranger. We were all in our late teens, but though we had all matured considerably, they had lived in a stagnant environment whereas I, without really realizing it, had gone through a more dynamic period of time. I looked different too: my hair was bleached very blond by the Indian sun, and I was one hundred and fifty pounds of muscle. Because I was so tanned, my mismatched eyes – one blue, one brown – really stood out, and my teeth looked dazzling white against my dark skin. Enid later said I resembled Errol Flynn in his 'Robin Hood' days; whether I was that handsome is a moot point, but I was a man, while my friends were still teenagers. We had little in common any more.

But all too soon the leave was over and it was back to the Battery, this time in Aldershot which, with Bulford, would be home for the next year.

IF IT WAS true that London was the centre of the Empire, then it is equally so that Aldershot was the centre of the British Army. A soldier who had not been stationed there could not justifiably say that he was a member of the British Army, and he had every right to feel ashamed about this – at least, that's how those of us who *had* served there felt. Aldershot was a large town, and certainly there were civilians resident there: employees and camp followers. But the bulk of the population wore a military uniform.

Consequently, it was always a noisy place, and at weekends, doubly so. It is also a fact that there were more drunken fights on a Saturday night in Aldershot than there were anywhere else in the world, mostly based on regimental jealousy, or women, or frustration, or all three. There was nothing more deadly than living in a military environment twenty-four hours a day, and fighting was a great way to let off steam.

It was, therefore, an appropriate place for the 'Glasshouse' (the Detention Centre), an institution well-known to the delinquents of military discipline. Although most of its business arose from the local area, it also received offenders from all over the country. Its reputation as being the worst of the military detention centres was based on the severity of the punishment meted out. Prisoners were treated roughly, and appeared to have no rights at all: to utter a single word of criticism brought down the full wrath of the guards. At times they were treated like animals, and were in a continual state of exhaustion because everything had to be done on the double, on and off the parade ground. If a man passed out from exhaustion from repeated doubling (extra quick marching, or running), he was revived and subjected to even more doubling. I never 'served' there, and I concluded that it was a good place to stay away from, so I was determined I'd keep my nose clean.

It was regrettable that the Regulars, soldiers, and sailors and airmen – but especially the soldiers – had a reputation for raping, looting, thievery and drunkenness; they were generally known as the brutal and licentious soldierly. The image had flowered long before the days of Wellington, gathering foliage as time went by, to the point where the average citizen looked with scorn on the humble soldier. But we were not all the dregs of the streets; far from it. Like those who joined the Foreign Legion, there were men who joined the army to escape not merely the handicaps of being out of work in civvy street, even as a labourer (for there were precious few opportunities for even menial jobs at that time), but also those whose love affairs had faltered, or whose marriages had broken up. Certainly there were some who were evading the police for reasons better known to themselves, but the army's recruits came not only from the slums, where the most desperate living conditions existed, but also from the homes of the rich, where ambitious men were attracted by the potential for adventure, or others simply to escape the responsibilities of life.

I was in Aldershot only a few months before being moved to Bulford, but it was an exciting period for me; several significant things happened. First, the Battery was equipped with the new ordnance: the 25-pounder gun, which was a major step forward from the 18-pounder. The range of twenty-one thousand yards, and a platform and fixed trail provided, vastly helped the gun's manoeuvrability. Its potential destructive power was enormously increased. We also had a different vehicle to tow the guns, a Quad: it looked like an armoured car, though in fact it wasn't at all bullet-proof. However, it was a comfortable transport for the gun crew to travel in, being totally enclosed, yet well ventilated – no more the misery of galloping on horseback across the muddy rivers in the pouring rain or snow, not to mention the early morning rough exercises in the Welsh rains: it was an enormous step forward in luxury for the gun teams, and a decided improvement all round.

The second was the issue of new uniforms. For years the British soldier had been accustomed to wearing a heavy cloth uniform coloured according to the branch of service: the red coats of the Royal Welsh Fusiliers and other infantry units, and the Engineers; the green of the Riflemen and the blue of the Artillery. Many of the regiments wore mixed dress, and this applied particularly to the officers. In the Afghan Wars of 1878 it was common to wear heavy white summer uniforms which were exceedingly uncomfortable, and presented a conspicuous target to an enemy. It was not until the nineteenth century that a khaki (Urdu for dusty) uniform of lightweight cloth was adopted for tropical areas: it started in India, where the white tunics were dyed a greyish colour with tea. The headdress from the very early days was a white Indian helmet fitted with a khaki cover. In non-tropical areas the British soldier wore a slouch hat during campaigns, but this was replaced by the very restrictive peaked hat, with a forage cap for daily use. Puttees were the widely accepted dress for legs, again in regimental colours. These were worn (and endured) until just before the First World War. The whole lot together was a most uncomfortable garb, and the puttees the cause of early varicose veins in many an unfortunate man.

Khaki quickly became the standard colour of uniforms for units in action, but the traditional heavy serge high-necked tunic and slacks, still with puttees for the infantryman, or riding breeches for the gunners and cavalry, remained until 1939.

Then came a major change, with the introduction of the battledress: still of a drab serge material, it was in the form of a roomy jacket fastened by a belt at the waist, with thick serge trousers fastened at the ankle by gaiters, which replaced the puttees, and were far easier to wear. Webbing became the standard for carrying equipment on and around the body, loose-fitting and relatively easy to wear. The new battledress was introduced early in 1939, but not all the troops, nor even the officers, were pleased about it, especially the old diehards who'd been in the service for years. It was certainly more comfortable, and sensible dress for the sort of situations soldiers often find themselves in. But it was too casual for many of us, not at all military enough in appearance: too rough and tumble, too slovenly. Even I thought it was sloppy: we looked like Fred Karno's Army! Give me the dress uniform every time, many said, under their voices. The remarks were endless, but in the end everyone – at least all the common soldiers, NCOs and Warrant Officers – had to wear the dress, either off or on duty. But for the officers, it was still tunics, Sam Browns and peaked caps. Many of them continued to wear riding breeches, although horses had been retired months ago because of the mechanization programme, although this provided nothing more than the opportunity to slap their riding boots so that everyone was aware of their presence.

But when the guns began to speak, they too would revert to battledress. Like it or not, there it was.

The third important thing that happened to me was mustering gunner: a huge step forward, the climax to an almost four-year wait. I had reached the age of eighteen and was now reclassified from being a boy soldier to being a Gunner. It meant I had become a man in the eyes of the British Army – and myself, and my service would now count towards a pension from that day on. Much more important, though, my pay would leap from one shilling and twopence to the fabulous sum of two shillings a day. Now I could live like a king – or at least go to the picture house once in a while. It also gave me the chance to earn my first stripe.

And, fourthly, this first stripe came quickly, for within the month I was promoted to the rank of Lance-Bombardier, a high-sounding title for the first step in the long chain of command that exists in the British Army. I was just eighteen years old. It was both an exciting, yet almost sombre moment as I sewed the single stripe of authority on the upper sleeves of my jacket. I was excited because I could now order other people around (as well as being ordered around myself), and at the same time I could enjoy the prospect of higher command, perhaps even to the exalted rank of General. But the downside was the sense of the great weight now placed upon my shoulders, for I felt very encumbered by the new responsibility. Was it to mean a sterner outlook on life, and no more friendliness towards those with only the common rank of gunner? Perhaps I couldn't even talk casually with them, in case I became too familiar and lost their respect . . . all sorts of things assailed my mind. But it wasn't too long before I stepped into my new role more confidently and began to enjoy this new world; even the officers appeared to be impressed by me, though there were no special privileges or consequences, of course – I couldn't even dine in a separate mess, as the distinguished and illustrious group of sergeants and other senior ranks did. But that would come eventually.

Specialized training now took place, to familiarize the Battery with the new style of artillery. For me it also meant learning how to ride a motor-cycle and, after a very brief description of the mechanical aspects of the machine I, along with several other potential dispatch riders, was turned loose on the vast parade ground. It was six o'clock in the morning, a time when it wasn't in use for drilling. After an instructional period which lasted all of five minutes, we were evidently expected to perform as we might in the famed TT races on the Isle of Man – but the closest we came to that very popular sport was for four of us to lock wheels in the centre of that hallowed ground. The parade ground was of an almost astronom-ical size, and it must have required the greatest of skills for us all to meet in that unseemly fashion – or so thought the Sergeant Instructor, who offered his condolences with the few choice words, 'You stupid lot of bas-tards. Who told you to fucking well dismount? Get back on those bikes before I stick their fucking seats up your gonga pouches¹!' And so we did, with sheepish grins, to the very loud laughter of the sergeant and the bystanders.

Within a remarkably short period of time we were out on the road; miraculously, none of us were killed, though there were a few spills and some very upset civilian and military motorists. Then we graduated to the tank training grounds on the outskirts of Aldershot where, across

1 Urdu for backsides

that steep and rough country, we spent a month learning how to handle our bikes like professionals. Day after day we were expected to climb, on the motorbikes, up the steepest imaginable hills, so steep that at times the gradients caused the bike to topple over backwards onto the riders. It was a painful experience, but in the end we could ride with the very best.

I will never forget the day my bike broke down on the training grounds. Attempts to fix the problem failed, but I did ride it back to the barracks, though not in a style much to my liking. In a very matter-of-fact way the sergeant produced a twenty-foot-long towrope, instructing me to link my bike to his. With a casual shout to mount my steed, the sergeant roared off, dragging me behind him; it was the most terrifying ride of my life, for we sped along the busy roads at breakneck speed, with me hanging on for dear life, expecting to meet my Maker at any moment. But the fates were kind and though the hapless, petrified rider being towed was nothing but a mass of shivering jelly when we reached the barracks, I was still in one piece.

All this training – or lack of it – stood me in good stead later though, for one day I was to post the fastest lap of the Southern India motorcycle competition, over a distance of five miles, in the muddiest mud imaginable. So glutinous was the mud that at times I had to dismount and scrape it from the clogged wheels, which would not turn because of it.

But that was years in the future; for now, I was still learning. Part of the training was to go off by ourselves and ride around the countryside, which I enjoyed thoroughly. But like all the new riders, I tended to travel too fast and lose control. On this particular day I had rounded a curve in the road, swerved to miss an oncoming car, and had difficulty in regaining my balance and direction, with the result that I and my bike went right through the front gate of a house with a long pathway – up which bike and I travelled unceremoniously – to the front door, where we landed with a loud bang. As I lay there with the motorcycle on top of me (that was becoming a bit of a habit), the door opened and the elderly lady who appeared cried, 'Young man! What are you doing there, young man? What do you want on my property?'

In response, I managed to blurt out, 'I'm sorry to disturb you, ma'am. I was just passing by and I wondered if I could have a glass of water. I'm thirsty and would be much obliged to you.' But I didn't get the water. The door was slammed in my face as the angry lady withdrew and I recovered myself and rode off again.

AFTER A WHILE the Battery moved to Bulford, where it amalgamated with three other units to form A/E Battery and B/O Battery of the 1st Regiment Royal Horse Artillery. We were now ready for war, and Herr Hitler was about to oblige. All the events of 1938 pointed to this: Hitler announced himself as the Chief of the German Army, visited Italy to make a pact with Mussolini, and invaded Czechoslovakia. France had partially mobilized, and the British Navy totally mobilized. On September 29, 1938, Neville Chamberlain, the Prime Minister of Britain, returned from the Munich Conference, where Britain, France and Italy had approved the German occupation of the Sudetenland. Mr Chamberlain arrived in London waving a slip of paper and proclaiming that he had brought back peace in our time, and that it was peace with honour. Nevertheless, Britain established a Register for War Service. Events thereafter moved quickly. In March 1939, German troops occupied Bohemia and Moravia via Czechoslovakia and the USA withdrew its Ambassador in protest. Hitler renounced his non-aggression pact with Poland, prompting British and French support for the Poles. In April, Italy invaded Albania; Britain declared the conscription of men aged twenty and twenty-one, and Hitler denounced the 1935 limitations placed on Germany's naval power. In August, Chamberlain again warned Hitler of Britain's intention to support its treaty with Poland. France commenced the evacuation of Paris and England of London, and on September 1, England introduced the National Service Bill, calling to the Colours men aged eighteen to forty-one. Finally, at eleven o'clock on Sunday, September 3, 1939, whilst the church bells chimed, it was announced that Britain and France had declared war on Germany.

THE REGIMENT WAS out on exercises when I heard the news broadcast in which British Prime Minister Neville Chamberlain made the statement: 'As Germany has not met the demand to withdraw from Poland, a state of war now exists between Britain and Germany.' We'd been on the firing practice ranges at Larkhill on Salisbury Plain, and there was wild, excited conversation and great rejoicing on the number 22 wireless sets within the regiment linking the OPs to the gun positions. The prospect of actually firing our guns in anger was exhilarating, and it was hard even to finish the shoot in progress. There would be no more make-believe, describing a target as being enemy troops, when in reality it was nothing more dangerous than a flock of seagulls. The unit was quickly returned to barracks and there was a general muster for all ranks to outline the mobilization plans.

There was little time to prepare, because in short order a signal was received ordering the regiment to be ready within the week to embark at Dover for passage to France. We were to be part of the 51st Highland Division. The dull and all-too-often boring period of peacetime soldiering was soon to be over. The true adventure, and the most exciting period of my life that lay ahead was about to start.

And that was the fifth matter of consequence for me. Soon I would be on French soil. It was an eventful year.

chapter nine

BRITISH EXPEDITIONARY FORCE

September 1939 to May 1940

Ils ne passeront pas; On ne passe pas

The regiment did arrive in France, but ten days later, as predicted by Sergeant Smudger Smith, on Monday September 11, 1939, at six in the evening, to be precise. 'We are always bloody well late,' Smudger said, 'in the same way we always start our wars with a retreat. What can you shaggin' well expect when the pissin' officers say they can't go until all the mess furniture and the silver is packed. And we can't do that until the friggin' weekly Guest Night has been held next Monday. Mustn't miss that, you know, or people 'ud think it strange of us to be so unsociable, even if there is a fucking war on! And Captain Crapoff won't bleedin' want to go until he's got his polo ponies ready. Can't win a war without 'em, you know! And we all know that the Colonel has to go down to Brighton for his usual dirty weekend with his tart from Kidderminster. So what's the fucking hurry? The French are there to keep the pot boiling, and they'll be on about their bloody "On ne passe pas" even though the only thing they're capable of passing is the shit in their pants. But Gerry will make them do that in a hurry, you just watch.'

Polo ponies or not, the Captain did sail with the regiment from Dover (the Colonel was to follow on in a few days' time), and the behaviour of the men showed this ranked second only to watching the English football finals: we were in high spirits and we very definitely wanted to go to war. The laughter and the joking never ceased, and it was just as well that we left

England happily, because our return would be a pitiable one. Within two weeks HMS *Courageous* would be sunk and the Soviet Union would invade Poland from the east; soon after, the USA would declare its neutrality and HMS *Royal Oak* would sink in the British naval base of Scapa Flow, sunk by an enemy U-boat with the loss of the entire crew: eight hundred and thirty three lives.

A major battle of the Titans would occur on December 16 off Montevideo in the South Atlantic, with the *Graf Spee* being sunk before the very eyes of the residents of that city. She had been chased into the harbour, where the Captain sought and obtained refuge, but only for three days, after which, with the steering mechanism still unrepaired, she was obliged to set sail again. The big guns of the British Fleet would be waiting offshore. At the eleventh hour the Captain gave the order to scuttle the ship, then committed suicide. More than a thousand men, many training cadets aged around sixteen, were lost. The entire incident was captured by a visiting American news journalist, who reported the scene live in a radio broadcast over the telephone for all the world to hear. The chase by the British warships had been long and exciting, with costly penalties before the Germans sank their ship.

AFTER LANDING AT Calais the regiment camped out in a village near the town of Arras, some few miles south of Lille, where we slept variously in farm buildings, public halls – virtually any place which could provide a roof over our heads. It was rough living, straw for our beds and ablutions carried out in the open; that was to be typical of conditions for the next few months. At first the weather was obliging, but soon it turned bitterly cold – that winter in France was to be the worst in thirty years. Snow, icy-cold winds, constant gales straight from the steppes of Siberia, or so it felt: the wells from which we drew water were constantly frozen. Washing was purgatory and shaving an ordeal; we had to boil ice on open fires for water. But regardless of the discomfort, and the hazards of the climate, preparations for the impending battle with the Germans continued unabated.

Even the thick, heavy army overcoats failed to keep us warm, and open fires were not permitted in the barns where I slept, so the only escape was to the local estaminet – French bar – just like our predecessors in the First World War. They were warm and welcoming houses, where it was possible to buy a good meal whilst imbibing the best of France's wine and liquors. But the house most eagerly sought was the brothel, the first choice for most of the men. Rue de ABC in Arras was the principal centre for consorting with the ladies, and it was always crowded. The street must have been at least half a mile long, and every door of every house was wide open, rain or shine, with the most charming ladies offering: 'A good time for you, Tommy Atkins.' Though always broke, somehow the soldiers always found the money to patronize those mansions of sexual delight.

Relationships with the French civilians were very friendly and after a while more than one man found himself a home away from home; life became less unpleasant, especially for the single man. Just about everybody had their feet under the table of a generous family, who provided the best they could in the way of meals. Rationing was in effect by now, as it was in England, but they gladly shared what they had. Of course the ideal situation, which many of the boys strived for, included an attractive daughter to share, as well as her family's hospitality – and the girls were not unwilling to oblige. If the soldier was lucky, the casual question to a pretty girl on the streets, 'Voulez-vous promenade avec moi, mamzelle?' could sometimes be fruitful. I often wondered later just how many marriages this led to after the war. I wasn't so lucky, but my friend Gordon and I were fortunate enough to find a temporary 'Mother and Father', who dined us well.

But the same convivial relationship did not exist between the French Poilus and the British Tommy. The former was convinced, and all his friends were quick to point out to him, that the British soldier was actively seducing his wife whilst he was away in some distant place – and in some instances it was true, and he was in not such a distant place at that. The squaddie, in return, had a poor view of his French counterpart, believing them to be ignorant bastards of poor taste in whatever they did, said or ate, ill-disciplined, scruffy in their dress and dirty in their habits, and lacking in all matters concerning decency. In short, the British trooper did not think very highly of them; they were just lousy soldiers – but their women were all right! Well, that was Dodger Green's inestimable opinion, and he believed he spoke for the rest of the regiment.

Privately, the British officers also were of the same view, being most critical of their French counterparts. When asked his opinion of General

Gamelin's competence in the conduct of war, a very senior British officer replied, 'I think he is an awfully nice little man, who has exceptionally good taste in well-cut riding breeches,' or words to that effect. It was poor testimony to the man who was the Supreme Commander of the Allied Forces in Europe.

WHILST THE REGIMENT enjoyed the best and endured the worst, there was no escaping the reason we were there. The business of soldiering, preparing gun positions and establishing observation posts along the Belgian frontier, kept us busy. In the shocking cold of those first few months it was an almost impossible task; the days were spent digging, training, and digging again. The ground was frozen so solid that even the pick-axes were blunted from the tremendous force applied in trying to break up what felt like iron.

For the next eight months the situation between Germany and the Allies was static, with little or no ground activity. There were air raids by both sides, but no fighting on the ground and neither side saw an enemy uniform. The war became known as the *phoney war* because, on the European front it seemed to exist merely in the imagination, and only on the high seas did the Germans reap their harvest of sunken vessels. Instead, the regiment, like all units on the Belgian frontier, built gun position after gun position. We searched the landscape around the border endlessly for likely targets, and much silent registration took place. On one occasion another artillery surveyor and I actually walked a hundred yards or so across the border to more closely identify a possible target, and got chased back by the Belgian police, all four of us laughing. But all that work was to no avail. None of the gun positions were ever occupied to repel the Germans, nor were the potential targets in Belgium ever shelled.

Now that I was a certified artillery surveyor, I had to do some unusual things; one of the scariest was climbing a water tower for an improved view of the Franco-Belgian border, in order to do silent ranging. The dome of the tower was quite one hundred feet high and shaped like a naked inverted mushroom, with a narrow steel ladder leading to the top. At the point where the head of the mushroom started, the ladder bent over almost backwards, and the concave slope made me feel that if I failed to keep my feet firmly on the rungs, I would just dangle in space, and it was a long drop. It was an unnerving experience, as though one was walking upside down, and, with no head for heights, I was not at all happy about it. Steel helmet and accoutrements, including a large mapboard slung over the shoulder, were added impediments. Reaching the dome of the storage tank was no more comforting: it was simply a large, concave metal structure about twenty feet in diameter. There were neither rails nor guards of any kind and with the strong wind that was blowing, I felt very vulnerable, in danger of being swept away at any time. My mission was to carry out a more accurate assessment of potential targets in the Belgian territory. Having reached the top, the view was magnificent, and I was able to identify many areas hitherto unseen from ground level. But it was with a thankful heart and great relief that I made the equally terrifying descent and finally set foot on terra firma once again.

War has been described as long periods of boredom punctuated by short spells of intense activity. That wasn't true in this war: nary a shot was fired for eight long months, and we had not even a sight of a German. Rarely did one see an enemy plane. The single occasion which could have been described as 'intense activity' was when a Fokker fighter plane flew at a low altitude across the part of Lille where my regiment was then billeted. At the time I was standing outside the building we were staying in with some of my colleagues when one of them commented, 'That's a strange-looking aircraft. Doesn't look British or French to me.'

'No, it's not,' responded someone. 'It's a bloody German. Get the Bren gun out here on the jeldi!' There was a mad rush indoors to get the weapon, assemble it, place it on the stand and load the ammunition.

'Right, where is it?' exclaimed the Bren gunner. 'What took you so bloody long? We thought you'd gone back to Woolwich to get the fucking thing. The bloody plane is long gone and probably back in Berlin, where the pilot's having his supper laughing his fucking head off. That's where it is!' The Bren gunner crew were the object of much derision thereafter, becoming known as the chaps who missed a golden opportunity to cover themselves in glory by firing at an enemy plane, which was two hundred miles away before they could get one up the spout! The Battery Sergeant-Major also gave them seven days' jankers for their tardiness and four hours of Bren gun set-up drill. They were lucky: if the war had started in earnest, they could have been brought to court-martial.

For some reason, the incident reminded me of the story I'd heard about the German plane which flew over the British trenches regularly and without fail during the First World War, always at seven o'clock in the morning. And it was always successful in strafing the troops, without ever any effective response from the ground. So an enterprising gunner thought he'd try to shoot it down in an unorthodox way. Siting an 18-pounder field gun in the anticipated direction from which the plane was expected, he and his gun crew waited for the magic moment. Sure enough, and precisely on time, the pilot arrived and, at the right moment and on open sights, the gun was fired. It was a direct hit; those gunners take the credit for being the forerunners of anti-aircraft artillery.

Unbelievably, short leave was not all that difficult to get, and it was refreshing to go back over the Channel and hear the civilians singing the favourite songs, 'I'll be seeing you in all the old familiar places' or 'Wish me luck as you wave me goodbye' and the heartrending 'Somewhere in France with you'. The troopers' most popular song was:

> Apres la guerre finis
> Soldat Anglais partee,
> Mademoiselle in the family way,
> Apres la guerre finis.

I took a seven-day leave over the Christmas period and Dad proudly took me to the Highfield Road Public House, showing off his newly promoted son: I'd been made a lance-sergeant, not bad for an eighteen-year-old. There I was treated royally: one of the men who would soon be licking the pants off the Germans. It wouldn't be long before they learned just how premature their hopes were. It would be disappointing at that time, but there would be another occasion, when the beer would flow as I was toasted as an officer: a Captain.

Promotion came rapidly during those few months; a bombardier could expect to wait several years during peacetime to be raised to the rank of sergeant, but it was now often only a matter of weeks. The growth of the British Army was phenomenal, creating promotions almost overnight. I had been a lance-bombardier just a few weeks ago; now I was a lance-sergeant. Shortly after that I was able to put the gun above the three stripes, signifying the rank of full sergeant. I was nineteen. The next step would have been that of sergeant-major, but there would soon be other plans for me. In the late spring of 1940 the pattern of life was about to be radically changed.

THE MUCH-VAUNTED Maginot Line was a monstrous construction of steel and cement designed specifically to shield France from an invasion of Alsace and Lorraine by Germany. While considering how best to fortify the frontier against German advances, the French Army's Field-Marshal Pétain had suggested that the sector which included the Ardennes Forest was in no danger, and he inferred that any defence need not include that area. So the plan for the Maginot Line which was subsequently adopted excluded any special preparations for the Ardennes.

The interior of the complex was designed by an ex-army sergeant so the fortress could exist for several months without assistance from the outside world. Gun emplacements to house 135- and 75-mm field-guns, anti-tank guns and mortars were sited in well-designed and fortified areas, with excellent fields of fire. There were barrack areas for the troops, although the sleeping quarters left something to be desired – the ceilings were so low that the noses of the men in bed almost touched the roof. The dining rooms and recreational facilities were adequate and little had not been provided for. There was sufficient storage for ammunition, food and water and other essential supplies. It was very much a city unto itself, but in the end it proved to be of no value and did little to hinder the rapid advance of the Germans, for they came in from the north of where the Maginot Line ended at Longuyon, where France and Belgium met. Described as an impregnable fortress, which it was, it might as well have been built in the middle of the Sahara desert for all the use it was.

Pétain was living in a fool's paradise as far as his assessment of the country's need was concerned: when the Germans came, the Maginot Line played no part in the defence of France. It was simply and swiftly outflanked as the Germans came through the not-so-impenetrable Ardennes Forest.

THE DISPOSITION OF the Allied forces at the beginning of May 1940, extending two hundred miles from the North Sea to the Maginot Line, was as follows: the French First Army on the right of the line facing east; to the left the British Expeditionary Force (BEF) with the 1st Armoured

Division (which included my own 1st Regiment Royal Horse Artillery), then the Belgian Army and, on the west flank extending to the North Sea, the French Seventh Army. On May 10 (the day Britain formed the Home Guard) the Germans invaded the Lowlands, ending the phoney war. In accordance with pre-arranged plans, the Allied forces moved into Belgium to meet the spearheads of the German armour, much to the delight (and expectation) of the Nazis. The French First Army moved into their assigned position between the rivers Dyle and Meuse, but they were swept aside by the German Panzers, which rolled in like juggernauts, for the Germans had more than thirty divisions to smash their way through Holland and across the plains of Belgium. By sheer weight of massive armour on the land, and by parachutes and gliders from the sky, they overcame all and conquered Holland in five short days.

The Belgium Army quickly surrendered, thus exposing the Allies to the German might, which raced through the gap, easily brushing off any attempt to stop them. From that point all organized resistance ceased, and the fighting – although heroic by both British and French – was unco-ordinated; the writing was on the wall. Utter chaos reigned across northern France as refugees became intermingled with those troops who were still gallantly fighting on. None of us knew where the Germans were, although there were reports of them being here, there and everywhere.

Finally, the remnants of the Allied forces, many of my closest friends amongst them – I'd been lucky enough to be on the last ferry out of Calais – were trapped along the coast in a pocket approximately thirty miles by twelve miles. The Luftwaffe ruled the skies and soon the approaches to Dunkirk became graveyards for both men and machinery. In desperation, we had destroyed our guns and transport, to deny these to the German Army, leaving a scene of disaster unparalleled in the history of British warfare. And now on the beaches of Dunkirk on the French coast, where, on a clear day, the white cliffs of Dover could be seen, the remnants of our defeated force assembled, and we prayed for a miracle to occur. The dead bodies of both civilians and soldiers were everywhere, and the scrapped guns and vehicles cluttered the approaches to the west in increasing volume. It was to be the greatest defeat in memory for the British and French Armies. The numbers of soldiers on the Dunkirk beaches soared from a few thousand to tens of thousands.

With little protection, our troopers were exposed on those open beaches to the murderous Luftwaffe machine-gunning and bombing attacks. My regiment, positioned with the Norfolk Infantry, had suffered the humiliation of having to destroy our guns and now the men had little more than rifles and pistols to fight off the terrible onslaught of the Blitz from the air. In vain they tried to stave off the Messerschmidts, but those pitiful weapons were useless against the airborne terrors; it looked like the end had come for the British. They were about to be totally wiped out.

And then our miracle happened.

VON RUNSTED HAD ordered his armoured columns to halt in order to regroup and to replenish. They had fought furiously since their invasion of the Lowlands and now required time to prepare for the battle against the French in southern France, which he anticipated would be their next task. He believed that the armour had done its job and that it was now up to the infantry to finish off. Adolf Hitler had approved that order, and so the BEF stayed relatively securely within a small perimeter.

For the Allied forces this was divine providence, allowing the miracle that was to take place. The man who planned and consummated this miracle was Sir Bertram Ramsey, Flag Officer, Dover, and he carried out his scheme from his headquarters under Dover Castle, far underground in the impervious tunnels that had been used since Roman times. This labyrinth of tunnels was manned mostly by naval personnel, including a contingent of Wrens, who, amongst other things, ran the switchboards. It was said that those tunnels were haunted by three ghosts, one of whom was a Wren; she and her lover had committed suicide and were now constantly searching for each other. They were both frightened of the third ghost, who was reputed to be in love with the Wren himself and wanted to harm her lover. Many years later I visited those tunnels, and as I walked along in the Stygian gloom, I swear that I felt a hand touch my shoulder. I shivered as I wondered if it was the ghost of the lover, or the one who wished to kill him.

Operation Dynamo, as the evacuation by sea was known, though hurried, was not entirely unpremeditated. On May 14, boat owners had been asked by the British Government to register their craft, and the compiled list showing the disposition of these boats was given to Admiral Ramsey. An unbelievably wide variety of craft of all sizes was used to rescue the soldiers from those death-filled beaches. The Royal Navy was highly profiled, with cruisers, thirty destroyers, machine-gun boats and many smaller supporting vessels. Then there was a remarkable assortment of freighters, ferryboats, tugboats, coalers, yachts, ketches and sailing ships of all kinds. There were small motorboats and pleasure schooners. There were even paddleships, dinghies and rowing boats. Many of the larger craft, the destroyers and the ferryboats, had to tie up at the one available mole, which was nearly a mile long, although just a few feet wide, but even the larger vessels which had to stay offshore were a refuge for those of us who swam or sailed out in the tiny boats. There were long lines of soldiers snaking out from the murder on the beaches to the haven of those boats which were close enough to wade out to. All those who sailed across to our beleaguered army at Dunkirk were themselves heroes, for they too braved the German destroyers, the U-boats and the German Air Force, all of whom were present in great strength.

There were devastating losses amongst those brave British sailors as they plucked the men from the hell of those beaches. The casualty rate on the bombed ships, which were jammed with hundreds of troops on the open decks, was horrendous. Many of these vessels were sunk, and many of the sailors on them died in their brave efforts to save their fellow countrymen. It was a nightmare of strafing; at one time there were as many as two hundred Messerschmidts and Stukas bombing us on the tightly packed beaches. The noise of the machine-guns and the bombs, and the shriek of the aircraft as they attacked again and again was both deafening and terrifying. Though stoic, there were cries of help from the injured troops on the war-torn beaches, but little could be done for them.

At the beginning it was thought that only a handful of men could be rescued. It took guts to wait on those long, exposed beaches, where the only cover was the powdery sand. Though repeatedly machine-gunned, on the beaches and in the water, the soldiers stuck on those naked stretches showed an orderly discipline throughout the attacks of the fighter planes and the bombers, which came on, interminably, their only opposition the few rifles and machine-guns pointed at them. The pathetic scene of the waiting men amidst the carnage on the beaches was covered by great columns of smoke from the damaged and blazing oil tanks near the town, and the smell, mixed with the stench of the rotting bodies of the men and animals lying around, was overpowering.

By the blessing of God the seas were calm and warm, and the rescuers were men of great determination, many of them civilians, sailing their own small boats or yachts. Through their courage almost a third of a million soldiers, some of whom were French or Belgian, were snatched from the concerted efforts of the German Army, Navy and the Luftwaffe. Unfortunately, there were few of our own RAF areoplanes at the scene; they were operating further inland, intercepting the enemy at their bases. There was some bad feeling amongst the troopers about this; they felt they should have been given more protection by their own boys. So the Luftwaffe had a field day, on the beaches and on the water.

But it was those men who had waited so stoically on the beaches and got home despite all the Third Reich's efforts who were to be the nucleus of the army which would eventually defeat Hitler. They had been saved by the Navy and those courageous part-time sailors who risked all in their own small boats so they could fight again. Thus ended the débâcle in France, the scene of so many famous battles down the ages, at Ypres, at Waterloo and at Agincourt.

SO RETURNED THE remnants of the British Expeditionary Force and some French survivors: of the three hundred and thirty nine thousand rescued, one hundred and thirty nine thousand were French soldiers. Many still carried rifles, bayonets and light machine-guns as they walked down the gangplanks of the sea-going ships, or swam from the tiny coracles. Some required little assistance. Others were so badly wounded it was question-able if they would live. The hospital ships had sought the mercy of the Germans, but the U-boats had sunk them mercilessly. And then there were the dead to be taken ashore, to be buried on English soil.

The survivors were met at the south coast ports of England, where the loving and compassionate residents turned out en masse to greet and welcome home the men who, in their eyes, were not defeated soldiers, but heroes. And we all prayed for those who had made possible the escape by remaining on the beach: the men of the rearguard who had held the enemy at bay, who were left to the dubious mercy of the Germans, to the prisoner of war camps, and to the SS. It was June 2 and it was all over. It had taken just twenty-three days.

chapter ten

OFFICER CADET TRAINING UNIT

June 1940 to November 1940

The war had not gone well for us British soldiers so far. Crushed by the staggering weight of the German Blitzkrieg, which ended our campaign in a matter of days, we were driven back relentlessly to what was to become the most ignominious defeat ever suffered by the British Army. The French had surrendered and lain down their arms; Britain now stood alone, German invasion dangerously imminent. But we were short of both men and tools to stave off defeat; to rebuild and re-equip would take time which might not be available before the onslaught began. This was not to be the beginning of the end, but rather, the beginning of the beginning.

The free world must now look to the west, for that was the only forge capable of meeting the tremendous demands if the struggle was to continue. And the United States of America would not be found wanting in the need to meet this voracious demand for men and weapons of war: the trickle would start, and grow with increasing strength every day until it became a mighty river. Only then would the tide change and the now-defeated British Army regain its glory. In adversity, the resolve of the English was strong, but whilst that spirit was willing, the flesh – in the form of armaments – was presently very weak.

Winston Churchill, the new Prime Minister of Great Britain, said in his stirring broadcast, 'We cannot flag or fail. We shall go on to the end. We shall fight in France, we shall fight on the seas and on the oceans. We shall defend our Island whatever the cost may be. We shall fight on the beaches, we shall fight on the landing-grounds, in the fields, in the streets, and in the hills. We shall never surrender . . .' The effect of that speech, which he made on June 4, 1940, reverberated throughout the nation, and the response from the people of the whole of the British Empire, was unequivocal: there was a dedication and a determination by all, young or old, to stay and fight to the bitter end.

I HAD BEEN very fortunate. I had taken what was believed to be the last ferry from Calais, just hours before the Germans swept through the Lowlands. But my regiment had suffered badly; they had been in the same area as the Norfolk Infantry Regiment, which had been butchered by Storm Troopers with machine-gun fire when trying to surrender, and it was feared my colleagues had suffered the same fate. Those of my fellows who survived told me of how the guns – the Colours – were disabled, and of the heartbreaking scenes that triggered. Though many colleagues died, a number of my good friends did get home safely. But not Smudger Smith, one of my closest.

I had been told several weeks before those grim days that I had been selected to attend the Officer Cadet Training School. To hear on my arrival in England of the loss of so many of my friends, and of the dismantling of the guns, was a very sad start indeed to my new career.

I was to be stationed in Ilkley, and then at Filey on the north-east coast of Yorkshire, for six months of very intensive training. The pressure to cram in what would, under normal conditions, have taken several years, was enormous; I had barely a moment to think of anything else beyond the training, let alone the chance to mourn my lost friends and comrades. The work periods were from seven in the morning until five in the afternoon, then, after supper, we cadets would be out on the cliffs digging trenches by six o'clock. That part of the English coast was considered a likely landing place for a German invasion, and to man the great stretches of beaches was a major task in light of the few soldiers available. It was a common belief that when the invasion came, it would do so at dawn (the British Army always did things at dawn!) so all our careful preparations were based on that likelihood.

We cadets dug the trenches, sited to provide good observation and fields of fire across the ocean, and, having done so, stayed on duty in those trenches until first light. Shifts were organized to allow two hours on and two off, and during the off periods one could attempt to sleep in the misery of the damp trenches. Blankets, wet and muddy after the first night, were the only gesture of comfort for those of us using the holes in the sandy cliffs as bedrooms. There were few rifles; perhaps one man in ten had one, with fifty rounds of 303 ammunition at the most, and none in reserve. For the rest there were pick-helves and staves and precious little else. God knows how we'd have fared had the Germans come with their top-of-the-range machine-guns and all their other upmarket war kit. All that we cadets and the other soldiers and Home Guardsmen manning the coast-line of England had to offer were sticks, fists and boots, and a great deal of raw courage. It was hardly enough to stop the Juggernaut that would come with brimstone and fire.

After a very rough night, and as soon as it was light enough to see, it was back to the billets for breakfast, followed by the first lecture or exercise. In retrospect, I wondered how I'd ever managed to absorb the course material as there was precious little sleep at night and during the daytime there was the constant fear that the invasion fleets would be seen off the coast.

We had a lot of lessons about the hierarchy of the army, the organi-zation of the Infantry and their deployment, and, to a lesser degree, the Royal Air Force. The Royal Navy element was even smaller – quite micro-scopic, really. We looked at the structure of a corps, and an infantry division, down to the brigade and the battalion level; the composition of these units was considered in much greater detail, and we had many exercises where we were required to deploy them in various situations. The role of armour and artillery was dealt with in great details; we accompanied units actually rehearsing those functions.

The trainee officer was taught how to deliver an *Appreciation* – or assessment – *of a Situation*, detailing information under the headings of *Enemy* and *Own Troops*, designed to illustrate, amongst other things, posi-tions and strengths, followed by the *Intention*, which would show (either succinctly or in some detail) who would go where, what these were indi-cating within the stages of the plan, the order of battle, the boundaries, and so on. It would include the support available from artillery, engineers and armour. The intention was usually to attack the enemy (heaven alone knew what with!); it was rarely to retreat, because the British Army was already adept at that, having had lots of practice. The *Method* would describe the order of battle; this might be down to the section level, in the case of a company action, or at the higher divisional level, with the brigade or battalion status. Other components of the British Army ritual would follow.

This was great fun when the process was applied to more mundane things, like going out on the town in the evening: it took little imagination to appreciate the planning results of a typical evening which, for most of us, would require doing the pubs, the women, and the pubs again.

After the first few months, the tempo eased off a bit. All the slit-trenches had been dug and many filled in. The soldiers who had returned from France had now recovered enough to show some semblance of organization, and could at least participate in manning the beaches. The need to keep a close watch was also declining. With less pressure on us, we now had a little free time in the evenings and weekends.

Most of the course curriculum dealt with understanding the organization and methods of making war; I was surprised that it hardly touched on the human relations aspect within military organizations, or man management, as it was then known. Nor were we taught what relationship should exist between a King's commissioned officer and the men in the ranks, and how we should interact. So man management was unimportant, an aspect that was touched upon only cursorily: there was a war on, and the enemy was knocking on the door; *that* was what was important. (And anyway, everybody knew about the men being fed before anyone else . . .)

THE DEMAND FOR officers was, of course, quite enormous, in view of the extremely rapid growth of the British Army, so the necessary calibre and qualifications were not as stringent as they were in peacetime. In some ways, this was good; those selected from the ranks, like me, were not chosen for breeding or social status, but rather for their proven ability as leaders of men and knowledge of matters military. Those with university degrees and specialists in specific fields received preference in their appointment to the service branches like the Royal Army Service Corps or the Catering Corps, their powers of leadership a secondary consideration. Those appointed to the rank of temporary war commission came in all shapes and sizes, poor and rich, ignorant and learned. Civilian rank was of no importance for these war substantive officers, whether they served on the field of battle, in the technical trades or as backroom boffins. Officers newly commissioned from the ranks often found it difficult to integrate, especially when appointed to a regular unit in which most of the officers held peacetime commissions – or having earned their appointments in a 'more acceptable manner', as they were inclined to say. Sometimes they would receive only reluctant recognition from the Regulars, and were often snubbed for not being *real* soldiers, there 'merely' to fight in the war.

But I was lucky, and didn't meet any of these problems. I'd been a ranker, so I had a good idea of the feelings on both sides of the fence; if anything, I was the aloof one – after all, I was ex-Royal Horse Artillery, and that more than made up for any failings I might have had. Occasionally we new boys were looked down upon by those who believed they were of superior breeding, even though they were newly appointed themselves.

But that was in the early days of the war: when the drums began to roll in earnest, the shrapnel began to take its toll and the blood began to flow, it was a different matter, and soon all new officers were taken at face value. When you are the target of enemy guns, you don't stop to consider the breeding of the man next to you. Dunkirk had already demonstrated that an uneducated man of poor breeding from the industrial slums of England could exhibit not only competent military skills and bravery in the face of defeat, but could rise above a desperate situation with courage, whilst being an inspiration to others. And this was demonstrated time and again. Those who graduated from the ranks made invaluable contributions, because of their experience and their ability to soldier on in conditions of gross hardship. This applied throughout the Service: foot soldiers, gunners, cavalrymen, or the service component of the army; their knowledge and their ability to impart these skills was vital to the rapid expansion of the Armed Forces. They invariably had a positive attitude, in even the most adverse conditions, and proved to be towers of strength to those in the ranks who were new arrivals from civilian life.

Even in these grim times, to become an officer in the British Army was still a great accomplishment, not lightly attained. The prestige and pleasure it brought was enormous. For centuries the acquisition of a King's or Queen's Commission had been achieved chiefly by money; less than a hundred years ago George Bingham, the Earl of Lucan and a leader in the Battle of Waterloo débâcle, had a commission bought for him in the 6th Regiment of Foot as a sixteenth birthday present. With it went all the gay balls and other occasions graced by the presence of a flock of beautiful, cultured ladies. And there was the glory of Trooping the Colour, or marching along Pall Mall before thousands of eager spectators, wearing the gorgeous dress of an élite regiment, knowing that by virtue of holding the King's Commission, you owned a part of that regiment, even if you were just a teenager. Keeping up with the Lucans would be hard for his schoolmates; within ten years, again by purchase, he commanded the famous 17th Lancers. The cost of that cornetcy was twenty thousand pounds, about the going rate for a cavalry command.

Lord Cardigan, James Brudenell, also of Waterloo fame, and Lord Lucan's brother-in-law, was another who had a meteoric rise: his purchase into the 8th Hussars was made for him at the age of twenty-seven; he bought himself a captaincy just two years later. Six years later he paid forty thousand pounds to command the 15th Hussars. Within the year he was fired from the position but, through friends in high places, persuaded the Duke of Wellington and Lord Hill to grant him the command of the 11th Dragoons for another forty thousand pounds.

Here were people actually spending money to buy into the army, and into senior positions, whereas many of the rank and file, me included, often wished we could do just the reverse. But to find a hundred pounds – for that was what it cost to buy a discharge in my day – on an earning of a shilling and tuppence a day . . . my status as a humble trumpeter in the hierarchy of the army is clearly put into perspective. But I did make Captain at the tender age of twenty-two.

Some of the Officer Cadet candidates were chosen because of their peacetime occupations: bank clerks, car salesmen, factory supervisors. Those with engineering degrees or other technical qualifications were obviously eagerly sought. There were, inevitably, those upper crust types whose sole ambition in life was to spend their parents' money in as glamourous a way as possible; quite what glamour there is in war I have yet to discover. It was a surprising experience for me to mix with such a diverse group, because I'd never really been in contact with younger civilians, nor had I started work seriously in a civilian occupation, as these men had done. It was also surprising that we all got along so well together.

My voice by now had acquired almost a neutral accent, while most of the newly recruited civilians spoke with the dialect of whichever county they hailed from. A discerning observer could distinguish not only which county of Britain a person came from, but precisely which town, and sometimes even the neighbourhood. But one could not always easily tell whether or not a person really spoke the King's English, and this led to a great deal of fun unmasking people. We were all to find that the regular British Army was officered largely by *pukka sahibs*, most with Eton and Oxbridge education (and accent), and consequently, to be accepted one had to speak their language, or *bolo the bat*, as Smudger would have said. And they had trained at Sandhurst, that elite, fashionable establishment for officer soldiers.

Not all of these potential officers made the grade; they were failed for a variety of reasons, ranging from lacking the ability to command to general incompetence in the art of soldiering. It was a summary dismissal, which came suddenly, often as a surprise, to the unfortunate person who was returned forthwith to his unit, or RTU'd, as it was known. It must have been devastating, to say the very least, having to go back to your own regiment branded a failure; I wondered why they'd been recommended for officer training in the first place. Out of fifty of us at the OCTU, seven were RTU'd – I held my breath myself at times!

THEN CAME THE welcome day when the course ended. Diplomas were handed out and we were gazetted with little ceremony – there was another group of cadets waiting for our billets and classrooms. A week or so earlier we had been fitted with the officer's dress uniforms by Moss Brothers, the recognized provider to His Majesty's Army: serge tunics and trousers, shirts, ties, peaked caps and that crowning glory: the Sam Browne belt. We cadets would continue to wear the issue battledress in which we'd arrived for the course, but now we could remove the white lapels from the shoulder straps showing us as cadet trainees, and mount a single pip in their place. There was an allowance for the purchase of this clothing, which barely covered the cost, but I felt rich enough now to buy out of my own pocket a winter warm coat of a golden colour. I thought it made me look the part – even if I wasn't – and it was the best article of clothing I had ever owned. And to crown it all, I really broke out and bought a dress side hat in the artillery red and blue colours. Now I really looked like an officer.

In my new dress uniform with its gleaming solitary pip, brown shoes and cap complete with artillery badge, and the swagger stick I now sported, I looked most elegant; I was truly the *pukka sahib*. But as I wore my uniform in the billets that night, I, like many of the new officers, was overcome with a massive sense of inadequacy: how could *I* possibly carry the yoke of the responsibilities which now weighed so heavily on my shoulders? Looking like an officer of the King was one thing, behaving and being accepted as one was altogether something else.

There was a wild party that evening, and we forty-three new officers who were to make the British Army powerful once again hit the town. How we ex-cadets laughed at each other as we paraded the following morning, prior to going on a week's furlough. As we dispersed, we recalled the drunken debauch of the previous evening, and of the long months we'd spent together, and talked about a reunion after the war. And that was definite, there was going to be an *after the war*. But few of us would live long enough for that.

So away I marched in my new role, already feeling more secure, swinging my swagger stick and wearing my issue Smith and Wesson pistol. I also felt comforted about my commitment to the army: in order to be commissioned, first I had to relinquish the agreement I'd made all those years ago, to serve the country for nine years with the colours and three in reserve. Only then could I be offered, and accept, the King's commission – and that commitment was only until the end of the hostilities; then I would be free. Was it really six years ago that I had sat in front of the Recruiting Sergeant in Blackpool, the man who had generously signed me on for a lifetime in the army, for the measly sum of one shilling? Flushed with all the success of having graduated to the exalted station of a King's officer, and the new authority bestowed on us, we went off to join our new units.

DURING THE SUMMER of that year, Hitler had threatened that a sea-borne attack, codenamed Sea Lion, would be made on England in September; all that he was waiting for was the total destruction of the Royal Air Force.

Herman Goering had claimed it would be child's play for his Luftwaffe to eliminate the RAF from the battle in four days, and so he sent over a thousand bombers and fighters to destroy the British airfields, the British planes and the British pilots. But he failed miserably, finding the RAF stronger and more determined than he had ever anticipated, and those brave and skilful British airmen were able to save the day. Of immeasurable help was the development of radar by Robertson Watt, which meant that the air defence could now be organized to provide the maximum coverage of the most vulnerable areas along the coasts of England. Watt's timely invention provided not only the identity of the planes – whether they were German or British – but also the location, and the numbers of aircraft reported in a given area. This provided a significant advantage to the defenders and gave the RAF another opportunity to again save the day. So December passed without the Germans seeing Hitler's promise of England being invaded. With the failure of Operation Sea Lion, Hitler had truly missed the boat. And the writing was on the wall for him.

Edward, the Prince of Wales was very much in the news at the time. When the King of England had died in 1936, the Prince had been declared Britain's new King and assumed the throne, with plans for his coronation getting underway. Though fashionable, he was considered to be a fop, and as a bachelor had always had a weakness for married women; his commitment to the American divorcée Wallis Simpson, 'the woman he loved', soon placed his position in jeopardy. When Mrs Simpson eventually filed for divorce from her second husband, Ernest Simpson, about a year later, the King abdicated the throne and the couple were married in France. No member of the Royal Family attended the wedding. It was well known that Prince Edward and his wife were sympathetic towards Hitler, and people were concerned about the agreeable relationship they had with Nazi Germany.

When war was declared, the newly titled Duke of Windsor took a commission and gave himself a posting to Paris where, with Wally, he lived in high style. When France was occupied by the Germans after Dunkirk, instead of returning to England, as a serving officer should have done, the Duke and Duchess of Windsor moved to the south of the country, where they continued to live in luxury, whilst the rest of France and Britain suffered severely. So close was their relationship with the occupying

Germans that the Duchess's maid received Nazi approval to go to Paris, not only to recover some of their goods, but to do some further shopping. Later on, in Spain, it was noted that the Duke of Windsor appeared on the friendliest of terms with the Gestapo. The whole of Britain wondered about this, and questioned whose side was he on now – he was, after all, still technically a British commissioned officer.

The Duke of Windsor was finally appointed the King's representative to the Bahamas, where, throughout the rest of the war, he and his wife lived in opulence, travelling as freely as they wished; Wally even returned to New York to see a dentist. Many considered him a deserter from the British Army, because of his non-return to England following the occupation of France, and held that he should have been court-martialled. After the war they settled again in Paris, but travelled extensively, mostly to the United States. They did not visit England: the Duke never forgave the British Royal Family for refusing to grant the title of Her Royal Highness to the Duchess. In spite of the rift, the Duke and Duchess continued to live happily, in peace and luxury, wanting for nothing until the time of their deaths.

chapter eleven

134 FIELD REGIMENT RA: DURHAM TO FELIXSTOWE

December 1940 to December 1941

Few people had any high ideals when it came to fighting this war. Perhaps they'd began by joining up to fight for King and country, and for their homeland, and all that they loved – even to save the civilized world from the greedy oppressor. But the beliefs of those diehards changed quickly enough when it became clear that all these elevated motives were nothing more than pipedreams, and that there was a real danger that we would lose the war against Germany. It was no longer a question of God being on our side, or of saving the King and others whom we had worshipped for so long. We were fighting for our lives and, make no mistake, we developed a far more bloodthirsty outlook on life: maim or be maimed; kill or be killed. All was fair in love and war.

Yet in spite of this change, the attitude of the average British soldier or civilian remained that of *sans souci*, 'Couldn't care less'. If you were going to die, you were going to die, so there was no point in worrying about it. And you came to accept the fact that it could happen to you tomorrow, if not today. It's strange, but many people were happier during those days of struggle than they had been in peacetime. And you never thought about defeat: that was unthinkable. Instead, you worried about the unimportant matters: what was the weather going to be like, and could you afford to go to the flicks? To most civilians it would be, could the butcher be persuaded to divvy up a little more than the ration book allowed? And cigarettes, you just had to have them at any price, and it didn't matter if the Wicked Hun was winning or losing. That could wait, and you'd be there when the chips were down, and anyway, Jerry had it coming. But all in good time. In my hierarchy of needs, it was a question of whether or not I would be able to buy toothpaste or razor blades – or if the pubs would run out of beer: I had to keep things in perspective!

Britain was still weak: thanks to the defeat in France, we were no match now for our adversary; we'd lost the cream of our army and it would take time to rebuild before we would be powerful enough to meet the enemy again on the field of battle. There were no noble thoughts about saving the Empire, let alone the world, from the tyranny of evil, or fighting for the King with God looking on approvingly and on our side. We were fighting for our very lives now. The country was fast becoming a fortress with bunkers, pillboxes and road blocks everywhere. Towering iron girders in the shape of the letter X were sunk on the beaches as tank obstacles, and rows of coiled barbed wire piled six feet high and six feet wide were laid at intervals of twelve feet apart surrounding the island. Air raid shelters were springing up in the towns and the villages; many people were building their own individual shelters in their back gardens. As far back as 1938, in the town centre of Stockport in Lancashire, a labyrinth of passages was cut in the soft, red sandstone to provide an extensive system of air raid shelters. They were equipped with lighting, toilets and washing facilities, First Aid and Wardens' areas and bunk beds.

People were becoming accustomed to the air raid sirens and to the bombing, which was now increasing in intensity; to the rationing and shortages, especially of luxury items. With everything in short supply, the black market was beginning to flourish – if one had the money, nothing was unobtainable. Arising from this was the trite – though common – saying: 'Don't you know there's a war on?' If you went into a store and asked for a packet of cigarettes, you were most likely to be told, 'We don't have any. Don't you know there's a war on?' Coming from a civilian, that rankled, to say the very least. But if you placed a silver coin on the counter as you asked, more often than not cigarettes would magically appear. It was distasteful, but it could hardly be avoided.

With the arrival of petrol rationing, the black market in petrol coupons flourished; you could trade yours for just about anything you wanted. The allowance per car was sufficient to drive around fifty miles a week, and that was just at the beginning; later on, it got far worse. So you could almost ask your own price for a gallon of petrol. The military were up to their eyes in these rackets; it was a common sight to meet a soldier on the roadside offering a can of petrol for sale which, though at an exorbitant price, was usually snapped up. The hapless motorist, driving on and congratulating himself on his good fortune, would, more often than not, find two Military Policemen around the next bend, flagging him down and accusing him of improperly obtaining rationed petrol. In shock at being caught so quickly, and prepared to avoid what could be a severe penalty for such an illegal act, the poor driver would willingly agree to an instant fine of five pounds and confiscation of the cans of petrol. But if he cared to look back after he'd driven on a bit further, he'd have seen the petrol vendor had joined the bogus MPs, all laughing their heads off at yet another sucker having fallen into their trap.

Directional signs across the country had been removed, causing far more confusion to the residents than the Germans would ever have experienced. There were suspected spies in every nook and cranny, and posters in tube trains, on the buses, and in the toilets constantly warned you: *Even the walls have ears!* People were reporting seeing German soldiers walking and shopping in the Bond Street shops in London; one day two wags did dress in German Army uniforms and walked down Bond Street – and no one accosted them or even reported their presence!

President Franklin D. Roosevelt had promised that his country's arsenal would be freely available, and the wheels of industry were beginning to turn when the trickle of aid from the Lend Lease programme with the United States of America began to flow. The call-up of eligible men and women began to swell the ranks of the services. And on the land, agriculture took a stride forward as the Land Girls came into being. But there was a long way to go, and the country was still struggling to achieve a measure of preparation.

THE REGIMENT THAT I joined, 134 Field Regiment, was very much undermanned, and equipped with relatively ancient artillery pieces dating back to the end of the nineteenth century. When war broke out many of the men had neither uniforms, nor steel helmets, and continued to parade in mufti, whilst the regular soldiers amongst them wore the uniforms they had been issued with in peacetime. So we were a motley-looking lot to start with. Eventually the uniforms arrived and were issued, albeit in dribs and drabs, and then it was common to see a man wearing a regulation tunic and riding breeches and carrying a gas mask – WWI-style, of course – with his own civilian trilby and brown pointed winkle-picker shoes. He was a ludicrous sight, and when we marched in formation, it was hilarious to watch. But it was not all bad. The headquarters of one Battery were first located in a pub, then the other Batteries of the regiment also found it to necessary to find a similarly convenient place to hold their own briefing sessions.

I, and another officer also posted to the 134 Field Regiment, arrived in the early winter to see the 213 Battery practising gun drill in a large area that had once been a school playground. After standing unseen for fifteen minutes watching them bringing the guns into action, we smiled at each other, and I commented, 'They look a real shower, don't you think?'

Guy De Bouvre (he was one of the wealthy OCTU candidates, dressed in serge dress uniform, Sam Browne and riding breeches, with highly polished knee-length brown leather riding boots, and with an accent you could cut with a knife) said, 'Yes, they are rather, aren't they? But look at the material.' And he was right, they did look a fine bunch of men, and their alertness, if not their drill sequence, left nothing to be desired. 'We'll soon put that right,' he said. 'Or you will anyway, Penny, won't you?'

I smiled and promised, 'But of course. There's room there for a bit of the Horse Artillery dressing.'

The men were part of a territorial unit whose history went back a hundred years; they'd seen a variety of ordnance, including 4.5 howitzers and 25-pounders, at the outbreak of war. But they had lost the 25-pounders to a regular regiment, which had had to destroy the guns at Dunkirk, and now they were equipped with French 75-mm. These were nice enough guns with a good reputation, easy to manoeuvre and with a range of six thousand yards. But they suffered several deficiencies, not the least of which was there were only twenty rounds per gun available! And they had the most peculiar dial sights, which talked in terms of pillars and quadrants. This was, at first, deeply confusing to the gun detachments who, having lived so long with British dial sights and being accustomed to degrees and minutes, found them difficult to get along with.

Another major handicap was transportation; flatbed vehicles were commandeered, but loading the guns without damaging them wasn't easy, because their carriage weight was over a thousand pounds. Using the improvised loading ramps was a challenging and difficult procedure, to say the least. We had to take the greatest care, or they'd come crashing down to the ground again. Still, they were artillery pieces, and thus worth their weight in gold, shortage of ammunition or not. And beggars could not be choosers. It was also good experience for us, as one day we'd be man-handling guns weighing approximately two thousand seven hundred pounds, so at least we started developing the appropriate muscles now. I wondered where these 75-mm guns had come from; they were certainly not from Dunkirk, although the beaches had been littered with them, but I never did find out.

The territorial troops were a mixture of young and old, from all walks of life. Many were married and not at all happy about leaving their families to go to war. A good sprinkling of Regulars had been transferred in to provide the experience the Territorials sorely lacked, but this didn't always sit too well with the 'weekend warriors', as they were sarcastically known. But the old troopers were a tower of strength, and when they started passing on their soldiering knowledge, eventually the younger men began to welcome them. They soon became seasoned soldiers themselves and grew to be proud of their regiment. Guy and I were posted to different Batteries, Guy to the 340 and me to the 213.

We were both taken aback at first at how little the men knew or understood about artillery; we were soon in great demand as instructors, lecturing and demonstrating the arts of gunnery. This was especially true for me; having qualified as an Artillery Surveyor, I was able to discourse at length on a variety of technicalities: silent registration, coordinates, slide rules and logarithms to compute ranges, the conversion of bearings (grid, magnetic and true north), meteor reports – with allowances for wind, drift, and temperatures – calibration and droop (every gun is different), angles of sight, clinometers using sub-bases to compute distances and angles (one degree subtends to one hundred yards at a distance of six thousand yards) – at the tender age of twenty-one, these were all old hat to me now. Then there were the different charges for the ammunition to explain, all varying with the gun in question, the fall of shot and bracketing; barrages, static, rolling, and creeping. Gunnery topics were endless. And between leaving OCTU and joining the regiment, I'd spent a month training at the Army Communications Centre at Catterick, so I was in demand to lecture about wireless and field telephones as well.

There were lighter moments amongst all this intensive activity: like the occupation by my troop in a 'crash action' whilst training in the countryside near the city of Durham, which was famous for its beautiful, very popular golf course. I knew exactly what this action entailed from my Royal Horse Artillery days: when a crash action was called for, the guns were expected to be brought into action immediately, as there was a target urgently requiring attention – usually in support of the infantry. It was a sacred occasion, not to be treated lightly, and nothing must interfere with it.

On this occasion, when the order was received over the wireless, I went through the usual drill of identifying the coordinates of the stipulated position and plotting my route. At that moment, my troop was travelling along a narrow road running parallel to the locally revered golf course. The gun position lay on the other side of it, and it was abundantly clear to me that crossing the golf course was the quickest way to get there. It never entered my head to do otherwise.

Casting aside all doubts, I promptly led the troop off the road and made for that all-important plot of ground: the proposed gun position. I almost set a new record for my crash action, but instead of being praised for my masterly action, I was brought to task for committing an unforgivable sin. It had rained heavily for the past few days – rain is as endemic to that area as it is in Newport – and some twenty wide-tyred, heavily laden vehicles had roared across the course, leaving a trail of ruts twelve to eighteen inches deep, impressions not even an elephant could have improved upon. Much like any British Army parade square anywhere, the golf course was hallowed ground, and even before the troop was back in its billets the first complaints had been lodged with the Colonel.

At ten o'clock the following morning I was summoned to his office, where, in the presence of the Secretary of the golf club, an inquisition was enacted, in which I was easily the loser. The Secretary was obviously prepared to come to blows with me, and my CO was equally upset – he too was an ardent golfer. Pleading that there was a war on was to no avail; it warranted the reply, 'But dammit, is nothing sacred to you?' I wasn't a golfer, and could never understand how grown men could be so entertained by such a boring game when there were so many other worthwhile things to do in life.

The outcome was that I got a rocket for ruining the golf course, followed by a compliment for getting the guns into action so quickly! The Colonel and the Secretary promptly returned to the golf club together.

It was a busy life. During the day there were endless parades, exercises and lectures; in the evenings there were the pubs – when the all-too-frequent night exercises were not taking place. But soon it was time to say goodbye to dear old England and sail for Destination Unknown.

1941 HAD ALSO been a very busy year politically. In April the Germans had invaded Greece and Yugoslavia, both of which capitulated a few days later, and put the Eighth Army under siege at Tobruk. Hitler had invaded Russia, and Leningrad was also besieged; tens of thousands were to die on both sides. The massive British battleship *Hood* was sunk, losing with it all hands. Rudolf Hess had flown from Germany to England under conditions of great secrecy, and the reason was never made public. On the plus side, an intact Enigma machine had been seized from the captured German submarine *U110*.

At the end of the year there was a catastrophic attack on Pearl Harbor by the Japanese, which brought the United States into the war. There would be worse to follow. There was little hope of any great improvement; and the only happy faces in the world were Teutonic.

The air raid shelters all over Britain were in constant use, and no one got much sleep when the bombing was at its height. In London many people used the underground railway system deep below the surface; the tube tunnels were a godsend. Whole families would move in regularly after supper during the Blitz, with crying babies, toddlers refusing to let go of their tricycles or other beloved toys. Mums and dads would bring bedding, water and food, not forgetting their dogs and other pets. Home for them each night was the twenty-foot-wide concrete strip alongside the very busy underground railway lines, where trains were scheduled every few minutes from five in the morning until midnight. It was a noisy, dangerous environment, with the trains creating massive airflows, making it very draughty. The overpowering smell of humanity crammed into those tiny areas was at times reminiscent of the Black Hole of Calcutta, and the rows of makeshift beds were disturbed by frequent and stumbling visits to the toilets; the constant movement kept awakening people, making for a restless night for everyone. It was even harder on parents, who had to improvise to keep children occupied happily and quietly. It would be late when they finally settled in, and then morning came too soon; now they must pack up and be off to their homes to feed the family in time for the husband to go to work and the children to school. That was the daily ritual for many families throughout the Blitz.

Many people endured even worse. Enid, my future wife, and her sisters had moved to Birkenhead after being bombed out of their home in Liverpool. They had a five-mile walk across fields to the shelters under the sand hills, pushing their mother in a wheelchair all the way. They were not allowed into the shelters until ten o'clock at night, and were ousted at five in the morning for the two-hour walk back before breakfast. Enid then had to walk another two miles to get to the railway station to catch the underground train to Liverpool, then another two buses to reach her school. If she failed to produce her homework, or was late, she was severely chastised by the teacher. She'd won a scholarship to attend this school, and didn't want to give it up, but it wasn't easy keeping the standards that were expected; just because there was a war on, that was no excuse. Some people didn't know how lucky they were.

And there were many isolated incidents which seemed to us to typify the German nature. I saw a German fighter plane swoop down on the sleepy seaside town of Felixstowe one Saturday afternoon, machine-gunning the crowded High Street. Frantic women and children, for that was what they mostly were, ran hastily but fruitlessly for cover to escape the scything hail of lead. The Nazi pilot's cowardly action, perhaps born of frustration, killed and wounded many, many civilians. First aid was administered at the scene and the ambulances were busy that day. There were few troops around – we were on duty ceaselessly, with little time (or money) for personal shopping. The motive for the airman who needlessly machine-gunned innocent women and children was hard to understand. I later discovered that this was a not uncommon experience. It appeared that in wartime, literally any act was permissible.

chapter twelve

H M T *STRATHEDEN* :
DUNOON - DURBAN - BOMBAY

December 1941 to January 1942

My regiment sailed from Dunoon, on the Clyde, near Glasgow, to a destination unknown, although it was no secret in which direction we were sailing. We suspected we were going to south-east Asia, and we were pretty sure it would be a hot climate, because topees and tropical dress had been issued to all ranks.

The overnight train journey from southern England had brought us to the Scottish port in the early hours of a grey December morning. There was a hint of frost in the air. It would be Christmas soon; very likely it would snow – it usually did up here in the north and the festive season wouldn't be the same without it. But then, I mused, Blackpool always had fierce gales at this time of year, not snow, which we youngsters far preferred, of course. Perhaps I'd be wishing for just such a grey, cold day as this when I got to the end of this current journey; I'd certainly better start getting used to Christmases which weren't white again: the only snow I'd see for the next few years would be on the peaks of the Himalayas.

I didn't realize then that I wouldn't see these 'green and pleasant lands' for almost five years, though many of us were already sailing with heavy hearts: we knew full well that not all of us would return. The odds were overwhelming that too many of us would end up buried in a distant plot of ground that would then be *forever England.* But a few, mostly single men who'd never set foot out of England before, were enraptured at the thought of visiting foreign lands, meeting different people and experiencing new customs. For them it felt like a great adventure.

The convoy of some twenty-four ships shipped anchor from Dunoon at the start of our six-week voyage. I smiled ruefully to myself: this wasn't the first time that I had left my homeland for faraway places in the service of my country; I didn't know then, but it wouldn't be the last time either. The far-flung outposts of the British Empire had an insatiable appetite for servicemen, especially for soldiers, who often spent years in God-forsaken places remote from the civilization that they once knew as home. But our departure this day was very different to my last: there was none of the pomp and circumstance that surrounded peacetime postings overseas, no carnival atmosphere, no flags, streamers or balloons. Gone were the massed bands and the cheering crowds of families, friends and comrades shouting fond farewells and saluting their countrymen. Present emotions reflected the grim reality of the war, and of the imminent dangers to be faced in the submarine-infested waters which lay ahead of us: it was not a time for rejoicing. As we sailed, excitement was mixed with great sadness, which brought tears both to the few gathered ashore and to those of us who crowded the decks of the P&O luxury liner the *Stratheden*, which once had plied the England–Far East route for the pleasure of its wealthy passengers, and was now converted to a troop-ship in search of the enemy.

I looked into the grey waters of the North Sea that December day as my journey across five oceans began and reflected on the times I had already crossed these oceans – as a guest, and at the expense of the King of England, in all the questionable luxury of a military troop-ship then too. My first journey to Bombay, the gateway to India, the jewel in the crown of Britain's empire, was indeed memorable; how could I ever forget HMT *Neuralia*? She was so old that she was said to have served with distinction in the dispatch of troops for the East India Company during the days of Clive of India, in the eighteen hundreds. Of course, when I'd been on board, her lack of grace had been matched only by her discomforts; still, I had been very young – still a boy – and for me it was, however uncomfortable, a journey filled with the romance of distant countries, and the promise of an exotic life far from England's shores.

Awakened from my reverie by the siren blast of the ship, I recognized how different things were this time. Even the crystal-clear waters and the merrily crowded beaches at Blackpool were no more in wartime Britain. Now there was just the grim reality of sailing across oceans infested with German U-boats. Soon we'd be beyond the guardianship of the Royal Air Force, whose distant bases limited the boundaries of their operation. Our convoy would be venturing into the unknown, and we all knew how highly vulnerable we were to the predators lurking below.

The Nazi U-boats were the scourge of the Atlantic; the German submarines had played havoc with British convoys, striking wherever and whenever they chose, with devastating effect. Since sinking the old British battleship *Royal Oak* in Scapa Flow, our fleet's main anchorage off the Orkney Islands, in October 1941, and later the liner *Empress of Britain*, they had decimated Allied shipping. Within the last few weeks their victims had included the aircraft carrier *Ark Royal*, off the coast of Gibraltar; the battleship *Barham*, which went down with most of her thousand-man crew, and many other merchant ships. And just a few days later, on December 10, the *Prince of Wales* and the *Repulse* would be sunk off the Malayan coast. The Nazis called this Glücklichezeit, *the happy times*; and there was worse yet to come. This was a time none of us would ever forget.

Our convoy of two dozen vessels was to sail in a box formation of four columns. As we moved out into the open waters, we felt pitifully dependent on the meagre escort provided by the Royal Navy. The hearts of even the most experienced mariners quailed at the thought of the U-boats awaiting us in these rich hunting grounds; the wolf packs did not disappoint us. Nor did they to keep us waiting: within days our hapless convoy was struck by enemy U-boats, attacking us repeatedly. Even during the night the Nazi submarines penetrated our ranks and, in spite of the flares we fired to illuminate our attackers, the surfaced U-boats continued to torpedo us, claiming many victims. Even when they submerged to regroup, they stayed close to the surface, in constant readiness to strike again.

Even though we were living in permanent dread of being the next U-boat victims, we couldn't help imagining what it was like for those men trapped in the tiny tin hellhole that was the Nazi U-boat whenever we got our chance to fight back. As frightening as it was for us to see the wolves suddenly emerge from the depths, for those in the submarines, it must have been equally unnerving to hear the thumping of the piston engines growing louder, like the sound of an express train roaring through a tunnel, as hunter and prey drew closer together. And at the moment when the destroyer was directly overhead, dropping its depth charges, with the canisters exploding all around – sometimes even bouncing on the hull of the vessel – the submarine would shake all over, like a cat being worried in the mouth of a dog. The crew would freeze in silence, the tension extreme; they hardly dared to breathe, lest the ship above hear them. The display of power was enormous: whenever we thought of this, it made us realize the hell which must have existed for those in the submarines when they became the hunted instead of the hunter.

There were only three destroyers escorting our convoy, which was widely spread out, and they were late arriving. By the time the RN ships reached us, the U-boats had struck and were gone; though the destroyers fired depth charges, it seemed to us to be an utterly futile exercise, apparently succeeding in doing no more than ruffling the surrounding waters.

FOR THOSE OF us aboard the convoy it became habit, at the first light of dawn, to scan the seas to see how much destruction had been caused during the night. The count of ships was always fewer than the previous day. Every ship lost meant more of our comrades had left our ranks forever. Often the only evidence of the devastation visited on us by the Nazi U-boats was the distant smoke of a vessel in distress, which would never again rejoin our group. As I gazed across the endless stretch of ocean, I seemed to see enemy periscopes in every ripple of water; it required little imagination to spot torpedoes racing towards my ship.

And so it continued without respite as more than two hundred U-boats multiplied their victories in the Atlantic. There was also the constant threat of attack by German raiders – merchant ships converted to fighting ships, heavily armed and ready to pounce at any moment. We aboard the convoy could take no comfort in the knowledge that our losses, though severe, were but a fraction of the one-and-a-half million tons of shipping lost to the enemy by the end of 1941.

THE EX-P&O liner *Stratheden* was to be the last of the *wet ships*, as those ships that supplied liquor were commonly known – though on later sailings, it was surprising how the steward could usually find a drink if he were slipped a couple of bob. (It was even more surprising how many officers did have a couple of shillings, and more than once in an evening – in fact, there seemed to be an almost inexhaustible supply of those coins!) But soon the war would mean even the *Stratheden* would be dry, and it would take a miracle for Tommy to find a bottle of liquor aboard, certainly after the first week out. And this applied to all troop-ships: no more alcohol for the ranks.

But this time out I was an artillery officer, not a trooper, and it was a different matter for us. The officers and warrant officers on board were privileged, able to live in relative comfort. Although crammed four to a cabin originally designed for one, we enjoyed dining standards that most could only recall from pre-war days. Damask-covered tables were laid with silver cutlery, and the finest food imaginable was served by tuxedoed waiters: five-course dinners started with devils on horseback and finished with a soufflé. I had never dined so sumptuously, or in such an elegant setting. There was no sign of rationing here, of either food or liquor, and the prices were ridiculously cheap: you could get a double Scotch for threepence, and cigarettes were threepence a pack.

The protocol of seating was always observed, with the regiment's Commanding Officer sitting at the head of the table and his officers next to him in declining order of rank. I was almost – not quite – at the end of the table, where the regiment's second-in-command sat, facing the CO. And at the end of the meal the King was toasted: 'Mr Vice,' the Commanding Officer would say, 'The King.'

The second-in-command would respond, 'The King.' Then we officers would rise and, echoing the words, raise our glasses and drink a salute to His Majesty. The etiquette persisted throughout the voyage, as it did with most regiments throughout their service.

BUT THIS GOOD living was no compensation for the trials we endured on our voyage to the Far East, nor did it help against the constant attacks the convoy suffered from the Nazi wolf packs. We'd sailed seven thousand miles from the Clyde and were off the Cape Verde islands off the coast of Senegal, still a long way from the South African port of Cape Town. Although there were still fifteen hundred miles between Verde and the coast of Brazil, it was a relatively narrow stretch of water compared to the vast open areas we had been crossing, and a likely place for U-boats to gather. Our convoy was easy to find, and the U-boats promptly did just that, mounting a determined attack that left several more ships sunk or derelict. The attack continued as far as Cape Town, where we reached safety for a day, then it was off to round the Cape of Good Hope, where we endured yet another attack during our approach to Durban.

As before, the Nazi U-boats attacked again and again, mostly in the early hours of the morning. An early riser could sometimes see the torpedoes' tracks as they sped towards a doomed ship. It was all very nerve-racking; it became a morbid pastime of ours to count the vessels in view before darkness fell, and to compare numbers at breakfast time the following day; there were almost always fewer. It seemed rather incongruous to me that we officers of the regiment were living in the height of luxury – certainly we had a far better standard than was being enjoyed by many at home in Britain – whilst all around ships were being sunk and many sailors and soldiers were losing their lives. It was a terrible sight to go up on deck after breakfast and catch sight of a burning ship in the last throes of death. One day, at about nine in the morning, those on the top deck of the *Stratheden* actually saw two torpedoes weaving through the convoy, finally striking an oil tanker. The explosion was enormous and the ship was quickly engulfed in flames, erupting into a boiling cauldron. Men could be seen leaping over the side of the doomed vessel, only to meet their equally gruesome end in the flaming oil on the water. There were so few naval support vessels chaperoning the convoy that there was little they could do to stop the constant devastation.

The *Stratheden* was lucky to escape the deadly attacks of the U-boats. The convoy steamed at a slow speed, perhaps ten to fifteen knots per hour, and so we were all easy prey. There were no enemy aircraft in the skies, fortunately, for neither were there any British fighter planes; what little protection we had ended after we'd steamed two hundred miles into the Atlantic from the Clyde, and our shield didn't return until we reached the coast of India. There were few Allied aircraft off the coast of South Africa and although we understood the necessity for the planes to be in the North Atlantic, it served only to make us more apprehensive. During the course of the voyage we lost around ten ships and an unknown number of soldiers and sailors, despite the vigilance of our destroyers and their determined counter-attacks. Those few RN destroyers did a magnificent job; without them, none of us would have lived to see Durban, let alone the Far East.

The Royal Navy did its best to make a show of strength for the troops, and to promote a sense of security, and it was heartening to see the cruiser *Belfast* weaving through the convoy with a Royal Marine band on the fore-deck playing martial music. Dressed in white tunics, with white helmets and black leather belts, their brass buttons gleaming, the band members presented a picture of peace and tranquillity; it was a splendid sight, rather like a regatta in the Solent, or a day out on the river Thames. At that moment the war could have been a thousand miles away. *Belfast*, a symbol of invincibility with her huge 6-inch guns and enormous firepower, steamed parallel alongside each vessel, as close as fifty yards away, so that every-one could get a good view whilst the Marines serenaded the troops. As she sped away to the next ship the cheers of appreciation echoed after her.

There was great jubilation as the *Stratheden* rounded Cape of Good Hope and sailed into the harbour at Durban after four weeks on the Atlantic Ocean. The population gave us an incredible reception: the quays were crowded by civilians in their hundreds, who had arrived en masse with their cars – and their daughters – to greet the convoy. Standing on a fifty-foot-high platform, the eager troops gazing down on her from the *Stratheden*'s decks, Perle Sielde Gibson, the Lady in White, as she was to become known to the many thousands who passed on their way to the eastern battlefields, sang her heart out for us; songs like 'There'll be blue birds over the white cliffs of Dover', 'Wish me luck as you wave me goodbye', 'I'll be seeing you in all the old familiar places,' 'We'll meet again, don't know where, don't know when', and some of the jollier tunes like 'Roll out the barrel' and 'Doin' the Lambeth walk'.

Dressed in white, and wearing a white hat, Perle – who lost one of her own sons in the war – was reputed to have sung patriotic songs to a thou-sand troop-ships and more than three hundred and fifty hospital ships; in 1995 a statue to her was unveiled by Queen Elizabeth at that same jetty where she had reduced our hardened soldiers to tears. We were far away from home, and for all we knew, we would never return to our loved ones and our homeland. For a while, her songs took us home. The Lady in White was a great morale booster; she was idolized throughout the Armed Forces.

Hospitality was poured upon us; we were invited into the local residents' homes and treated like royalty. For me, a young officer, I was treated to lavish entertainment and a constant round of dinner parties; the brilliance of the star-studded heavens, a staggering canopy of beauty spread over the brightly lit open-air dances, left me breathless. It was a remarkable contrast for the soldiers who had endured all the privations of life at sea on a troop-ship, sleeping in close-hung hammocks, eating food so bad it should have been condemned and thrown overboard; they were certainly not in peak physical condition. After a month of being cooped up with nothing to amuse them and precious little exercise, Durban was a veritable oasis of pleasure. Nothing was too much trouble for the Durbanites, who even arranged sightseeing trips for the troops, all at their own expense. For a time we could forget reality; the war felt like a figment of our imagination. We lived only for today.

I took the opportunity to visit a gold mine on the outskirts of the city. The face of the mine was several thousand feet below ground level and reached by an antiquated elevator. There was room for ten passengers, and as we filed into it, we were in our usual boisterous mood, joking about this being our last ride, and maybe we'd stay at the face of the mine until the convoy had sailed, escape the war and live in luxury off our local benefactors. The shaft to the first level of excavation was two thousand feet, and as the cab rattled down at what appeared to be a high speed, we were still joking about *What if.* As if reading our minds, the cab came to a sudden and jarring halt, causing us all to fall to our knees. We picked ourselves up, no idea of what had happened; the irrepressible Battery wit was the first to break the pregnant silence with, 'All change for Wigan Pier.'

Someone offered a more concrete suggestion: 'This'd be a grand time to have a couple of women aboard, so we could play strip poker to pass the time away. Someone should telephone to the surface for them.'

Unfortunately, there was no emergency telephone, so not only could we not order up a couple of half-naked girls – to make the game go quicker – but it meant we also had no means of finding out what had caused the elevator breakdown. At first we weren't really worried, but as the minutes passed and the cab remained stationary it rapidly became more nerve-wracking; our levity turned to tense anxiety. For half an hour conversation followed the normal pattern, but soon the jokes began to fall a little flat and it was clear that everyone was edgy. However, as abruptly as it had stopped, the power was on again and the cage started to move, with sighs of relief all round.

Down below it wasn't what I had expected; it was quite different to the coal mine in Craghead in Northumberland I'd visited; that was a dark, oppressive place with narrow corridors where the men worked. The miners there were black with grime and all looked permanently apprehensive, as though they expected the worst to happen at any moment. Here it was the reverse: the traffic areas were wide and bright with electric lighting, the miners more cleanly dressed and a hum of activity prevailed. If you had to work underground, this would be the place. The sight of the finished gold bars spawned a number of would-be robbers, but the security was too tight to even think about it.

ON THE EVENING of December 6, 1941, unknown to all except the Japanese themselves, a great Japanese armada of aircraft carriers was steaming east, at a speed of over twenty knots, to their attack point two hundred miles from Pearl Harbor. By the early hours of the morning the aircraft carriers were in position to carry out their mission, the destruction of the United States Navy, although no state of war had as yet been declared between Japan and the United States of America. Air reconnaissance had enabled the Japanese to verify that the American fleet was in the harbour, and at the expected strength. At that very moment negotiations between the governments of Japan and the United States were in progress; the Americans were confident that the differences between the two countries could be resolved.

At dawn on December 7, 1941 the Japanese aircraft struck, literally out of the blue, with devastating effect. Virtually every major warship anchored in Pearl Harbor was sunk, and only two aircraft carriers, which by the grace of God were at sea on exercises, remained of the once powerful American fleet. The base was absolutely unprepared and resistance was ineffectual, so the two hundred Japanese planes had been able to carry out their attack systematically and without hindrance. The assault was totally unexpected, other than for one radar sighting, the report of which was botched, failing to reach defence headquarters, and within a few moments American naval power as an effective fighting force was destroyed. However, by this act the Japanese caused a self-inflicted wound, almost amounting to hara kiri: they had awakened a sleeping giant and in so doing had ensured their own ultimate and final defeat. The world was plunged further into a state of chaos, and the war was to last almost another four years.

THOSE FEW SHORT days of respite in Durban passed very quickly, and all too soon it was back to the crowded decks of the ship, the miserable conditions and the awful food, for the common soldiers at least. We all had fond memories, thanks to the hospitality of those wonderfully generous South Africans, but four of the officers had more enduring happiness, returning to Durban when the war finished to marry the girls they had met there – officers of the regiment were nothing if not opportunists.

Of course, I nearly missed the final leg of my journey as I boarded the wrong ship by accident. I'd got to the end of the *Mauretania* gangplank and still hadn't realized my mistake; luckily, the ship's Military Policemen were paying more attention than I was and helpfully guided me back to my own vessel.

The convoy sailed east again after that wonderful period of rejuvenation. We hadn't known, but we had been bound for Hong Kong, but this was about to be changed by the fortunes of war. For some completely inexplicable reason, the regiment's guns and equipment had been transported in the *Stratheden*'s sister ship, the *Strathmore*, which also carried a few of our gunners. We occasionally sailed close enough to see people on deck; we'd stand at the rail and try to recognize some of these figures, although we were never successful. But shortly after sailing from Durban, whilst I was looking across at the ship, I saw the disturbed pattern on the surface of the water which marked the passage of torpedoes. There were four such trails, each following the other in rapid succession. The first three hit square on and in seconds the entire ship was engulfed in flames. She sank almost immediately; at no time was there any sign of life aboard her, or in the water. Within two minutes there was simply an empty space where, a few moments previously, had sailed a 20,000-ton vessel. Only the flotsam remained to mark the passing of two thousand soldiers and sailors and their equipment of war. It was eleven o'clock in the morning.

But for me and the other soldiers aboard the *Stratheden*, this tragedy turned out to be a blessing in disguise. We found out our destination was to have been Hong Kong, but having lost all our field-guns and equipment, we were no longer an effective fighting unit, and instead were diverted to Bombay.

ON DECEMBER 10, 1941, both the *Prince of Wales* and the *Repulse* were sunk, and this was a bitter blow to the British Navy. Hong Kong was attacked by the Japanese on December 19 and occupied on Christmas Day; they had already landed in Burma and Malaya, in the Philippines and Luzon. My regiment had come so close to being massacred by the Japanese, like the other British troops in Hong Kong; at best, we'd have spent the remaining days of the war as Japanese prisoners of war; for too many, literally a fate worse than death. We thought it far better to be exposed to the unpleasantness of the Indian climate and spend perhaps another two years of boredom soldiering in almost peacetime conditions, although that wasn't what the men of the Territorial Army had either expected or wanted. We really all wished we could just fight and get the war over so that we could return home.

The journey to Bombay was shorter than to Hong Kong, but we lost more ships in the remaining days at sea. The war was getting closer. For some peculiar reason, I felt good about that, perhaps because I was a regular soldier, and wars were part of soldiering.

We were still well over four thousand miles from Bombay, with several days to go. The excitement and pleasure of Durban had faded and the weather became hot as we passed Madagascar and the Seychelles (another punishment station for the British soldier) and approached the equator. We had endured almost six weeks at sea in the close confines of the ship, with that one short break in Durban, and it felt like an eternity. As we passed the Seychelles and entered the Arabian Sea, the attacks ceased; the Nazi U-boats had obviously found other prey. The days were beginning to drag: we were all anxious to have done with the ship. At last the west coast of India hove into sight. There was a flurry of activity; now that dry land was again in sight, life took on a more cheerful aspect once again.

A hot and muggy day welcomed me back to India. As we prepared to carry our kit-bags ashore, we knew without question where we were. Never in a thousand years could I have forgotten the scent of India; I would have known her had I been blindfolded, or journeyed around the world. And returning gave you a sensation unlike anywhere else, quite unmistakable, quite unique to India. No matter the love/hate relationship you had with the country, arriving back made you feel almost as if you had never left, even had you wished never to return. India was a compulsion, a magnet, that drew you back.

And for those who had not been before, even if there was no real desire to be in India, for you would rather be back home in England, yet still there was a fascination to see this mysterious land the old soldiers talked about so much. Some had said it was a paradise: the beer was cheap, the women were free and easy and you never had to work because the wogs did it all for you – what more could a soldier ask for? But there were those who heartily condemned it as the graveyard of the British soldier: boredom, discomfort, frustration and misery. All this was in the smell which wafted over us as we were preparing to disembark.

BACK AT HOME, boredom was the last thing on anyone's mind. After the attack on Pearl Harbor, the world had changed dramatically. We were aware of some of what was going on elsewhere, thanks to the ships' radios, but I don't think any of us then realized the true scale of what was happening because of Adolf Hitler's insane plans for world domination. On December 6, 1941, Britain had declared war on Finland, Hungary and Romania. Five days later, Germany declared war on the United States of America, the Dutch government-in-exile declared war on Italy and the Polish government-in-exile declared war on Italy. The following day, on December 12, Romania in turn declared war on the USA and Haiti, Honduras, Panama and El Salvador declared war on Germany and Italy. On December 13, New Zealand declared war on Bulgaria and Bulgaria declared war on Britain and the United States; Croatia followed suit the next day. South Africa declared war on Bulgaria. The Czech government-in-exile rounded it all up by declaring war on all countries at war with the UK, USA and the Soviet Union. Nicaragua got into the picture on December 19, coming out against Bulgaria, Hungary and Romania; on December 20 the Belgian government-in-exile declared war on Japan. On Christmas Eve Haiti also declared war on Bulgaria, Hungary and Romania.

On Christmas Day Hong Kong fell to the Japanese.

Now it was truly a world war.

chapter thirteen

RETURN TO INDIA: BOMBAY TO MADRAS

January 1942 to September 1944

You could sense India long before you walked on her soil. You could smell the mystic East, a mixture of every conceivable odour blended together. And there was the tower, the famous Gateway to India, looking as forbidding as ever, I thought. The only time it took on a pleasant aspect was when it was viewed from the stern of a troop-ship bound for old Blighty – but that wouldn't be for a while now, and it would be better to think about the immediate future here in India, rather than to speculate about our return.

Now that Singapore and Hong Kong had fallen, how long could it be before India also fell? But I still had a way to go before I finally met the Japanese in battle. The regiment had made the almost ceremonial walk down the gangplank; already many were wondering how long we'd serve in this strange land before we could walk back up a gangplank. There was no kissing the cement paving of this Bombay dock as there would be upon our return to England.

The troop-trains were waiting. Regulations authorized a limited number of Indian vendors be within the military dock area, but this was obviously ignored: the thronging crowds of Indian box wallahs were already at the heels of the troops, offering for sale everything from chah and wads to trinkets suitable to 'Send home to the girl you left behind.' It was a novel experience for many of the men, who at first were entranced at this welcoming reception. But it didn't last: their captivation soon turned to annoyance and they would be as quick as we oldhanders with phrases like 'Buck jow, tum sewer cabutch.''

Many soldiers had been given a short primer on soldiers' Urdu; whilst I was stationed at Meerut and Sialkot I had been taught Urdu, which, amongst all the thousands of dialects on the sub-continent, was the language used most between the Indians and the British. Although I never had a really good command of the language, I, like most soldiers, excelled in all the slang phrases. And we all knew that if the natives didn't understand what you were saying, you just had to shout louder! My men liked to gather around me to hear me speak the *Hobson Jobson* to the locals. Soon they too became proficient in the lingo, able to put together a few sentences – and some were even capable of talking eloquently to the wogs, as Taffy described them. Though the natives invariably failed to understand what was really being said to them – most of the words were still soldiers' blasphemy – they usually managed to get the drift. They had become quite accustomed to being referred to as *You son of a pig* and other, less complimentary terms doled out by the troops.

The bands were there to meet us of course, for England always rolled out the pomp and circumstance when her troops arrived overseas, not so much to welcome the soldiers, more to impress upon the locals how mighty was their army. Unbelievably, despite all the army officials, there was a pimp standing near the engine of the train, as black as the proverbial 'lassie from Madrasi', offering the best in the country – according to him – for the princely sum of two shillings (a day's pay for me). 'Bibi mongta Sahib. Very good woman for you. Is doing what you want, Sahib.' Where the 'bloody big Madrasi' was hidden was a mystery and likely to remain so, for the Military Police were present in full force, and whilst they might close their eyes to some things, this was decidedly not one of them. There were moans of despair and cries of shame from some who could hardly contain themselves after those long weeks at sea dreaming, as Bombardier Wally Jackson would say, of things to come. For he was one of the deprived, and perhaps if he were quick and silently slid away, escaping the searching eyes of the MPs, he could have a quick look in the engine's coaling tender. And then, if he were lucky and she *was* hiding there in the coal, he might

1 Go away, you son of a pig!

have time for a *jeldi duffey*[1]. Although the prospect of going into action amidst the coal lumps was distracting, it was nothing ventured, nothing gained; needs must and it's any port in a storm, he maintained. Perhaps the Military Police could be bribed. That could be worth trying. 'After all,' continued Wally, who knew how the wheels were greased in India, this being his second time around too, 'bribery abounds at every level; and nobody's above it.'

It was true: from the Maharajas and the Generals, all the way down to the lowest ranks of the sepoy, everyone was at it; even the Indian Civil Service at the most senior levels was not above a bit of corruption, though they were renowned throughout England and India for the forthright manner in which the British members conducted affairs. But it was there all the time; nobody was immune, and if you failed to take advantage of this enriching practice, you were thought a fool. Contracts of every description were bought and sold on the 'cross my palm with silver' principle. There were backhanders for every transaction; nothing was accomplished without it. The award of a multi-million-rupee project, the supply of boots, uniforms or foodstuffs, the construction of a building, or a concession to the char-wallah to set up shop on the bungalow porch at the barracks: it was all grist for the mill. The Indians were past masters in the arts of bribery and corruption; they called it 'dastar' – the custom. It started with the giving of presents like flowers and fruit, then with services for favours received. From there it was just a short step to money and land, and favours of a different kind. Many senior employees of the East India Company retired as rich men after only a few years in the country; Clive himself was not above it. So why should not the common soldiers embrace the practice?

It had been a way of life for centuries, and many were made rich by it, both Indians and British, said Wally, who still wondered if he should risk tangling with the Military Police. But he decided life was too short, no matter how great the charms of the hidden bibi: in a few days' time we'd reach our camp, and then there'd be ample opportunity to sample the delights of the country, so the five fingered widow must continue to serve for now. Meanwhile, the possibility of Wally making any progress with the pimp had been great entertainment for his fellow soldiers, for they all had one-track minds as far as women were concerned.

1 A quickie

Their fun was short-lived and Wally's potential 'romance' halted as the sergeant-major was screaming at the top of his voice, 'Pick up your kit-bags and bunducks[1] and get fell in facing the train!'

THE JOURNEY TO Bangalore was a dismal one for the new boys, who were as shocked as I had been when I made my first train journey. They found it hard to believe the poverty and dreadful conditions in which the natives lived, and they realized that India was not going to be a good place to serve in. The contrast with South Africa, the little they'd seen, was incredible; they had assumed that the conditions in all the eastern countries would be similar. But they had seen only Durban, and few had ventured beyond the luxuries of the beautiful estates where they had been wined and dined so sumptuously. For the men fortunate enough to be living in a pre-war cantonment of India, it was a comfortable enough place to soldier, but this was not to be the case for me this time. My men had been aghast at the plight of the Indians; now they – and I – were about to sample the rigours of life in 'Inja' without the trappings of civilization ourselves.

Because of the events in Hong Kong and Singapore, and the subsequent change in our destination, our arrival at Bangalore was totally unexpected, so no preparations had been made for us. Not for us the comforts of the cantonment barracks and all the luxuries that went with it; we had to sleep on the ground of the maidan, in tents, but without beds or charpoys[2] of any kind. The sandy gravel was alive with red ants, and there weren't any mosquito nets. After a night of extreme discomfort, during which few had slept, we were a sorry-looking lot when dawn came, our bodies covered in mosquito and ant bites.

Nobody was very hungry for breakfast – which was just as well, for the cook was incapacitated, having suffered the embarrassment of being stung in the bum. Shaking out your boots first thing in the morning was almost a ritual in India, because they were a favourite hiding place for scorpions, and if you were bitten by one, it was usually fatal. In the case of head cook Bombardier Tich Evans, it wasn't a scorpion which caused his agony, but a centipede quite two inches long which had reposed the night in his trousers, which were also lying on the ground. Poor Tich's plight was about the only source of amusement for the regiment that day; luckily for him there was

1 Rifles   2 String beds

no lasting damage, other than being unable to sit in comfort for a week or so. And the lads had a good laugh, which they desperately needed.

By nightfall the officers and senior NCOs had acquired charpoys and mosquito nets sufficient for all, and our second night on Indian soil was much improved.

IT FELT LIKE only yesterday that I had first been here; in fact, it was almost exactly six years. My first tour of duty was in the northern areas of the Punjab and the United Provinces; now it was to be exclusively in the southern part of the country, beginning in Bangalore, six hundred miles southeast of Bombay and, at an altitude of three thousand feet, a popular hill station for the British. Set in the rolling hills of the Deccan it gave pleasant relief from the scourge of the Indian summers, although not quite so much as the stations in the far north which, at six or seven thousand feet, had a much cooler climate. Its population at that time was in the order of a million souls, including the native and the cantonment population. Not far from the cantonment was the beautiful Palace of the Maharaja of Mysore, an extremly rich man, who was also reputed to be paid his weight in gold every year by the population. He was apparently gross in stature, so the pickings were substantial. Bangalore was somewhat cleaner and better planned than the average Indian city, and the cantonment was easily one of the finest British facilities in India.

There were churches of most denominations, the oldest of which was the St Andrew's Kirk, on the north side of the great parade ground. To the east were St Xavier's Roman Catholic Church, and the Anglican Church of St John – in the cemetery of which lay the body of General Cleveland who died at the age of ninety-two, after serving seventy-five years in the Madras Army. Close by was a statue of Sir Mark Cubbin, who served for twenty-five years. Standing high above sea level, Bangalore's favoured climate perhaps contributed to the longevity of these two gentlemen. To the west were the Wesleyan, St Mark's Anglican, the Trinity and the All Saints Churches, which stood close to the mile-long general parade ground. There was a cinema, many European-style restaurants, a YMCA, and two well-staffed and equipped hospitals. But whilst there was plenty of beer in the canteens, there was little else to entertain the men, apart from the ubiquitous brothels.

In the centre of the cantonment, dominating the surroundings, stood a huge statue of Queen Victoria, whom the natives called 'Queenie Vitoria, velly good man!' The magnificent Bangalore Fort – a mile long by a mile and a half wide – was close by; it was captured by Lord Cornwallis in 1791 in the face of Tipu's large and superior army. Tipu was an Indian Raja who clashed with the British in four separate Mysore wars, the first in 1767. He was known as the Lion of Mysore; the many atrocities he committed against the Hindu people won him the reputation of a complete barbarian. The third time he went to war against the British, he was forced into a treaty at Seringapatam by Lord Cornwallis, and lost half of his realm, including the Bangalore Fort. Never one to give up, he tried again seven years later – and this time, in 1799, he was killed, at Seringapatam, the site of another extraordinary fort, this one with double ramparts, one face over a mile long.

Later, we met the chee-chees in Bangalore, which I'd already decided was not an unpleasant spot, as it was cooler than the plains. I began to acknowledge that there was a place in this world for the Anglos, and felt a little bad about my previous attitude towards them. They had been discriminated against, in very bad taste, and made to feel like outcasts.

The troops were soon beginning to feel the pangs of deprivation brought about by the lack of female company. No one thought to organize supervised establishments, so the problem of VD was ever-present. Since there wasn't on-site provision for their needs, the men were quick to find out where the local brothels were; such information travels with the speed of light in any military organization. They were quick to share their discoveries, too: 'Hey, mucker, I found a good screw tonight, she's a real humdinger, does it like a rabbit on heat. Can't go wrong with her, does whatever you want for a couple of chips. Works in that crummy Chinese restaurant dump next to the charnel house. On the other side is the pig-slaughtering place, so you can't miss it. If you decide to have a go, just don't go in the wrong door or you might finish shacking up with a corpse – or, worse still, a pig. And watch you don't get stuffed yourself, there's a lot of randy Sikhs working in the area.' There were few of us who didn't know that the red light district in Bombay was called the Cages; in Poona it was the Nage – troops have fabulous memories, at least for the important things in life.

AFTER ABOUT A month, my regiment was abruptly moved to the west coast for combined operations training, which surprised us, for we thought we'd move closer to the Burma border, ready for the reconquest, which was thought to be imminent. Beginning to feel like wandering nomads, we found ourselves in Nasik, a busy city a hundred miles north of Bombay. It was a pleasant enough spot, two thousand feet above sea level, and a very holy one for the Hindus, being situated on the banks of the sacred river Godavari, or the Ganges of the Deccan, as it's known, for the Ganges and the Godavari are believed to rise from the same source via an underground passage. At the point where it is about two hundred feet wide the river is lined with steps on both sides, and there are always hundreds of people bathing in the holy waters. Of far greater interest to us was the fact that Nasik was the home of the famous (or infamous) Nasik whisky and gin. Maybe the holy waters, tainted with the hordes who habitually bathed there, gave these drinks such a noxious taste. They packed a vicious punch, but it was all alcohol, it was both cheap and plentiful, and therefore Nasik was a good place to be.

The Sundar Narayan Temple stands at the top of the hill, shining prominently in the brilliant sunshine. Sixty-eight steps wind tortuously up the steep hillside to the summit where the temple stands. Built in 1786, it cost ten lakhs – a lahk is one hundred thousand rupees; pre-war, the rupee was nearly fourteen to the pound sterling, so ten lakh then was £72,000; two centuries earlier it must have been a large fortune, but it bought a true work of art. Surrounded by numerous small temples, the main temple and the steps are brightly lit by the Kartik full moon. Nasik is steeped in religion (like many places in India); on the east side of the town is Sita's cave, which only Hindus may enter, from which the goddess Sita was carried away to Ceylon by the mendicant Ravana. Rama passed his banishment there and God is said to have bathed at the sacred Rama Kund, where the dead are taken. Close by is the semi-hill station of Deolali; the cantonment was used for the transfer of troops to and from England. It is there that one might have contracted the famous 'Deolali tap' – the fervent hope, and often the pretence, of many soldiers, hoping that they would be diagnosed as mentally unbalanced, and so returned home.

FROM NASIK THE regiment moved down to Madh Island, just off the shores of the Bombay coast, for a period of combined operations with the Navy. Working with seamen was an adventure in itself, even a supposedly simple thing like climbing down the side of the ship on rope ladders into a landing craft: if your rifle did not become entangled in the ropes then your leg would. Or your web belting, or your backpack, or ... And what was worse was becoming so caught up that you'd find yourself swinging by the heel of one leg, head down, and dangerously close to the butt end of your neighbour's rifle, who was also in a similar position and equally unable to extricate himself. With a heavy sea running, one moment you were level with the landing craft, and the next you would be twenty feet above. I could only conclude that making a sea-borne landing in this manner was more hazardous than meeting the enemy on the beaches.

Then it was back to the mainland again, and living under canvas. Early one morning we were greeted with the surprising sight of a huge white mushroom cloud in the east, which was followed within twenty seconds or so by a loud sound like thunder. The tent lines were quickly crowded with men, all wondering what had happened. We soon found out, for a signal was received ordering us to the Bombay docks at once. An ammunition ship had caught fire and there had been an explosion. This ship, HMS *Stikine* had actually been ablaze whilst out at sea, but, foolishly, it had been brought into Bombay Harbour, where it promptly erupted. The ship had just docked alongside the other vessels in the wharf abutting the city's crowded bazaar when it blew up. The force of the explosion had scattered the boats along the quay as if thrown by a giant's hand. Liberty ships of tens of thousands of tons were lifted completely from the water onto the dock pavements and were lying around haphazardly. We arrived to a scene of utter devastation. The whole place was a shambles, in absolute chaos. There were dead bodies everywhere; the most grotesque sights greeted us: in one gutter was a hand – a white hand – and in another was the head of an Indian man, still with a look of horror on his face. And the most memorable sight was that of the thousands of chaplis – sandals – littering the streets in the immediate vicinity of the disaster, where they'd been kicked free so their owners could run for their lives. The fires were blazing out of control in the bazaar and in the go-downs, and people were still walking around in a daze. There was little we could actually do for those who were injured and still lived. The few ambulances and medical teams ordered to the scene were totally inadequate to cope with the huge numbers who required medical attention, so the wounded were unceremoniously placed in the back of the regimental vehicles and taken to the already overcrowded hospitals.

My regiment took part in the rescue: we fought the fires and shot the looters who were already ransacking the shops and the storage areas. At one point there was a strong rumour that a second ammunition ship was about to explode and this resulted in renewed panic. I will always remember seeing the crews of two fire engines, feverishly hosing down a ship alongside the dock, simply drop the hoses, water still spouting, mount their vehicles and speed away without disconnecting them; in other circumstances it would have been funny, for they continued to lash around in all directions like headless snakes.

It was whispered that one of the devastated vessels, either the *Stikine* or another British ship, had been carrying gold bullion, and of course this set off a feverish search. All the likely – and unlikely – places were searched, but to no avail. By all accounts none of my people found the gold bars, but it was said that one of the officers was seen leaving the scene, and walking with some difficulty, as if he were carrying something heavy.

The regiment was there for three days helping to bring order. It was a harrowing period and we were glad when it was all over. After we returned to the camp, it was noticeable that a large number of men were displaying new wristwatches, and the charpoys in their tents were stacked with boxes of cigarettes – Indian-made, admittedly, and not very palatable; but who is going to turn down a free cigarette? And an unusually high proportion of those who had taken part in the rescue were making application for extended leave passes to the hills; a sure sign that they had received a bonus of money from somewhere.

BUT WE WERE on the move again, now to Madras, four hundred miles north from the tip of the sub-continent, where the British domination of India started three hundred years before. We were based near the small village of Khodumbakkam, twenty miles to the west of the city. The camp, sited in a mango grove, was pretty unpleasant; without the comforts of the cantonment, we were all feeling the effects of the weather far more than on my first tour of duty in India. Being under canvas, everything was constantly sodden, inside and out. We had no punkah wallahs or ice, nor refreshing cold showers, nor the cooling effects of the high-ceilinged bungalow. The weather was hot and humid and unbearable; I could never forget the discomfort of squatting in my tent in the evenings writing home to Mother, so hot that the sweat pouring from my forehead literally smeared the ink so badly that the letter became unreadable and I had to start over again. Soldiering in the Madras area was truly unpleasant, boring and monotonous.

The camp was virtually in the middle of nowhere; the nearest sign of life was in the village about a mile up the dusty track, elegantly named Poonamalee High Road. The town of Poonamalee itself was just a few more miles along that apology for a highway, which was now knee-deep in ruts, thanks to our heavy vehicles, which meant it was almost impassable in the wet weather. The bullock-carts which had been the main users for the past few hundred years were severely hampered. The jungly scrub covered miles in all directions. There was little arable land; it was a most unattractive landscape. There was little incentive to go exploring, for all we'd find were more dismal villages filled with inhabitants who, like all their brothers and sisters throughout the country, would pester us mercilessly for baksheesh. In spite of two years' service in India now, and the constant hounding for hand-outs, it was surprising how many of the men continued to give money to the beggars – it was always hard to ignore the pleas, especially of the underfed children. The British soldier was noted for his generosity; the men of my regiment were no exception. Here the begging was not as highly organized as it was in the cities, where it was specialized; it wasn't uncommon there to find children who had been intentionally deformed by adults, in some instances, in a shockingly dreadful manner. The mutilations ranged from dismemberment to blindness; a child could lose the tongue and have its face distorted. The most hardened of men found it difficult to close his heart to a child so severely disabled. But such sights did little to endear the soldiers to the entreaties of the adults who were the wilful architects of these loathsome infant deformities.

As usual there was little contact with the natives beyond the purchase of foodstuff and, inevitably, the women, though few men cared to take advantage of the opportunity presented by the locals. They preferred the delights of nearby Madras, which was well able to serve their constant – and essential – sexual needs. There were many establishments providing such services, offering girls from around the world, or so the touts would have one believe. In fact, most of the prostitutes were Indian, with an occasional girl from one of the other Eastern countries. It was highly unusual to see a European girl offering herself for sale – if there *was* a white woman, she was likely to be haggard and well-worn. By and large the brothels were of a high class, and they functioned under the jurisdiction of the Military Police – indeed, it was rumoured that the Provost Marshal himself was a partner in the business, receiving a very handsome share of the profits of those establishments he smiled upon. He was destined to end the war a rich man; and no doubt he himself was a frequent visitor, like his policemen.

In some respects, though, for me and the other officers, Madras was a veritable paradise: this came in the form of the Connemara Hotel, an oasis for those of us lucky enough to enjoy its sanctuary. It was a place of the past, the present and the future: time here did not exist. Once inside, I felt like I'd entered another world, sheltered from the soul-destroying existence which had become our way of life in the unforgiving land of wartime India. Here we were free from it all: the apparently wasted days of routine in the mango groves, where nothing worthwhile was ever accomplished.

The Connemara offered escape in many ways, not least the chance to sleep long and soundly in a bed made up with clean sheets mashed soft on the rocks on the banks of the Godavari River by an energetic dhobi[1], then to awaken to hot and cold running water instantly available at the turn of the tap, and chota hazri[2] in bed. Perish the primitive charpoy out in the wastes of Khodumbakkam: here we were far from the monotonously plaintive call of the fuchu bird and the raucous echoing of the mynah birds as they fought for the scraps in the nearby village, free from the dust and the heat (the hotel was air-conditioned, an unheard of luxury in southern India!). The welcoming arms of the hotel embraced us and offered us hospitality, and the comfort of cleanliness, a much-needed reminder that there was another world far removed from that which was presently our unfortunate lot. Did such a place exist anywhere else in this vast country? Certainly not in the south. Within these four walls, ignoring the ghettoes on the outside and the ever-present colony of ants parading

---

1 Laundryman   2 Small breakfast

across the floor, with an occasional divergence up the legs of the bed into your presence, was nirvana. Here we could get life back into perspective.

A call to the bearer who lived outside your door day and night, guardian and servant, brought the luxuries of civilization in a trice. That wonderful invention the bathtub was always there, to wash away the trials and tribulations endured under the mango trees, and to sober us up for further drinking sessions; not for us that abomination, the wretched canvas camp bath. An unlimited supply of liquor – albeit most often Nasik's rotgut whisky and gin – and at incredibly low prices, was ours to enjoy; after the first glass or so it became surprisingly palatable. And if our heads felt a little topsy-turvy in the morning, it was nothing that a Bombay oyster could not put right: two freshly broken eggs in a tumbler of vinegar well laced with salt and pepper would put anyone back on the straight and narrow in very jeldi time.

We spent long weekends at the Connemara: the days could be spent relaxing in bed, some enjoying the delights of an Indian bibi provided by the enterprising bearer, who appeared to be aware of one's most intimate needs, and, at the drop of a hat, you would be besieged by one or more attractive 'Indian girls of high caste I am getting for you, Burrah Sahib.' In the evenings, there was, inevitably, the bar, and – surprising above all things – a band, so those few officers who were capable could tread the light fantastic. Those long weekends' escape, often lasting from Friday to Monday, enabled us to return to the mango swamp and continue the sordid routine, but with perspective temporarily realigned. That was the Connemara sedative; what a wonderful time it was.

But it was one thing for us officers to enjoy all the luxuries of the good life; for the rank and file, a night in town in a hotel worthy of being patronized was far more expensive than they could afford. Their only option was to rent a room in some sleazy hotel, which boasted neither bar nor dance floor. There were good brothels, clean, and with desirable women, but they had to be out of there by eleven at night; the Provost would see to that. So the troopers had to take their pleasures back at the camp, in the tents and the mango groves and the murderous temperatures. Still, they organized concerts, the biggest hits always the scenes where men dressed as women, and in spite of the heat and the humidity and the squalor, they usually had a roaring time. And there was always the singsong, which keeps the British soldier going no matter how hard the road. Wherever you are, the Sergeant-Major, that most beloved of comrades, is a popular subject, but for my men in India, high on the list whenever despondency reigned was 'When this bloody war is over'. The tune for the song was taken from the Hymn 779 in the Anglican Book Of Common Prayers, better known to civilians as 'What a friend we have in Jesus':

When this bloody war is over
What a friend we have in Jesus,
Oh! How happy I shall be,
All our sins and grief to bear.
You can tell the Sergeant-Major,
What a privilege to carry,
No more soldiering for me
Everything to God in Prayer.

No more church parades on Sundays,
O what peace we often forget it,
No more asking for a pass,
O what needless pain we bear,
You can tell the Sergeant-Major,
All because we do not carry,
To stick it up his f —— arse
Everything to God in prayer.

It was always sung in a melancholy way, and always with great gusto. The natives from the villages used to gather on the roadside by the mango grove and would attempt to join in the chorus – the troops learnt a fair amount of Urdu from this.

BUT THINGS WERE changing fast. The Yanks were beginning to monopolize the services in India, as they were elsewhere, including Britain. Their military rates of pay far exceeded those of the British, so they could outbid the prices we paid for services; that meant they had first choice in the hiring of cooks, bearers, and servants of all kinds, and a host of other artisans. The Eurasian girls were obviously attracted by the Americans' ability to spend money so lavishly – the same thing was happening at home –

and so most of the girls were lost to the British soldiers. They were also in a position to hire the best prostitutes, and the British soldiers were deeply embittered about that too. They cornered virtually all the liquor, including beer, whisky (Scotch, the best), while Tommy was relegated to the local brews, absolute rotgut by comparison.

The consequent fights between the Allies in the bars and in the streets were probably not a great deal worse than they were in England, but they were bad enough. The difference in pay rates was not the only thing that caused jealousy. The Yanks got far better quality food; we never ceased to be astonished by the luxuries, including ice cream, provided to the Americans, even in the forward battle areas. And whilst the British had to be satisfied with inferior food, cheap liquor and cigarettes made in India – tasting like sour weeds – their counterparts had it all, including the prime smokes, made in the USA.

THE MONSOONS HAD paid little heed to the passing of time and still arrived with monotonous regularity, although earlier than I'd experienced on my first tour in the north of the country. In the south they started in early June, then swept across the sarai, the grasslands of northern India, about a month later. Their arrival brought a great deal more discomfort than I had previously experienced; our troops were more vulnerable to the ravages of the storm. There were many times when the tents collapsed through the sheer force of the winds, or the incessant, heavy rain. We'd heard that the wettest place in the world was Cherrapunji, in Assam, where four hundred inches of rain a year was normal. But everyone was prepared to gamble that Trichinopoly and Madras must be serious contenders for the title in southern India. Doubtless the elephants were happy about the rains, for they need no longer resort to blowing dust over themselves with their trunks as protection from the rays of the sun. We didn't feel quite so sanguine.

With the rain came all the usual unpleasantries, including the increased mosquito activity and the mouldiness caused by the perpetual dampness of one's clothing and equipment. The flies, the usual pestering nuisance, seemed to have increased in number; they were very much part of India and the white man's burden. The anthills came to life, a hive of activity, and the stink bug made its appearance. It was enormous, well over an inch in length, black and shiny: not an unpleasant insect to look at, but it made the foulest possible smell when killed. Unfortunate was the man who did accidentally squash one, especially if he did so upon his personal possessions – or anyone else's, for that matter – for the stink proved impossible to eradicate and not even your best friends would speak to you, for the longest time afterwards.

The temperatures remained in the high thirties and often in the low forties and the scrublands became marshes, and a haven for birds visiting from around the world. Not until September did the rain stop and normality return to the land.

IT WAS ABOUT that time of the year that concentrated training – realistic training – took place in the jungles of southern India. The monsoon season was chosen intentionally, because the regiment had become soft from easy living in relative peace, and most of the 19th Indian Division's training had been confined to the arid plains, so that the troops had never been subjected to the difficulties of waging war in the wet weather. It had been the general understanding that the war should stop during the monsoon period, because of the impossible conditions the weather created, and the widespread disease that invariably attended the torrential rains. However, the Japanese had shown a remarkable ability to live and to fight under those very same adverse conditions, so there was no longer reason for the British not to do the same. And whilst this might have felt damned uncivilized to us, the war had to be got on with, and as the jungles of southern India were capable of equalling almost anything that one might expect to meet in Burma, the 19th Indian Division was sent there to train.

The conditions during that period of training, unpleasant though they were, were of a short duration, and there was always the knowledge that the peaceful and luxurious life was just around the corner, and accessible at a moment's notice. The hotels in the major cities – Madras, Travencore, and Trichinopoly in Tamil Nadu – were within striking distance; at the first sign of sickness the ailing were whisked away to a modern and well-equipped British General hospital, offering high standards of treatment and care not so different from those of the famous London hospitals. There were no corner shops, of course, or restaurants, or cinemas, or football fields, or pubs or women (the ultimate sacrifice!); in fact, almost all the essentials of life to keep a soldier happy were very much absent. But however bad it might have been in relation to soldiering on the plains, it was a paradise compared to what lay ahead.

Living off the land was part of the training for self-sufficiency, and for the first time the men had to go without their usual beef suppers. We took very few provisions with us, and there were no fresh vegetables, or meats, so corned-beef stew made with whatever could be gathered together became the staple. We did live off the land quite successfully though, and it was surprising that such luxuries as eggs and chicken were found to be so liberally available at the gun positions! And there were plenty of wild fowl to shoot and to eat. The British soldier – if not all soldiers – is capable of living in a state of wellbeing even if parachuted into the middle of the Sahara desert or the wastes of Siberia, as long as one didn't question the source of supply.

To compensate for the lack of fresh meat and as a change from the perennial bully beef, there was goat, made possible by taking live goats along with us whenever we moved – goat meat on the hoof, so to speak. It made a tasty enough meal the first time around, but the honeymoon ended after the second day; the meat was tough and sour and by no means to everyone's liking. The novelty bloomed and faded overnight, so it was quickly back to the bully beef stews again. But however boring or taste-less, we had enough to eat, which would not always be the case when we entered battle with the Japanese.

Living off the land was not an unpleasant experience, for most of the time the regiment was within access to the beaches of southern India. Away from the polluting cities and villages, the beaches were beautiful: golden, hard-packed sand washed by the bluest waters imaginable – almost as perfect as those at Blackpool! Those who were lucky enough to bathe in the waters of the Bay of Bengal, thought it adequate reward for the hardship suffered that month. At the end of it, most of the men returned to the Madras camp refreshed, in body and spirit, and with a different outlook on life; we'd been away from the British Army environment of Aldershot, and the regimentation that governed our every waking moment. The exercise had shown us a little of what we'd be facing in the jungle, and the difficulties of fighting during the heavy monsoons. We'd learned how to be independent, and faced the realization that if we failed to provide for ourselves, nobody else would.

What that training couldn't do was to show us the reality of close contact with a ruthless enemy; at that time we had no conception of the constant feeling of uneasiness – of fear – not knowing where or when they would strike next.

I was not quite so lucky as my men, and was unable to revel in that carefree period, for I was packed off to attend a jungle warfare course organized by that well-known Chindit jungle fighter, Colonel Michael Calvert, popularly known as 'Mad Mike Calvert'. He was a man with an enviable reputation, a born and experienced leader, fearless and imperturbable in battle.

The reports reaching us in India of the Japanese brutality were blood-curdling and, linked with the stories of their successes in battle, painted a grim picture for us: young British soldiers in India, we awaited orders to leave for Burma. By all accounts we were to fight not an ordinary soldier, but a Japanese 'supersoldier': a natural jungle fighter, who lived in harmony with nature. He carried a small bag of rice at his waist, which would sustain him indefinitely: he was able to live off the land, eating bamboo shoots, leeches, snakes and monkeys if necessary. The British, on the other hand, had been raised on meat and potatoes and were accustomed to eating three square meals a day. The Japanese soldier had the courage and the heart of a lion, and was said to be capable of meeting any challenge. His weaponry was excellent, but he preferred to use the steel of his sword and bayonet to defeat his enemy, for to him 'the sword was his soul'. He was invincible, yet not afraid to die, preferring death before dishonour. Our chances of defeating him appeared slim.

The Japanese could trace their warrior roots back down the centuries; even now the modern soldier holds strongly to the tenets of his warrior race. He would rather die than surrender; to be captured or to surrender alive is contrary to Japanese beliefs, and in the eyes of the Emperor, an unacceptable act. To capitulate was therefore unworthy of him, and if he did, then he had lost faith with his homeland and could no longer be recognized as a person entitled to the rights and privileges of a human being. So there was no alternative but to die. By the same token, the Japanese believed that the soldiers of other nations who allowed themselves to be captured should also forfeit the right to live, and that belief was reflected not only in the Burma Campaign, but wherever and whomever the Japanese fought.

The Japanese despised surrender as cowardly behaviour; whenever a soldier – be he British, Indian, Gurkha, or American – was captured alive, he was usually murdered. On the rare occasions they weren't killed outright, their Japanese captors were brutally, inhumanly cruel: the punishment for being captured. Because the foreigners had tarnished the hallowed codes of honour, the consequent abhorrent actions were carried out with impunity. Prisoners were subjected to forced marches, where many of them died from exhaustion, or disease or starvation, or from the tortures inflicted upon them daily. Those who did fall en route were bayoneted and just left to die. Thousands more were put to work in the slave camps, building roads or airfields, or slaving in the mines in Japan.

So we were presented with a daunting – even terrifying – image of our enemy. Most of the lads about to enter the fray were only about nineteen or twenty; I myself was still only twenty-three, but I'd already achieved the rank of Captain, and had a well-earned reputation with the Infantry as a gunner. For the younger soldiers, it was probably their first time away from home. Apart from that month of training, they – and I – knew little about fighting in the jungle; after all, we'd all been raised in the bricks and mortar cities of Manchester or Liverpool or Birmingham, and there was little jungle there! The fact that there is no jungle around Tokyo, and that the Japanese were as ill-experienced in jungle terrain escaped most British soldiers. And the Japanese travelled light; we did not.

Clearly the British lacked the know-how of jungle warfare in which the Japanese now excelled. This was not easily acquired and required special training in the appropriate conditions; several training schools were set up across India, instructed by men who had already met the Japanese in battle in Burma; it was one of these that I was sent on whilst my men were themselves learning a little about jungle survival tactics.

Deep in the southern Indian jungle, totally isolated from civilization, I spent six weeks learning guerrilla warfare tactics whilst surviving in the most hostile of conditions. We officers had to learn how to supply and conserve both ammunition and food, not just for us as individuals, but for our men's sake too. We learnt how to use nature's bounty: food which, though not always palatable, would provide sustenance. Where we were, much of the plant life was edible and the rivers teemed with fish – though the crocodiles were fierce competitors. Wildlife was prolific: I discovered snake meat was quite tasty when roasted over a log fire, and how to catch mongoose and small rodents, and larger animals like deer and even monkeys. Water was carried in pigskins or chaguls, and strictly rationed, just as it would be in the battle zones.

It was easy to become lost: even using a compass for a bearing and noting the paces as we progressed could give unreliable results in the dense surroundings of the jungle, so we had to use more primitive methods of direction-finding: quite often we went by instinct or by guess, and by God – who wasn't always receptive to our wishes. The sun and the moon were rarely visible, so we couldn't use them to compute directions either. To be unsure of your position, or just lost, wouldn't be comfortable if you knew the enemy was in the area.

A FEW WEEKS later, in Burma, when I was travelling in a Jeep along what were nothing more than animal tracks, I did become lost, and in the presence of the Japanese. Realizing I was out of my depth, I told my driver to stop and consulted my map. At that moment a Japanese patrol appeared, and – fortunately – saw us too late. Quick as a whip and without a word from me, my driver spun the steering wheel and executed a very smart about-turn and the Jeep roared away at breakneck speed back along the track. At the time I was armed with a Sten gun, which was notoriously unsafe, a cheaper version of the Thompson submachine-gun I was to receive later in the campaign. The Sten was well known for its propensity to discharge even with the safety catch on, and as I fell from my standing position, the gun fell and, sure enough, it did fire, with the unreliable safety catch on and all! Dropping the map, I grabbed the windshield, but the gun chose to send a burst of three rounds, not at the enemy, as one might have wished, but just past my head and into the windshield. By the grace of God I escaped, though the windshield, which was totally shattered, was never the same throughout the campaign. Nor was my ego. Luckily for us, the Japanese didn't have time to respond, but it must have made their day, for they burst into paroxysms of laughter. And I had the added embarrassment of having to explain the shattered windscreen to my colleagues.

THE CAMP HEADQUARTERS was a rambling old building, which also served as a mess on the very few evenings we were allowed to dine there (mostly we ate wherever we happened to be in the jungle), and on these occasions, after the protocol of the evening meal, we had 'games'. These were common enough in a regimental mess, but infinitely milder than those we played at the jungle training camp: using live ammunition whilst playing hide-and-seek in and around the building, for example. There was the hunter and the hunted and, as the latter, Mad Mike thought it added realism to an otherwise civilized meal, but nobody else was amused by it, for several officers returned to their units via hospital with gunshot wounds. Marginally less dangerous was his version of rugby; the dining room, cleared of furniture, made an excellent 'field'. The two teams would line up and at the whistle were expected to score a goal using whatever tactics they wished, rough or otherwise, but mostly the former. Here too severe injuries occurred, for the ball was a steel helmet, and its sharp rim accounted for many a broken nose or lost teeth. Calvert was not every-one's idol by the end.

On the lighter side, there was training with elephants, using them to carry 3.7 Howitzers and machine-guns which were stripped down for the purpose. Properly trained Indian mahouts drove the animals and we 'students' merely practised dissembling and assembling the equipment. Some of the officers were invited to act as mahouts, but that didn't work out, due the objections of the elephants, who failed to appreciate the signal honour! The elephants were prepared for active service, complete with regimental and divisional signs of forty mph and the gunners' logos stencilled on their coats in large letters. It was a lot of fun but, in the event, wasted time, for neither I, nor any other officer from my course had occasion to use elephants in Burma.

As well as learning self-sufficiency and jungle survival, we had to study Japanese tactics. They were masters of infiltration and at nights as I crouched in my foxhole, on the gun position or with the infantry, unable to see or hear my neighbours, I felt very isolated. It was nerve-racking; we had to keep quiet and well down, for the enemy's objective was to locate our position. Our response to their taunting calls could well end in disaster. Typically, the night would be filled with sporadic Japanese rifle fire to attract the gunners' attention, but we were taught to respond only by throwing grenades in the direction of the voices and the fire. They would be back again, tonight, or tomorrow night, or the next. It was their way.

The Japanese were also adept in the art of the ambush. They would set up a roadblock in front of an advancing force and, when contact was made, engage it just strongly enough to stop it. When on the move, the British typically sited their major power at the head of the columns, and the Japanese were aware of this. They also knew of the British habit of bringing forward any additional 'rifles' they had, thus denuding the rear. Having halted the column, the Japanese would then swing around with a left hook action and, mounting a more powerful attack on the now-vulnerable rear, take out the whole column with ease. This left hook ploy of the Japanese was invariably successful, and the British took too long learning to keep the entire column protected, and not just the front of it. It was a costly lesson. And there were many other tactics for us to adjust to and overcome.

It was not all work and no play: one night I went on a tiger hunt. The local villagers thought there was a tiger close by, for several of their cattle had been killed the night before. Hurriedly mustering a party of four to hunt for the animal, we set out with our rifles, Dusty carrying his faithful shotgun – for whatever good that might do. We searched the area where the animal was believed to be, but could find no trace. Undismayed, I elected for a night shoot, so we sat in a machin, a platform hide, perched high in the largest tree we could find. It was a pleasant evening and we settled down for what we thought would be an exciting time. At the foot of the tree was tied a calf.

As the darkness gathered, bringing with it the coldness of the night, we began to feel a little apprehensive – none of us had ever attempted anything like this before, and the only advice we had was from my own recollection of hearing two of my officers, quite five years ago, during my first time in India, telling of their similar exploit, when they had indeed seen and shot a tiger from the security of a machin. It was not to be for the present hunters; we were bitten incessantly by mosquitoes whilst waiting fruitlessly for the rustling sounds and scent which heralded the approach of the tiger. But all we could hear from our uncomfortable perch twenty feet above the ground were the whimpers of the wretched calf tied to the tree; the small machin grew smaller and smaller, and more and more vulnerable – at least in our minds. As dawn broke, and the wicked rays of the sun cast long shadows around us, each had reached the conclusion this was the first and last time we would go tiger-hunting. The only winner was the quivering calf, which was now released, hopefully unaware of the reason it had been tethered there. Arriving back at the camp, I had to face the ribbing of my fellow officers as they sat at breakfast, laughingly deriding my tiger-hunting abilities, shouting for the bearer to bring bacon and eggs and a slice of my newly shot tigermeat sautéed in red wine! I sat silently, thankful, like my three comrades, to be back where the bites of our comrades were less harmful than being torn to pieces by an infuriated tiger.

In spite of these rare occasions, it was six weeks of gruelling activity and most of us were glad when school closed and we could return to the relative peace of our regiments.

AFTER A WHILE even the attractions of the Connemara and Madras lost their glamour: a sense of frustration was creeping in. Monotony was our constant companion. We'd spent two years without hearing or firing a shot in anger and we were anxious to get into the war and fight. We'd had two years of training: so much that we were becoming stale. The war had raged all around us: battles were being fought in Europe, in Africa, and the Pacific, and we wanted in.

But Burma was waiting for us; we would have more than our cupful soon enough.

AFTER THE RESOUNDING success of the Pearl Harbor strike on December 7, 1941, Japan had started on the next step to expand its Empire: an ambitious conquest of the Asian countries. First was Malaya, with its valuable oil fields; the task of the Japanese Twenty-Fifth Army. Then, following in quick succession after Hong Kong, the Japanese Fourteenth Army would strike at the Philippines and, from Thailand, General Lida of the Fifteenth Army, with the Twenty-Eighth and Thirty-Third Armies, would march into Burma. All these campaigns were won with relative ease: the defenders were totally unprepared and inadequate. In Britain, both senior officers and politicians appeared indifferent in the face of reality, in their heartfelt belief that Britain was invincible and, anyway, 'When the chips are down, we'll be there.' Meanwhile, the general attitude was, 'Let's have a another cup of tea', or 'Mine's a pink gin.' Who could doubt there would always be an England in the face of this *laissez faire* attitude?

In Malaya, the British garrison consisted of one hundred and twenty thousand men, British and Indian, well equipped, with a preponderance of artillery and tanks. On the surface, it was a formidable fighting force. But when the Japanese swarmed in from Thailand, the British were unprepared: they had expected an attack from the sea at the southern tip of the island, and had made no provision for invasion elsewhere. Neither the roads nor the terrain were conducive to the deployment of the larger British force, so the superior strength of four to one was useless: by the time the British had organized themselves, it was too late. With the element of surprise, the Imperial Guards Division and other seasoned Japanese troops overran the poorly trained defenders and swept through the mainland, brushing aside all resistance. The fanatical determination of the Japanese meant they'd stop at nothing even if the British troops had been ready: they were undeterred by any obstacle, always ready to improvise or to change their tactics to deal with unforeseen situations. If their vehicles couldn't use the roads and tracks, then they were quick to use bicycles.

The British, on the other hand, were uncommonly slow to act decisively in defence and were quite overwhelmed by the ferocity of the Japanese attack. With the fall of Johore, the end was near; they were forced to retreat to Singapore and, after futile attempts to blow up the causeway, awaited the onslaught, which came on February 8, 1942. The defence of the island was also predicated on the belief that any invasion would be sea-borne from the southern tip of the Peninsula, so only a few areas of the north coasts were fortified. General Percival, commanding the eighty-five thousand men stationed there, had no choice but to surrender to the thirty thousand Japanese attackers, doing so on February 15. It took only a few days for the city to fall; the Japanese troops were themselves surprised by both their rapid advance and by the British decision to surrender so quickly. It was a nightmare as the Japanese raped and looted as they pleased. Even Singapore's famous Raffles Hotel, known both for its pink gins and its bar, the longest in the East, was not sacred.

The British had already lost twenty-five thousand men during the mainland campaign; now wholesale massacre was inflicted on both military and civilian personnel. The medical and nursing staff at the

Alexandra Hospital were killed and the sick and wounded were savagely bayoneted to death in their beds. The detestable and unforgivable behaviour of the Japanese there was beyond description, and typified their attitude towards the countries they overran and raped. It was said they had learned a great deal of bestiality in China, where it was common practice to lash civilians to the trees for bayonet practice.

Tens of thousands of British and Indian troops were captured, and those who were not instantly murdered were sent to prison camps in the Far East, to Japan or, worse, to the death railway at Kanchanaburi near the Burma–Siam border. There, they lived in the worst conditions imaginable and suffered cruel punishment for the slightest of reasons. The Japanese gained especial notoriety for the treatment accorded to the thousands of British, Indian, Gurkha and Burmese forced to build the bridge over the Kwai River. The men worked like slaves for eighteen hours a day, with little rest or nourishment of any kind. Neither sickness nor disability was an excuse: the backbreaking work under the cruel Burmese sun must continue and the penalty for failing to meet the work quotas was instant flogging until the blood ran red. Worse, the transgressors were denied water and locked in isolation, perhaps until they died. Death was never humane or speedy; only torture and long-drawn-out demise appeared to satisfy the unbelievably sadistic whims of their captors. The Geneva Convention, which sets out minimum requirements for the treatment of prisoners of war, was ignored. Records later revealed that the shocking, ruthless savagery inflicted on prisoners was unparalleled in the history of warfare; worse even than the treatment of prisoners in medieval times. On that three-hundred-mile railway line and on the bridge at Kanchanaburi alone, more than sixteen thousand British, Indian and Gurkha troops and one hundred thousand native slaves perished.

The taking of Hong Kong began in the same ruthless and determined way, giving no quarter to soldier or civilian – man, woman or child. The Japanese attacked soon after Pearl Harbor, racing down from the Chinese mainland where they had been stationed since the capture of Canton in 1938. This was quite contrary to the expectations of General Maltby, the Garrison Commander who, as in Singapore, expected an assault to be seaborne from the south. Accordingly, all the fortifications were concentrated there, with the huge gun emplacements pointing out to the sea and sited to enable only a 50-degree traverse left and right of due south. The military planners' myopic view caused the quick downfall of the island. Hong Kong was far from impregnable: not a shot was fired from those guns. The Japanese sliced down through the New Territories on December 18, smashing through the Royal Scots, who were positioned on the so-called Gin Drinkers' Line – the demarcation line between China and the New Territories – and soon had complete control of the latter. Withdrawing, the British and Indian troops – the Royal Scots, the Middlesex Regiment and the Rajputs – were ferried across to the main island and by December 8 there were no British forces in the New Territories on the mainland. The small garrison was supplemented by two battalions of untrained Canadian infantrymen, the Winnipeg Grenadiers and the Royal Rifles, who disembarked, straight into the jaws of death, a bare week before the invasion. Though valiant in their contribution, most had never fired a live round of ammunition; their presence did little to alter the outcome for the hopelessly outnumbered garrison.

Hong Kong was now under heavy bombardment preparatory to the Japanese attack, which came on December 15; within three days they had landed eight battalions on the island. Again the element of surprise helped the Japanese forces' rapid break-through; resistance was sporadic and uncoordinated. The Japanese occupied the Repulse Bay area and moved into the Stanley Peninsula, where there was fierce fighting. The British were in absolute chaos; they suffered heavy casualties, finally surrendering in total defeat. The Japanese flag was raised over Hong Kong on Christmas Day, 1941. The widespread rape and murder of nuns started on Christmas Eve at St Stephen's Hospital: the medical and nursing staff were first raped, then together with the patients, butchered by sword or bayonet; a repeat of the Singapore atrocities.

chapter fourteen

BURMA:
CROSSING THE IRRAWADDY

September 1944 to February 1945

The Burma Campaign was recorded as the longest retreat in the history of the British Army; it was also the longest campaign the British Army took part in during the Second World War. Its defeated forces were pursued over nine hundred miles through rice paddies, jungles and mountains, from Rangoon to the Indian border. It began on December 8, 1941 when the Japanese Army landed on the border of Malaya and Siam (now Thailand), four hundred miles north of the British naval base of Singapore. Storming across Thailand and capturing Rangoon almost unopposed, they put to rout the small numbers of British, Indian and Burmese troops who were poorly equipped and, strangely enough, untrained in jungle warfare.

The occupation of Burma was not so very different to that of its neighbouring countries, except that the native Burmese were almost anxiously awaiting the arrival of the Japanese. The British first started to exploit the country in 1826; in 1886 the final annexation took place; leaving Burma in an almost constant state of political dissension and turmoil. The British had to send in the troops to keep the peace: the Burmese strongly objected to being treated as a province of India, which they had always considered to be an inferior nation, and to being classed as Indians. There was also great protest against Indian immigrants; a seriously violent riot in 1930 left many thousands dead. Overtures between Burma and Japan started in

1935; there were promises to support the Japanese, should they invade the country. The younger Burmese were supportive of the Co-Prosperity scheme, in the belief that the Japanese could help them gain the independence they so yearned for.

But the country also suffered from internal strife: when Japan did invade, the Karens and the Nagas were dealt with most severely by the Burmese. Many tribes kept their faith with Britain throughout the war, but the Nagas actively fought with us. Tough and determined warriors, they gave their help willingly, in spite of the severe treatment they received from the Japanese when they were captured. During the 1942 retreat they pursued the Japanese, though facing torture and death, and the burning of their villages, as punishment for their activities. When the British returned, victorious, they fought and died alongside us. Led by British officers, they repeatedly ambushed the Japanese, and fought valiantly. For their unswerving loyalty, their active participation in the fighting, and assistance in carrying wounded Allied soldiers to safety, the Nagas earned the undying gratitude of all who were fortunate enough to have had them by their side.

When the Japanese attack came, the Burmese cities were heavily and indiscriminately bombed, but the residents forgave their potential redeemers for this, receiving their conquerors with open arms, showering them with flowers and gifts. The Japanese were treated as saviours by the Burmese, who felt downtrodden and ill-treated by the British. But they were quickly disillusioned: not only did the Japanese treat them as badly as any of their other conquests, but they soon made it quite clear they had no intention of granting independence to Burma.

They wanted Burma not just to protect their new prize, Malaya, from the British bases in India, but also for the rice fields, and the sorely needed oilfields of Yenangyaung. They could also now stop the passage of supplies from India to China through Northern Burma, which were presently being shipped from Rangoon up the Irrawaddy and over the mountains to Lashio, thence by the Burma Road to Kunming. In 1941 they had asked Britain to close that supply road to China, and received a polite 'no' in response.

Others initially welcomed the Japanese incursion: Subra Chandra Bose, the leader of the Indian National Army – deserters from the British

Indian Army – and of the Free India Movement, which was sweeping the country, was anxious to lead the revolt against the British Raj. He wanted the Indian National Army to be the spearhead of a Japanese invasion of north-eastern India, so the Indian population would welcome the Japanese. However, he received only the most cursory attention from the Japanese, and the INA played an inconsequential role in the future.

There was little opposition from the meagre British garrison in Burma, or the Chinese troops, flown into the central area by order of General Stilwell, and who eventually also fell back. Apart from some volunteer organizations, there was only the 17th Indian Division, which had fought in the deserts of North Africa, but they knew little of jungle warfare. They were out of their depth.

A further disastrous decision by the British, on February 23, jeopardized the safety of the 17th Indian Division. The Japanese Fifteenth Army crossed the Siam–Burmese border, entering Burma through Moulmein and heading for Rangoon, but there was a major obstacle: the Sittang River, would soon be in full spate. They planned to cross by the bridge between Bilin and Pegu, about a hundred miles north-east of Rangoon. To deny this bridge to the Japanese would impede their speedy taking of Rangoon, and would help the British in the withdrawal of their troops. Major General Jackie Smyth, the Divisional Commander, knew how vitally important the bridge was and, in considering its destruction, realized also the grave consequences to his own troops. Unless the most careful timing was observed, they would be exposed to immense danger. But if they failed to destroy the bridge, they would face death at the hands of the Japanese – or, possibly worse, captivity. After much soul-searching, and with the support of his staff officers, Major General Smyth ordered his engineers to destroy the bridge. It was a mistake; by his poor judgment he alienated himself from his fellow officers, who believed he had erred sadly in his decision. It also ended his career as a Field General, for he was sent home immediately and relegated to relatively menial administrative duties.

The timing was indeed poor, and the bridge was destroyed whilst two-thirds of the Division was still on the east side of the river, isolated from Divisional Headquarters and faced with imminent action by the Japanese. What happened to those three thousand British, Indian and Gurkha soldiers was never known. Many were probably swept away by the fast-flowing river, others killed in battle, or, worse, captured – the cruelty of the Japanese was already well known. A handful reached the other side using bamboo rafts, or by swimming across.

Meanwhile, the Japanese pressed on to Rangoon by a slightly different route and entered the city without further difficulty. The effectiveness of the remaining British forces after this setback was reduced to the point where any resistance offered not even the most forlorn hope of success, but the Japanese diversion meant they missed their chance to completely anni-hilate the British forces trapped in the area. There was only one squadron of British fighter planes, and though supplemented by American Flying Tigers, they were no match for the Japanese Zeros. Rangoon and the adja-cent airfields were bombed on December 23; the Rising Sun flew over that city on March 8, 1942.

AFTER THE JAPANESE invasion by General Iida's First Army on January 20 and the Sittang disaster, followed by the occupation of Rangoon, events moved very quickly. On April 25 the British were given the order for a general retreat. Meanwhile the Burmese Voluntary Forces, ostensibly allied to the Japanese, suddenly sprang into being and spent most of their time hindering the British retreat, and looting, raping and murdering the Burmese Indians.

For the soldiers of the Raj it was as bitter a defeat as Dunkirk had been a year earlier for the British Expeditionary Force routed by the Germans. By and large the general retreat was completed within a few days, heavy armour, field-guns and vehicles having been abandoned earlier on. The majority of the men walked nearly nine hundred miles north, across the Ava bridge at Mandalay, which they then destroyed, on through Shwebo towards the Indian border. The last hundred and fifty miles of this gruelling journey were a real struggle, to Ye-Hu, across the chaungs [1] to Shwegan, by boat along and across the Chindwin River, thence to Kalewa and the malig-nant Kabaw valley. It was along this same route that three years later the vic-torious Fourteenth Army would return to defeat the Japanese and recapture Rangoon.

It is estimated that more than thirteen thousand British soldiers and countless thousands of Burmese civilians died on that weeks-long journey.

1 Streams

They were often in danger of being cut off by the fast-moving Japanese. They were poorly fed, and often without water for days; when they became too weak to walk, they crawled, and when they were past crawling, then they died where they fell. Those who fell behind were massacred by the Japanese, whose passion was to kill all in their path that moved. Those fortunate enough to reach India did so with bodies ravaged by disease and jungle sores that never healed. They had struggled over razor-backed mountains, crossed fast-flowing rivers – where men were swept away and drowned – and were tormented by mosquitoes, leeches and deadly snakes. They suffered from malaria, dysentery, black water fever, beriberi, and a host of other afflictions to body and mind that only pernicious jungles could cause. It was a sorry mass of humanity that, reaching the border, sought refuge. They stumbled across exhausted and haggard and almost at death's door, fearing not only the pursuing Japanese snapping at their heels, but also the nearing monsoon, which would mean certain death for those still trying to escape.

General Bill Slim later said that when the main body of the retreating army left Kalewa, halfway between Mandalay and the Indian border, heavy rainfall caused sheer misery. Toiling up the hills in the inches-deep slippery mud, shivering, ill-fed and suffering with fever, it was a time of Purgatory. At night their only rest was on the sodden ground under the dripping trees. But whilst the rains added immeasurably to the discomfort of the fleeing troops, they also helped to slow down the Japanese pursuit.

In his book, *Defeat into Victory*, Bill Slim said, 'The first of the army survivors to reach India were an undisciplined mob of fugitives intent only on escape, and on the last day of the nine-hundred-mile retreat, I stood on a bank beside the road and watched the rearguard march into India. As the British, Indians and Gurkhas walked by, all were gaunt and ragged as scarecrows. Yet, as they trudged along in pitifully small groups, they still carried their rifles and kept their ranks, and were still recognizable as fighting units. They might look like scarecrows, but they also looked like soldiers too.' And so, unwashed, unshaven and very bedraggled, they returned to fight another day.

It was touch and go whether or not the Japanese would be able to surge across the border and into India to continue their murdering and plundering; there appeared to be little to prevent them from doing just that. In the end, sufficient force was gathered to repel the Japanese at the very edge of the Indian border and the country was saved the horrors of occupation by a ruthless enemy.

So ended the longest retreat in the history of the British Army. And the Ledo Road to China – the supply route for arms, ammunition and food for the Chinese – was closed.

THE SUMMER WAS ending at Madras as my regiment loaded guns and vehicles onto the flatcars of the North Eastern Railway, which was to carry us more than a thousand miles along the typhoon-prone east coast of India. Most of the gunners travelled on the open flats with the equipment, sleeping, eating and drinking tea surrounded by their weapons of war. Piled alongside them were the exposed 25-pounder ammunition shells. Brewing up tea on petrol tins filled with sand and fired by a small amount of petrol poured in (an idea copied from the Eighth Army in the western deserts of North Africa) was a common practice, even in the proximity of live ammunition. To the onlooker it must have presented quite a picture: to see all this taking place with such a total disregard for safety; mind you, they might have been more appalled by the men themselves, who had divested themselves of all their clothes in an effort to keep cool as the train rolled along the track. Not that we passed through any so-called 'civilized areas' – and anyway, the native women were thought to be not averse to the sight of a British soldier displaying his manhood.

The scenery was ever-changing as we passed from the lush greenery of Tamil Nadhu in the south to the hills of central India, across the arid flatlands, then the jungles of the north-east. And wherever we were there were always the crowded and mean-looking villages inhabited by undernourished people, the children with bellies swollen from hunger.

It took several days to traverse the famine-stricken Vellore, Vizagap-atam – once a Dutch possession – Cuttack, and Balesore, a coastline forever being punished by the typhoons that swept in from the Bay of Bengal every autumn. Cuttack, about two hundred and fifty miles south-west of Calcutta, sits on the Khatjuri River which, during the rains, pours down a prodigious flood, creating havoc in the town. The Cuttack Fort, built in the thirteenth century, was taken by the British in 1803 from the Raja of

Nagpur. It now lies in ruins and all that remains is a gateway. A hundred miles on is Balesore (an unsavoury name; its correct name is Baleshwar), some one hundred and fifty miles south-west of Calcutta. Once of great commercial importance, the English, the Danes and the French had factories there, and in 1634 it was a Portuguese stronghold and slave market. The inhabitants of the area were accustomed to their homes and possessions being ravaged by the brutal weather, and surviving on a consequently meagre diet.

The train bypassed Calcutta to the south, then we headed up to Assam, later, when India was partitioned, to be renamed Bangladesh. After crossing the mighty holy river Ganges, we reached the even mightier Brahmaputra. At Gauhati the men, vehicles, guns and equipment were ferried to the southern banks of that wide and fast-flowing river and loaded onto the narrow-gauge railway that was to take us on to the railhead at Dimapur.

The Americans now ran the railway system, and on the latter part of the journey the train was manned by three swashbuckling Yanks, hard-living, hard-swearing men who seemed to live only for, and thrive on, Scotch whisky, from sundown to sun up, and often before and after. How they obtained it in this remote part of the world was a mystery, especially in the prodigious quantities they had acquired: the greater part of the coaling area behind the engine cab was given over as storage! I assumed there was an American Air Force base in the area. But they certainly deserved what little comforts they could find, for theirs was a lonely and dangerous job. The route was through a very active dacoit area, and they had none of the luxuries of civilization awaiting them at either end of their journey. However, they were generous with the liquor, handing bottles to me and each of my fellow officers, saying, 'You'll need this where you are going, God help you!' This last kind act by the Americans was greatly appreciated.

Also, quite miraculously, someone had produced a fairly good supply of beer, which was hung in saturated straw bags on the side of the flat-cars, swinging as the train moved along and almost dragging along the sleepers of the railway track. Icy cold, it helped the parched gunners enormously. Standing at the side of the tracks during one of the many halts with the Quartermaster, I asked where the beer came from, but the QM expressed complete ignorance of the source. Smiling, I retorted, 'Good show, Q, I knew you could be relied on for the beer to have been delivered by the fairies! Make sure you keep in touch with them and let them know that the officers are not averse to drinking beer either – even if it was "lifted" or "borrowed". We'll do our best to see you get your reward in heaven!'

The mystery of how the beer found its way aboard the train was never solved, but perhaps those generous Americans knew something about it.

Though accustomed to enforced boredom, the troops were nevertheless tired of the long inactivity as they entered the eighth day of the train journey. All the popular songs had been exhausted and everyone had sung the current favourite – 'I'm going to buy a paper doll that I can call my own, a doll that other fellows cannot steal,' – so many times that they were quite prepared to give her away free to the first person that came along. They were tired of the train and itching for a change, and it was about to come, albeit in ways for which we were all quite unprepared. We would soon be in action against the Japanese; now it was time to get ready for the fighting.

We were now approaching Assam and Manipur, which had been the scene of a recent major battle. This wasn't the kind of country one would choose to hold a battle, for it was, as General Slim observed, 'Some of the world's worst country, breeding the world's worst diseases, and having, for half the year at least, the world's worst climate.' Set in this very unpleasant landscape, Kohima was a far cry from England's green and pleasant land: it was definitely *not* one of the world's more delightful places. The depressingly ugly plain was alive with mosquitoes carrying malaria, dysentery and most other diseases known to man. Hot and unpleasant, the undergrowth, the chaungs and rivers were infested with all manner of creatures.

At the time, the Japanese were closing in on Kohima and Imphal (the capital of Manipur State); both were some forty miles inside the Indian border, but sixty miles apart from each other. Imphal was an important British base with an all-weather airfield and supply dumps; losing Kohima would also mean the loss of Dimapur, our destination, the railhead through which all supplies flowed to both the Fourteenth Army and to Stilwell's Chinese forces in the north. The Japanese, in the form of General Sato's 31st Division, had already forced a roadblock between Imphal and Kohima, which was itself besieged. In Dimapur, Slim asked Major General Ranking,

Commander of the base and rear areas of Assam, what the strength of his command was, to which he replied, 'Forty-five thousand, near enough.'

Slim's next question was, 'How many soldiers out of that lot can you scrape up?'

The discouraging answer was, 'I might get five hundred who know how to fire a rifle.' Meanwhile two additional brigades had been brought in, so now the opposing forces were about equal in numbers.

There were many battles in the area surrounding what was to be the major scene of conflict: in the village of Tamu, fifty miles south-east of Imphal, a tank battle continued for three days, resulting in heavy casualties. A Gurkha battalion captured an entire Brigade of the Indian National Army fighting under the flag of the Rising Sun. It was a bloodless encounter – the INA surrendered without a shot being fired; the Commander of the Gurkhas commented, 'Never have so many been routed by so few.'

And it was in Kohima that a small group of some five hundred British infantrymen, the 4th Battalion of the Royal West Kents, fought a vicious battle against the fifteen-thousand-strong Japanese 31st Infantry Division of the Fifteenth Army, commanded by General Mutaguchi. The Japanese were well-equipped and flush with the victories which they had recently enjoyed. Defeat for them seemed an impossibility. In fact, Mutaguchi was so confident of the outcome of his planned attack at Kohima and Imphal that he had arranged for geishas to be flown in as comfort for his troops. (In the event, the girls did arrive, but they were too late; there is no record as to which side they serviced.) Mutaguchi had forecast victory within three days, but the siege lasted three weeks, after which the gallant West Kents were reinforced after holding out against his vastly superior force. In his book (*Defeat into Victory*) General Slim makes reference to Major General Tanaka's directive to the men of the 33rd Division, which stressed the importance of the Japanese capture of Imphal. Tanaka said: 'Rewards and punishments must be given on the spot without delay.' Failure to do their duty would result in the severest of penalties, he said, and 'A commander may have to use his sword as a weapon of punishment, although it is a shameful thought to have to shed the blood of one's own soldiers on the battlefield. On this battle rests the fate of the Empire.'

In fact, the focus was on Kohima, where the battle raged for eleven days. British and Japanese trenches were within yards of each other; there was no avenue of escape to lead the wounded and the dying to quiet areas. The designated evacuation area, for want of a better name, was behind the stone walls of a bungalow, and some casualties were hit again and again. At one stage the tennis courts of the local Governor's residence on the outskirts of the town became the focal point of the fight. It was close-quarter action all the way, fighting hand to hand, with the British dug in at one end of the courts and the Japanese at the other. And so it continued for several days, with British artillery gunfire being brought down on the far courts, only a few yards away from our own troops. Artillery and mortar fire fell incessantly, and the advantage see-sawed repeatedly: most of the time the score was Love All. The opponents were crammed in such a confined area and so close that it was said that when a Japanese soldier threw the soil out of his slit-trench, it landed in a British soldier's pit. They could clearly hear each other talking, and a fair amount of blasphemy was constantly shouted in both languages. Though neither understood the words of the other, the meaning was abundantly clear.

The phrase 'Fight to the last man and the last round' has long been a cliché applied to any desperate situation, though in military terms the order has been used only two or three times in the recent history of the British Army. During the First World War, Colonel Heston said there was only one degree of resistance: to the last round and the last man. More recently, the order was given at Dunkirk in 1940, when the German juggernaut was overrunning Western Europe and the freedom of the world was in jeopardy. And that was obeyed. The next occasion was at the battle of Imphal, and this was also a crucial moment in history. This final order had been issued at the most desperate moment, just hours before the last man did fire the last round – but at the height of the battle the 161st Brigade reached the beleaguered West Kents and a Punjabi regiment was the first to enter the fight.

So the order was never consummated, and the last man lived, thanks to the Punjabis (and to the heartfelt relief of the brave West Kents). On the following day, 6th Brigade of the 2nd Division relieved the garrison and Colonel Richards, of the Royal West Kents, handed over the command he had so gallantly held and collected his men. General Slim wrote, 'Three hours later they marched out, and just down below what had been the hospital, they found lorries waiting to take them from the dust, din, and stench of death in which they had lived for eleven days. Sieges have been longer, but few have been more intense, and none of the defenders deserved greater honour than the garrison of Kohima.'

Some of the fiercest, most ruthless fighting of the Burma Campaign took place at Kohima before the British successfully repelled the Japanese in an action that would long be remembered by the participants. It received widespread publicity throughout the British Army, and was always the subject of discussion whenever famous battles were talked about. The cost in lives on both sides was enormous: as many as sixty thousand Japanese and twenty thousand British casualties were reported. In the end the Governor's house was totally demolished; for a hundred yards around the trees were stripped of their foliage and branches, and the ground was a series of miniature dead volcanoes from the intense shelling by British and Japanese gunners. It would be a long time before tennis was played again there; the sounds of battle would endure even longer.

A memorial was erected at the heart of the battle place, sculpted by a Naga tribesman at the request of the British 2nd Division, which bore the brunt of action at the Battle of Kohima. It reads:

> When you go home,
> Tell them of us, and say
> For your tomorrow,
> We gave our today.

The author of these words is believed to be the Greek poet Simonides, who wrote them in the year 500BC to honour the three hundred Spartan soldiers who successfully held a mountain pass at Thermopylae against the Persian King Xerxes' huge invading army. Although surrounded, they fought to the last man, and so allowed time for their main army to regroup behind them. Simonides wrote the famous epitaph under the title, 'The Three Hundred who fell at the Battle of Thermopylae.'

THE WIDE AND swiftly flowing Chindwin River had been crossed; soon the world's longest Bailey bridge, of eleven hundred and fifty feet, would be assembled there, in the space of twenty-four hours. The regrouped British forces now pressed on relentlessly, with a part of the Fourteenth

Army advancing south from the Imphal area towards Shwebo and Ye-Hu. Soon it would cross the Irrawaddy. This force consisted of the British 2nd and 20th Divisions, plus an infantry brigade and a tank brigade. 4th Corps, under General Messervy, would sweep down the Gangaw valley, followed by the 7th and 17th Indian Divisions and the 255th Indian Tank Brigade. The strategy there was to simultaneously forge separate crossings of the Irrawaddy, both to the north and to the south of Mandalay. The four divisions of the Japanese Fifteenth Army had been decimated in the north and at Imphal and now numbered only twenty thousand men; this was typical of the destruction suffered by the other Japanese Armies. The Fourteenth Army now held a vast superiority. To the north and on the Salween fronts the Allied force consisted of five Chinese Divisions, commanded by General Joe Stilwell, the British 36th Division, Merrill's Marauders and, in Yunnan, twelve Chinese Divisions. They were operating in the Ledo Road area, where the Americans, with thousands of coolies, were building a road through to China from India for supply purposes.

Those working on the Ledo Road were isolated, living in primitive conditions and always open to attack by the Japanese. Disease, including the dreaded cholera, was rampant. The country was mountainous, covered by jungle, and in the monsoon season the conditions were horrendous. It was an impossible place to build a road, particularly during the rains, but it was desperately needed and eventually completed, and the first convoy of arms and supplies arrived in China a year later. Meanwhile the ferrying of arms and supplies to China was conducted on an enormous scale by air, 'Over the hump', as it became known, though it represented but a fraction of the needs.

Vinegar Joe – also known as Crusty Joe, for the same reasons – didn't get along very well with his British counterparts. He thought of them as novices, with little knowledge of soldiering and even less about the conduct of modern warfare. In his opinion, they were ineffectual and indecisive, and he was quite open about this. His nicknames were most appropriate: they reflected so well the sharpness of his tongue and his bitter attitude to all things British. Oddly enough, he took a shine to Bill Slim, publicly saying he 'wasn't a half bad guy' – high praise from such a man. The British in return were too well-mannered, of course, to say what they felt about Joe – but he did have a way of getting what he wanted. And he got results. He was very proud of the Chinese Division, which he had scrounged with the help of Chiang Kai-Shek and trained in India, thanks to money from Britain (and the ear of Lord Mountbatten); he was always ready to support them in all their actions. In the opinion of many of the British troops, however, they were poor soldiers, scruffy, ill-disciplined and badly trained. Their equipment was inferior and their artillery had the reputation of firing ammunition which frequently failed to explode upon impact. Taffy Jones bluntly described them as 'a fucking shower', which was about the most derogatory condemnation a British soldier could make about anybody.

On the west bank the two Divisions of the Japanese Twenty-Eighth Army had to prevent the British 15th Corps from attacking the Japanese communications in the rear of their main forces in the Irrawaddy valley. This force had an impossible task, for their two Divisions of perhaps thirty thousand men were faced with West African and Indian Divisions with five times their numbers, and they were forced to withdraw.

MY REGIMENT, NOW in support of the 19th Indian Division, had travelled down the narrow and winding roads – often nothing more than animal tracks – with the dust so heavy that it mixed with the sweat on our faces and turned to mud; we could hardly see the vehicle ahead, though it was only a few yards away. The route was littered with the debris of the ignominious retreat of 1942: rusting guns of all calibres, tanks and all the paraphernalia of war. Here, a mountainous stack of 303 rifle ammunition; there, in equal proportion, 3-inch mortar shells piled high alongside the dirt tracks. A rusting bayonet and a steel helmet, an unopened tin of bully beef, and a tattered tunic with the stripes of an artillery sergeant . . .

In pursuit of the enemy regiments, we had passed through Tamu, Kalewa, Ye-Hu, Shwebo and other villages with strange and fascinating names. We had also passed through the Hawkuang valley, an area reputed to be the most pernicious jungle in the world; it was here that my regiment suffered its first casualties: the troops, attacked by diseases the like of which we'd never before experienced, fell like flies. Many of the men were returned to the hospitals in India for treatment, and never saw action against the Japanese.

There were more casualties crossing the many major rivers, when our home-made bamboo boats collapsed. But the worst was yet to come, for we had now arrived at the western bank of the Irrawaddy River and there were few boats available to attempt the crossing of this enormous river, which ranged from a thousand to four and a half thousand feet wide. We had only a dozen or so LCTs – Landing Craft Troops – and these were quite inadequate for the task that lay ahead. As with all other war supplies, priority was given to the battlefields closer to Britain. The Fourteenth – the 'Forgotten Army' – must make do with what it had. We were too far away, and too tiny, in comparison with what was happening in the European theatre of war. The government and military leaders believed our part was sufficiently inconsequential to justify the lack of any vital supplies. Our action could not be compared, for example, with Stalingrad, where a German Army of three hundred thousand was decimated in a short period of time, or Normandy, where enormous casualties were suffered.

The few boats which were available to us had been damaged in other crossings, and there was not a single bridge the entire length of the Irrawaddy, for the only crossing at Ava had been destroyed by the Royal Air Force in 1943. Guns and heavy equipment cannot cross rivers without bridges or boats. So the determined General Bill Slim took control, gathering his engineers around him and saying, 'I believe that God helps those who help themselves. I want a hundred more boats to force the river.' Pointing to the huge trees and thick bamboo, he went on, 'There are the materials. You have four days to build them!'

Out of sight of Uncle Bill, as he was affectionately known, the engineers, shaking their heads ruefully, mustered their resources to meet this seemingly impossible task . . . which they did, making Slim's pronouncement a catchword for the Fourteenth Army.

Approval for the plan proposed by General Slim to finalize the Burma Campaign was a convoluted procedure involving army groups in south-east Asia and the Planning Chiefs of Staff in both London and Washington. Codenamed *Extended Capital,* the idea was to destroy the Japanese Fifteenth Army in a vice created through General Stopford's 33rd Corps crossing the Irrawaddy above and to the west of Mandalay, and General Messervy's 4th Corps broaching the river to the south and west of Mandalay. In this manner Slim proposed to trap the Fifteenth Army, isolating them from other Japanese forces further south. It would also place elements of Messervy's command ready to strike at the Japanese base of Meiktila. There would be four points of attack across the river, with the 19th Indian Division – commanded by the fiery Welshman Pete Rees, who won the Military Cross in the First World War, spoke several Asian languages, stood five feet two inches tall and wore a flamboyant red silk scarf – crossing at Singhu, some thirty miles north of Mandalay and storming the Japanese head-on. West of the city and thirty miles distant, the 2nd British Division would cross at Ngazun. About ten miles downstream, the 20th British Division would strike at Myinmu. Finally, a further seventy miles to the south-west, Nyaungu would be taken by the 7th Indian Division.

Upon the completion of the crossings, the 17th Indian Division (that same 17th Division which lost most of its men to the Japanese on the Sittang River in the 1942 retreat) would pass through the bridgehead gained by the 7th Division and race the eighty miles to Meiktila. General Punch Cowan would successfully do this, heavily thrashing the Japanese forces in Meiktila on March 1. The 7th Division went on to capture the oil wells at Chaulk; they'd been destroyed by the British during the retreat, but the Japanese had rebuilt the plant and the wells were now found to be in good order. The Irrawaddy crossing by the 19th Indian Division went well, patrols in boats locating Japanese positions at various points. Then, on the night of March 14, we made an entirely unopposed, stealthy crossing at Thabeikkyin; a whole battalion was dug in on the far bank by sunrise. At the same time the Division made its major crossing at Singhu and within twenty-four hours had two battalions over with little opposition from the Japanese.

A heavy counter-attack followed quickly, but after vicious hand-to-hand fighting, the Japanese were repelled. Calling up two additional divisions, with more artillery support, the Japanese attacked again and again, in suicidal efforts to dislodge the two brigades of the 19th Indian Division. This went on for almost three weeks before we were able to strengthen our bridgehead and muster sufficient force to make the Japanese retreat. Casualties on both sides were extremely heavy; the Japanese division of twenty-one thousand men who had fought at Kohima just a short while before was now reduced to a fraction of that number. Other units suffered similar casualties.

To provide an element of surprise, Stopford was to feint further down river at Nyaungu, with other, most elaborate diversions created both up and downstream, as far as ten miles away from the true proposed crossing. Strategies to create deception included unusually heavy wireless transmissions, some in clear; the movement of troops and vehicles on the riverbanks to make dust and noise to give the impression that here were the intended crossings; boats set at various places along the river, and constantly moved. Reconnaissance party crossings were also made to the enemy-held banks, to strengthen their belief that we would land there. These places were heavily shelled and mortared, whereas the intended crossing was not, nor would it be until minutes before the assault was made. We resorted to every trick in the book to avert attention from our real intention.

I HAD BEEN seconded to the 2nd British Division to provide artillery support for the crossing which was to take place on February 23. At my assembly point, absolute silence prevailed, with no visible movement of any kind during the hours of daylight. Not even a cigarette was lit. Only the noises of the jungle were to be heard. Waiting a short distance from the riverbank, still in my Jeep and concealed in the bushes, I could sense the tension in the two signallers who were to accompany me on the crossing. The wireless operator appeared to be under considerable stress. When I asked him, he admitted that he was scared; he was obviously about to have a breakdown. Without hesitation I signalled to his troop for an immediate replacement operator to be sent up, dispatching to the rear the man who had been my signaller for three years. He had to be replaced at once; this was no time for any weakness in my party, not even by a young man in his late teens with long service behind him. The company of infantry was poised ready for the assault.

I and my OP Ack – my Observation Post Assistant – and signallers were to be in the first wave of the crossing, and in the same boat as the infantry's Company Commander; Robin and I were old acquaintances, having met frequently during training exercises; we'd shared drinking sessions in the Officers' Club at Poona. I knew him to be both resolute and aggressive.

The mood amongst the men was tense as we knew the night ahead was wrought with danger and many of us would not survive. The Padre made his rounds, quietly moving from boat to boat. And meanwhile the preparations for the assault continued.

BURMA: DENSE, PESTILENTIAL jungles and razor-backed mountains to the north; to the south, the open paddy fields from the rice bowl of Mandalay to Rangoon. And riddled with rivers: the Chindwin, the Salween, the Shweli, the Sittang, the Meiktila . . . Burma is truly a land of rivers: and now the greatest of them all, the Irrawaddy, rising in the Kachin hills in the north, stretching over thirteen hundred miles down the length of the country to the Rangoon Delta: it is one of the world's mightiest waterways. Its source is the confluence of the Meihha and the Malinka rivers, some thirty miles north of Myitkyina, an area where the roads are little better than narrow tracks. It is at once so rugged and jungle-clad as to be almost impenetrable, deterring anyone from journeying to the cradle of the river. To the north it is quite shallow, but before it reaches Bhamo, where it is joined by the Mogaung River, the snow thaws create a huge lake, with the water rising as much as forty feet. South of Bhamo at Sinkan, during the rains, the depth of the water can reach one hundred and eighty feet; in the defiles it becomes a raging torrent. At Katha it is joined by the Shweli River entering from China, which is heavily used for logging. On past the great Shwebo plain and Mandalay, the river turns west for a distance of fifty or sixty miles, before veering south again towards Ngazun, Pakokku and Pagan. There was only one bridge along the entire length of this powerful river, and that was at Ava, once the capital of Burma. It served not only the road joining east and west Burma, but also the railway line from India to Myitkyina. In 1943 that bridge was destroyed by the British; now the only way across was by boat.

It was at Ngazun that I was to make the stormy crossing of the Irrawaddy.

The assault troops who were to undertake the hazardous crossing of the river were fortunate enough to have the guidance of the Sea Reconnaissance Unit, more commonly known as the Frogmen, a small group of superbly trained swimmers, to assist in amphibious crossings. They were men from all three branches of the services, of diverse nationalities, who learnt their craft in California, in Britain and in Ceylon. Of the four sections comprising the Unit, two were with the 19th for the Irrawaddy crossing, the third would be on Ramree Island, and the fourth here with the 2nd British Division. Their job was to reconnoitre the river and to lead the first wave of troops: that meant actually swimming across the treacherous waters of the Irrawaddy to explore the beaches on which the proposed landings were to take place.

First they had to determine whether the far side of the river was occupied by the Japanese, and if so, to what extent. Then they had to find out the strength of the current, the water levels, the gradient of the beach, whether or not the ground was suitable for tanks, and a host of other data. They would make the crossing as many times as was necessary to gather this information, working closely with the Commanding Officers of the troops making the assault. It was an extremely dangerous task, whether carried out by day or by night, and they were very vulnerable, as they would be fully exposed and readily visible to the Japanese, especially at night when the moon was full. As they crossed on their paddle-boats which were similar to surf boards, about ten feet long, there was always the possibility of meeting Japanese patrol boats. And there were the more natural but no less deadly hazards of the river: the strong and unexpected currents and the giant water snakes which lay on the beaches waiting for unsuspecting prey. On the north-west coast of Burma there were the man-eating estuarine crocodile-infested chaungs to navigate in order to carry out their missions. The Frogmen had the most dangerous job in the British Army; it was a brave man who would volunteer for those duties.

Now they had to explore the beaches for the three separate crossings by the Worcesters, the Cameron Highlanders and the Royal Welsh Fusiliers, doing so over two separate nights prior to the actual crossing. The leader of this section was Flight Lieutenant Harry Avery, of the Royal Canadian Air Force, who was awarded the Military Cross for his bravery, as was his second-in-command, Lieutenant Turpin of the Royal West Kents. During one of the explorations, a very startled Lieutenant Avery emerged from the water to see a senior Japanese officer standing on the beach, looking across the river in the light of the dawn. He was equally shocked to see the water-dripping Avery; he dropped the briefcase he was carrying and fled. Avery was quick to seize it and swim back to his own bank, but it contained nothing more important than the Japanese order of the day to resist the British crossing of the river.

He returned the following night and carried out his reconnaissance in preparation for the Worcesters' crossing. After dusk the next night, February 23, he attempted to swim to the far bank to post beach lights to guide the troops across, which was the normal practice, but Japanese patrols prevented him. On this occasion, Avery didn't lead the crossing, as he normally would have done, because the Worcesters' loading area was visible from their start point. As they left in the early hours of the morning under a bright moon, they were greeted with heavy machine-gun and rifle fire. They had a difficult time of it, and there were many casualties.

Both the Worcester Regiment and the Cameron Highlanders had fought for England throughout the centuries. The former saw service in many parts of the far-flung Empire, including Gibraltar in 1727, in the Pyrenees in 1813, Corunna and Salamanca in the Spanish Wars. The Camerons are first mentioned at Blenheim in 1709, Malplaquet in 1709, Pondicherry in 1760, Copenhagen in 1807 and, with the Worcesters, at Salamanca in 1812. They were both in the South African wars earning battle honours; wherever the British were fighting to capture foreign territory, or to retain lands already acquired, one or the other were there with the flag. It is said that one of the more onerous duties the Camerons had to undertake was to act as guard to the Duke of Windsor and his wife Wally in Nassau whilst he was the Governor of the Bahamas; considering the Duke's friendship with the Germans, the Camerons seem to have been given a difficult task – but then, they were used to fighting at a disadvantage, and winning. Now both the Worcesters and the Highlanders were facing an implacable enemy; they would need all their skills and experience, honed through centuries of warfare, if they were to survive.

Tomorrow would be February 23, 1945, and at first light we would cross one of the most dangerous rivers in the world to attack the Japanese. We knew it would be a day to remember: a day filled with violence and fear, against the vicious and ruthless Japanese.

IT WAS NOW after dark that evening, and, in my role of Forward Observation Officer providing artillery support to the Worcester Regiment of the 2nd British Division, I and my two signallers were making last-minute preparations. There was some optimism about the crossing, and expectations that it would be a relatively bloodless one were being freely voiced – but the optimists were wrong. We would be under surveillance by the Japanese the whole of the way across the water, without protection; it was to be a bloody journey, with the full moon making us easy targets for the Japanese. The famous Cameron Highlanders, who were to land on the adjacent beach, were to fare no better.

I was dressed like most of the men, in jungle-green battledress, with shirt sleeves rolled up in spite of the mosquitoes. I'd worn this uniform for six months and the jungle had taken its toll on what was now a very bedraggled-looking outfit. It was but a poor memory of its original dark green, faded and patched here and there; it was threadbare at the knees and torn at the back where the bamboo had caught it. It hadn't been washed in weeks, and didn't appear to be long for this life – much like me! But looking around, I saw we were all the same. And it didn't bother anyone; nothing lasts long in the jungle. A few men even wore shorts, which was contrary to regulations because of malaria, but nothing was said; there were other things on our minds besides our dress.

It was unusually quiet now. Even the chattering of the monkeys was subdued, and there were few other animal cries to penetrate the deathly hush. It was a long wait to the small hours of the morning, but at 02:00 hours the boats slipped quietly away from the shore to start the two mile trip across the Irrawaddy. All we could do was to hope for the best, that the Japanese wouldn't have time to strengthen their position before they realized that the Worcesters were upon them. The crossing was expected to take about twenty minutes, with the landing on the far beaches coinciding with the first light of day. Unfortunately the water levels had fallen dramatically during the night and the crossing proved to be extremely hazardous. There were now many more sandbanks and several boats would obviously be delayed, or even prevented from reaching the far shore.

There had been no element of surprise and we were dogged by the vicious Japanese guns all the way across the river. Firing back from the boats was pointless and we could only pray.

I was also under fire, like the rest of the men in boats, all of which were already filled to overflowing. My mind was in a state of chaos, but I had to concentrate on reaching the far bank. With the confusion of orders being shouted and countermanded, many of us were despairing. Most of our boats were of bamboo but a few were factory-made. However, these had been used the previous day for the 20th Division crossing downstream at Myinmu, and many of them were badly damaged. They had already been used extensively before that in Europe and were in pretty poor shape when the 20th got them. By the time we got them, they were very much hand-me-downs; the 2nd Division felt like poor relations – that didn't help when we knew we had a tough job to do. Even now we were under heavy machine-gun fire and, in our exposed position on the moonlit Irrawaddy, many of the Worcester infantrymen died, easy targets for the enemy.

I was in the leading wave of the assault and now it was my turn. As the shore was reached, at the order 'Kedge down' – lower the ramp – the kedge of my boat struck, and it too received the attention of the machine-guns. Now we were faced with twenty yards of sandy beach which rose steeply for thirty feet before being topped with thick elephant grass. Razor-sharp and taller than those who got ashore, the grass was a treacherous obstacle, and more men died from the same withering fire trying to get to it. But it also offered sanctuary, for once you gained its cover you were hidden from the eyes of the probing machine-gunners. All around, other boats were landing, with the occupants racing up the beach seeking the haven the grass presented.

The target was to be the enemy machine-guns situated on the promontory a few hundred yards to the flank, which dominated the landing of the assault craft and was responsible for the near-failure of our landing. It could be seen only from the exposed beach, so it was *once more into the breach* for me as I stood there unprotected, directing the fire. Three ranging rounds from a 25-pounder were all that were necessary before I ordered gunfire from the Troop's four guns to silence those murderous machine-guns. As the smoke and the noise cleared, so did the strafing along the beach. But there were still the Japanese mortars to deal with and, being obscured by the elephant grass, it was not possible to see them. Accompanied by a section of Worcesters, I crept along until we'd cleared the grass, after about fifty yards and saw open country. And there were the mortars, perhaps half a mile away. Once again I ordered the gunners' response, but this time with the guns of the whole Battery, which replied with devastating fire, and the Japanese mortar fire ceased. And so the status quo was restored. The bloody hand-to-hand fighting continued, with the bridgehead taken only at great sacrifice by the men of the Worcester Regiment, and the day was won by the narrowest of margins.

About a hundred yards upstream, and outside the perimeter of the ground now held by the Worcesters, another drama was unfolding, for a stray boat was being washed ashore. It was one of several which had been stranded on a sand bar and was now reaching land. The men, many of whom had been wounded by the machine-gun fire, which was also the cause of the boat going astray, had clambered out and were struggling to reach the beach. The moment they reached the edge of the shore, they were viciously sabred by the Japanese who were waiting for them. As the victims held their arms above their heads in surrender, the merciless Japanese cruelly hacked off their limbs, leaving their bodies writhing in the yellow sand, which quickly turned red with blood. It was too far away to hear any sounds and the slight breeze was blowing in the wrong direction anyway, but it was evident to me, as I looked through my binoculars, that the men were pleading for mercy as they were cut down; their faces showed the immense agony they were suffering. But the Japanese officers continued with the slaughter, their swords flashing in the sun as they rose and fell. As our men lay there, the vicious Japanese plunged bayonets into the bodies, again and again, long after they were dead. Almost a dozen unfortunate men were dispatched in this manner; there was nothing I or the Worcesters could do, only stand by helplessly, watching the grisly executions. It was a brutal carnage, which would be reciprocated tenfold by the onlookers at the earliest opportunity.

By a miracle, one man was able to break loose and run along the beach to the safety of the bridgehead. On that narrow stretch everything was being done to help the wounded, but there were no skilled doctors; the only medical attention was what first-aid we could provide. Medical supplies consisted of nothing more than the field bandages which every man carried sewn into his battledress trousers, and perhaps a shot of morphine if the First Aid Corporal could be found – if he too wasn't dead. This was of little help to the man who lay a few yards away with both of his legs blown off by a land mine, still conscious, though in a state of shock. Nor would it help the man on a makeshift stretcher, with a gaping hole in his stomach and blood spurting from his mouth, his body riddled with Japanese machine-gun bullets. His blood was so red, so outstandingly vivid, that the deep red colour of the sun setting over the west bank of the Irrawaddy was a watery shadow by comparison. It might be an hour or so before a Medical Officer crossed the river; those two soldiers would be dead before he arrived, and buried with little ceremony on the banks of the Irrawaddy. There would be no gun carriages to carry their bodies, no marching bands, no volley of rifle fire as a last salute, no 'Last Post' blown by the bugles as the flag was lowered. And I thought: this is what war is all about, the killing of men, and all too often the killing of women and children.

The company was about to move on now, and the two men, along with others whose wounds were not considered life-threatening, would remain there in the care of an NCO until the main body of the regiment arrived. For them the war was over; those who lived would probably get a Blighty ticket and soon be on the boat. As with all soldiers, 'roll on the boat' was always on their mind, but this was not the way they had expected to earn their ticket home. With a last look at the poor devils, I helped my signaller gather the equipment and we moved off with the infantry to whatever lay ahead.

The position had been consolidated and the next waves of troops would be on their way across the river. The new group of British infantrymen would be busy as well, for the elephant grass still sheltered many Japanese and there would be a lot of mopping-up to do. But I was safely across that stretch of water, and in spite of our bad start, my signallers and I were on the eastern shores of the river and in pursuit of the Japanese again.

THE FIRST COUPLE of months of 1945 were momentous. In January, US forces captured Mindora Island in the Philippines, the British started a new offensive in Burma and the Germans in Budapest surrendered to the Soviets, who also liberated Warsaw, and the death camp Auschwitz in Poland a week later. American troops took Iwo Jima with heavy casualties. US bombers laid a carpet of incendiary bombs on Tokyo by low-level bombing, and the inferno created by the Allied bombing of Dresden in Germany killed sixty thousand people in one night. And now we were off to recapture Mandalay.

chapter fifteen

BURMA: THE CORPS SHOOT

March 1945 to April 1945

Luckily, I was still alive and uninjured – what more could a soldier expect? Not every venture across the river was uneventful, and there had been more casualties than we'd anticipated (or hoped). There had been several dismal failures at other crossings, caused mainly by the boats we had to use. Old and already damaged by previous rough use, they were floating death-traps for many of our men. Leaking badly, breaking up on sandbanks, they spilled their occupants into the dangerous, fast-flowing waters of the Irrawaddy. Helpless, like those who were lost in the crossing with me, they were easy targets for the Japanese machine-gunners who seemed to be everywhere. And if they were lucky enough to escape that merciless hail of lead, they were dragged down by their heavy equipment as the swirling currents swept them downstream. It was a far from pleasant death, to be sucked under by those evil-smelling, disease-carrying waters, where the flyin'-fishes most decidedly do not play, contrary to Kipling's assertions[1]. It was very questionable if they could survive the filth and the muck the river had gathered from the shores of countless villages it had passed on its long journey before it finally emptied in the great delta on the Andaman Sea south-west of Rangoon. To share the same waters, where so many bodies now floated – British, Indian, Gurkha, Burmese, and too few Japanese – all mixed with the rotted, bloated carcasses of animals, was not a worthy or befitting end for a British soldier. Yet they have died under worse conditions, perhaps given to the women of the Pathan

1 'Mandalay', *Barrack Room Ballads*

310

tribesmen on the North-West Frontier, and subjected to the most horrific torture before finally being put to death –

> *When you're wounded and left on Afghanistan's plains,*
> *And the women come out to cut out what remains,*
> *Jest roll to your rifle and blow out your brains*
> *An' go to your Gawd like a soldier.*[1]

Or worse, to the Afridis . . . Kipling again. British soldiers were mutilated and died at the hands of the Zulus in Isandlwallah, South Africa, unable to defend themselves because the ammunition boxes were bound with copper bands and under lock and key, by order of the Quartermaster back in England – he had said they would have no need for them. They had only single-shot rifle ammunition, for the Treasury Board said clips of five would merely contribute to waste – and anyway, the rabble they were fighting were only simple blacks who should easily be defeated. In the rat-infested military hospital at Katari, in the Crimea, they died not from their Russian-inflicted wounds, but from disease from the open sewers and appalling conditions at the hospital. Not even Florence Nightingale's ministrations could help them. They too were a long way from England, and did anyone care?

MAP-READING WAS difficult in the jungles, and even on the plains of Burma. In the great rice bowl below Mandalay I could at least see far enough to try to find an identifiable feature and so orient myself, but reference points were not too plentiful, so it meant a lot of guesswork. But it was much worse in the jungle: we were lucky if we could see even a few yards in front of us. Climbing trees sometimes offered opportunities, but they were few and far between and often it was necessary to engage a target based on the sound of the shells landing. We had to hope that the first round did not land in our own area, but they often did. A company commander might ask me to engage the nearby enemy, knowing only that they were thought to be a hundred yards in front of his troops. If there was time, I'd go forward, often alone, into enemy territory, and attempt to determine the location more accurately myself – one reason why there were so few forward observation officers left at the end of the war. I'd then

1 'The Young British Soldier', *Barrack Room Ballads*

try to fix my own position on the map, almost impossible to do with any accuracy in dense jungle, but if the support of the guns was requested, we made an educated guess based on the last known position (by adding the distance we had travelled since then, usually in paces, and using a compass bearing to project our new location).

Once there was a round on the ground, it was then a matter of ordering corrections to creep slowly on to the target. It was a rough and ready procedure and there was none of this nonsense of applying any scientific gunnery calculations. It was very much by guess and by God, and not all that different to the way a target was engaged a hundred years earlier, except no one had to peer along a gun barrel. It took only a small error for the next shell to land in our own area, so we held our breath when the final rounds were fired. It was also rare to see the smoke from the round striking the ground, so there was no visible assistance there. We also had to be careful not to waste ammunition, though this was difficult when using this method to engage a target, because supply lines were often far distant and the terrain made it difficult to bring the ammunition forward. Where the supply was by air, a gun might be limited to ten rounds a day, or even less.

On one occasion, when shells were strictly rationed – and, incidentally, when there were some choice targets to engage at the time – an overseas radio broadcast announced that a dockers' strike at Liverpool had paralysed the shipping of supplies to the Far East, and this included ammunition for our guns. That day the dockers in England would have hung their heads in shame, had they heard the blasphemy of the men of the Fourteenth Army.

Forward observation officers were always out in the front of the battle, always where the action was. They were usually artillery captains of a troop of four or eight guns, and their lifespan was considerably shorter than that of a subaltern at the gun position. Because of the high casualty rate, the promotion of subaltern to captain was often very quick, though they in turn could not expect to last long. It was an exciting and sometimes frightening job because you were always within rifle-shot of the enemy and more often than not at close quarters in the jungle. But I, like all forward observation officers, learnt to stomach the tension and, in time, came to accept it as routine; that sinking feeling in the pit of the stomach gradually mellowed.

Of course, there were respites when we were relieved: someone else carried the torch and we returned to the Battery to rest. I was fortunate and although engaged in hand-to-hand fighting on occasion, never had recourse to the bayonet – that was about as close as you could get to the real gut-tearing sensation you could experience as an infantryman. And when it happened, it looked unreal, to watch the man behind the bayonet now transformed to a killer as he lunged at the throat or the stomach of his victim, twisted and withdrew and thrust again. There would be a sudden rush of blood as now, with his face flushed and distorted in a snarl, eyes bulging and with the weapon held well forward, he went savagely in to the kill. The blade would sink but a few inches into the naked stomach, and the victim would sink to his knees, gripping the shaft of the bayonet as his eyes looked with disbelief at his killer's unforgiving face. With nothing more than a sigh as the bayonet was withdrawn and once again thrust into a now suppliant body, the blood slowly seeped as it fell headlong to the ground. He might lie there in agony for a long time before he died. There would be other screams around you, sometimes English screams (though they all sounded the same), and chaos would reign for a while. It was not pretty to watch, or to listen to.

And you could be overrun, and when that happened and it looked like you were going to be submerged, you brought down fire on your own position. You would do that with the concurrence of the company or battalion commander you were supporting, and there was nothing heroic about doing so: it was often the only counter-attack available, and desperate situations called for desperate measures. And I learned just how terrifying shellfire can be when you are on the receiving end of it.

Most FOOs carried a rifle or an automatic submachine-gun. I usually toted the latter, a Thompson machine-gun which could tear your guts to pieces, or occasionally a rifle, but I was lucky: I never once used it in anger; other than to practise on some empty bully beef tins. I never got used to the sight of the dying Japanese squirming on the ground, uttering unintelligible words, while the raucous sounds of the disturbed birds seemed to constantly express their objection to what was happening. Or worse, of watching the agonies of a mortally wounded infantryman and the desperate efforts to save him – or of the Last Rites being read over him. But these things were all part of just another day in Burma, and when the heat of the moment passed I was busy preparing for the next incident. It never ended, and nor did the fingers running up and down my spine.

AT EVENING, IN the half-light at the gun position, the Japanese would occasionally show themselves, to tempt our fire; whenever that happened, I knew that a restless night lay ahead of us. Typically, the night air would be filled with the jeering and the taunts of the Japanese, but we'd all been there before and responded only by throwing grenades in the direction of the enemy voices. Dawn usually brought an unpleasant scene: the many Japanese bodies lying dead or wounded testified to the accuracy of our gunners' aim with grenades. All we could hear were the awakening jungle sounds and the cries of agony. Once I saw, almost within my reach, a Japanese officer in the last stages of death, with the entrails of his stomach falling out. As the darkness dissipated fully, I saw the ghostly figures of the Japanese now withdrawing, pausing as they passed several of their wounded to drag them away. None of the wounded who were left were willing to surrender, and it was gruesome to see them commit suicide rather than face the dishonour of a prisoner-of-war camp. Some, even though grievously wounded, tried to fight on, forcing our men to shoot them: we had no other choice.

But the Japanese would be back again, tonight, or tomorrow night. It was their way. All we could do was squat there in our slit-trenches and lob a few grenades their way, hoping they would get fed up and leave us in peace for an hour or so.

MY BIG MOMENT as a gunner came soon after the bloody crossing of the Irrawaddy, in the area of Kyaukse, close to Ava, the old capital of Burma and thirty miles south of Mandalay. It was one of those rare moments that all gunners looked forward to. Most of the time when I called down artillery fire, it would be that of my own troop, or perhaps all the guns of the Battery. A major target would qualify for the response of the entire regiment, thirty-six guns in all. Corps' targets are altogether something else, and stories about them are long and legendary because there were so few of them. Only the most deserving situations justified such mighty firepower, for up to five hundred guns or more would be employed. You rarely met a gunner who had the privilege of directing, or even witnessing such devastating force against an enemy. And now my time had come to wield this devastating force . . .

In my usual role as the forward observation officer with the advanced infantry patrols now entering the open country of the paddy fields, I saw from the crest of the hill where I stood the rapid movement of figures, about a thousand yards away. There were so many people herded together that at first thought I thought they were the inhabitants of a nearby village attempting to escape from the violence of the war which was fast approaching them. It was but a momentary thought, though, for I suddenly caught sight of a glint of steel flashing in the midst of the gathering – which was now moving quickly – and that could mean but one thing. Unmistakably, the steel was bayonets. Japanese bayonets. And a veritable forest of them now, glistening like ice on winter trees. A brief discussion with the patrol commander was followed by my issuing of a series of preliminary fire orders to Regimental Headquarters. Within seconds of the order, the Regimental CO, learning of the potential magnitude of the target, and following a subsequent discussion with Corps Headquarters, placed the guns of the entire Corps at my disposal. My knowledge of the enemy strength was limited to my immediate surroundings, but Corps Intelligence had a much broader picture of the whole enemy front. They believed that I had seen the remnants of a Japanese division, perhaps several thousand men, withdrawing in total disarray. I was wildly excited at this information, and I knew my excitement would be shared by all the Corps' artillery units.

Bringing fire to bear on enemy transport or tanks or gun positions was one thing, but to shower gunfire on defenceless enemy troops, out in the open with nowhere to hide and no possibility of escape, was altogether something else. I could picture the feverish activity on the gun positions; few men would rest there now. With me at the observation post were the company commander and his platoon commanders; they'd joined me to witness the impending massacre. Crouching in slit trenches some four feet deep, we all had an excellent view of the panorama lying before us. Several miles to the north was Mandalay, from where the Japanese had come; they were now emerging from the low, scrub-covered hills about a mile away, to the left flank of us observers. Facing them was a vast area of open paddy fields, which provided no cover of any kind. They were broken only by the low irrigation bunds and ditches the natives had dug to water the crops. Flat as far as the eye could see to the east, bordered by hills sprinkled lightly with trees, the land was already covered by the shimmering haze of the sun. The enemy were moving in loose formation south across the rice bowl, towards the cover of trees about two thousand yards away. They didn't know it, but they had entered a death trap.

The tension at the OP was building: there was some apprehension as well, as this strong enemy force, although in disorder, was close enough to easily overrun us, if they so wished. Assessing the information for the issuing of the fire orders wasn't easy; amongst the casualties from our hurried escape from the phosphorus grenade-damaged boat were our range tables and maps, so essential to these calculations. But this was no time for textbook perfection: I must rely on a gunner's instincts and my desire to totally destroy the Japanese division as an effective fighting entity. Looking at the patrol officer's map, I quickly established our present location, took a rough compass bearing to the centre of the Japanese mêlée and estimated its distance from our own location. There would be none of the niceties of peacetime gunnery as practised at the School of Artillery on Salisbury Plain, that temple of learning to which all aspiring gurus of gunnery seek admission. And what would they think of me at Woolwich? They'd be squirming and shaking their heads in disapproval at my primitive methods – odds were the gunnery instructors would snub me altogether!

On the other hand, nothing succeeds like success, and I was about to savour that. Allowances for wind, temperature and other meteor report information droop would all be ignored. Transmitting this information in speech to the guns by the number 22 wireless set was sufficient to get a ranging round down on the ground, hopefully within the huge area that was the target. Speed was of the essence, for the Japanese were streaming towards the distant cover of the large wooded area on the right flank. Once they reached that sanctuary, they'd be more difficult to find again, let alone to engage successfully.

The first round was a gunner's dream, for it fell smack in the middle of the horde. There was no need for further ranging, no need to set fuses or to concentrate the guns to obtain a narrower fall of shot. It was child's play now: I could almost close my eyes and let events take their course.

There was enough room, enough of the target, for all to fire at, regardless of the guns' individual peculiarities. 'Five rounds gunfire' was the only logical order for me to give now – even the most senior instructor must agree on that! I did it willingly. First, the crack of the guns as the rounds were fired, and oh! What a beautiful sound it was to hear those shells screaming overhead like so many express trains, and to watch the hundreds of high explosives, shells of all calibres, 25-pounders, 6-inch and 5.5 howitzers, meet the disorderly ranks of the fleeing Japanese. And as the first rounds fell, the Japanese became utterly panic-stricken; bunching together like so many sheep, in groups of fifty or more, making them even more vulnerable. Just one shell exploding in such a tight formation would have a devastating effect. I was not sure how many guns were allocated to the target, but it looked like all the artillery of the entire British Army was responding.

Through my binoculars, I could see our enemies' bodies being flayed and flung into the air by the tremendous power of the bombardment, limbs torn apart and scattered as if to the four corners of the earth. What had been a placid scene, of moving figures across the open paddy fields, was suddenly transformed: it was as if a hurricane had struck unexpectedly, with murderous fury. The figures became agitated; now they were running hither and yon, in all directions, some flung in the air helplessly, like rag dolls thrown by a child. The few trees in the area were violently uprooted and the air was filled with dust and debris created by the exploding shells. Only the violent thunder of the explosions was to be heard, but it required little imagination to guess at the cries of agony and despair within that deadly sector. Death and dismemberment were everywhere, on a huge scale. There was no escape from the fury of our guns.

There was a deathly silence around me as the infantrymen looked in awe at the spectacle: the decimation of a division; of an enemy once feared – those supersoldiers with no equal were defeated, their flesh and bones scattered across the arid rice bowl of Central Burma, within earshot of the whispering sounds of the great Irrawaddy River.

But it was not yet finished, for as the last salvos roared overhead, I received a message over the wireless from Regimental Headquarters authorizing a further five rounds of gunfire. There was a look of incredulous disbelief from those nearby who'd heard the order, but I was quick to comply, and the shelling started anew. As quickly as it had started, it was all over. And as the sounds died away and the last remnants of smoke dissipated over the scene, the group at the Observation Post broke up. The parting words of the Company Commander were, 'Jolly good show, Penny. I'll buy you a drink at the Club when we get back to Poona.' Robin himself still had a job to do: he and his infantrymen had to move forward to begin the mopping-up process, not an enviable task at any time, much less now when they'd be working amongst hundreds of Japanese bodies in various states of disrepair; some alive and still dangerous, for the Japanese never gave up.

Suddenly I felt very tired. I wished it were time to go home. It was only ten o'clock in the morning, but it was already hot, and a full day's action lay ahead. April and May are the two worst months in Burma: hot and humid, reaching the high forties in the afternoons. It promised to be another scorching day. The stress and excitement of that shoot, being in control of the Corps' guns, had exhausted me more than I'd realized; the sweat was pouring off me. The carnage I'd created hadn't been a pleasant sight – I wasn't squeamish, and I certainly wasn't sorry, but the fearsome results of the slaughter I'd set in motion were enough to turn anyone's stomach, no matter how much one loathed the Japanese. And the sleepless nights were catching up with me – the persistent night attacks with the Japanese trying to locate you by your response, calling out in the darkness, 'Tommy, American GI soldier now having good time with your wife in England, and jig-a-jig every night while you fight for him!' It was eerie listening to them in a silence broken only by the animals of the jungle, and you never became used to it, or lost that sinking sensation in the pit of the stomach. And there'd been weeks and months of ceaseless battle in an unfriendly and debilitating climate. I began to wonder if I'd actually make it.

OUR CAPTURE OF Mandalay is an epic story. Sweeping down from the north, Brigadier General Pete Rees's 19th Indian Division had crossed the last major obstacle, the Chaungmagyi River, and merged with the 20th British Division, which had moved to the south-east of steaming-hot Mandalay. By March 8 they were on the outskirts of that bustling and noisome city, fighting in sporadic actions. As expected, the Japanese Fifteenth Army was fast approaching the anvil that was the 4th Corps at

Meiktila, and the hammer of the 33rd Corps racing from the north. Meiktila was the nerve centre of the Central Japanese command in southern Burma, and the major supply area for ammunition and supplies. It was also a major air base; destroying it would severely hamper the Japanese Thirty-Third and Fifteenth Armies' ability to wage war.

Extermination was now inevitable for those much-vaunted Japanese supersoldiers. They were misled by Slim's deviousness and fell neatly into his trap, suffering ten thousand casualties. Just forty-seven men surrendered: the cracks were beginning to show. Now at the threshold of the city, the Gurkhas of the 19th Division were already engaging the Japanese on Mandalay Hill, which rises several hundred feet above the busy market centre. There are eighteen hundred steps to the temple on the top of the hill, and it was a long and thirsty climb for the British on that hot and dusty day. The Japanese were well ensconced amongst the profusion of temples and pagodas, and it felt like every single one of them was a Japanese machine-gunner's nest. The battle raged all that day and throughout the night; it took the arrival of two more British battalions to finish the bloody fighting. The most savage hand-to-hand fighting left both sides suffering huge casualties.

And now Fort Dufferin itself was under siege. The fanatical Japanese were entrenched in the buildings, and remained so, although heavily shelled and bombed from the air. The ferocity of the fighting increased, but it appeared to have no effect on the enemy. They refused to be dislodged from the tunnels in which they were hidden, even when met with a hail of hand-grenades and doused with barrels of petrol set alight with flame-throwers by the Engineers. Obstinate to the very end, few emerged, and when they did, they came out fighting. This stubborn and suicidal opposition meant the infantry failed to penetrate the upper levels of the Fort, where the Japanese remained in strength, until eventually the Gurkhas went in, bayonets at the ready, in a determined effort to winkle them out. But they weren't able to scale the walls of the Fort, however. It was time for heavier measures: the gunners were called in.

Four of the guns from my regiment were brought up and, in true siege style reminiscent of Corunna, were placed in action three hundred yards from the Fort. Firing with open sights, the 6-inch howitzers blasted the thirty-foot-thick walls with high explosive and armour-piercing shells, but they were so strong that hours of pounding failed to breach them, although the guns fired all night. During that time the gunners were prime targets for the Japanese snipers and machine-gunners, and we suffered a number of casualties.

Nor was the low aircraft bombing any more successful the following morning.

It was time to send the Gurkhas back in. During the early hours of the dawn, they made an assault through the sewers leading into the wide moat surrounding the Fort, only to find the Japanese had escaped during the night: they'd put up a very aggressive resistance, but once it became clear that their position was untenable and that the Gurkhas were not to be defeated, they had fled.

AND ON MARCH 20, 1945, the Union Jack flew over the Fort once again, proudly hoisted on the flagpole by the Battery Commander of the guns which took part in the siege, with General Pete Rees looking on triumphantly. The 340 Battery of the 134 Field Regiment, the one-time Sussex Militia Unit which had fought with the 19th Indian Division since the beginning of the campaign, made a name for itself that day.

But the fight for Mandalay was not yet over: the Gurkhas and British troops still had to clear the honeycombs and the cantonment with their bayonets, and it was a bitter struggle. Still fighting fanatically, none of the Japanese surrendered; few of them escaped from the British troops, who emerged victorious. General Slim described the campaign as a soldier's war because of that close-quarter fighting, which was typical of our battles in Burma.

One unfortunate outcome of the battle for Mandalay was the total destruction of the Golden Palace, a beautiful building in the Golden City built, in 1859, entirely of teak. Occupied by the Japanese, it was demolished – much to the distress of the Burmese – by British gunfire. Fortunately, King Thibaw's throne – the Lion's throne – had been confiscated by the British after the Third Anglo-Burmese War, and was still in their possession; it was their intention to return it after the Second World War ended. The throne, made of wood and almost thirty feet high, is inlaid with gold and precious stones: that, at least, was one piece of booty the Japanese were unable to gather – and one that Tommy Atkins could not plunder either.

How unglamorous was the war in Burma: in the Middle East or in Europe, a victorious army could expect to be greeted with open arms as the returning conquering heroes who'd driven back the tyrannical invaders; welcomed with flowers strewn across their path, and with kisses and promises of much more from the grateful girls. In Europe or the Middle East, you might be offered a glass of wine, or get invited to a humble home for a meal in celebration of the triumph. And they probably spoke a language that you understood, and perhaps even looked like you. Here in Burma there was none of that for us. There had been for the Japanese when they arrived in 1942: the Burmese had danced in the streets, giving them a reception as generous as that soon to be given to the Allied troops in Belgium. They had looked forward so long and so eagerly to the moment that British domination was at an end.

The jails were always full and over-flowing during the British régime. Mandalay Prison could accommodate a thousand prisoners, but when the British were driven out, it held fifteen hundred, only a few of whom were political prisoners. Now, under the Japanese Co-Prosperity Scheme, it held three thousand, virtually all of them political criminals condemned by Japanese oppression. The Japanese fist had been hidden inside a velvet glove; Burma's love for them quickly changed to hatred and the country once again descended into a state of turmoil. In 1943, Burma was offered a form of self-government, but this was a complete farce as the head of that government was answerable to the Japanese Army, so no proposal that contravened Japanese wishes was ever passed. Now the glowering locals accepted the British as a returning oppressor, even though we'd never treated the Burmese as harshly as the Japanese had.

THE RIGOURS OF battle in the jungle were by no means enjoyable. March was the hottest time of the year in the country, when you could expect to see temperatures reach 48 degrees Celsius. And then the rains would come, bringing unbearable humidity, and we would be faced with the steaming heat, the ubiquitous bamboo, and filthy rivers strewn with carcasses, both human and animal. And the vultures were always there, ready and waiting. Not for us the babbling brooks of England, or cricket on the village green with a genteel group of onlookers exclaiming, 'Oh! Jolly well done, sir!' And, 'Leg before wicket,' or, 'Well caught, Sir,' with cups of tea held delicately in one hand and a plate of mustard and cress sandwiches balanced in the other. There were no church bells calling to us on Sunday mornings, to attend St John's Church at the end of the Barrack Square in Woolwich, or the promise of a bit of grumble and grunt in the afternoon. And no quick escape from the rigours of soldiering to the home town, by way of the Fylde Coast Express from Euston, either: all we got was a foreign faceless village consisting of nothing better than a collection of hovels occupied by resentful residents.

There were no friendly faces or welcoming smiles, and we knew it would always be like that, whenever we 'liberated' a town or a village: the Burmese had been openly hostile during the retreat, acting as spies for the Japanese and reporting our whereabouts whenever they could; there were even reports of them forming quasi-military groups and attacking the retreating troops. The Kachins in Northern Burma were one of the tribes which remained loyal; of their own volition, they ambushed the Japanese. We had far fewer privileges here than we had in India, and those were few enough there. The sound of the Bow bells of East London was an eternity away; it was unlikely some of us would ever hear them again. And Rudyard Kipling had written:

> There's a Burma girl a-settin', and I know she thinks o' me;
> For the wind is in the palm-trees, and the temple-bells they say:
> 'Come you back, you British soldier; come you back to Mandalay!'[1]

What heaven it would be to shed the nearly one hundred and thirty pounds of equipment that I carried: to lay aside the Thompson sub-machine-gun and the pistol, to strip naked and lie on a golden beach far from the sounds of the battle, hearing instead the gentle lapping of the blue ocean waters in a place far away from Burma, where the land was free of dead and dying soldiers. Perhaps I'd be served an ice-cold beer by a dusky maiden who didn't glower at me, and then, later ...?

The monotony of battle and the ever-present piles of dead men could be borne for only a limited time before the enormity of the senselessness made us realize the futility of it all. However, like it or not, now was just another day in Burma, and tomorrow I could look forward to more targets, more Japanese to shell and to kill – always providing I was still alive myself,

1 'Mandalay', *Barrack Room Ballads*

of course. And after a while we began to feel blasé about the whole business of war; what elation we felt at first when we saw our shells land on target and decimate the enemy had long gone: now we were just doing a day's work. Shelling the Japanese, or even the Germans, for that matter, was an impersonal affair: you simply dropped a round or two amongst them and then called for five rounds of gunfire. Normally you saw the results but heard nothing beyond the scream of the shell overhead and the terrifying explosion when they landed, never the screams of those trapped in the hail of gunfire, and if you thought for a moment you did, it was probably only your imagination. But I had to admit that, after the ceaseless butchery on the beach at the Nyaungu crossing, which was still fresh in my mind, I derived a savage pleasure from watching and listening to the Japanese who were subjected to that immense shoot. I wasn't close enough to hear their desperate cries, but imagining them provided the sweet music I longed to hear. Hatred was dominant, and I felt no remorse in what I was doing. And there would be no regrets. Ever. They were cruel, inhuman bastards who deserved to die; the Corps shoot had given most of them a far kinder death than those they had doled out.

Carrying such a heavy load was just one of the major differences between the Japanese and the British soldier. When dressed and equipped for battle, that is, in Field Service Marching Order, which included one hundred rounds of ammunition, rifle, water-bottle, hard tack rations and other essentials to stay in the field for a prolonged period, we carried about one hundred and twenty pounds – almost twice as much as our Japanese counterparts. (There were exceptions, for example some senior Japanese officers were issued with bullet-proof vests.) Every Japanese soldier was trained to fight as an infantryman, unlike either the British or American Armies; even Japanese medical staff in the field were equipped with side-arms and swords, and they executed their sick and wounded if capture was imminent. British and US troops carried a substantial food component, notably the K-ration (soup which could be warmed, biscuits, chocolate and chewing gum), our enemy simply carried a bag of rice at his waist.

Even our personal habits were quite different: the British soldier was expected to shave whenever possible; the Japanese soldier was not. They were indifferent to personal hygiene and were unkempt in their habits. When they were overrun, their camps were found to be chaotic and ill-cared-for. Yet I did find anomalies: when the pockets of dead Japanese officers were examined it was quite common to find vitamins and medications, though never once did I see them issued with toilet paper! (Our allocation in peacetime was based on six sheets a day per man.) The Japanese Guards, of magnificent physique, were the exception: they were immaculate at all times.

I had heard that the Eighth Army in the desert in North Africa were a slovenly lot, who dressed as they pleased and washed only when the spirit moved them. (Mind you, I had also heard that during the fighting they were rationed to a pint of water a day – nearly as bad as us in Burma – so they too needed to conserve that precious liquid.) Few of the Eighth Army officers wore regulation uniforms: it was more likely to be yellow corduroy slacks, a sweatshirt, neckerchiefs and a pair of old brown boots or sandals. They wore a variety of hats, even bowlers and Indian headdress. And that very regimental soldier General Montgomery was the most colourful deviant: the only apology he made to the military uniform that he wore was by way of his hats, for he sported a variety, reflecting the various units under his command. And he too had a penchant for bright scarves. Though desert wallahs truly dressed like nomads, their lack of military apparel didn't impede their progress as they eventually kicked the Germans out of North Africa.

We jungle wallahs in Burma were no less imaginative in our dress, and we too gained our share of victory.

In peacetime, one prepared for war by spit and polish; I understood that was a keynote of the British Army, largely because it was believed to be a worthwhile contribution to the making of a competent soldier (or so they claimed). As a gesture, some of the bull was eradicated, but it stopped short of whitewashing the stones around the perimeter of the camps. Not to be clean-shaven daily was not to be tolerated in any circumstances, because a daily shave was said to contribute to a man's wellbeing, and consequently improve his fighting ability. Pride in one's appearance was essential. They also said that when an army was serving in a peacetime role, cleanliness was of paramount importance for, amongst other things, the public was sensitive to the appearance of its soldiers, but Burma was a far cry from the perennial dress parades in peacetime, where anything less than perfection in turnout was severely punished: a faulty tunic button brought the most dire penalties and a twisted bootlace almost a court-martial. The Germans though, even on the field of battle, were always in full Field Service Marching Order: they needed only to fasten the top button of their tunic to be ready for an unexpected inspection by Herr Hitler. But look what happened to them – as many as two hundred thousand surrendered at Tunis within a few days; unlike the Japanese they were well fed, well dressed and undismayed at the thought of surrender, whilst the Japanese would never consider throwing in the towel.

In the jungle we didn't have the time – or desire – to express our individuality: we wore the jungle-green uniform, thankful that it was serviceable and not torn to shreds by the bamboo, without thought – probably without a shirt and damn the mosquitoes – and didn't bother with our tin topees. We were careful to remove any badges of rank, for the higher the rank the worse the punishment if captured. And if we felt like shaving, and had the water, we did so.

In some battlefields around the world, the misfortunes of the Fourteenth Army in Burma and of the Eighth Army in North Africa paled into insignificance. On the Eastern Front in Europe the Russians suffered unbearable hardships: they had little transport and had to march long distances in deep snow. Their clothing was quite inadequate against the icy-cold winds of the appalling winters, when the temperatures would plunge to minus 40 degrees Celsius and lower. Some men were even without boots, and severe frostbite was rampant. Fortunately, they too were incredibly tough men who survived in spite of the terrible climate and the lack of adequate clothing.

The Russian's food shortage was most serious: much of the time he was often reduced to eating raw vegetables, or chewing on the leg of a frozen dead horse. What price soldiering in Burma at 45 degrees above? At least we had bully beef – on the other hand, the 'Ivans' never had to worry about having their blood sucked dry by leeches.

Every battlesite, anywhere in the world, had its own particular problems.

Though, initially, the Japanese were victorious at the beginning of every campaign, they were finally defeated because the Allies had more men and equipment. So perhaps it is nonsense to say that a cleanly dressed and well-shaven soldier will be superior in battle – but, being British, I, like the rest of us soldiers, will continue to believe in the RHA image: however a man surely requires more than the appearance of a shining knight in armour to win wars: he needs self-discipline and the belief in God. And it has to live within.

IT WAS ODD to think that one day in the future, perhaps ten or twenty years away, pleasure trips to Burma would be the order of the day, with luxury cruises along the Irrawaddy: all the comforts that civilization could offer. Visits to notable battle areas, like Myitkyina and Imphal, would be made by the sons and daughters of those who died there; some governments, the Canadian and the Americans particularly, although not the British, would organize pilgrimages (at no cost) for the men who did return home from the Burma war, to refresh their memories and to pay homage to those who were buried there. The Canadian government would sponsor only those who were of Canadian birth when they joined the British Army, held a Canadian passport at the time, joined the army whilst in Canada and were demobilized in Canada. Those British men who, though not born in Canada, yet who had lived, in some cases, for as long as fifty years as naturalized Canadians, were not eligible: there was much bitterness over the decision, which excluded many who had seen real action in Burma.

Yet to see the beaches of the Irrawaddy in peacetime circumstances would give little indication of what it had been like for us who crossed to the other side during that time of bloody fighting. It was hard to picture the setting of the assault across that river, or to see the bodies of the living and the dead amidst the roar of gunfire, of the machine-guns or the flame-throwers – even for those who were part of it, for the years would dim our eyes. The sightseers would never know the true jungle, for there was always a meal ready and a bed in an air-conditioned room in a safe environment. Many preferred not to return; they had no wish to be reminded of that time.

BUT THAT WAS for the future; for now, I was still in the middle of a war zone, and liable to be killed at any moment. In an hour or so it would be blistering hot and the flies would be out in full force to torment us. The early showers of the monsoon were now here, and trying to sleep in the glutinous mud was virtually impossible, in spite of groundsheets. Even in the absence of the rain, the ubiquitous dampness of the jungle seeped through to the bones. And it didn't matter how wet, or sweaty, or uncomfortable we were, how plagued with mosquitoes and leeches: we still had to be on our guard every moment of every day, for if we were moving off, we could expect to be ambushed, for this was the Japanese speciality – and they were very good at it: machine-gun fire would greet us as we went along the track, and whilst we paused to retaliate, they'd sweep to our rear and shoot us down in a surprise attack.

When I returned to the gun position later that day, after being relieved from the OP for a breather, I paused to admire the drill of the men serving the guns. Stripped to the waist, their muscles gleamed in the sun which filtered through the trees, their bodies bronzed or even black, faces grey with gunpowder from the repetitive gunfire of the afternoon, eyes red rimmed from lack of sleep and yellowed by the mepacrine, and with a strip of rag around their necks to absorb the sweat streaming down their faces, they toiled at the guns. It was hot, exhausting work serving the guns in the steaming jungle, with the ever-present broiling sun made worse by the intense heat thrown back from the searing-hot gun barrels, which were fired as quickly as the shells could be loaded into the breech. That could be a round every seven seconds as, with great enthusiasm, the gunners pumped the deadly metal at our despised enemy.

As new orders were given for a troop target, there was increased activity. During the process of ranging, the gun layer could expect to receive correction orders to both the range (elevation) and the bearing. The OP officer would try to get a 'bracket' on the target in both instances: for the range, for example, one round plus and the next round minus of the target. Depending on the target, this bracket would be reduced to four hundred yards, or perhaps eight for a widely spread target or, in the case of a precision target, just fifty yards. Where the target was not in a direct line with the gun position and the OP, the corrections to the line (bearing) would be more difficult. If the OP/target gun position was at a 90-degree angle, observing the fall of shot for the bearing meant that the range needed to be determined first by rounds on the ground, and a line established between the OP and the target. Often the only way to know where the shot was – plus or minus, or left or right of the target – was to observe the drift of the smoke as the shell landed. If it obscured the target, then you knew the fall of shot was to the right, and then you would try for a round on the far side of it, narrowing the angle until it could be converted to a distance in yards from the target. If the target was troops out in the open, you might be satisfied with a one or two degree-change, depending on the range. At six thousand yards, one degree subtended to one hundred yards, so the accuracy could be readily determined. Every OP officer carried his *Range Tables* booklet, and used it – when it was practical, of course.

A gun detachment for the 3.7 howitzer consisted of six men; 5.5- and 6-inch howitzers got seven to ten men, under the command of a sergeant. If necessary he, with the help of his Number Three, would manoeuvre the trail so that the gun was aimed roughly in the required direction. The gun layer of each gun had to try to keep his head whilst the gun position officer gave his orders, which were repeated by the sergeant, quickly setting the bearing of the target on the dial sight, the range on the cone-shaped range instrument and the angle of sight on the clinometer. There might be some additional movement of the trail, and then the layer made the final settings. All this was done with the utmost speed and precision, but sometimes in error: the possibility of death or injury from friendly fire was always there. The gun crews had always to work feverishly and in perfect harmony, which was achieved only by countless hours of practice.

The ammunition was stockpiled a few yards from the gun, and it was Number Six of the gun detachment's job to bring forward the shell, handing it to Number Five. It was then passed to Number Four, who had the most demanding task of all: he loaded the shell, firmly ramming it home in the breech, before loading the separate powder canister which would give the shell flight. He had to make sure that it contained the charge exactly as ordered and, if necessary, remove unneeded cordite bags accordingly; there was a choice of six separate charges, including the super charge, which enabled a range of fire of over ten miles. The discarded bags would later be split open in a safe area, with the cordite forming a trail and then set afire. The palms of his hands were calloused by the constant use of the ramrod, the mark of his trade. With the sweat pouring through his shirt he would load and ram the next round home before the recoil was completed, and within a second a canister charge would be loaded. Number Three operated the breech, closing it when the loading was completed.

The gun layer was then tapped on the shoulder, to confirm the gun had been loaded and, after making final adjustments, he would report 'Ready' to the sergeant (Number One) who stood at the trail of the gun. He in turn would report 'Number One ready, Sir,' raising his right hand as he did so. Upon the order 'Fire', he placed his hands to his ears and his back to the gun and the shell was away. Had the initial order been 'Gunfire', he'd have ordered fire without further instructions.

It was all done very slickly, as a team, a performance demanding perfection.

All this was going on simultaneously, every minute. I smiled, thinking, not bad for a one-time Territorial Unit: these weekend soldiers were now as good as any regular artillery detachment. Well, perhaps not quite up to the standard of the Royal Horse Artillery, but given time . . . Serving the guns was demanding work; the men were certainly earning their pay now. And in the appalling heat a man developed a thirst that could be assuaged by nothing less than a few pints of Watneys' Pale Ale – that was our beer of choice then, but such elixir was eight thousand miles away, and no more attainable than a night out with a ravishing blonde at the Palais de Dance on Kensington High Street.

The noise on the gun position was deafening and distracting. The constant shouting of the fire orders from the Command Post and the acknowledgements by the Gun Sergeants sometimes made it difficult to hear. The men fought to exclude the surrounding noise of the gunfire and the clang of the brass canisters as they were ejected from the breech onto the trail of the gun. And there was no time to bother with ear mufflers in the heat of battle; they had been lost several hundred miles back in earlier action.

Enemy fire was not the only danger to the gun detachments. Our own guns were just as likely to kill us; this was especially true of the 5.5 howitzers, which were inclined to 'prematures' – these were usually caused by faulty fuses on the shell which exploded whilst still in the barrel of the gun, invariably killing the detachment members. This happened so frequently that the firing of a 5.5 howitzer was often done only by means of a very long lanyard from the safety of a slit-trench, where the detachment would take cover. This wasn't the only hazard either: 'hang fires' constantly posed a threat as well, when the main charge failed to ignite immediately, and if the gunner didn't wait a few seconds to make sure it really was dead, it might still go off: it could, and often did, explode whilst the breech was being opened.

Satisfied that all was well, I went back to the wagon lines where the vehicles were parked – 'went back' was a bit of a misnomer as it was only a hundred yards away. In open warfare, it would more likely be a mile to the rear, but here we kept a tight circle to avoid infiltration: the enemy was all around us. Today the Jeeps which towed the 3.7 howitzers were parked cheek-by-jowl, to narrow the perimeter as much as possible.

During the campaign, my regiment utilized a variety of ordnance; as I talked to the sergeant about the various vehicles we used to tow the wide variety of guns, I was remembering that the old 6-inch howitzers had been found in the Kirkee Arsenal in Calcutta just before we moved into Burma. We had a good supply of ammunition for them and they were in excellent condition so, as 5.5 howitzers were in short supply, my regiment got assigned them – and that made us a medium regiment, rather than the field regiment we'd been, using the trusty 25-pounders we'd trained with for several years. (There were a few heavy regiments in the British Army; they used the monster guns like the massive 8-inch howitzers.)

Though we'd become a medium regiment for a short period of time, being Fourteenth Army artillery, and changing from one theatre to another as required, there would be times when we'd use other calibres. We used the 6-inch howitzers for the crossings of the Irrawaddy at Sagaing and Ngazun, the latter where I had crossed that raging river. The 5.5 howitzer was a relatively new gun, developed between 1940–42 to replace the 6-inch howitzer, but I preferred the 6-inch howitzer myself. In our arsenal were 25-pounders, 3.7 howitzers, 6-inch howitzers, 5.5 howitzers and 4.2-inch mortars, for use depending on the terrain – jungle, open paddy fields, or mountainous country. My regiment's knowledge and experience of guns was probably equal – if not superior – to any other artillery unit in Burma. And of course, I had served with 18-pounders in the 1930s with the 1st Regiment Royal Horse Artillery, and the French 75-mm in the dark days after Dunkirk.

Burma taught all us gunners everything we'd ever need to know about the science and application of gunnery: General Bill Slim said of the artillery, 'Burma was the most difficult theatre of war in which to operate because of the impenetrable jungle and the razor-backed hills, the few metal roads and rough tracks which became virtually impassable during the monsoons, turning the ground into a quagmire.' It wasn't that long before that I'd watched six-horse teams draw the 13- and 18-pounders in Newport and India. Then the horses gave way, in Bulford, Larkhill, and France with the British Expeditionary Force, to the 25-pounders, firing a twenty-five-pound shell to a maximum of seven miles, which were towed by Quads – and ugly-looking vehicles they were too. Before my time, a hundred years ago, the horse artillery moved with the forward cavalry; it was different from the ordinary artillery in that all the men of the detachments rode horses, whereas the latter would ride on the limbers, or even march alongside their guns.

The 5.5 howitzer had a range of over ten miles, firing a hundred-pound shell, but the gun itself weighed twelve thousand six hundred pounds – eight times heavier than the 3.7 howitzer. In the early days of fighting in Burma, we used the huge Scammel lorries to tow the heavy 6-inch how-itzers, and later on the giant 5.5 howitzers, across the open country of lower Burma. The difference between the weapons we used was that how-itzers fired a heavier shell at a lower velocity, and at elevations of more than 45 degrees, and so were ideal for engaging targets on the other side of hills. A gun like a 25-pounder fired a lighter shell at a higher velocity, in a relatively flat trajectory. Our mortars fired only at elevations above 45 degrees, but they were cumbrous weapons, even though Jeeps had replaced the mules which used to pull the 4.2-inch mortars in the jungle-covered razor-back mountains. They were not exactly a toy, nor an inferior weapon: with a bomb rated at twenty pounds and a range of four thousand one hundred yards, they were also very effective at firing on the unseen sides of the mountain. But it wasn't always possible to use the Jeep to transport them, and then it became heavy work for the men and the mules – when we still had the beasts. Broken down, the mortar weighed ninety-one pounds, the tripod forty-six pounds and the base plate a hundred and twenty pounds.

Right now our task was to tow the smaller 3.7 howitzers, which were most suitable in the hills because of their high trajectory and easier to deploy in the jungles. Although they had a range of only six thousand yards and fired a light shell, they did a sterling job in Burma. These were the screw-guns, with gun barrels in two separate portions, which allowed them to be dismantled for pack carrying – they were made famous by the North-West Frontier campaign, and by Rudyard Kipling, of course: what gunner didn't sing the praises of the 'Screw-Guns'? The mules had done a sterling job, but sadly, many were lost: they were often overladen and missed their footing, plunging over the sides of the cliffs. Many men fell to their death in the same manner, for they too carried heavy loads, often weighing far more than a hundred pounds, over the murderous slopes coated with impenetrable jungle.

I HAD LONG been fascinated with the methods employed in the olden days to destroy a captured enemy gun, or to deny the use of one of our own guns if it had to be abandoned. In those times it was common practice to spike a muzzle-loading gun by hammering a nail firmly into the vent so that it couldn't be removed, thus preventing the ignition of the propellant. In later days a means was devised of reversing the spiking procedure by the use of a 'spring spike', which was removed when necessary, and this was frequently used when the danger of being overrun was imminent. And, of course, there was also the practice of destroying the gun completely by using its own ammunition. And just this opportunity presented itself to us one day.

The local battle in Central Burma had been won and the Japanese had retreated in a hurry, leaving a gun and a lot of their dead comrades in the clearing where I now stood. It was a small field-gun – a galloper-gun, capable of being horse-drawn – which was a standard weapon of the Japanese infantry, used alongside their mortars. In their haste they had abandoned the gun, complete with ammunition and stores, and our British troops had continued the pursuit. Whilst waiting for the Battery to arrive, I, together with my OP Ack and signaller, were now alone with this fine-looking piece of ordnance, which was apparently in good shape apart from the scratched-up paint work – and everyone knows that the jungles of Burma were no place to keep anything in a pristine condition, let alone a 70-mm field-gun! There was neither inclination nor opportunity for spit and polish, no matter how regimental you were – even if you were Royal Horse Artillery.

So there it was, standing in the open clearing on the fringe of the jungle, beckoning so invitingly: as nice a looking whiz-bang gun as you could wish for. (It was commonly called that by the British troops because of its low muzzle velocity of about seven hundred feet per second: a 3.7 Quick Fire mountain howitzer was almost one thousand feet per second and an older 18-pounder QF field-gun was one thousand six hundred feet per second.) It had an effective range of one thousand five hundred yards, and when fired at almost point-blank range, the shell was at your feet long before you heard the sound of its departure from the gun – almost as if it had arrived before it left the muzzle. We looked at each other and the expression on all our faces was the same. The nearest village was about a mile away and there were no natives around, so there was no danger to anyone – except to ourselves, of course. This was the golden opportunity of a lifetime: an abandoned artillery piece with no observers to criticize or to say no, or to even witness if anything went wrong. After all, the gun had been captured by British troops, so it rightfully belonged to the King of England now. However, he might not see things my way, so the fewer people who saw us, the better. We had no other pressing engagements at hand, and the temptation was just overwhelming.

So it was with great enthusiasm – and a slightly queasy sensation in my stomach – that I invited my team, 'Let's have some fun and blow this bloody thing up.'

Now, I had always understood that if a round was placed at both ends of the barrel – one up the spout and one in the chamber – and fired, the gun would be utterly shattered. But I was about to discover that was not so. To really make it disintegrate completely, it needed a shell loaded backwards in the chamber, with the explosive at the rear, which was quite a different procedure. We didn't realize this, so we loaded a round only in the breech, in the normal manner. Then, after using the ramrod – which had been so conveniently left by the side of the gun – we rammed another down the muzzle. Attaching a length of D3 telephone wire to the firing lever – we weren't entirely foolhardy! – we withdrew, carrying the spool and unwinding the wire as we went. Reaching the cover of the trees about fifty yards away, we sheltered behind the trunk of the thickest tree we could find. As we made our final preparations, it felt like there was a great silence all around: the perpetual background noises of the jungle and the far-distant crack of rifle fire from the Gurkhas who had now caught and engaged the

Japanese faded away. At my word, my signaller jerked the wire and there was a tremendous explosion. For what felt like an eternity, pieces of the gun whizzed through the air with a screaming, whirring sound, falling like a shower of shrapnel, landing with great force in and around the trees where we crouched. When the fall-out stopped, the silence was accentuated as we emerged from our place of safety and went to inspect what was left of the little field-gun. The entire barrel had been shattered, from the muzzle almost down to the breech, though the breech itself was left intact. Much of the carriage had been heavily damaged by the huge pieces of flying metal. Truly immobilized now, the barrel of the gun was stripped like a banana. In a way, it was a sorrowful sight: quite beyond all repair. It would never speak again; not even the Japanese artificers, with the best of Tokyo's facilities, would be inclined to rebuild it.

It may have been an ignominious ending for the gun, but it was a great experience for me and my men. And as the Battery arrived, we left with a feeling of great satisfaction. It wasn't often we got the chance to do a thing like that; those gunners of a hundred years ago, with their hammers and nails, would have been envious!! And now we had a good story to tell the lads back at the gun position, or in the mess, surrounded by the new subalterns, after the war . . . if there was an after, that was.

IN MARCH, HAMBURG and Cologne were pulverized and Montgomery's armies crossed the Rhine. The Red Army entered Austria and took Danzig, followed, two weeks later, by Vienna. Okinawa was taken by American troops, who suffered extremely heavy casualties. President Roosevelt died on April 12, and Harry Truman became the President of the United States of America. On April 28, Mussolini and his mistress were shot by partisans in Milan, the Germans surrendered on the Italian front, and Russian and American forces linked up at the Elbe. Hitler married Eva Braun in their Berlin bunker and on the last day of the month shot himself. He was aged fifty-six.

chapter sixteen

FROM BURMA TO BLIGHTY

April 1945 to July 1945

We were out on the move again; the company of Gurkhas that I was supporting had laagered down[1] for the night after a day of heavy fighting,
straddled across a track in a jungle clearing not more than a hundred
paces wide. We were relaxing; our skimpy meal was finished – we'd not
eaten since breakfast, and that was only hard-tack – sentries were about to
be posted and a game of football was in progress, when a small armoured
car came bumping into the bivouac in a cloud of dust. Although unexpected, no one paid much attention at first, until the shout went up,
'Japanese Wallahs!' There was a moment of pregnant silence as the Gurkhas
and the Japanese looked at each other in stunned disbelief. Then, within
a second, the four Japanese officers in the car – for that was what they
were – were galvanized into action, running hard for the cover of the
jungle, hotly pursued by the Gurkhas who, with a great roar and lusting
for blood, threw down their rifles and automatic weapons in favour of
their kukris. Now both the Japanese and the little men from Nepal were
all in the cover of the jungle, and the high-pitched screams clearly
indicated that the Gurkhas were obviously using their beloved weapons to
the fullest extent. By the time any of the white Gurkha officers arrived at
the scene, the carnage was all over and the men had resumed their
football game – but now they were using the heads of the Japanese, which
had been unceremoniously lopped off. They were unabashed when
reprimanded by their officers – for having thrown down their rifles

[1] 'Circle the wagons': form an all-round defensive position – a Boer War expression

and resorted to their knives – they just smiled and continued their game. It was all in a day's work for them.

The Gurkha kukri is a beautifully styled knife with a rosewood handle; its symmetry is pleasing to the eye. And this attractive weapon is lethal in the hands of a Gurkha, who uses it for everything from chopping wood to chopping off heads. The stem of the handle is two and a half inches long, and one and a quarter inches thick. It curves slightly for a further two inches at the same thickness, widening at the hilt to two inches. The twelve-inch blade is one and a quarter inches at its narrowest and almost two and a half inches at its widest, narrowing to a deadly point at the end. At the base of the blade is an indentation similar to a rifle sight; it's not a sighting device, though it looks like one, but a lock to engage an enemy blade. The kukri curves exactly 30 degrees from the stem of the handle, weighs just over two pounds and has a fetching heft; it swings easily in the hand. Sheathed in a leather holster in which are also mounted two 'skin 'em and eat 'em' replicas four inches long, it is the Gurkha's favourite weapon. The sight of a Gurkha with kukri drawn is always a terrifying sight: his enemy knows he either kills him with his first shot, or runs for his life – that's if he's still capable of running and hasn't already lost either head or limb. Contrary to popular belief, if a Gurkha draws his blade, he doesn't have to draw blood before he sheaths it: the kukri is no supernatural weapon, just an excellent fighting man's tool.

I had first-hand experience with the kukri when I was involved in hand-to-hand combat with the Japanese, when I was attacked by a Japanese officer wielding a sword. The Gurkha unit I was supporting had been overrun by the Japanese, and although I attempted to defend myself with my Tommy gun, I was too late to stop my cheekbone being lacerated by the sword.

As the Japanese officer prepared for the coup de grâce, a Gurkha Naik (corporal) standing nearby distracted the swordsman and promptly dispatched him in a timely manner by lopping off his head – as welcome a demonstration of one-upmanship by the Naik as I could have wished for. He, of course, got yet another head to add to his daily quota; I had a deep scar on my cheek to remind me of my close call for the rest of my life.

The Gurkhas were the exception to the rather distant relationship between the British soldier sahibs and the Indian sepoys: there wasn't necessarily any unfriendliness between the two, but there was no real intimacy. Rarely did they address each other by Christian names. It was the reverse with the Gurkhas, whom the squaddies called Johnny; the Gurkhas in turn addressed us by our own nicknames. We had a very free and easy relationship; it was quite common for us to spend our leisure hours together, playing sports. It wasn't so with the Indians, who were a race apart: we didn't share the same camaraderie. The Gurkhas had been part of the British Army for fifty years; they and the white soldiers were as one.

A Gurkha patrol was dispatched to a lake in Northern Burma to capture two Japanese officers who were known to fish there regularly. Their mission was to escort the prisoners to Divisional Headquarters, where they were to be questioned about local troop movements. Somehow this was not explained clearly to the Gurkhas, who returned two days later carrying a large wicker basket. Ushered into the General's tent, the Gurkha leader smilingly raised the lid of the basket and empted the contents on the floor of the tent. Out rolled two gory Japanese heads and several fish, all mixed together. The General, deeply disapproving, complained that he'd wanted the Japanese alive, not dead, and ordered the Gurkhas to instantly remove the heads from his presence. Unabashed, the Gurkha leader asked the General-sahib if they could also take the fish, which they wanted for supper. The General screamed, 'Yes,' and ordered them out of his sight at once. Picking up the fish, the Gurkhas obliged.

I was invited to a Gurkha *ramsamee*, a form of religious ceremony – but to all intents and purposes, it was a giant bacchanalia. Many officers from other regiments were invited and the party, which started early in the evening, lasted for three days. The food and the wine were nonstop: the festivities were punctuated by individuals going back to their unit, sleeping, sobering up and returning to the marathon. It was all conducted decently. The Gurkhas gave dance demonstrations – similar to that of the Scottish Highlanders, except that for the most part they dressed as women, and occasionally performed in the nude!

The highlight of the event came on the last day, when a ceremonial sacrifice took place. With a great show of suspense, a Gurkha, short and stocky, with a perpetual grin, like most of his fellows, came to the centre of the gathering – there were at least a hundred people standing, sitting or lying on the maidan – leading a goat. There was a great deal of shouting and banter from the crowd as the animal was prepared for the occasion, but a silence fell when the ceremonial kukri was brought in. It was almost identical to the general issue kukri, with two exceptions: it was double-handed, and thirty-six inches long. The goat was positioned and the executioner made ready. The silence was profound. With a cry, raising the gargantuan weapon high above his head, he brought the heavy blade down squarely on the back of the goat's head. With that single blow the head rolled to the ground. The noise of the crowd was now released, as if by magic, and the sounds of appreciation echoed around for miles. With a wide grin on his face, the executioner proudly made his exit and the party continued.

I, together with other officers of my regiment, attended a party given by the Royal Welch Fusiliers[1] – not a special occasion, but an ordinary social event, though the setting was not unlike that of the Gurkhas' recent ramsamee. Everyone was having a great time, moving from marquee to marquee exchanging pleasantries, when the Fusiliers introduced their regimental mascot, a goat with a brown-and-white flecked coat and a long white beard. The goat was allowed to roam freely around the tents. It was frisky by nature, and this evening it was particularly active: it made a habit of jumping up on people's chests, rather like a dog, and it was quite accustomed to taking liberties in whatever way it wished. On this occasion it appeared to have developed an affection towards my subaltern, Gallows and was making much of him, pawing at his tunic and then his trousers. The Welch Fusiliers were very generous hosts and Gallows, like everybody else, had partaken of a few drinks and was feeling no pain. At first it was just a friendly wrestling match between him and the goat, but suddenly the animal became extremely agitated, tearing at his pants and spilling the contents of his pockets onto the ground. Seeing what it thought was a tasty morsel, the goat started chewing on Gallows's identity card – a very important document indeed.

Sobering up very quickly, Gallows threw a headlock on the goat's head, at the same time vainly trying to extract the card from the beast's mouth, but it was too quick for him and, realizing that it was about to lose its meal, wrenched itself free and promptly swallowed the card. With a great

---

1 'Welch' is the old English spelling; during the Boer and Great Wars the official spelling was 'Welsh'; Army Order No. 56 of 1920 finally confirmed that the official spelling should be 'Welch'.

roar of anguish, Gallows renewed his headlock and drew the ten-inch knife he wore at his waist. The knife was already at the goat's throat and the deed was about to be done when the goat's guardian – the battalion sergeant-major – leapt forward and flung Gallows to one side before he could disembowel the goat to retrieve his valuable document. Within seconds the place was in an uproar as the Welshman subdued Gallows before he could do any damage. The air was filled with vituperation; just as a major brawl was about to break out, the goat, by the grace of God, regurgitated the identity card and the man's cry of triumph and relief was sufficient to restore the friendly atmosphere – though Gallows's coolness thereafter towards the goat was distinctly noticeable.

The Gurkhas were superb fighting soldiers; the only criticism anyone could have had of them was their insistence on using their kukris at the drop of a hat. Their expertise was encapsulated in the tale of the sceptic who didn't believe a head could be lopped off by a single blow: the Gurkha lunged forward with his kukri, swinging it at the man's head. 'Ha! You missed!' exclaimed the sceptic. 'I knew you couldn't do it!' Whereupon the Gurkha stepped forward, touching the man's head, which promptly fell from his shoulders, and retorted, 'Guess again!'

But they were beautiful little men; their presence made us all feel secure. Regardless of the severity of the situation they were always prepared to engage a superior force, always eager to move on to the next battle, and were ever cheerful, in even the most adverse of conditions. And their courage was second to none.

They were ordered to take part in an airborne landing behind the Japanese lines; their eyes lit up, though none of them had used a parachute before – all Gurkhas loved new experiences; they were always ready to try something different. They were told that to achieve the maximum surprise, they were to jump from a height of only five hundred feet. The Subadar Major could see from the men's expressions that they were troubled, and asked the Major Sahib if he could have a private discussion with them to see if they had a problem with the order. This he did, and returned a few moments later saying, 'Sahib, while the men do not like the order, they are prepared to jump, but would prefer to do so at a lower altitude.'

Aghast at this, the Major responded, 'That's downright dangerous. There won't even be time for the parachutes to open at that height.'

The Subadar's expression changed from dismay to one of supreme joy. 'Sahib, you mean we shall be using parachutes?'

I was lucky to be attached to the Gurkha regiments on a number of occasions, but I must confess that I felt equally secure when the Cameron Highlanders were my companions: these Scottish Highlanders were all regular soldiers, and a breed unto themselves. Rough and ready and foul of mouth; not every mother would want their daughter to go out with one, let alone marry one: but in battle you couldn't wish to soldier with a finer group of men. They knew how to use their boots as well as their fists and entered every fight kicking, screaming and swearing. Like the other Scottish regiments who were labelled the Ladies from Hell (they wore kilts), their reputation was well earned. Knuckle-dusters and cut-throat razors were as familiar to them as haggis, especially those who were raised in the Sauchiehall Street area of Glasgow. Solid as the Rock of Gibraltar, they could be counted on – before and after the chips were down. Some of the finest troops in the British Army, of all nationalities, were serving in Burma and the Far East.

WE'D BEEN CAMPED about a hundred miles south-west of Mandalay when the Japanese had arrived in our clearing and been decapitated by the Gurkhas. We were close to Mount Popa, an extinct volcano that last erupted about the fifth century BC. During the second week in April, the 5th Indian Infantry Brigade of the British 2nd Division, consisting of the 7th Worcester, the 2nd Dorsetshire and the Cameron Highlanders' Regiments, moved into the Irrawaddy valley from Myingyan. It was not until we reached Mount Popa, about fifty miles away, that we met any strong opposition from the Japanese, who were firmly dug in there with a number of field-guns.

Mount Popa rises almost five thousand feet above sea level: it's an ugly sight, dominating the surrounding desolate plains. Naturally it made me a wonderful observation post, offering a commanding and unobstructed view for miles around, in all directions. I put it to good use, for I could now see the Japanese transport vehicles withdrawing to the south, and I was able to keep my guns, which were about a mile away, fully occupied. The mountain, riddled with tunnels, provided a good hiding place for the retreating Japanese, who were reluctant to come out and join in the fighting. Rather than the infantry going into the tunnels to winkle out the Japanese, which would have been a messy job, my troop was invited by the Infantry Commander to fire our guns directly into the tunnels. My gunners were more than pleased to relieve the infantry of that little chore, and two of the guns were called to the scene. We had great fun firing the 5.5-inch howitzers over open sights into the tunnels at a range of two hundred yards – this was the second time we'd had the opportunity to fire with open sights; Mandalay was the other – and it was a welcome change of pace for us. When we'd finished, there were no Japanese soldiers to be seen around the outside of the tunnels, nor did any come out subsequently.

I knew that Mogaung and Mogok were famous for rubies, jade, sapphires and emeralds, and I'd already collected a few stones, both cut and uncut – they looked very impressive in the dazzling sunshine, even though, when I had them valued in Calcutta later, they were found to be worthless. In those negotiations the Burmese had been cooperative, even calling me *Thakin*, the equivalent of the Indian Sahib. Now here we were at Mount Popa, famous for the pagoda stones mined from the mountain. When cut and mounted, they really do look like one of the many pagodas scattered so profusely across the area: set on a pearl-white background, they make very fine and distinctive rings. It was said that Winston Churchill wore such a ring, but I doubted he got his the same way I did, trading with the locals.

From Mandalay to Pakokku, fifty miles or so to the south-west, the Irrawaddy can be very treacherous: the currents run fast and the sand banks are constantly changing. Bordering the river is the most fertile land in the country, a major rice-growing area. To the north-west, just a few miles distant, lies the town of Sagaing and the Kaunghmudaw Pagoda, one of Burma's most prominent temples. Built in 1636 on the north side of the Sagaing Hills, the lavish, ornate building stands one hundred and fifty feet high. Its bells are deafening as they ring out constantly. It is steeped in religious history, and is reputed to hold the Buddha's 'Tooth of Kandy'. Though I, like many other passing soldiers, looked long and hard to find the tooth, I was unsuccessful – but at least I could tell the folks back home that I had walked in the presence of the Buddha.

The lake just beyond the Pagoda was, at first glance, tempting enough for me to contemplate swimming, but on closer inspection I decided to give it a miss: it too had suffered the woes of war and was covered with floating corpses, mostly Japanese, but also a few Burmese civilians. It was still unusual to find any uncontaminated lake or stream; on the rare occasion we did find clean water, we made the most of the opportunity to bathe, and to scrub our filthy uniforms that otherwise went unwashed for weeks on end. Drinking water, equally difficult to find, was strictly rationed to eight cups a day – for all purposes; there were times when even this was not possible. It led to real hardship in the jungle's stifling heat.

The journey from Sagaing to Mingum was a veritable paradise for pagoda lovers: on the western bank of the Irrawaddy, every hill and crest sported its own temple. But though they were all beautiful, set amidst bougainvillea and frangipani, none of these enchanting pictures compared with the famous temple of Sagaing. In spite of the noise of the battles being fought all around them, the thousands of monks who lived in the monasteries went about their business as usual, chanting their mantras, seemingly unconcerned; gathering in groups under the banyan trees. Further along the street the beggars sat with their begging bowls under the shade of the palm trees, their saffron robes adding further colour to the glittering scene, soliciting even the British troops as they passed by: 'Thakin, baksheesh, Thakin.' Their counterparts in Calcutta would have said, 'baksheesh, Burrah Sahib, baksheesh. Um boat booka hie. Humco dayo ack rupiah. Mer barney, Mer barney, Sahib Log. Sir, please give me money, I am very hungry. Please give me one rupee, Sahib Log.' Whatever the language, the pleas were the same.

The mangy pie dogs searched frantically for the scraps of food dropped by the soldiers, snarling and snapping at each other. The Burmese also had difficulty finding enough food to survive; the streets were always crowded with brightly clad, hurrying natives seeking food for their families who had not eaten that day. The transient British and Japanese soldiers had disrupted the markets and there was a dire lack of produce. Many of the locals pressed their shoddy wares upon the British soldiers who responded, as they were accustomed to do in India, with a sharp tongue; an oath tinged with anger, or an actual threat, were usually sufficient to send a clear message. The constant clamour of the crowds thronging the streets and the endlessly ringing temple bells continued unabated far into the night, and my OP party and I were glad to reach the solitude of a temple on the outskirts of the city.

Not far from Mount Popa is the ancient, beautiful city of Pagan, a religious centre for the Burmese whose origins were reputed to date from the year 100AD. Once the capital of Burma, in the days of the Shan kingdom, about 1300AD, it was moved to Ava (Innwa) and became known as the Golden City of four million pagodas. It is renowned as one of the most remarkable cities in the world. The first two thousand temples were built in the twelfth century.

But Burma's history, like that of India, is one of constant strife and conquest, especially in the thirteenth century, when the Shans and Mons tribes fought for dominance. When Kublai Khan invaded with his hordes, there were some thirteen thousand temples in Pagan, but to fight off his holocaust, several thousand temples were demolished so their stones could be used to strengthen the perimeter walls. Now the city lay in ruins. The desecration, both manmade and natural – in the form of terrible earthquakes – left just two thousand temples. Now deserted, this capital is still heavily studded with pagodas of all shapes and sizes, which stretch endlessly across the great plain of Pagan.

It was an arresting sight for all the British Tommies, including me. When we were amongst the temples, we could feel their sacredness. Rising above all others was the Thatbyinnyu Temple, rising to two hundred feet. Close to the banks of the river is the Thandawgya Image, an enormous figure of Buddha almost twenty feet tall. Many of the interiors of the stupas also contain effigies of Buddha; they're decorated with wall designs reputed to date back before the days of Kublai Khan. The most unusual is the Shwegugyi, built in 1100 AD: unlike all the other temples, which face east, it faces north, to the Royal Palace. The Minglazedi Pagoda, acknowledged as having the finest architecture of them all, is certainly one of the most beautiful.

We British soldiers could see the magnificence of those ancient works, but we were more concerned about the protection they could offer us rather than their beauty, as were the Japanese too. For several nights my team and I lived and planned in one; although of little value as an obser-vation post, it was convenient and spacious and offered a good measure of security from the enemy gun and rifle fire; the fighting amongst the pagodas was fierce. At night, in the darkness, there was less chance of a Japanese patrol stumbling over us; in fact, there was greater danger from the snakes which abounded in the area. They sheltered in the temples and were quick to seek the warmth of a body in preference to the cold cement floor. But that was a risk we had to take: it was still better than tangling with the Japanese. Generally, the pagodas were in a great state of disrepair, because Burma was prone to severe earthquakes. (The most devastating disturbance was yet to come; in 1975, this revered city of Pagan would be virtually obliterated.)

The countryside around was quite magnificent; it was a wonderful feeling of release to be away from the depressing atmosphere of the jungles. And the scenery was simply beautiful; in the evening the landscape was bathed in the red and yellow rays of the sunset and the dust rising from the wheels of the oxen-carts moving slowly along the rough tracks. The view across the city was breathtaking. When I stood on the eastern banks of the Irrawaddy, the gun fire ceased for a moment and watching the sun set over the ancient city of Pagan, I experienced an almost transcendental feeling; I could easily have been persuaded that Buddha did indeed once walk on those holy lands. There were pagodas as far as the eye could see; it looked as if a giant had rolled dice, scattering them across the land. The spires of their myriad white and ochre temples reaching for the sky and glistening in the sunlight conveyed a message of peace, in spite of their often forlorn and abandoned condition.

Sir James Scott wrote, 'Pagan is in many respects the most remarkable religious city in the world. Jerusalem, Rome, Kiev and Benares cannot boast the multitude of temples and the lavishness of the design and ornament that make marvellous the deserted capital on the Irrawaddy: the whole place is so thickly studded with pagodas of all sizes and shapes, and the very ground is so heavily covered with crumbling remnants and vanished shrines, that according to the popular saying, you cannot move foot or hand without touching a sacred thing.'

Though I could recognize there were places beside England's green and pleasant lands worthy of admiration, my heart would have been uplifted all the more had I been watching that same sun sinking over the golden sands on the coast of Lancashire, or highlighting the smoking chimneys of the dark, satanic mills of Wigan – or even over the gas works just around the corner from Mum and Dad, who were probably sitting in their small council house, wondering where their boy was. Not by even the wildest stretch of their imagination could they have pictured me spending the night in such a romantic setting.

But I was unmoved by the yellow moon in a sky sown with emeralds, for the ugly hand of war was upon the land, though sometimes hidden from the casual observer. All it required was a single shell to explode in this beautiful countryside for the illusion of tranquillity to vanish – and at that very moment the shells did indeed begin to fall on and around those majestic pagodas: the battle had recommenced.

After a series of withdrawals, the Japanese had begun their counter-attack. This was to be a determined effort on their part, for retreat was anathema to them. Sure enough, after five minutes of concentrated gun-fire, they swarmed into the temples now occupied by the Cameron High-landers, screaming bloody blue murder. But we were ready for them, and cut them down with such vicious machine-gun fire that they were halted dead in their tracks, literally. Facing the Scotsmen's withering fire, they had no alternative but to retreat – or die. Strangely enough, this time many of them chose to live, and so fell back to their start line. With hardly a pause they then very rapidly withdrew even further, fully expecting the British to seize the moment and vigorously follow-up – we did just that, but because they had run away so far and so fast, they escaped the fury which would otherwise have rained down upon them. Once more the battleground became still and quiet.

THE ROYAL AIR Force and the American Air Force were doing a sterling job throughout the whole of the Burma Campaign; they tried always to be there when needed. One evening I was laagered down by the side of a river with the Japanese on the other side; the Gurkha regiment I was sup-porting was under heavy artillery and machine-gun fire. The Japanese had the dominating position and could see us clearly, but we could see hardly anything. Battalion headquarters was informed of the situation and within a matter of minutes British and American fighter-bombers were on the scene. Flying P57 Lightnings, the pilots proceeded to saturate the target area with napalm bombs; although we couldn't get a clear view of the ground being attacked, we knew the planes must have been flying at almost ground level. The attack lasted just a few minutes, but the wide-spread jellied gasoline flames and black smoke indicated the enormity of the strike: the effect of the jelly is like that of a flame-thrower, and the fragments of phosphorus bombs become embedded in bodies and continue to do damage long afterwards – not a very pleasant ending for those Japanese on the receiving end of the Allied blitz. This was a typical example of the splendid cooperation and rapid response by the Air Force to a request for fire-power: with a waggle of wings, the pilots were on their way back to the base. The Gurkha position was now peaceful again and we were able to get on with our business: fortifying the area we occupied, especially to prevent the Japanese creeping up silently at night.

We set booby-traps to discourage their attention. Hand-grenades fitted neatly into an empty tin of bully beef with the firing lever securely in position, but with the safety pin removed, requiring only a slight pull to detonate the grenade. Strung between two trees, these produced the most rewarding results when the wire or string was tripped. Another popular method was the use of panji pits: a trench about seven or eight feet deep, wide enough to receive one or more bodies, with a number of bamboo stakes sunk in the bottom. Burma has some of the strongest bamboo in the world, often thicker than six inches in diameter, and in plentiful supply. It was ideal for use as a booby-trap, and an individual falling through the pit, which was covered with natural undergrowth, was liable to be impaled as he struck the stakes. Cut to a fine point and then hardened over a fire, the tips were like steel and, placed at strategic places around the laager, they were very effective indeed in deterring unwanted visitors. It was an agonizing way to die; we had to ignore the screams of the injured in the pit until dawn broke.

THOUGH I EMERGED from the Burma Campaign miraculously unscathed in body, the same could not be said for my mind. I would never be able to forget the evil I had seen, and I would always hate the Japanese, even in my declining years. Ask any man who fought against the Japanese in that campaign: we all carry the same abiding hatred; it would be a rare man indeed who could ever forgive their cruel, barbaric behaviour. Our British soldiers came from the mill towns, or the slums of Liverpool or Glasgow, or from the south-west of England. There were a goodly number of fighting Irish, Jocks and Taffies. And there were fishermen from the harsh north-east coast, and Cockneys from within the sound of the Bow Bells. Our troopers were, by and large, simple men, accustomed to working hard in the mines or in the fields, or braving the angry oceans. But they had to be harder than nails to endure the rigours of the war in Burma, fighting an implacable, inhuman enemy, knowing that their chances of ever getting home, to Ireland, to Scotland, to Wales or to England, were slim indeed. But every man soldiered on with a do-or-die attitude and took the knocks as they came. They were typical British soldiers.

For the infantryman, the paramount task was to kill; both sides had this same objective. And having killed, you moved on to the next man before he moved on to you. And whatever you might think, it was all very impersonal: it was just you and him – or rather, just you *or* him. There were no Marquis of Queensberry rules here, just stab and kick; thrust the bayonet into the stomach, then foot to the chest to withdraw that steel blade. Kill and kill again, for the Japanese were evil bastards, worthy only of death, and these were the thoughts and actions that drove you on. There was no hope for mercy – no 'love thy brother' – no serenading each other with Christmas carols, as did the Germans and the British in the First World War.

The casualty rates were enormous.

We paid a lot of attention to the war in the vast open spaces of the deserts of North Africa: it was such a different world. In the desert you could see your enemy, though you could not hide from him. In the jungle, it was the reverse – that was clearly elementary, my dear Watson. In the desert, there were large numbers of men involved: with lots of armour, their columns covered vast distances in short periods of time. Hacking our way through the jungle was a long, tedious process, and progress was often measured in yards, not miles. In Libya, the fighting was on a relatively massive scale, and so were the casualties. For the gunners there, it was tremendous barrages and concentrated gunfire all the time, because of the openness of the country; rarely were our own troops killed by 'friendly fire'.

In my war it was so different, for often we couldn't see our target clearly. We mostly fought in small, isolated groups; often I'd be shelling an unseen enemy, perhaps just a few hundred yards away, but totally obscured by the impenetrable jungle. In Burma far fewer men were involved, but by the nature of the terrain it was very personal and, as neither side could easily see each other until they were on top of one another, the fighting was often hand-to-hand. And it was ruthless, because of the enormous enmity between the Japanese and us. It was very different for those fighting in Europe: there was not the same degree of hatred between the British and the Germans.

It wasn't natural for British troops to so loathe their enemy, though there were certainly men who did just want to kill for the sake of killing, as there are everywhere, in every century. Most of us were God-fearing men, accustomed to going to church on Sunday. But eventually, even the most decent British soldier became as ruthless as his enemy, and returned in good measure what had been dealt to him – this particularly applied to the Gurkhas, who made no bones about their disgust at the brutal treatment they received at the hands of the Japanese. We always knew which troops had gone first by the manner of desecration of the Japanese corpses at the side of the tracks: the Gurkhas' delightful trademark – they had a wonderful sense of humour! – was either cutting the penis off and laying it horizontally across the body as a battle honour (dishonour?), or chopping off the testicles and thrusting them into the mouth – often it was both. If they had the means, they sewed the lips together.

Nor had our troops any compunction, later in the campaign, when it came to bayoneting injured Japanese: by now, we had discovered for ourselves how merciless they were. One of my mates would say, 'Skewer the bastards so you can see right through them.' We all felt the same. The Japanese rarely took prisoners; those they did take were punished mercilessly for their weakness in allowing themselves to be captured: they were tortured, or tied to a tree and used for bayonet practice. The Japanese had a great deal of experience in this latter practice in China, as they'd murdered thousands of Chinese by this method.

So it was no wonder that we gave no quarter to the Japanese.

THE BURMA CAMPAIGN was like a collection of incidents, rather than one constant and continuous fight. Often days would go by when we had no contact with the enemy; the world was a different place then, with the silence broken only by the commonplace sounds of the jungle and the troops' everyday activities; the reverberation of gunfire was eerily absent.

We were always glad of the respite; doubtless the Japanese were too. But there were not many days of inactivity; there was always something else around the next corner.

What happened to me after a peaceful night with the Camerons was typical: as dawn broke, a withering barrage of fire was directed at us. The company commander and I soon located the source: a Japanese machine-gun position some four hundred yards away had, unbeknownst to us, been dug in during the night. Rapidly I passed fire orders for a section of two guns to engage the target, realizing that nothing less than a direct hit on the machine-gun would stop its deadly hail. It was a precision target, and the element of luck would play a great part. After five ranging rounds, I knew that I wasn't going to succeed in hitting it, for the fall of shot was too wide, even though I'd achieved a bracket of fifty yards.

There was another solution. I radioed to the tank support unit and within fifteen minutes a tank had arrived on the scene. As it approached, I signalled for it to halt under cover of a nearby tree and, going to the rear of the machine, I picked up the external telephone by the rear hatch. Quickly I described the nature of the target and, within a minute, the Sherman was pumping round after round at the Japanese position. The fourth shot was a direct hit: we could see parts of the Japanese and their weapon flying through the air. Their machine-gunning was over; strangely enough, no other Japanese position took up the fire. It appeared to be an isolated position set up by the Japanese quite some distance from their main body – they did some odd things at times!

At the end of the shoot the hatch of the tank opened and the red head of Captain Ian Percival looked down on me, saying with a grin, 'Glad to know we're indispensable: you gunners can't do it all!'

Percival was a long-time acquaintance of mine; I retorted, 'Good to see *you* do something useful once in a while, rather than hiding away in your tin box, no doubt swigging beer unseen, while we poor foot-sloggers soldier on! So long, Ian, I'll see you under the fig tree.'

The Japanese knew how to deal with tanks. They trained Human Destruction Teams, whose sole purpose was to destroy our armour, even if it meant being killed themselves in the process. One team was dedicated to the destruction of tanks; they'd do this by strapping high explosives to their chests and allowing the tank to pass over them, exploding the device at the right moment. It was a gory business, and the removal of the resultant mess of blood and guts from the tracks was an unpleasant and unnerving chore.

The distinctive rattling sound of enemy tank tracks was always unsettling, especially at night, when we couldn't see them. The ominous noise told us they were out there, and we knew that we were directly in their path, and that they'd be coming unerringly straight for us – that thought alone was enough to send shivers up our spines. If we were in a slit-trench at the time, we had even greater cause to worry: the Japanese Whippet tanks, although very small, packed a nasty punch, and they manoeuvred quickly, so we had to stay constantly alert to avoid being caught unawares.

After this incident, the Camerons moved on to make contact with the main body of the enemy, but were forced to halt at a place I'd shelled a few day earlier. It was a small copse, providing the only cover from the eyes of the Japanese, but unfortunately, several corpses were rotting there: the bodies were Imperial Guard who would never use their steel swords again. They were in an advanced stage of putrefaction, and the sweet cloying smell of death filled the air. Some had died from shellfire, and some, who were a ghastly sight, from the torching of a flamethrower. The flamethrower was one of the most frightening weapons in the history of warfare; to be sprayed by the flaming oil was a terrible way to die, and a horrible sight to witness.

This was the first time I'd seen the results of this dreadful weapon at first hand, but it wasn't to be the last: a mass killing which took place near the end of the war turned out to be an even more appalling spectacle, when flamethrowers were turned on escaping Japanese as they broke away from the Pegu Hills. As they scrambled through the scrub country where they were trapped, they were incinerated in their droves by the searing heat of the British Engineers' flamethrowers. It was a blood-curdling sight watching the bodies become burning torches, and to see them staggering forward like robots in their last desperate death throes before they shrivelled into a burning mass on the sandy ground. They were exterminated ruthlessly and expeditiously, though it was not a sight that many men cared to see – witnessing the death of a human being in such a manner, even a Japanese soldier, would be etched forever in one's memory, together with the smell of burning flesh.

In spite of the unpleasantness – the smell of burning flesh pervaded the copse – our overriding thought was still, *Fry them up and serve the bastards to the crocodiles,* such was our loathing of these inhuman men.

IN THE NORTHERN part of the country the Chindits were addressing the myth that a military unit was unable to fight isolated from the main body of the army during the monsoons, or without the traditional lines of supply. This Chindit strike force was assembled during 1943 at the orders of Winston Churchill and Lord Louis Mountbatten. Their mission was to strike at the heart of the enemy, to inflict casualties and to harass and deflect their attention from the American-led Chinese, who were engaged in operations on the Ledo Road. The first expedition led by Brigadier General Orde Wingate, the architect of the Chindits concept, was by the 77th Indian Brigade, which was divided into seven columns of four hundred men each. The principals in this revolutionary venture were Wingate – a man experienced in similar military operations in Eritrea and other parts of the world, a leader in the techniques of jungle warfare, who, tragically, was to die in a plane crash near Imphal on March 24, 1944 – and Major (later Brigadier General) Michael – Mad Mike – Calvert, whom I'd met at my Jungle Warfare training camp; I was more than willing to testify to the appropriateness of his nickname! The Chindits – their name was derived from the mythological *chinthes,* the lions guarding the Burmese temples – were a few thousand strong only: the unit comprised infantry-men, gunners and engineers. The Lancashire Fusiliers, a battle-hardened battalion which had fought the Japanese for more than two years, were a key component. I was particularly interested because my father had served with the Lancashire Fusiliers during the First World War. The artillery units, also well-seasoned soldiers, were converted to foot soldiers and trained in jungle warfare: the whole became an entirely self-sufficient fighting force.

The task of Mad Mike's column – there were seven columns in the Chindits – was to destroy two railway bridges and the important Japanese supply centre at Nankan. It struck hard, inflicting severe casualties on the Japanese, and taking some losses, and did so quite independently, some two hundred miles from the main British forces near the Indian border. It lived off the land and relied entirely on air supply for the replenishment of ammunition and other essentials, including fodder for the mules. The airmen who carried out these supply drops did so under the most dangerous and difficult conditions, and because of this the crucial fodder drops often missed their targets. Mules were the prime means of transporting the 4.2 and 3-inch mortars and other heavy equipment. Apart from this, the force was self-sufficient; the men carried everything else on their backs. There were no vehicles; the two hundred miles each way were covered on foot.

The Chindits had blown up bridges and railway lines – including Myitkyina Railway, as ordered – and disrupted the supply lines to the Japanese on the northern front. But their attempt to cross the Irrawaddy to cut the Mandalay–Lashio line was unsuccessful, both because they were exhausted and because of the difficulties of being supplied by air. After completing their mission, the columns broke into small parties to return to the base: of the almost three thousand men who started with the Wingate expedition, nearly four hundred were lost to enemy action and sickness. In a later expedition, Mad Mike commanded the brigade which flew in to 'Broadway', near Indaw; many of the gliders crash-landed, but although casualties were heavy, he succeeded in establishing the unit there and building an airbase. The Japanese retaliation destroyed a number of Spitfires on the strip, but failed to dislodge Calvert.

The Japanese had great respect for the Chindits as a fighting force, probably because they fought the Japanese on their own terms and did so with little service support. Every man was a soldier with a rifle, no matter what his job was. There was no massive artillery or large-scale armoured support, nor were there rear echelons to supply their every need. They lived and fought in an isolation experienced by few soldiers. They were perhaps, in the opinion of the Japanese, the only soldiers equal to them, men who would face death rather than defeat, the principle the Japanese themselves lived by. To surrender was, in their eyes, unworthy and dishonourable; that was their rationale for treating a defeated enemy who still lived as inhumanely as possible. Because the Japanese recognized the Chindits as a strong fighting force, they were anxious to destroy them – but they were unable to do so.

For his bravery and leadership, Mad Mike Calvert was awarded both the DSO and bar. However, Slim would later write that the damage the

Chindits did to Japanese communications was quickly remedied, and it had no immediate effect on their plans.

It was first intended that this Special Force would coincide with a major Chinese offensive, but this didn't take place, and lessened the unit's potential for success. Whilst saying that the raid was a failure, Slim continued, 'There was a dramatic quality about the raid which, with the undoubted fact that it had penetrated far behind the enemy lines and returned, lent itself to presentation as a triumph of British jungle fighting over the Japanese. We had beaten them at their own game. This was important to the troops in Burma, and to them it was the first ripple showing the turning of the tide.'

The Chindits operated in various areas of central and northern Burma and were to share in the glamour surrounding Brigadier General Merrill's Marauders, the Chindits' American counterparts, who operated in a similar manner with the Chinese: both groups had a mystique not unlike that enjoyed by the French Foreign Legion. The Chindits' capture of Myitkyina became renowned; the operation used the codenames Blackpool, Broadway, Aberdeen and Piccadilly for the features of the ground. Mogaung, about fifty miles from Myitkyina and well known for its ruby mines, fell then too; though Stilwell credited the Chinese with its capture, it was in fact the Chindits who liberated that British hill station. Somewhat miffed at being ignored, the column commander sent a signal to Vinegar Joe, saying, 'If the Chinese had indeed taken Mogaung, then the Chindits would take umbrage.' Vinegar Joe's response was not recorded.

Merrill's Marauders, known officially as Force Galahad 5307 Composite Unit (provisional), engaged in similar activities, although on a smaller scale. There were three battalions – three thousand men – representing the total number of American troops in Burma. However, unlike the Chindits, they were not already battle-hardened. Three weeks earlier they'd been in the United States, where they were selected from volunteers from various branches of the US Army. Yet their exploits, conducted under the most arduous conditions, were no less sensational than those of the Chindits: they performed valuable work in the northern parts of the country, working with thirty thousand Chinese troops. Much of their work was in the Hukawng Valley supporting the 32nd and 38th Chinese Divisions, a hundred miles north-west of Myitkyina.

The Galahad force had successfully – though with difficulty – taken the airport, putting the Japanese to flight. Having suffered severe casualties themselves, they were resting and regrouping, preparing to meet the retaliatory attack which they knew the Japanese would launch on the vital airfield. It was at that point that General Stilwell ordered Galahad's Colonel Hunter to dispatch two battalions of Chinese to assist in the attack on Myitkyina. If anything, Hunter had expected Stilwell to send reinforcements to *him*, in anticipation of the counter-attack. En route to Myitkyina the Chinese became lost and, meeting the Japanese unexpectedly, were forced to withdraw. When they did resume the march, the two battalions entered the town from opposite sides – it's believed they ended up attacking each other, so had to be withdrawn once more: it was a fiasco the likes of which Dodger would have revelled in: 'A right bloody mess.'

Subsequently, Force Galahad – Merrill's Marauders – had taken the airfield and been prominent in helping Calvert's 77th Brigade to capture the well-defended town. The fight was a bloody one, and not an easy victory: ten thousand determined Japanese defended that town for almost three months, against far superior forces. The Marauders were sorely beaten: they lost more than half their force, killed and wounded, against an equal number of Allied troop casualties. The occasion marked the outstanding courage and determination of the Japanese in their resistance, which was subsequently noted in both British and Japanese military history. There were desperate men on both sides: it was by no means an ignominious defeat for the Japanese.

The Galahad group had been dubbed Merrill's Marauders by a news reporter – Brigadier Frank Merrill was the unit's commander – who was looking for an arresting title to catch the attention of his readers; he'd been impressed by the group's stealthy infiltration tactics and lightning strikes against the Japanese. Though the Brigadier's tenure was a short one, with Colonel Hunter, the second-in-command, assuming the role, the name stuck. Under Hunter's inspiring leadership, they overcame the hardships of fighting a vastly superior force in an alien environment. Only eight weeks earlier they'd been volunteers. They fought on in spite of rampant disease, with inadequate arms and equipment, and took that severe mauling at Myitkyina. Valiantly they struggled against far superior odds, but they were applauded by General Slim and earned the respect of the Fourteenth Army.

The Marauders had become known for their gallantry and tenacity. Eventually, however, the deficiencies in their equipment and supplies, and the poor support given to them, proved too much. They suffered enormous casualties. These factors, and the fatigue of ceaseless conflict against a ruthless enemy, the hostile jungle, the sleepless nights and the shortage of food and water, all conspired to the breakdown of morale, as did the fact that they were a long way from home, where nobody seemed to care about them. The final straw was the demand for the sick and wounded to return to the struggle, because of the desperate situation that had developed in Myitkyina. Then came rumours of insubordination, and refusal to return to action. The insinuations gathered strength, following which the unit was withdrawn from Burma and the eight hundred proud survivors were returned to India, where the unit was disbanded. Future consideration of the part they played in those difficult engagements exonerated them from all blame. They had done well.

The Chindits also were to receive approbation for they too, like the Marauders, suffered heavy casualties. The fighting in which they were engaged was the most vicious: it was hand-to-hand combat on an individual basis. This typified the Burma Campaign: and both sides were determined to kill each other.

The hardships the brave men of the Chindits and the Marauders endured were enormous. They fought in some of the worst possible conditions: jungle-covered mountains in the torrential monsoons. In their isolation, they coped with the sick and the wounded as best they could; medical facilities were nonexistent, so treatment was rough and ready. It was frequently necessary to abandon those unable to keep up with the column: these men were left under a tree or by the side of a chaung with a water-bottle and a pistol, waiting for death – which was assured when the Japanese arrived. And discipline on the march was brutal: it echoed that of the Spanish Wars.

When the Chindits returned to base from their foray they were a sorry sight, looking more like scarecrows than the fine fighting body of very professional soldiers they were. Ill-fed, they had all lost too much weight. Their uniforms were soiled and bedraggled, ripped, with buttons missing, hats lost. The men were unshaven, their hair dishevelled. Their boots were rotted from the dampness of living in the jungle under the most primitive of conditions during the three months of the expedition. Most of them were suffering from malaria, and their eyes were yellow with jaundice. Dysentery was rampant; on their faces was written the agony caused by pain and the fever. For three months – on too little food – they had endured sleepless nights, forded rushing rivers, and hacked their way through the thickest, razor-sharp bamboo jungle in the world. And their minds were frayed from the need to remain constantly on the alert for the ever-present Japanese.

But as they marched in to base, they had a certain air about them. Their decrepit appearance belied their supreme confidence: they were men who knew they had faced adversity, and done so with courage. They had fought the jungle as well as the enemy, and had succeeded in a bold venture. They had shown us all that the British soldier could survive out there as well as the enemy; they had reinforced the belief that the British soldier was second to none on the battlefield. They had made history proving that the British soldier could successfully fight under the most adverse conditions, even in the pestilential jungles of Burma. And their forefathers who had fought at the Somme, at Minden, at Coruna, at Talavera or the Battle of Hastings would have been proud of them. The cheers as they arrived showed the admiration in which they were universally held. General Montgomery once said that the finest thing that a British soldier could say was that, 'He marched with the Eighth Army against the Germans.' General Slim offered the same praise when he said to his men that they should be proud to say they fought with the Chindits.

Having completed their mission they, like Merrill's Marauders, were disbanded. Both groups had been asked to do more than was humanly possible, and their ordeal had been harsh.

GENERAL SLIM HAD MORE than straight warfare to consider during the Burma Campaign. Two political matters sorely tested his powers. The more troublesome was Aung San: in the 1930s Aung San had been a student at Rangoon University where he formed the All Burma Student Movement, their purpose: to oust the British Government. These Marxist students led a strike against the British educational system; Aung San soon became the Secretary of the Nationalist Majority Group. Sentenced for leading a political uprising, he spent seventeen days in Rangoon Jail before escaping. In 1939 he fled to China on a Norwegian boat, seeking help to gain independence for Burma. The Japanese, sensing a potential future ally, indoctrinated him into the Japanese Co-Prosperity Scheme for Asia philosophy and trained him in the Japanese Army. Returning to Rangoon in a Japanese freighter Aung San selected thirty of his student friends – the 'Thirty Comrades' – to be trained in guerrilla warfare on Hainan Island. Then at the head of the Burma Independence Army (BIA), Aung San and his men – some three hundred of them – led the Japanese invasion of Burma from Thailand in January 1942. During the great British retreat and defeat, the BIA worked closely with the Japanese, fighting, ambushing, harassing and killing the British forces.

As the strength of the BIA multiplied – the Bamar tribes were the main volunteers, though some, like the Kachins and the Chins, remained loyal to the Crown – BIA civil administrations terrorized local minority populations and, fed up with mobs getting out of hand, the Japanese disbanded it and set up the Burma Defence Army (BDA), headed by Aung San, now a Major-General in the Japanese Army. The BDA became the Burma National Army (BNA) on Burma's independence from Japan in August 1943.

In 1945, however, when it was clear that the Japanese were losing the war and would soon quit Burma, Aung San, now BNA's political supremo and minister of defence, openly defected to the British side. (The previous year he had secretly formed the Anti-Fascist Organization, which ran resistance against the Japanese.) He offered his support to General Slim in May of that year. A meeting between the army commander and the defector, arranged by Force 136, a clandestine group composed of Kachins led by British officers, took place on May 15. Aung San was a very charming individual; he'd had little difficulty in persuading the Japanese of his continued support and good intentions, even whilst he was talking to Britain of defection. In his early thirties, he had a wealth of experience with the government of Burma and a reputation for successfully motivating people. He was a natural-born politician, and he knew not only what he wanted, but how to achieve it with a minimum of friction. Is it any wonder that he was able to persuade the British to forgive and forget and welcome him into the fold?

Slim, after some deliberation, accepted Aung San's offer to swap sides and to place the BNA at the disposal of the Fourteenth Army, to fight the

Japanese. He did tell Aung San that he was a traitor, and really should be shot, but he recognized the value of the offer, for the Japanese were now at their most vulnerable and Aung San's ten thousand troops would be useful in their extermination. So the arrangement was consummated and approved by Lord Mountbatten, and the BNA worked closely and successfully with Slim's troops – although they seemed to spend more of their time murdering their political opponents than fighting, perhaps unknown to General Slim.

After the end of the war, Aung San concentrated on politics; he signed an agreement in London in January 1947 that led to Burma's independence in 1948 – but, ironically, he and six of his ministers of the interim government were assassinated by political opponents on July 19, 1947, before true independence began. He never saw what he'd fought his whole life to achieve.

SLIM ALSO HAD to deal with Subra Bose and his Indian National Army (INA). Of the hundred thousand British troops captured in Malaya, there were many Indian soldiers who, not wishing to face the rigours of a Japanese internment camp, elected to serve under their Japanese captors. This renegade group defected and assembled under the name of the Indian National Army, their purpose to gain freedom from British rule for India. Subra Bose, an Indian educated at Cambridge, and a one-time President of the All India Congress Party, wished to lead this group of freedom fighters and, after escaping from prison – serving time for his political activities in India – he made his way to Germany, thence to Japan by submarine. He volunteered himself to the Japanese as the man of the hour to free India. Japan accepted his proposal in February 1942 and Bose's recruiting campaign across Asia gained more Indians to the ranks of the Indian National Army. His grandiose vision was to personally lead his INA divisions across the Burmese border into India, acclaiming himself as India's saviour, and introducing Japan as the redeemer. In the event, the Indian National Army did take part in the Burma Campaign serving under the Japanese, but the INA lost confidence and became disenchanted with Bose, and he and his provisional Indian government party were relegated to a lesser prominence, and did not reach India until 1944.

In all there were about fifty thousand Indian troops in the INA, and their record suggests that rather than being helpful to the Japanese, they were in fact a liability. They took little part in the fighting against the British and were quick to surrender, especially when the tide turned, and on occasions disgraced themselves. They did, however, cause some concern to the British troops because, on Japanese orders, they would frequently wear their British uniforms. It was very disconcerting for a British patrol to meet this apparently friendly force, only to be shot at by them, as I myself experienced one day. By and large, the attacks by the INA and other Jiff units were invariably unsuccessful. As Japanese defeat grew closer, many of these deserters readily offered to surrender, but their traitorous behaviour meant we bore them no love, so they were shot. Slim issued a directive that the British and Gurkha troops should 'take a kinder approach to them' – but no one was much inclined to do that.

THE JAPANESE ARMY was presently in disarray, forming isolated groups rather than a cohesive force, and susceptible to annihilation. Now desperate and in full retreat, with their lines of supply cut behind them, they fled wherever they were able, often into the hands of the waiting British. The final Japanese break-out occurred in July; the end was close, and the mass killings were about to commence. The thirty thousand troops of the Japanese Twenty-Eighth Army, once an élite battle formation, now a tired and disorganized rabble, were hiding in the Pegu Yoma mountains. In their desperation, they were attempting to break out and cross the Sittang River to join other retreating Japanese forces. A copy of their plan for this break-out, showing precisely the chosen routes, fell into our hands, and wherever the Japanese turned, the Fourteenth Army was waiting for them, and ruthlessly hunted them down. The Sittang flowed parallel to and east of the road from Mandalay to Rangoon. As they hurried across the railway line at Nyaunglebin, between Pegu and Toungoo, a hundred and fifty miles north of Rangoon, and were about to cross the river, the British, Gurkha, and Indian Brigades of the 17th Indian Division were waiting for them. Firmly entrenched along the road and the railway with the full support of artillery and tanks, they slaughtered these ruthless enemies in their thousands. The Japanese Thirty-Third Army came from the east to help their comrades, but they were too late; they also became embroiled in the break-out and thousands were killed, with fourteen hundred being taken prisoner.

It was a complete disaster for General Sakurai and his Twenty-Eighth Army as they tried in vain to cross the very river they had so victoriously taken three years earlier. As the British Commander, General Scones had watched the futile attempt of his two brigades of the 17th Indian Division to swim the fast and swollen Sittang in 1942. Now General Sakurai watched as his men suffered the same fate. And this also caused the failure of a last, desperate attempt to defeat Slim's Fourteenth Army, by regrouping to join with the remnants of the other two Japanese Armies in Burma. Their attempts to cross the monsoon-enraged river were suicidal: many were either drowned or eaten by crocodiles – a fitting end, many of us thought. The British played cat and mouse on a large canvas as the swirling river swept the Japanese away like matchsticks. Those who tried to negotiate those waters using banana leaves as rafts went without sleep and food for the several days they were afloat, but those who survived that nightmare voyage did so only to meet death along the swollen banks of the river from the heavy carpet of fire laid down by the British artillery and RAF fighter planes. The Japanese were killed in their thousands. The Burmese guerrillas also took part in the retribution, ambushing and killing to the last man every enemy unit they encountered. The Japanese reaped what they had sown.

The enemy had no medical facilities available as these had been destroyed by the USAF and RAF as they tried unsuccessfully to move eastwards. The wounded Japanese must lie where they fell and take their chances on living or dying, as the British forward first aid posts and the mobile hospitals were too busy attending to our own. We were still taking casualties because of the Japanese's bloodyminded refusal to surrender.

Very few units of the Indian National Army were engaged in a fighting role, and those that did were ineffectual, and reluctant to engage with the British. Thousands of them had thrown down their arms at Pagan, just south and east of my own Irrawaddy crossing, when it was evident that the Japanese were now losing the war: they were quick to surrender and return their allegiance to the Raj, although their reception was not warm. It was expected that at the end of hostilities those who returned to India would be court-martialled and severely punished, maybe even sentenced to death. But because of India's political situation – it was the eve of India's independence – none were executed, or imprisoned, or penalized in any way at all. Indian history would acclaim them as the 'Liberators of India' and 'The Freedom Fighters'; they were revered accordingly across the country. Subra Bose escaped with his Provisional Government of Burma to Bangkok by way of the Death Railway along the river Kwai: far from being punished for his traitorous behaviour, he was lauded by the Indian Government. One of the streets in Calcutta was even renamed after him – but he had once been mayor of that city.

I HAD EARLIER been on an exterminating trip with a battalion of infantry of the 2nd British Division, this time to the south-west. There were thousands of Japanese troops in isolated pockets of resistance in the Henzada area, where the railway line and the road to Gwa met, eighty miles northwest of Rangoon and back on the west side of the Irrawaddy River. And it was here, crossing the bridge over the river, that we found hundreds of them. Like those later trying to cross the Sittang a hundred and fifty miles to the east, they were in very poor condition. They were as fanatical as ever, fighting on in spite of exhaustion and hunger. And they suffered the same fate as their colleagues trying to escape elsewhere: we cut them down. Although I had only a troop of four 5.5-inch howitzers with me, I used them to great effect. There was no counter-battery response from the Japanese, because they'd abandoned what artillery and armoured vehicles they had as they had neither fuel nor supplies.

These were easy targets, and we shelled them at our leisure: it was rather like an exercise on the Royal Artillery firing ranges on Salisbury Plains, but without the usual barrage of criticism from the gunnery instructors. And whilst the Japanese went hungry during their slaughter, my friends and I ate the usual M&V tins of stew and brewed up copious quantities of tea.

Smoking a cigarette whilst directing the gunfire was a bit unusual for me; normally this was strictly taboo. But these were unusual times, casual times – even a bit light-hearted, strange as that sounds. We had plenty of cigarettes, for welded to the rear panel of the Jeep was a 303 ammunition box full of them; like the ammunition and food, they'd been shipped up from the rear echelons. There was even a bottle of Scotch whisky in there – purely for medicinal purposes, of course, and too precious to use otherwise. The Japanese were enjoying none of these luxuries; they were too busy dodging the hail of shells and machine-gun fire and trying to stay alive to continue the fight. Yet for all the hopelessness of their situation, they never gave up: *Death for the Emperor* was their cry. When capture looked imminent, they had only one choice: death; to die by the British guns, or to commit suicide. And if the guns failed to oblige and they were being overrun, unable to accept the consequences of losing faith with the Emperor and their people, they chose the latter: suicide was the Japanese way. Few of them carried rifles or side-arms, although most of the officers still wore their swords; we paid special attention to them, because the swords were prized keepsakes, and in great demand back in Calcutta, where the Americans were prepared to pay exorbitant prices for them – so much so that the Royal Engineers were doing a very good trade with the Yanks using the excellent facsimile swords they were making from Jeep springs!

Large numbers of Japanese were now committing suicide, and a few British officers thought they should be stopped from doing so – though no one had any suggestions as to how this might be done. General Bill Slim issued the following order to all ranks, 'That any Japanese officer wishing to commit suicide would be given every facility.' The slaughter had now become commonplace across southern Burma as the Japanese tried to break out: seventeen thousand men died, less then a tenth of that number were taken prisoner. During this period, the British Army lost ninety-five men: later described as the most disproportionate battle of the war. Because the Japanese refused to surrender, the slaughter continued unabated, even after the ceasefire on August 15, 1945. It is thought that a few survived in the hills and the jungles, where they started new lives, protected from discovery by the isolated terrain.

It was a bitter defeat, and an ignominious ending for an army which, for a short period of time, was lauded as the finest fighting force in the world. The Japanese were now reaping the evils of the harvest they had sown. After they surrendered unconditionally on August 14, 1945, General Kimura publicly handed his sword to General Slim – yet it was three weeks before the last remnants of the Japanese Army were destroyed, and many more British soldiers were killed whilst the world rejoiced in this hard-won peace. The last Burmese river had been crossed. We prayed the next one would be the Mersey.

IN CONTRAST TO the stark and unpleasant conditions the Fourteenth Army endured in Burma, our parent body, the South-East Asia Command, was headquartered on the small island of Ceylon. Lying a few miles off the south-east tip of India, it was a veritable paradise for those fortunate enough to serve in that vast organization. Administered by Britain since 1796, the capital of Ceylon is Colombo; Trincomalee had long been a major naval base. Lord Mountbatten chose as his headquarters the town of Kandy, in the centre of an island in a small artificial lake surrounded by hills, described as some as, 'A scene of beauty which cannot be surpassed.' The British barracks were well-established; even the rest houses far exceeded the comfort of their counterparts in India. Lord Mountbatten chose well, for the climate was most tolerable, and his top-heavy organization of several thousand people were able to enjoy every conceivable luxury: no bashas or tinned bully beef for them, it was ham and ale all the way. Lord Louis insisted on this, for he loved the good life and wished to be sur- rounded only by that which pleased him. Every conceivable facility was made available; it must have been wonderful for the servicemen to see white women once again – in the shapely, if official, forms of WAAFs, WRENs and the ATS. Kandy was an infinitely more enjoyable spot to serve in than anywhere else on the planet, particularly the jungles of Burma. We were told about the numerous dances, where the women were dressed in the most enchanting ballgowns in a lavish, glamorous setting second to none, even in peacetime England. The Oxford and Cambridge accents were very much in evidence, and Lord Louis' retinue of suave – and effemi- nate – young equerries in uniforms of a smartness unsurpassed in any army, tended to his every need. There was a decadent air in Kandy; a visiting Brigadier, summoned from the fighting in Burma to attend a high-level conference, was aghast at what he saw, fearing that if the pomp and splen- dour of the headquarters were to become known in the forward area of Burma, there would be mutiny. General Slim must also have been appalled at what he saw when he visited, though it was a paradise any man in Burma would have given his right arm to enjoy.

LATER ON, I discovered that whilst the war in Europe was almost finished, the most spectacular campaign was still in the making: the destruction of the Japanese in Manchuria, where their Kwantung Armies of more than a million men were based. The United States and the Soviets had agreed earlier that, at the appropriate moment, the latter would declare war on the Japanese. They would then march on this massive conglomeration of armies, which consisted of forty infantry divisions, eleven hundred tanks and five thousand field-guns.

But first the Red Army had to be redeployed, for the majority of its resources were on the Western front fighting the Germans. It marshalled its own even-more-gigantic force of one and a half million men, five thousand, three hundred tanks and twenty-five thousand field-guns, moving them over a vast distance – more than five thousand miles. The Red Army envisaged no trouble in wiping out the Japanese.

On August 8, 1945 the Russians did indeed declare war, surrounding the Japanese on a perimeter three hundred miles long. The following day, they struck hard with an even mightier force, making a two-pronged attack deep into the Kwantung Armies. Within a few days the Japanese started to surrender; by August 15, the fighting had ceased. The Japanese admitted defeat on August 26 and surrendered totally on September 2. It was a unique feat, on a scale unprecedented in the annals of war: the enormity of the logistics pertaining to rations, fuel, ammunition and the supplies necessary for such a campaign must have been breathtaking, not to mention the superb control of troop movements and vehicle convoys in order to prevent the terrible nightmare of everyone becoming hopelessly entangled.

During the short battle, the Japanese fought with their usual tenacity. Brutal to the end, they mutilated the Russians whenever they could, as was their inhumane custom.

AFTER PROVIDING HEAVY artillery fire to the infantry during the extermination exercises at Henzada, I returned to the regiment, which was now in the area of Pyu, thirty miles south of Toungoo and about two hundred and fifty miles from Mandalay. Rangoon was a further two hundred miles to the south. We were now in the last week or so of our war, and the regiment was to be flown out of Burma to Dum Dum airport at Calcutta: our part of the battle was ended. We were told to take only our personal equipment and weapons, leaving the guns to be taken down to Rangoon by the rear party, which would consist of just a few men, sufficient to escort the eight howitzers, the twenty-four 25-pounders and the vehicles. They'd go by road to the docks at Rangoon, and thence by boat to Calcutta. Much to my dismay, I was chosen to lead this party – I too was anxious to be out of the battle zone, and desperate to savour the delights of Calcutta, that huge and dismal city. But there was no arguing, and the day that my regiment boarded the old Dakotas for the relatively short flight, I started the long drive to the south.

At least I wasn't expecting it to be an unpleasant journey: I was optimistic that it would be free from the tensions we'd lived with for so many months. I led the gun train at a leisurely pace, for the road was heavily damaged by gunfire and the RAF's bombing, and we reached the town of Pegu that evening. We were nearly halfway to our destination, which, I sincerely hoped, would culminate in a very comfortable voyage of seven hundred miles back to a better civilization, with plenty of liquor and good food available to while away the time.

Pegu had been the scene of fierce fighting when the 17th Division swept down from Toungoo and met strong resistance. Before surrendering the town, the Japanese had released almost five hundred British prisoners, who were fleeing in a disorganized group. Unfortunately, they were mistakenly identified as Japanese, and the RAF killed or wounded many of them with bombs and machine-gunfire. The monsoon broke as the forward elements of the 17th Division captured Pegu; the consequent flooding of the river halted any further advance.

When we had captured Rangoon, the remnants of the Japanese Army fled the city, so very little fighting took place there. To our great disappointment, the British 2nd Division – to which I was attached – and the 20th Division (which made up 4th Corps) were deprived of being in at the kill; we were relegated to a passive role, dashing our hopes to be the first British troops to capture Rangoon. We had raced south from Meiktila, although running low on supplies and being serviced by airdrop; so strong was our desire to be there for the final battle that we sacrificed food for ammunition.

But we were too late, for Rangoon had to be taken before the monsoon set in. The glory went to 15th Corps, when a battalion of Gurkhas parachuted into Elephant Point on May 2, 1945. On the landing ground they met thirty Japanese, who were quickly dispatched, but unfortunately the Gurkhas suffered heavy casualties – from friendly fire from US bombers. The following day the 26th Indian Division went in, in an amphibious assault codenamed Operation Dracula. But though 4th Corps didn't have the honour of capturing Rangoon, we were the true victors: we'd set the stage and driven the Japanese out of the country.

The major fighting in Rangoon ended on May 5. The British prisoners of war, about a thousand of them, had waited anxiously for their liberators' arrival, writing on the roof of the jail: 'Japs gone. Extract digit.' Most of the Japanese had indeed gone, five days earlier; just a handful remained, but when the Gurkhas arrived, that handful had a pretty bad time, paying the penalty for the brutal, inhumane behaviour of their whole army. When a British officer reprimanded a Gurkha for summarily dispatching a wounded Japanese, the Gurkha replied, with an innocent air, 'But Sahib, I was only putting him out of his pain.'

Some of the prisoners of war were in very poor shape, especially those who had been confined since the retreat in 1942. Many more had died during that prolonged period of suffering. Poor devils, they were in a sorry way, worn with hardship and riddled with disease, some suffering every conceivable affliction. Often toothless, and without limbs, it was tragic to see them lying on their rough charpoys, or, those who were capable, slouching aimlessly or hobbling around the grounds, still in shock and disbelief that they were free. They were infested with lice but they were deliriously happy to be decontaminated, fed and given medical attention, then clothed in fresh uniforms and clean clothing. It was a wonderful day for them when those Gurkhas entered their lives. Now the priority was getting them back to the hospitals in India, and thence to Britain, to families desperate for news.

As it turned out, invoking 'Dracula' was the correct decision, for by doing so the ports were reactivated a week earlier than they might have been. I wasn't unduly sorry about not being in at the kill; there were other pleasures awaiting me. The Japanese had been defeated; all that remained (apart from the mopping-up operations) was for the atom bomb to be dropped on Hiroshima on August 6, and on Nagasaki three days later, and the formal declaration of surrender by the Emperor on August 15.

The last time that Britain had conquered Rangoon was in 1885, when Burma was being annexed. Britain had been warring with the country for some time, but was galvanized into more serious action by King Thibaw's cavalier attitude towards British traders in Burma. Sorely miffed by his impertinent attitude, the British stepped up the war, dispatching a force of several thousand men – mostly Indians – to attack Rangoon. This they did quite easily (and on the same day and month as my own birthday!) – although they lost almost two hundred officers and men; that wasn't a great loss compared to the present bloody strife, but the big difference was that Britain got to rule Burma for close on sixty years that time around: the conquest this time would last but a few months.

I wasn't aware of the speed at which things were happening to the south. Travelling down to Rangoon, my gun party got a major shock: we'd driven some distance south and I'd decided to halt for the night, stopping at an unusually large and attractive house standing in its own grounds. The place was deserted; the locals had fled. It was clearly a property owned by the Government – perhaps the local District Inspector – so I decided to occupy it. Though sparsely furnished, both my subaltern Gallows and I had separate bedrooms of quite eight hundred square feet, in which were king-sized charpoys set on two-foot-high platforms; they could well have been ceremonial beds, they were so grand. It was pleasantly cool, thanks to the high ceilings and the tatty matting hanging at the entrances. After months of sleeping on jungle ground, we were delighted at the prospect of a good night's sleep in reasonably safe surroundings. After posting guards and eating – a bully beef stew, of course, though the best the cook had made in a long time – the men were happily settled down and we prepared for bed ourselves. I was interrupted by the arrival of a signaller, who came into my room and announced, 'There is a signal for you, sir.'

Expecting it to be nothing more than a routine message in response to reporting our position to Divisional Headquarters, I told him to leave it on the table and I'd deal with it later. With some hesitation, the signaller responded, 'I think you had better read it at once, Captain.'

With raised eyebrows, wondering what on earth it could be to warrant such insistence – after all, the war was just about over bar the fighting – I ordered him to read it out loud. The signaller obliged: 'To Officer i/c 134 Field Regiment Gun Party. Your guns are required for further action. Report your status and remain where you are. Repeat, remain where you are until further orders. Acknowledge.'

Stunned by the words – and their implications – I immediately shot

PICK UP YOUR PARROTS AND MONKEYS

back my reply, that the regiment was down to bare bones: we had only the
guns, no ammunition, dial sights or important stores. Further, there were
only two officers, one warrant officer and thirty-six NCOs and other ranks,
and no gun teams: as an effective artillery unit, my little party could be of
no value whatsoever in participating in further action. Gallows and I were
aware that the Japanese were still breaking out in great numbers, stream-
ing east from the Pegu Yomas and north from Rangoon. Although I anticipated hearing that the order had been rescinded, there would obviously be
some hazards in continuing on to Rangoon. We were so close to freedom
we could also smell it; it would be a dreadful twist of fate if we had to
rejoin the battle at this stage. Neither Gallows nor I slept well that night,
despite our palatial setting; nor did those of my men who knew what was
going on. It wasn't until the early hours of the morning that we received a
further signal cancelling the order, instructing us to proceed to Rangoon
as first planned. Heaving great sighs of relief, we ate a hasty breakfast and
were on the road within thirty minutes, before anyone on high could
change his mind.

We drove those last few miles with some trepidation, aware that we
had no close contact with any of our own infantry, and knowing that if
any Japanese, desperate as they were, engaged us, we'd be alone and at
their mercy. But by the grace of God we finally reached Rangoon, unscathed,
and were met by the Military Police, who installed us in a suburb in the
north of the city until I could finalize shipping arrangements. Once these
had been palatial homes for the British civilian population, but they'd
been bombed pretty badly – and the Japanese had also contributed to the
damage of the buildings. The need for caution was paramount; if we didn't
wish to die at this stage of the war, it was necessary to search each house
thoroughly for the booby-traps that had been scattered in such profusion.
One likely place to find them was in the flushing systems of the toilets:
pulling the chain before inspecting the system was usually tantamount
to pulling the plug on yourself!

And of course there were still Japanese roaming around the place,
singly and in small groups, killing and looting.

The Japanese had re-established the Burmese Government *their* way,
and that included the currency. The Japanese commanders of every formation had at their disposal travelling mints, with which they printed out

as much Burmese money as they wanted. And they *wanted* a lot: we found the evidence lying in the streets of Rangoon, where the gutters were filled with sodden piles of paper currency. One could scoop up a sackful in moments; now this worthless trash served only to plug up the city's drainage system. Nevertheless, my lads were quick to gather up handfuls of this pseudo-money as a souvenir; there was little else worthy of looting. The Japanese had cleaned everything out long before.

So once again it was the same miserable entry into a wretched, drab city. But though there was little to gladden one's eyes, still there was reason to be jubilant: the war was over and my side had won.

AS SOON AS I was settled I, like everybody else, was off to see the fabled Shwedagon Pagoda, one of the most famous pagodas in the world. It was on the outskirts of Rangoon, so I had to thread my Jeep through traffic heavy with military vehicles and filled with swarming crowds of Burmese. It was a very hot day and the slight breeze blew the dust around, causing great discomfort. I was surprised to see so many people: it looked like the whole of the Fourteenth Army and all the residents of Rangoon had chosen this very moment to visit the holy shrine.

The Shwedagon's golden roof and spire stretched far into the sky. The entrance was guarded by two thirty-feet-tall *chinthes*, part lion, part beast and part man-eating ogre – it was from these mythological figures that the crack troops known as the Chindits took their name. The chinthes were also to ensure that visitors removed their footwear before entering on bare feet. The pagoda was an impressive sight, and truly beautiful. It was once described as, 'Being of a wonderful bigness and all gilded from the foot to the top. It is the fairest place, as I suppose that is in the world. It standeth very high, and there are four ways to it, which all along are set with trees of fruit, such wise that a man may go in the shade above two miles in length.'

Legend has it that two disciples, brothers, met Gautama Buddha in India, when he was close to enlightenment. In appreciation of their visit he plucked eight hairs from his head. Though half were stolen on the journey back to Burma, the brothers placed the remaining four in a golden casket and buried it on the Rangoon hillside, in the tomb which contained relics of the three previous Buddhas. In later years the tomb was excavated; when the golden casket was found it, remarkably, contained the original eight hairs – and when the casket was opened, the hairs emitted a brilliant light, radiating to all the corners of the world, and the Heavens cried aloud, the thunder roared and the lightning struck, and the trees which were out of season blossomed and gave fruit. Other miracles occurred at that moment: the blind could see, the dumb could talk and the lame could walk.

The grave was then covered by a gold slab and a small pagoda built upon it.

As the years went by, the pagoda was refurbished and rebuilt until it reached its present size, towering almost three hundred feet into the sky. I was told there was more gold on the roof than there was in the Bank of England's vaults: there were eight thousand gold slabs on the outside. The tips of the spires were garnished with rubies, sapphires and topaz, while a huge emerald embedded in the middle caught the rays of the sun as it rose and set. Surrounding it, there were many smaller pagodas and bells. Still enshrined inside are the Buddha's eight hairs and the relics.

The building had suffered a great deal in the past from the elements – storms and earthquakes – and vandalism; it was pillaged twice by British troops. The gold leaf that glistened so beautifully under the hot Burmese sun was easily damaged by the heavy rains of the monsoons and was in need of constant replacement by a string of benefactors down through the years, like Queen Shinsawbu, who gave eighty pounds of gold. Her successor, Dhammazedi, gave four times his own weight in gold. He also gave a bell thirty feet in diameter; the bells of the pagoda spoke a great deal of its history. Dhammazedi's bell was plundered in 1608 by the Portuguese. They'd intended melting it down to make cannons – but whilst trying to ferry it across the Pegu River, it sank and was never recovered. Singu, Dhammazedi's son, gifted the pagoda with a twenty-three-ton bell, but the British pillaged it in the war of the eighteen hundreds and the bell suffered the same fate, sinking in the river. Several British efforts to raise it were fruitless; when the British agreed that it be returned to the pagoda, the Burmese successfully floated it to the surface by ingeniously building a bamboo frame around it. It stands today by the side of the Shwedagon Pagoda, together with the forty-ton bell given by King Tharawaddy, and others which were subsequently donated.

But though I was impressed with the exterior of the pagoda, I was sorely disappointed when I went inside. I could accept the tawdry merchants selling all manner of goods outside the pagoda, but I hadn't expected the inside to be similarly desecrated: it was even more crowded; there was a constant babble of chatter and the floors were awash in rubbish. You could scarcely see the faded beauty for the garish souvenirs – not only of the temple itself, but a good number of 'Feelthy pictures for you to take home, Sahib. Perhaps to show your girlfriend, Thakin.' I was appalled. The jostling crowds made it impossible to see the place properly; I was deeply disenchanted. I paused briefly to inspect some of the many inscriptions on the walls, but gave up without seeing the various levels inside. The Burmese, in their own way, were repeating the rape of Kublai Khan.

THE ENGINEERS AND Military Police were quick to restore order in Rangoon, but it was quite a week before there was any semblance of authority, especially in the dock area. We had to be self-sufficient; if we wanted something, it was up to us to make things happen. That applied to food too: we ate whenever we could find a willing host. Slim's motto for the Fourteenth Army was still very pertinent: *God helps those who help themselves.* I combed the docks ceaselessly for three days before I was able to find an American captain of a Liberty ship who agreed to take the guns to Calcutta. This was great news, for the competition for boat space was fierce, but the budding warm relationship between the captain and me was somewhat marred when, whilst loading the guns by crane, the jib gave way, and a 25-pounder field-gun fell several feet, embedding itself in the deck of the ship. I'd looked forward to eating meals in a civilized manner with the ships' officers, instead of resting a can of soup on the dashboard of my Jeep – which I seemed to have been doing for most of my life – but the seamen were rather aloof after that. I was a bit miffed: after all, it wasn't my fault their ship had been damaged!

Once my men were settled in, I went to the bunk the captain had provided for me. The small cabin had a porthole, so I was able to watch the feverish activity on the dockside. More vehicles and troops were being loaded and as the tempo reached its peak, the ship's siren sounded long and clear.

Once again I was aboard a ship bound for distant places.

The main deck of the small 10,000-ton vessel – at the time it looked like a huge, ocean-going luxury liner to me – was packed with men taking a long last look at the country in which they'd fought so brutal a war, a land of enduring, vivid, often bitter memories, where so many had grown to manhood. And above all, a place where many thousands of friends and comrades lay buried. Many a battle-hardened man felt his eyes mist over for those who had died alongside us. Hearts softened as thoughts turned to wives and families, the parents, the girls and the children who had been waiting so long to greet those men who would never return home. And we all prayed for our comrades, who had given their all for their country, and to save the world from an evil beyond imagination, now gone to a better place.

THERE WAS GREAT elation, in London and Washington, and all over the world, when the Japanese surrender was announced. But that elation was certainly not reflected by those still on the ground in Burma, for whilst the world rejoiced, the British soldier still had to fight on against the diehard enemy. Though their chiefs had thrown in the towel, the Japanese soldiers, true to the end, refused to acknowledge defeat and battled on bitterly. For three more weeks after the formal ceasefire the fighting and slaughter continued; only when there were but a few Japanese left did the resistance finally stop.

Several of my friends, including two from my own regiment and the Company Commander with whom I'd made that stormy Irrawaddy crossing were killed during that period of uncertainty. And then it was truly the end at last, and it was homeward bound for the boys who had survived the privations of jungle warfare for so very long. For me, the Fylde Coast Express was a step nearer.

Our ship was to sail at seven o'clock, with the evening tide, and there was just time for a quick burrah peg or two before dinner. Tonight I would dine off a white linen tablecloth, rather than from a mess can. There'd be no toasting the monarchy, though, for this was an American ship. And after a repast I had dreamed of for weeks, we downed a few more drinks and listened to the horrors of each other's war before saying goodnight. It seemed like everybody I spoke to had been in the thick of the fighting, for each had his own tale to tell of how he'd won the war! And so to bed, for tomorrow was another day.

The long, tedious war in Burma was ended, and it was surprising how quickly one readjusted, and how one's perspective on life changed. The world was a brighter place almost instantly – no more need to bed down on the wet jungle ground at night listening to the animals, or worse, the Japanese, wondering whether you'd be dead by morning. Or living in a slit-trench with Delhi-belly, or watching the flow of blood match the setting sun. And whilst I thought of the past, I wondered what had become of the tens of thousands of British and Indian troops who hadn't been put to death by the sword in the retreat. I knew many had been sent to prison camps in the country of their capture, to Malaya, or other parts of South-East Asia, or to Japan. Those who remained as prisoners in Burma perished at an unbelievable rate; the most infamous of these camps were located along the river Kwai, two hundred miles north-west of Bangkok.

The Japanese gathered together almost a quarter of a million men, women and children to work on linking the existing railway between Bangkok and Ban Pong to Burma for a supply-line for the Japanese Armies. It was to connect the village of Thanbyuzavat, where a line already ran, to Moulmein, where the Japanese had invaded Burma on that fateful December day in 1941. Using primitive tools and equipment, this unskilled labour had to carve out two hundred miles, through dense, malignant jungle, scrub-land and deep gorges which were almost impossible to negotiate. This daunting fourteen-month task started in 1942. It followed the river Kwai, and numerous prisoner-of-war camps were established along its banks. Of the several hundred bridges built, the one at Kanchanaburi – three hundred feet long with fourteen spans, at the confluence of the Maekhlaung and Kwai rivers – was designed to be permanent, being made of steel. And in this village, as in many others, the most heinous crimes were committed by the Japanese. Comparable to those atrocities committed by the Germans at Belsen and Auschwitz, this behaviour, perhaps the most atrocious in the twentieth century, earned the Japanese their deserved reputation as sadistic and brutal murderers who were callously indifferent to their prisoners. Aptly, the project became known as the Death Railway.

The work quotas were devastatingly high, far exceeding those expected of a Durham coal miner. In the heavy monsoon rains, the labourers, many without boots or even clothing, had to march several miles to the work site, where they would toil for twelve hours or more. Failure to meet the required work standard invariably met with punishment: a beating with a rifle-butt, or the breaking of a limb, or a bayonet in the stomach. The Japanese soldiers appeared to delight in the cruellest of punishments, deriving sadistic pleasure from the practice. Exhausted and hungry, often without food or water, with perhaps half an hour to eat the small portion of rice provided at midday – which was never sufficient – the prisoners would return in the still-drenching rain to the miserable campsite. At most of the camps, officers were expected to work too; refusal meant severe punishment, often death. And any Japanese guard who was suspected of even the slightest gesture of sympathy or kindness towards the prisoners was attacked and beaten by his comrades.

In a four-kilometre stretch at the notorious Kanchanaburi bridge alone, seven hundred British soldiers died, and for every sleeper laid on the line between there and Thanbyuzavat, a prisoner of war or coolie gave his life. If a bridge collapsed, the men had to work throughout the night to repair it, often up to the chin in water. For the white man, the conditions were unbearable. For the coolie they were abysmal. They worked longer hours – often eighteen hours a day, seven days a week – and slept in the most abject conditions, usually in the open, in spite of the torrential rain. The British tried to exercise some control over hygiene in the cookhouses and open-pit latrines; this wasn't done in the coolie camps, which were infested by insects and creatures, with devastating results.

Both British and coolies perished because of the conditions they endured during the hot Burmese summer. They died from the contaminated water, the lack of food, the impossible workloads, and the most stringent, brutal discipline by the vicious Japanese. They died from malaria, dysentery, beriberi, scrub typhus, black water fever, scabies, and from the sword and the bayonet. And from the constant rains of the devastating monsoons, and God knows what else. There was no medication; the few doctors in the camps executed the most complex operations in the most rudimentary fashion. There was a minimal quantity of quinine, but it wasn't given to the doctors; instead, it was used as a currency. And when the dreaded cholera struck, it spread like wildfire along the river, and the prisoners fell in their thousands: in some camps as many as thirty bodies a day were burned on fires of bamboo and scrub waste. There was no escape; the ocean and the jungles surrounded them. Weak and tired, with no hope, no letters from home, no Red Cross, lost to the civilized world, their isolation eventually broke the morale of all but the very strongest.

There was one shining light in this tragic story of unimaginable suffering: a doctor, Selwyn Clarke, and his wife, who devoted themselves ceaselessly to caring for the sick, under the most dreadful conditions. His eventual death by execution for alleged treason shocked the whole community along the railway line.

On October 25, 1943 the railway line was opened with a flourish. The bands played as the Rising Sun was displayed the length of the line. The officers and men of the Japanese Army turned out in all their finery – still wearing the swords with which so many had been murdered. For the prisoners, a day of rest was declared, and a few men were issued with tinned food and cigarettes they had not smoked in many months. But the dying continued to die: in all, some one hundred and thirty thousand people of all nationalities perished. And the others, those who eventually returned home, would bear the marks of their ordeal for the rest of their lives. The world should never forget or forgive the Japanese for the barbaric acts they committed along the river Kwai.

Who ever thought, then, that in fifty years' time, you would be able to take a sightseeing holiday to see where these men and women suffered and died in agony. The train leaves Bangkok for the three-hour journey twice a day, and you need not even alight at Kanchanaburi, for a few minutes later it will conveniently stop at the original elevated bridge over the Maekhlaung at Tamarkan. You could, if you wished, go by bus, although it is a less comfortable way to get there, but it will stop at the bridge for an hour so that you may make a close inspection of the site. And in the town there are two war cemeteries, one adjacent to the bridge on the east side and the other to the south. The former is still well-kept, and not far from the modern luxury hotels where you may rest after the tiring visit before you move on to different, less emotional vistas. Before you do so, however, you might wish to experience the River Kwai Massage Parlour, reputed to cure whatever ails you. That might be appropriate for those who wish to try what happened, for it is said that when the line was opened in 1943, the first train carried geisha girls.

Or you might stay at one of the sumptuous palaces conveniently close to the bridge. They will provide every comfort you could possibly wish for, and you may gaze at the bridge, built on the agonizing deaths of countless thousands, white and black, from the inestimable luxury and security of your verandah. Perhaps you might think of the sixteen thousand prisoners of war who died just across the way from where you are so that you might live ... and when you tire of that vista, take a cruise along the Irrawaddy, in the luxury boats which now sail those waters, and enjoy a standard of service unseen anywhere this side of the Ritz Hotel in London.

Think again of those who died for you on those stretches of muddy waters. To end this journey down bitter memory lane, take the long trip up to Kohima and Imphal, to see the memorial where the valiant few hundred held thousands of Japanese at bay, and paid the price. Remember that they were all in their late teens and early twenties, and perhaps you will have reason to commiserate with their ending. And when you go home, you will truly understand the message they wished to convey, 'When you go home, tell them of us and say, for your tomorrow we gave our today.'

I SAILED AWAY from the most exciting period of my life, an episode which had felt like a lifetime, and one which, hopefully would not, ever, be repeated. The few days it took to reach Calcutta were like a dream. And when we arrived in port, I had a few nights on the town before I had to leave for Ranchi to rejoin the regiment.

Calcutta was known by many appellations, the sweetest of which was 'the arsehole of the Far East'. Winston Churchill once visited, and when asked if he was glad that he had been, and why, he replied, 'Yes, indeed, I am very pleased that I did, for it means that I shall never have to go there again.' The origins of the city's name are obscure; some think it comes from the village of Kalikat, where Job Charnock opened his factory all those years ago; the Indians themselves believe it's from the city's Kali Temple.

In spite of Churchill's remarks, there were some very attractive areas in Calcutta – though the native quarters were deplorable and no person in his right mind would think of sight-seeing there. In the centre the British had built many fine buildings and statues during the last two centuries. The residence of the Governor General, Lord Curzon, was one of the finest examples of British architecture: in 1805 he spent two million rupees to build a mansion in the likeness of his home in England. The six-acre site was, appropriately, located near the Strand. (The British left their marks with Strands and Malls and Barracks Roads all over the British Empire.) Close to that work of art was St John's Church – where Job Charnock is buried; both are just a stone's throw from the River Hoogly, and close to Chowringhee. A few miles out from the city centre is Dum Dum, where, from 1783 to 1883, the Bengal Artillery had their headquarters before relocating to Meerut. The famous parade ground, the maidan, was adjacent to the Strand, extending from St George's Road to the north to Babu Ghat – almost two miles – and from the Strand eastwards at its widest point for a mile. Bounded by the Hoogly and Chowringhee, it was the cultural centre of the city, well known for its beauty and its officers' clubs. The beautiful Garden Reach, once renowned for its magnificent homes, sat close by Government House; it was a popular gathering-place for the mem-sahibs, who would dress in all their finery to discuss the gossip of the day. To the west of where the old fort was, at the new Fort William's St George's Gate, stood the statue of Lord Napier.

The new fort, with the river on one side, occupied almost two square miles; the excavation of the thirty-foot-deep moat that surrounded it contributed material for the building. The moat could readily be filled with water from the Hoogly; it had six gates with such romantic names as St George's, Plassey, Treasury, Calcutta, Chowringhee, and Water Gate, and it was never attacked successfully. In the centre of the complex was the church of St Peter's, built in 1828. By the south-east corner of the maidan was the one mile, five furlongs race course. St Paul's Cathedral, built in 1847, with a spire two hundred feet high, stood at the extreme south-east of the maidan. King George once landed in Calcutta on the Hoogly, at the Strand, at the aptly named St George's dock. Further downstream was the memorial to the Indian Lascars of Assam and Bengal, who gave their lives in the First World War – there were monuments galore: the Gwalior Monument, in memory of those British soldiers who fell in the battles of 1843. In the Curzon Gardens, north of the maidan, the Ochterlony Monument, to commemorate Sir David Ochterlony, who won the Nepalese War in 1814. Across from the racetrack at the very north-east corner of the maidan, the Victoria memorial with its impressive Cenotaph: this magnificent stretch of land was steeped in history, both of the British Empire and of India.

It was a Mecca for most of the troops who were stationed in the cantonment or there on sick or normal leave. Every possible luxury had been imported, from the four corners of the world, and in profuse quantities: wine, women and song were the order of the day. It was a poor man who was unable to find whatever special vice he enjoyed – providing, of course, that he was prepared to pay for it. No matter how rife your imagination ran, still you would be unable to plumb the true depths of the decadence that was possible. And just about every country had its representative contingent of heaven knew how many thousands amongst the burgeoning population of fifteen million natives. They came from the United Kingdom and the United States – who appeared to outnumber us, and were still increasing, day by day. There were Chinese, Australians, New Zealanders, French (what were they doing there? They lost Madras a hundred years ago), Poles, Czechs, West and East Africans and Uncle Tom Cobley and all – and they all had money to burn. The streets were jam-packed solid with the buyers and the providers. Just say what you wanted and it was yours in a flash – but be wary, for you could as easily get your throat cut and end up dead in the labyrinth of alleys for which Calcutta was noted. And everyone was looking for easy money, at any price: there were gangs galore, both white and coloured, and the local constabulary was too small to cope with them. As well as preying on the tourists, there were no end of gang rivalry fights.

Chowringhee, the Piccadilly of Calcutta, was the centre of the maelstrom; at times it was literally impossible to move along the sidewalks. Firpo's, a popular bar and restaurant purely for the Feringhees (officers only), and renowned throughout India, was packed solid day and night; it was as much as you could do to get inside the door, let alone to a table. But after a great deal of pushing and shoving, I managed to get in. I carried with me the Japanese flag, the Rising Sun, which I'd acquired whilst with the Gurkha regiment. The man who had formerly carried it was no longer in a position to do so: a Gurkha had slit his throat. I found a ready American customer for it – they had voracious appetites for these things, and were in the mood to buy anything from the war in Burma.

Three days there were quite enough for me and my contingent; I was glad to move on to Ranchi, in Bihar, where my regiment was. But before leaving, I sold the Samurai sword formerly worn by the Japanese soldier who had almost killed me, but who was himself killed by the Gurkha who saved my life; that scar would remain with me always. The sword also went quickly, also to an American, and I got an excellent price for both it and the Japanese flag. Not so the rubies and other precious stones I'd so carefully collected on my nine-hundred-mile journey, by foot and by Jeep, from the Indian border to Rangoon. When I had them appraised, I was told they were valueless.

Our sojourn in Calcutta was short, our freedom ended, and it was off to Ranchi for the final episode in our Burma war saga. At two thousand feet above mean sea level, and two hundred and fifty miles to the west, I was once again in what had been a hill station and the summer capital of the Bihar Government, and a rest camp for British troops. During the war years, it had become the Burma group headquarters, from where all the activities of the Burma Campaign were coordinated. Just a few miles away was a mental hospital, the largest in the world, and many a wit discoursed upon the subject of the Deolali tap, or madness.

It was a pleasant place for me to end my sojourn in the Far East. It was good to be away from the constant threat of malaria, dengue, cholera and black water fever, not to mention the leeches, crabs and hookworm, and the jungle sores that never heal. I'd had my fill of those, including the amoebic dysentery and malaria. You could be put on a charge for failing to take the mepacrine (even in close action), so I'd taken it religiously (in spite of the yellow eyes one developed), but it hadn't staved off the malaria, which would recur frequently for many, many years. I was destined to awaken at night, shaking uncontrollably, sweating profusely and running a temperature, even years after returning to England. And I was glad to leave behind the hot and humid weather, which was sheer bloody murder.

And it was purely wonderful to escape from the loathsome smell of the Japanese, who were often all around us, for there were no front lines in Burma. Did they never wash, or cleanse their backsides?

For a short time the monotony of cantonment life was most welcome. I was there for a month, awaiting repatriation to England, and it was a leisurely existence. There was little to do, no more exercises, no more gun drill – the guns were still somewhere in the Calcutta area, and would never again be handled by those men who had used them so effectively. There was some sadness about that: with those guns, the regiment had earned a magnificent reputation: we'd often been in action for days on end, using the cooks, the drivers and the runners as reliefs for the exhausted teams.

General Slim said we had done a superb job, and had done more than anything else to win the battles. And our men could go home, knowing that they would be the proud recipients of the Burma Star Medal, and that more Victoria Crosses were won in Burma than in all the North Africa campaigns. There were thirty-one Victoria Crosses awarded: eleven to the British (seven to Officers and Warrant Officers, four to Other Ranks), ten to the Gurkhas (two to Officers and eight to Other Ranks), and ten to the Indians (all to Non-Commissioned Officers and Other Ranks).

And, unbeknownst to me at the time, I was to be awarded the Military Cross myself – which arrived, rather disappointingly, in the mail a year after the war was over. No presentation at Buckingham Palace for me; perhaps it was just another demonstration of how we truly were the Forgotten Army.

At the beginning of June there were rumours that we'd hear soon about our repatriation. Uppermost in everyone's mind was the question: when would the troops go home? This was the news that everyone had been waiting for. The word flashed like lightning around the cantonment: what would the order be, and who would go first? And when? Most men had been in India and Burma for three years and more, separated from their families for the entire time. Because of the vast distances, the time spent apart, and the difficulties of adequately expressing their feelings in writing, some marriages or engagements would have been broken; many more would simply have drifted apart. It must have been difficult for the wives, who had to live monogamous lives while separated from the men they loved by seven thousand miles. The glamorous life being offered by others – especially the American servicemen who had inundated Britain – must have been tempting.

And life was very short; death was always waiting around the corner in war-torn England as well as in Burma. With the constant bombing, the V1 and the V2 rockets, the incendiaries and the high explosive bombs that fell incessantly, everyone was acutely aware that he or she might well be the German Luftwaffe's next target. It wasn't a question of whether or not your number was on one of those missiles, but just when and where would it find you. And apart from the nightmare of bombing raids night after night, there was the sheer drudgery of everyday living, and the struggle to keep food on the table when practically everything was rationed. It was desperately hard, even with the pittance from a soldier's pay allowance, to try to find nutritious food to feed the children, and to keep them clothed when there were not enough clothing coupons to go around. Many children had never seen a banana or an orange – and this would continue for years, long after the war was over.

AND WHAT OF General William Slim, our 'Uncle Bill'? On March 19, 1942, he was sent to Burma, with the rank of Lieutenant-General, to command Burcorps, the Burma Corps, comprising the 1st Burma Division, the 17th Indian Division and the 7th Armoured Brigade. His stubbornness and determination saw a large part of the army returned safely across the border to India (when Burcorps became part of 4th Corps), and he was to return victorious in three years' time, at the head of the newly formed Fourteenth Army, to drive the Japanese back whence they came. The son of an ironmonger who rose from the ranks, General Bill Slim is acknowledged the most successful commander, and the best general, in the Second World War – even Lord Louis Mountbatten said as much.

We all loved him, our Uncle Bill; he was unique in the British Army. He'd started his military career as a Second Lieutenant in the Royal Warwickshires, graduating to commanding a Gurkha regiment, and in the First World War he was awarded the Military Cross. He spoke several languages, including Pushto and Gurkhali. A soldiers' general, he knew how to get the best from his troopers: he always spoke to us as man to man. Early on, he told us: 'When you go home, don't expect anyone to recognize your Fourteenth Army badge, or even the Burma Star medal you wear. They have never heard of you, or your exploits in Burma, for the land you fight in is a long way from England, and they are preoccupied with the war in Europe, which is on their doorstep. You are the Forgotten Army and will remain so for many years, until your story is told. But I will tell you this, that when they do hear of your exploits and the conditions in which you fought a cruel and unforgiving enemy, you will be praised and honoured.'

With that little speech, he raised our morale as it had never before been raised. He was already ready to pay a compliment where it was due; he always looked serene and confident, even when you knew things were not going well. And he could be as casual as a trooper; he had the comforting characteristic of hitching up his pants whenever he met you.

And Bill Slim had a great sense of humour: at a particularly critical moment in the campaign, when one of his staff commented that the situation was not good, the General said, 'Oh, I don't know, it could be worse.' When asked how it could possibly be worse, Uncle Bill replied, 'It could be raining.' And of course, it immediately started to rain.

One evening he visited a famous regiment for dinner; the officers' lifestyle there followed that of peacetime Aldershot. This applied to mess etiquette, with promptness for meals, proper dress and the observation of precedence in seating in the Officers' Mess, all strictly observed by the officers, who were sticklers for doing the right thing. The English pukka sahib attitude was still very much alive, as the General discovered that evening. After a pre-dinner sherry, the Colonel of the regiment took the General into the mess tent, where the officers were already seated. Then, with a few introductions and the usual banalities, he was offered the seat at the head of the table where the Colonel usually sat.

Before accepting this gracious offer, the General looked to the far corner of the tent, where a group of officers sat in isolation, and asked, 'Who are those officers, and why are they sitting over there?'

The Colonel, a little nonplussed replied, 'Oh, they are Indian Army chaps; they cannot sit with the King's Commissioned Officers.'

With an expressionless face, Slim replied, 'Well, that solves the problem of where I should sit. I will join the outcasts. You see, I was Indian Army myself.'

Thereafter, the only levity throughout the meal was in that remote corner of the tent. The table where sat the pukka officer sahibs was silent, their red faces filled with dismay. And the Colonel's was the reddest of them all. It was rumoured that the regiment had a new Commanding Officer a few days later.

The million men of the Forgotten Army which he commanded – the largest army in the British service – would testify to his consummate ability; he was a superb and popular leader. He was a great General, and it was an honour to serve under him.

ON JUNE 7, 1945 the Secretary of State announced that the period of service in the Far East was to be reduced to three years and four months as far as repatriation was concerned, and that any man who had exceeded this was to be sent home at once. With this news came wild excitement, and the celebrations were even more pronounced than they had been when greeting the formal statement that the war was over. Those who failed to meet the requirements for immediate repatriation were frantic; they did everything in their power to persuade the authorities that their service in the East had started earlier than the records showed, but it was to no avail, and they were reduced to calculating how much longer they must serve before their turn came.

The wheels were set in motion immediately and within days the first batch of men was en route for England. Most of them sailed home, but a lucky few – me amongst them – were to fly. I had served for three years and nine months in India and Burma. With me were three other officers, and a few NCOs and troopers. The monsoon was ending, and it was a very hot and humid day as we boarded the plane at Dum Dum Airport in Calcutta – and discovered that, though privileged to be the first away, it was not to be a luxurious journey home.

The aircraft, a Lancaster bomber, had been converted to a troop-carrier by the simple expedient of placing benches around the equipment wherever possible. It was by no means a professional job, and had been carried out in great haste. The seats were narrow, barely wide enough to accommodate the buttocks, and the bare wood made it even more uncomfortable. We were crowded in together like the proverbial sardines in a can. Once we reached the higher altitudes, it would be bitterly cold – 'Cold enough,' as Smudger would have said, 'to freeze the balls off a brass monkey.' And I thought the area where I was seated – the bomb bays – was infinitely more suitable for its original intended purpose of bomb storage. There were about a hundred of us crammed into that dark, confined space; at times it was almost impossible to be seated, and if you stood, then your head was in constant conflict with the roof. If you manoeuvred carefully, it was just possible to peer out of a port-hole – although vision was limited, you could just about get a glimpse of the outside world.

But Gallows, who was also on board, had the right attitude: he said he'd willingly have travelled on the wings of the plane; he didn't give a monkey's shit as long as he got back home to the Sheilas, and the booze, and his Granny's farm on the eastern cliffs of Scotland. He wasn't sure if he wanted them in that order, but was quite prepared to take things as they came – as long as he got them all.

The first leg of the journey, about a thousand miles, was to Karachi for refuelling, then on to Lydda in Palestine, where we had a three-day break. Our reception there was by no means as welcoming as that we'd been given in Durban on our journey east, almost four years before. Palestine was a very unsettled state, with unrest between the Arabs and the Jews and the British. But there were compensations and there was time enough to savour the delights of Tel Aviv, to swim in the gloriously blue waters of the Mediterranean, or to lie on the pure golden sandy beaches. The city was also famous for its beautiful women, who were apparently always ready for a good time, much to the delight of the troops, who were desperate to associate with fair-skinned girls again – and who had enough money (forcibly saved) to meet the girls' needs. We spent the following, fascinating, day at Bethlehem visiting the sepulchre; I will never forget that dark cave, the entrance of which was typically cluttered with hawkers selling all manner of merchandise, as was the practice throughout the East in temples and other holy buildings. Just like the Shwedagon Pagoda, their wares included not only pictures and effigies of the tomb, but also dirty postcards – wherever you went in the East it was always the same, in the pagodas of Burma or the fire temples of India. Once inside it was dark, lit only by flickering candles and oil lamps, and religious chanting filled the air. Priests in white clothes hovered near the ledge of the tomb. The stench of the burning incense, the candles and the press of human bodies was overpowering. Forcing my way through the crowd, I was glad to get outside again. My few minutes at such an important place was pitifully inadequate; I couldn't do justice to an opportunity I knew would never occur again.

The gardens of Gethsemane were disappointing too: I had expected to see a well-tended place filled with a profusion of beautiful flowers, but it turned out to be nothing more than a neglected, weed-filled patch of ground that looked as if it had been ignored for years – perhaps it was another victim of the war.

We were living under canvas and when I got back from Bethlehem and went into my tent I realized I'd been robbed – something I would regret for the rest of my life. My suitcase had been opened and the contents scattered around, as had Gallows's, who was in the same tent. I had – stupidly – left a pistol in my case, one I'd carried for many years, and I knew at once that it had been stolen. With my heart in my mouth, I frantically searched through my possessions for it, but it was gone.

Cursing the Arab who'd stolen it, I stormed through the camp shouting, 'You black bastard, where are you?' But my search was fruitless: the thief, and with him my gun, was long gone and the odds of retrieving it were nonexistent. I realized the futility of informing the Military Police of the loss, not to mention the embarrassment of explaining the circumstances, for I should have known better than to leave the weapon unattended, so I decided not to say a word. I discussed it only with Gallows, hanging my head in shame at having committed such a grave crime. In later months I felt this deep sorrow even more, when the anti-British violence erupted in Palestine and British troops were shot and wounded; particularly when two British sergeants were hanged publicly in the streets. I have forever wondered if my loaded pistol was fired at my comrades; my guilt was long-lasting.

On the morning of the departure on the next leg of our journey, we all wondered if the plane would actually become airborne, as it was so heavily laden. England had seen little fresh fruit during the war years, because of the shipping restrictions that had allowed only supplies essential to the war effort. Here in Palestine there were oranges, bananas, mangos and other exotic fruit in plenty, and we were intent on taking every possible advantage of that abundance. The area surrounding the plane looked like a fruit market, for every man was carrying huge baskets of fruit. The plane became horribly congested as we squeezed in a last bag of grapefruits or box of clementines – but no one stopped us. The plane took off very sluggishly, barely clearing the runway, with the wheels brushing the treetops, but it made it into the sky and we were away. We settled in with a sigh of relief for the several hours' flight to Benghazi in North Africa.

Benghazi was well known for the legendary battles between the British and the Germans, which had taken place there over the past few years, and for the ebb and the flow of the victors' occupation: the names of

Montgomery and von Rundstedt had become equally well known. As the engine became quieter in the landing approach, I could just see the green lights bordering the tarmac, between which the plane was now flying. Almost at the point of the wheels touching the ground, the engines suddenly roared back to life and the plane surged ahead, overshooting the runway and climbing back into the sky again. The pilot had misjudged the approach because of the weight of all the fruit. Up and around again we went for another attempt, and down we went again, with exactly the same thing happening. Once again we saw the red lights and heard the angry roar of the engines, and the moans of concern from the occupants, who began to despair of landing safely. There were some who truly believed the end was near: after years of surviving the horrendous fighting in the jungles, we were to die in peacetime on the North African deserts, and all because of a surfeit of oranges and bananas.

By the grace of God, and the skill of the pilot, on the third attempt he got it right and we put down safely on the ground.

But this stop was just to refuel, so we weren't allowed to leave the airport; in a short time we were back in the air for the final part of the journey. Across the Mediterranean, Italy and France, home to our beloved country we flew, softly singing,

Six long years you loved my daughter,
Now you go to Blighty, Sahib.
May the boat that takes you over
Sink to the bottom of the pawnee, Sahib!

and hoping those words were not prophetic. They were not, we were safely across the oceans and nearly home.

WE LANDED AT London Airport, where documentation took place, pay arrangements were made, and leave and railway passes given, with posting instructions at the end of our leave. Wearing the clothes in which we had left India – jungle-green uniforms, chaplis and bush hats – we were driven to the centre of London and deposited at Piccadilly Circus. The reception we were given by the Londoners was unbelievable: they treated us like conquering heroes. Gallows and I, and two other officers, were immediately ushered by several civilians into the nearest pub, where our health was drunk innumerable times. And so began a glorious party in London, the centre of the British Empire – indeed, the centre of the world, as it was then. I remember very little of that evening, other than that it was a glorious time, with people milling around congratulating me and my friends on our achievements, and lavishing praise and liquor on us. Events were rather hazy after several rounds of drinks, not one of which were paid for by me, or my colleagues. No one would take our money.

I awoke the following morning in a hotel near Euston Station, which was very convenient for the Fylde Coast Express, which was still running at the usual time, just after noon. I was laden down with kit and my hard-won basket of fruit. Sitting opposite me was a woman with two children, who whispered constantly, and couldn't take their eyes off the basket. So nothing would do but for me to give each of them an orange and a banana. Their eyes sparkled as they ate the fruit – that first bite was like tasting the nectar of the gods; it made me feel great to be able to give them what had been denied all those years.

And some four hours later, at the appointed time, as the train left Preston, where I'd joined the British Army as a boy bugler eleven years – a lifetime – earlier, the Blackpool Tower showed its face. It dominated the skyline, as if shouting to me, 'Welcome Home.' I was truly home. It had been a long journey.

But it had been a longer journey for those lads who never came back. May we always remember them.

chapter seventeen

GERMANY:
BAOR TO DEMOB, AND BEYOND

July 1945 to 1981

From London, where I'd been treated like a hero, I went home for two weeks' leave, and to a surprisingly tumultuous reception. Bill Slim had warned us that the people of England knew little about the war in Burma, and that we returning soldiers should not expect to be lauded publicly: to most people, it was a pretty insignificant campaign. Burma was on the other side of the world, and their lives had been in constant danger from an enemy much nearer at hand. Slim had told us that it might take some time before our story became known, but that one day it would be, and we would be the Forgotten Army no more. Well, it appeared that the news had spread much quicker than anyone had expected: Britain had already heard how her young men had become seasoned fighters, second to none, and no one was slow in expressing thanks at every conceivable opportunity.

Nothing was too good for the Fourteenth Army men; we were soon very much the 'Remembered Army', treated like returning heroes, with flags and banners appearing everywhere, in our homes, on the buses, in the streets and the cinemas, the shops and the pubs: 'Well done. Welcome Home. We love you.' What more could a soldier wish for? It was a great feeling to be truly appreciated, and slowly, the horrors of Burma faded, though they would never completely vanish for any of us.

That leave was different from any I'd ever experienced before: I was praised wherever I went, and it made all that effort feel worthwhile. Though I met few old school friends – like on my previous leaves– my father took great delight in taking me into all the pubs within his parish, and the beer there flowed stronger and tastier than anywhere else in the world. My relatives descended from miles around, all wanting to see their brave soldier-boy, returned home safely, against all the odds. They all tried to pump me about what the war in Burma was *really* like: the newsreels and radio broadcasts and newspapers had told them something of the horrors we'd faced, and of the terrible jungles infested by dangerous, lethal creatures. I was glad to tell them they were quite right, and how terrible it had been – and I laid it on thickly, with my tongue firmly in my cheek: it was clear no one knew whether to believe me or not! They listened, awestruck, as I recounted some of my adventures, like when food was so short we had to eat snakes – and eat them raw, at that. And as for my story about capturing two geisha girls and taking them back to my gun position, well, there was no end to the questions as to what happened to them; when I said, straight-faced, that it wouldn't be proper to tell them any more, it left them gasping. But Uncle Tom, himself an old soldier, saw straight through my stories quickly enough; he didn't crack a smile as he asked if my Military Cross had anything to do with the capture of those two geisha girls. I was quick to reply, 'No, that was for personally capturing Lieutenant General Kotuku Sato, Commander of the 31st Division, at Kohima'.

That was greeted by silence, broken only when I added, grinning, 'But I had a whole battalion of Gurkhas with me at the time!'

'Well! Fancy our Joe doing all those things,' said Aunty Alice. I think they all found the enormity of what I'd been through rather too much to contemplate.

All too quickly my leave was over. I was astonished to receive a letter from Woolwich, informing me that I was now posted to Germany, to join BOAR (British Army of the Rhine) and that I was to leave immediately. I tried in vain, by telephone, and then by personal visit to the War Office, to have this order rescinded, on the grounds that I'd spent the best part of four years soldiering in the worst possible conditions in the Far East, and I should be allowed to remain in England, at least for a time – especially as there were countless thousands of men who'd not even left home during the whole of the war.

But my pleas to stay in England fell on deaf ears at the War Office, and off to Germany I went.

MY POSTING WAS to an unusual unit, an Enemy Ammunition Dump Control Unit, which turned out to be – unsurprisingly – just that: handling the destruction of German shells and ammunition of all kinds, including V2 rockets, bombs, artillery shells and rifle ammunition. It didn't sound a particularly exciting or rewarding job to a soldier who'd once belonged to the élite Royal Horse Artillery. It was really a very boring job being Officer-in-Charge, as my sergeant-major did all the organizing; in effect, he ran the whole show – sergeant-majors always did! – supervising the fifty German prisoners of war. In some instances, the ammunition was, literally, blown up, and the fact that it was enemy ammunition was poor compensation for the tedium of sitting in my office listening to explosions day after day. So I had a leisurely, if boring, time of it. Many of the heavier shells were sent to the coastal ports, where they were loaded on ships and dumped in the North Sea; at that time no one speculated on the effects this might have on the world's oceans.

On the bright side, now that hostilities had ceased, there was little point in doing any training, so, to everyone's great relief, we were done with the square bashing. We still had to keep our men occupied, though, without resorting to the mind-numbingly repetitive inspection parades, so someone on high decreed that sports were the road to contentment. So we had a sudden outbreak of games of all kinds. Leave camps were arranged, at a minimum cost and with free transportation; one of the most popular was in the mountains at Bad Harzburg. Brussels was an extremely popular place to visit; during their occupation, the Germans had nourished it, using the city as a centre for their troops and keeping it prosperous, ensuring a plentiful supply of luxury items. Now it was the turn of the British Army of the Rhine. The shops were full of goods which had been unobtainable for years except in the US or Switzerland; we flocked there for presents for friends and families at home, who'd been denied luxuries for so long.

The British Army of the Rhine, administering twenty million people, was truly an Occupation Army: the rule was *arm's length*, we were to have no close contact with the residents. The blanket order that there was to be no fraternization with the Germans wasn't very popular; and it led to a very secluded existence for both sides. We would have enjoyed mixing with the natives on a friendly basis, for that was always the nature of the British soldier: it would have given us all a chance to see that, at the end of the day, we were all human beings and we'd all suffered very badly thanks to the evil of one man. But worse, the no fraternization rule meant no dating – at least, not ostentatiously, otherwise the law would come down heavily on the lovestruck troopers, in the not-so-lovely shape of the heavy hand of the Military Police. Of course, it was virtually impossible to enforce the law completely: soldiers and women, regardless of nationality, go together like soldiers and beer, and are equally inseparable. No matter how strict the rules, men and women always found a way to meet. And it wasn't just the troops: more than one officer of the Army of Occupation went home with a German bride on his arm.

The country was completely devastated: what the Allies had not wrought was finished by the retreating German Army, who did a comprehensive job of blowing up roads and bridges, amongst other things. The scale of damage was unbelievably massive. Major cities like Hamburg and Hanover were razed to the ground. Every town was in an absolute shambles, with hardly two bricks of any building left together anywhere. There were a few exceptions; like in Hamburg, where a very large hotel was miraculously intact, while all around the city had been flattened as though a giant had run wild, scything all before him in anger. Though the roads were partly clogged with rubble and difficult to negotiate, the hotel was still accessible and, first things being first, it was immediately designated as an Officers' Club and, being both sumptuously furnished and well stocked with the necessities of life, was well patronized by the British. It was an oasis in a desert of destruction. The plentiful stocks of liquor and food made it also the chosen rendezvous for visiting Russians, though they made themselves very unpopular by their lack of grace and filthy habits and created much resentment amongst the cleaner-living British and American officers. We particularly objected to the Russians' insistence on wearing side-arms whilst dining; this was contrary to the British custom of removing their weapons before entering the mess. This ill-bred behaviour led to many fights, none of which, luckily, were very serious.

As for the German locals, they were a pathetic sight; one would have needed a great deal of hatred and lack of compassion not to sympathize with their misery. All that was left of the population appeared to be older adults and children and, to the latter at least, the British Tommy was generous, freely handing out chocolate and fruit. I, like many others, gave more substantial food and clothing where I could. There were Germans searching constantly for missing family members, friends and relations, and the countless notice boards everywhere were filled with the most harrowing and plaintive messages. New York after the terrible events of 9/11 – September 11 2001 – echoed those desperate searches; more than one old soldier was forcibly reminded of post-war Germany as he gazed on the thousands of pleas for news that covered every billboard, wall and empty space in the city.

And many people were on the move, going in all directions, sometimes aimlessly. The trains were in great demand, and so crowded that the people swarmed and clung like ants to the sides and the roofs of the carriages. Inside the coaches they were packed like sardines, and it reminded me very much of the trains in India. And like the Indians, the Germans were also becoming emaciated. The lack of food – and clean water – was becoming critical. Although the occupying forces, both British and American, at least, were genuinely concerned about this, and about rebuilding the country, the infrastructure, including transportation, was chaotic. British armies had always excelled in acquiring countries not already shown on the map in red, and occupying without ceremony any unoccupied land, but they did not seem to have the knack of restoring a defeated nation to normality. The population was living like rats – and *with* them – in the basements of their shattered homes.

In spite of our best efforts, lawlessness flourished as gangs roamed freely around the ravaged cities. The gang members were not all Germans, either; there were many different nationalities involved, including Poles, Russians and, it was said, even the occasional British and French were not above looting. Weapons were readily available, so the gangs were well-armed; our Military Police were woefully inadequate to handle the situation because of the magnitude of the problem. Whilst it was reasonably safe to walk the streets if you were armed, you had to be extremely careful going indoors. I went into a barber's shop for a much-needed haircut, but all the time I was sitting there, I felt as if I were in one of Sweeney Todd's chairs – especially when the barber raised his razor for the final trim. I kept my hand on the Smith and Wesson strapped to my side the whole time, even though I was acutely aware that if my throat were to be cut, I'd be dead before my gun could speak.

The Black Market had reached its zenith and the most lucrative deals were now being done. A Polish Army interpreter attached to a regiment near me had gone well beyond petty transactions: he was now buying up houses and other real estate – he proudly told me he owned nearly the whole of a nearby village outright! He also kept a locked steel trunk under his bed, filled with British, US and German currency. The sweetest deal I knew was the acquisition by a Colonel (who shall remain nameless) of a convertible Mercedes Benz sports car. It was red, and a real collector's model – and all he paid for it was half a bottle of Scotch! Nobody knew where the vehicle came from, and though it wasn't possible to take goods out of the country then, this was of no concern to him. He'd worked as a salesman before the war and had travelled extensively in Europe. He still had many friends in Germany, and one of them, as a favour, stored the car in his garage until the time when the Colonel would be able to legally claim it and take it back to the UK. I often wondered if he succeeded.

Regardless of the restrictions, many English warriors managed to get goods across the Channel to Britain – one friend of mine said he'd not only seen the Military Police close their eyes to a soldier unloading a washing machine off the ship at Harwich, but they'd actually helped him to do so. There were probably more fortunes made in those few months after the war ended than in any other time in history, though the dealing that took place a few months later in Government-supplied war surplus goods probably ran it a close second. At that time you could buy anything from topees to tanks, helmets to howitzers, bullets to Bangalore torpedoes, medals to missiles and Dakotas to dartboards – even a mobile laundry: 'Why hang out your washing on the Siegfried Line?' Want a good German Stuka with a few fresh Spitfire bullets in the fuselage, or an anti-aircraft gun to shoot it down? The list was endless, and you could buy them all for next to nothing. The Middle-East countries were prominent customers, making large purchases in order to attack each other in later years. The London spivs did extremely well; you'd be approached at every street corner by one selling a particularly juicy ex-military item – it might be at an exorbitant price, but you knew you couldn't live without it . . . and people *were* buying. Who could turn down land mines at a penny each? Or 'Pinky Pawnee at tuppence a bottle' – allegedly for cleansing the private parts after a session with a questionable lady of the night; 'You never know when you'll need it, sir,' they shouted after us. Best-sellers were US ration packs, army blankets and groundsheets, which enhanced many a camping trip for years afterwards.

I spent the better part of a year in Germany, and even by the end, there didn't appear to be any great improvement in living conditions. It was March, and it had been a bitterly cold winter: we played football endlessly, even with two inches of snow on the ground and snow still falling from the sky. As I looked beyond the goal posts, I could see the trains passing by, still clothed with people from engine to caboose. There was now a sprinkling of younger men who'd returned from the prisoner-of-war camps, but there was little employment for them. It would be years before the wheels of German industry gathered any momentum; right now the rebuilding was in its infancy. The situation in the Russian sector was even worse, and things didn't look encouraging.

FOR THE FIRST time in ages, I had been able to go home for Christmas: I spent a very happy fortnight's leave with my family, and we were all able to recover a little from the rigours of the last several years. Taking advantage of my backlog of leave, I went home again in March – and this homecoming marked another great turning point in my life. I found the love of my life. I'd taken my mother to a dinner dance in one of the Pleasure Beach hotels and we entered the ballroom just as the band struck up and the gentlemen were choosing their partners. Pushing me forward, Mum said, 'Well, go on, ask someone.' Obediently I ran my eyes over the crowded seats around the dance floor, and saw this outstandingly beautiful young lady, at that moment alone. As I walked over, my heart was beating fast lest someone else beat me to her. When I asked if I might have the pleasure of the dance, her lovely brown eyes shone as she smiled radiantly and accepted my offer. She was not quite as tall as me, but was both elegant and poised. And as she stepped gracefully into my arms, I, almost breathlessly, danced into the beginning of my new life.

Whether or not I was prepared to acknowledge it, I'd fallen in love then and there: me, a hardened, brutal and licentious member of the military, a common soldier who knew little of courting cultured women. I'd spent most of my time in the last few years living in less than salubrious environments where white girls, beautiful or otherwise, were few and far between and I knew more of brothels than of ballrooms. But I was home now, and pretty English girls were two-a-penny – and I was a hero; I could have had my pick.

Whilst we were dancing we exchanged names; she was Enid Pover. The conversation flowed easily as we talked, mostly of mundane matters, though I was startled when she told me she came from Liverpool, for she spoke with a cultured, musical accent which sounded quite unlike the other girls from Lancashire I'd met. She'd been evacuated to her older sister's in Blackpool when her Liverpool home was bombed out; she'd even attended my old school, although I'd been long gone by then.

Life is often governed by coincidence; the circumstance of our meeting was no exception. When I told Enid I had just arrived from London, en route from Germany, on leave, she was astonished: she too had travelled up on the one o'clock Fylde Coast Express that day, to spend the weekend with her sister. That clinched it. It was obviously no coincidence but the hand of Providence that had brought us together. And she seemed to like me too – though perhaps that was the glamour of the uniform and the three pips and Military Cross. (And I later discovered the Sam Browne played a key role in her initial attraction to me, though she had not then recognized the ribbon of the Military Cross.) I knew I had found the girl of my dreams; I would leave no stone unturned until she was mine forever.

The evening went by in a whirl, as did the next two days. It was an enchanted time, wherever we were: at the pictures, or dancing, or simply walking along the promenade and talking. For the first time in my adult life I felt at ease with a member of the opposite sex. Army barracks and battlegrounds do not, after all, offer many opportunities for meeting well-brought-up young ladies; I'd learned how to ride, to shoot and to fire a wide variety of big guns, but lessons in conversational etiquette and proper courtship were never on the army agenda. I'd been surrounded by men since I was a boy-drummer; although they'd been protective of my innocence, in their rough way, I knew more about the seamier side of male and female relations than I did of 'dating' – this was a whole new world to me, and I revelled in it.

All too soon our idyll came to an end. It was now the end of March, and though neither of us were looking forward to it, I had to return to Hamburg and Enid to her typing pool job in London. We met briefly in London before I left and I told Enid I'd have something to ask her next time we met. We'd known each other four days.

Once back in Germany, Enid was never far from my thoughts and I pondered my future endlessly. Now I had met Enid – though I'd not yet won her – should I continue in the army, or resign and find civilian work? I was still thinking about my dilemma when I bumped into my former Battery Commander from my time in India, when he'd been a Major and I, a fifteen-year-old trumpeter, his horse-holder. In those far-off days he'd always slipped me a bar of chocolate or a slug of tea from his Thermos flask – a real luxury – even though I was the lowest of the low in the ranks. Now he was a very senior General, adorned with red braid. I'd been horribly afraid that he'd been a prisoner of the Japanese, having surrendered the Commonwealth forces at Singapore when it fell. Until I met him again in Germany, I hadn't realized there had been another officer of the same name, and *my* Major was safe and well.

The General insisted that I should stay in the military: the British Army wanted me, and I'd have the prestigious job of senior gunnery instructor at the School of Artillery in Larkhill – a very choice position indeed. I prevaricated, still not sure that I wanted to stay in the army, because there were no guarantees about anything, and I might well end up posted to some other God-forsaken country at the other end of the world. I'd had enough of that.

The General then suggested a job in Assam, managing a tea plantation – he had a good friend there who would oblige him, and I'd be a natural because of my Indian experience. The downside was that I would not be able to take a wife there until I'd completed two years of service. Though he strongly recommended the position, it wasn't on, not just because I was on the verge of getting wed, but also because it would have been hellish for Enid. Apart from the normal tribulations of living in India – and I was very familiar with those! – tea planters were usually stationed in remote areas where the next-door neighbour might be ten miles or more away. And Enid was only seventeen: she deserved to have fun, and that wasn't likely on a tea plantation in the middle of nowhere.

I wrote frequently to Enid, but she was young and innocent and I'd spent years in charge of troopers, so I was used to making decisions. Though I knew I'd have a good future in the army, and Enid would have been perfectly happy being an officer's wife, I'd had enough of army life; I decided that I should resign and take my chance in Civvy Street. Though I hadn't yet proposed to Enid, we talked as if I had; it had been like that from the beginning of our relationship. And I rectified that little oversight by proposing the very next time we met: we got engaged in June 1946, and I came out of the army.

I'd spent twelve of my twenty-six years in the British Army; it felt like a lifetime. To start the demob process I went first to London, to hand in my papers (and where quite a lot of pressure was put on me to remain in the service), and then on to the demob section of Fulwood Barracks at Preston. It hadn't changed a bit since I arrived, a newly signed up four-teen-year-old innocent, all those years ago. There, alongside hundreds of others, I chose my civvy clothes: suit, shirt and shoes. I was allowed to have a dark grey suit specially ordered, so that at least it fit me, which is more than could be said for a lot of the demob suits. I was allowed to keep the battledress that been issued to me, and I'd bought my officer's serge outfit, so of course I kept that. With a carton of cigarettes, a few bars of chocolate and pay for six months' leave, I was on my way.

I'd walked in an officer of the British Army; I walked out a civilian. Outside the barracks the spivs were waiting, trying to buy our newly issued clothes and other items (at a fraction of their cost) from us now ex-soldiers – many took up their offer for the hard cash. The cord had been cut and I was ready for a new life. A new adventure had started.

I WAS MARRIED to Enid in October 1946, at St John's Church, Blackpool, and then started the arduous task of looking for a job, which wasn't easy: my qualifications were few and employers weren't really interested in my gunnery talents, or my ability to kill Japanese soldiers. There wasn't much call for those skills now, but I knew little else. I tried a number of occu-pations, like working for Courtaulds' in Preston, and then, after a stint as assistant laundry manager, opened my own laundrette, but there was a lethargy throughout the whole country and everything got bogged down. Government restrictions were a throttle on enterprise, the paperwork for approval to do anything was enormous, and finding materials of any kind virtually impossible. You wouldn't have known it was peacetime, everything looked so grim.

For a while I missed the army: the lack of responsibility for both the present and the future, the lack of worry about money: if you didn't have it, it didn't matter. I'd never had to panic about how to put food on the table, today or tomorrow, and my health had been ensured thanks to free medical treatment and inoculations galore – though the inoculations were not always effective, and your teeth would fall out just the same. And it was true that sometimes the Medical Officer was indifferent to your problem, or simply didn't know what was wrong with you, in which case the prescription would be for the totally inadequate Number Nine medication – at least this pill could do no harm, other than have you camping out in the latrines.

In the army, clothing was free, though that didn't guarantee its comfort (or its style: the high choke collar I was often subjected to was distinctly reminiscent of the previous century), and it always provided a roof over our heads – albeit that could be as little as a canvas roof in below-freezing temperatures, without heat or electricity, or maybe just a basha we'd built ourselves of banana leaves, deep in a jungle in a faraway place, that collapsed in the first heavy downpour.

In the British Army, your future was secure, and if you kept your nose clean, you could rely on promotions and a little more money with each step up, and a pension later on – of course, I knew that I'd still be entitled to that: it wouldn't be large, but it would be certain and regular.

But above all, I missed the comradeship and the easy relationship I'd had, both with my men and my fellow-officers. We supported each other, and shared in the good times, as well as the bad and the indifferent. There was an easy-going atmosphere which prevailed most of the time. On the other hand, there was also the strict discipline, which could at times be cruel, and the incessant demand for spit and polish, and endless inspections to make sure it was so.

Join up and see the world, the advertisements said. But they didn't mention the loneliness and the isolation, or the malevolent places one might be dispatched to. And all in all, when I weighed up the pluses and the minuses, I knew I'd made the right decision – and in any event, I had traded it for the most important thing in life: true love.

THE PROSPECTS FOR a young couple setting up married life together in Britain were not bright. The Government was not generous in the resettlement programme for its returning men, and it kept quiet about the few things it did offer. In North America, the USA's GI Bill and the Canadians' similar programme offered low mortgage rates, job opportunities, education and a host of other useful benefits. Here, though, there were few rewards for returning soldiers – but then, Britain was never kind to her soldiers, either in war or peacetime.

I soon realized that we had little chance of ever getting a house of our own, or even a flat. Everything was either rationed, or in short supply. Newly married couples received a tiny ration allowance, which was supposed to help them set up home together. In our case, we ended up with a blanket; thank God we were given sheets and pillowcases as a wedding present, otherwise we'd have been sleeping on boards. It was almost as if shopkeepers were still saying, 'Don't you know there's a war on?' Food was still severely rationed, as was petrol. Enid was barely eighteen when we married and still had a child's ration book – that would have entitled her to a banana every now and then, if only there had been any bananas. It certainly didn't help our day-to-day existence.

FRIENDS OF OURS had emigrated to Canada a few months earlier, and had written glowing reports: the country was full of vitality, and was thirsting for good people. In Liverpool, Enid and I met with Canadian Immigration officials, and in May 1951, we set sail on the *Scythia* for Montreal, in Quebec.

But even then, the long arm of the British War Office reached out for me. I was on the Class A Reserve list, which meant that I could be called up for further service in the event of any emergency so designated by the Government. The growing situation in Palestine certainly qualified as that: the Palestinians appeared ready to wage war with Britain unless certain impossible demands were met. They demonstrated their wrath by publicly hanging two British Army Sergeants. The telegram demanding my service arrived the day Enid and I caught the boat; by nine o'clock of that May morning, we had already set sail, and my mother took great delight in informing the War Office that her son was unable to help because he had gone abroad, to an unknown destination. (I followed the course of events in Palestine, of course, and was pleased to see that the mighty white sahibs were able to deal adequately with the situation without me.)

We started our life in Canada in Ontario, where I worked as a hospital Laundry Manager, then we moved to Saskatoon, Saskatchewan, finally coming to Victoria in British Columbia, where Enid and I raised our son and daughter. For three years I studied every evening and weekend on hospital management courses, coming top of the group throughout the whole of Canada, and became Director of General Services at Victoria General Hospital. Eventually I joined the Provincial Government as a hospital planner.

Though I left the British Army, the army – and particularly the Second World War – never completely lets go. I helped to found a local branch of the Burma Star Association, and our fifty members still talk of those perilous, desperate times, which imprinted themselves forever on my heart and memory. And I still attend reunions in Britain, though many of the men who served in Burma are now over eighty years of age. But we're a tough old bunch of comrades – we had to be, to endure what we went through in Burma. We're survivors.

I still think of the India I knew before the war. Though I talk with my old comrades of Burma, I don't recall that time with any fondness, nor my time at the Depot, nor wartime England. It's always India that raises my heart: it's, 'Tope kana[1],' and, 'Itherow towards me jow[2],' or 'Tum sewer kabutch[3]'. Never, 'Murbarnee[4].' I never did say 'thank you' to the Indians I had had dealings with, and deep down, I know that I should have. I'm sorry about that. Perhaps one day . . .

THERE COMES A time when a man begins to ask himself what his abilities really are. At the age of sixty-two, was I over the hill? I wondered if I still had the guts – and the staying power – to travel around the world not only cheaply, but with a minimum of baggage, so that I could be fully mobile. This trip would take me to new and faraway places, but above all, it would

---

1 Come here   2 Come here, towards me go   3 You son of a pig   4 Thank you

allow me to fulfil my long-standing dream of visiting that country I had had a love/hate relationship with for so many years: India. Once I'd made the decision, I embarked upon my circumnavigation of the world.

The key issues were that I would travel alone and light – a soft carry-on bag weighing around twenty pounds – and I would complete the trip in six weeks. My budget was ten dollars a day for food and accommodation, and I'd travel with Thai Airlines, east to west and staying north of the Equator. My journey would be Vancouver, Tokyo, Taipei, Hong Kong, Singapore, Calcutta, Delhi, Frankfurt, London, Copenhagen, and back to Vancouver. I'd taken extended leave from work, but tagged on an extra few days by agreeing to investigate central food service systems whilst in Germany – although that meant I had to carry a jacket, trousers and shirt suitable for business meetings in Germany.

So early on February 26, 1981, on a typical dreary, rainy winter's morning in Victoria, I walked across the road to the bus which, for fifty cents, would take me on the first leg of my odyssey: to the airport for the plane to Vancouver. My shoulder bag contained all my worldly goods; I had a bunch of credit cards in my pocket and a prayer on my lips. And away I went to start my trip, with Japan as my first stop.

Accommodation that night was the benches at Tokyo Airport, where I was awakened every few minutes by Japanese airport security demanding to know what I was doing. I had no pre-booked accommodation anywhere, but I had a great time in Taipei, Hong Kong and Singapore. But there was a magnet, drawing me back to India, and I was loath to linger more than a day or so anywhere en route.

Then at last it was Calcutta, and for all I thought I was well prepared, I was still shocked: I had forgotten the turmoil and congestion in that teeming city, once described – for good reason – as the cesspool of Asia. Jostling with so many people, the relatively mild 85 degrees Fahrenheit felt almost impossibly hot. But though Calcutta was my first port of call in India, it was that other India that was calling me: the India of the cool hills and rushing mountain streams and icy torrents. So I spent just a night in Calcutta and then, first thing in the morning, I rushed off to the railway station to purchase train tickets to Darjeeling, in the hills.

The setting and the town of Darjeeling were exactly as I had remembered – with one exception: the people who frequented it. The narrow

winding streets were no longer filled with the white faces of British soldiers and their white women – wives, daughters – who were escaping
from the scorching plains for the summer months. Now I could see only
Indians thronging the streets; though doubtless drawn there for the same
reasons. However, just like I found in Simla later on, I could hear the
bugles and the trumpet calls, sounded now by the Indian Army and not the
British, who had left some thirty-five years earlier.

I lingered in Darjeeling long enough to have tea with Sherpa Tensing,
of Everest fame, whilst visiting his Mountain Institute, which had become
a Mecca for mountaineers from all around the world. Whilst there I enjoyed
the luxury of a hotel where a bearer slept outside my door in case I should
require anything during the night, all for the princely sum of just over
five dollars a day – of course, that price included all my meals. A brief
detour to Tiger Hill, about five miles from Darjeeling, gave me one more
glimpse of Everest at sunrise, in all its spectacular beauty, before I joined
the train to Delhi.

Here I should have been on familiar ground once again, but after all
those years, it all looked new to me. I strolled down Chandi Chauk like a
tourist, shopping for silks and souvenirs to take home before booking
into the YMCA for the night. And though I paid just one rupee for my
night's accommodation, it was here that I dined like a prince in the palatial home of my Indian friend: some months earlier I'd read about Patwand
Singh, a Sikh who was piloting a health care unit on the outskirts of Delhi
and was looking for hospital equipment. I'd spoken to him from Canada,
and when I called on my arrival in Delhi, he invited me to that memorable party, where I rubbed shoulders with local dignitaries and senior
military officers – it was all very different from my previous visits, when I
was just a raw boy soldier of fifteen, or a young captain training to fight
an evil and deadly enemy. No char and wads for me here: I was wined and
dined by Patwand Singh in the finest style before being delivered back to
the YMCA in his own Rolls Royce.

During my few days with Patwand Singh, I attended a cricket match
and lunched with several Indian Army officers; we had lots to talk about,
and I came away with a far better understanding of the problems India
was facing. The splitting of the Indian Army when the British left was as
fraught with agony and bloodletting as was the division of India.

And finally, it was off to the khuds again, to visit Simla in all its glory and beauty. I hadn't the time to visit Meerut or Sialkot, but a day-trip to see the Taj Mahal provided some compensation. These moments were indeed everything I had ever hoped for.

I left India from Delhi, where I discovered the airport was just like any city in India: hot and filthy, with floors so heavily coated with grease and the muck of the years that your feet stuck to them. In spite of the filth and hellish heat, it was a sad parting for me, and I realized that my relationship with India, that exotic, filthy, beautiful, depressing country, remained the same: I hated it with a passion, but I loved it just as fiercely.

HAVING FULFILLED MY need to see India again, I then had to decide whether or not I would visit Burma. It wasn't that difficult a choice: I made a conscious decision not to go back. I had too many unhappy memories of that country, not just of the comrades I had lost, or the ungracious, treacherous attitudes of the natives we were there to save, but of the truly shocking behaviour of the Japanese, which was evil beyond measure. Going back to Burma would serve no purpose except to reopen old wounds that had never quite healed over.

So instead I flew on to Germany and Britain, before taking an SAS flight from Copenhagen home to my beloved family. I had had my once-in-a-lifetime trip to revisit my old haunts and relive old memories, and I was satisfied. I had joined the British Army not just to adventure in faraway lands, but also to serve my King and protect my country. I was proud to have fulfilled that promise I made so very many years ago, and I was proud of all those men who fought and died beside me so that our world would not be overrun by an evil beyond imagination. It had been a long journey, but it was one I could never forget.

I HAVE CROSSED a lot of rivers, and there are many more still to cross. In their own way, they could be as perilous as the Irrawaddy, but I am no longer alone, and with Enid beside me, I need not hesitate to cross the widest river on that journey that lies ahead.

CLIVE'S INDIA

A part of India steeped in folklore, superstition and religious rites, Madras was also the scene of great strife within the British and Indian armies, and featured prominently in the history of the Honourable East India Company. A large and prosperous city, Madras lies on the east coast, about four hundred miles north of the tip of the sub-continent. It is bisected by the rivers Cooum on the north and the Adyar on the south.

In 1644 Francis Day, of the Honourable East India Company, negotiated with the Raja of Chandragiri for land at Chennapatmann, about twenty-five miles to the north, where he built Fort St George as a trading post, or factory, and quickly attracted a large native population to work and live there. In those turbulent days the fort was unsuccessfully attacked, first by Aurangzeb's generals in 1702, and then by the Marathas in 1741. Some years later it was held to ransom by the French for four hundred thousand pounds, which was duly paid, but when they attacked again in 1756, the timely arrival of the British fleet of six men-of-war quickly disposed of the French, forcing them to retreat after a two months' long siege.

Several years later the settlement was constituted by a charter at the order of His Majesty James II, under the East India Company's seal. Also established close to the fort, with great haste, was St Stephen's Church, where the churchmen proceeded with dispatch to convert the local heathens.

When The Honourable East India Company received its charter from the Queen of England in the year 1600, it was for the purposes of trading in the Far East for cloves and cinnamon and other spices, and perhaps to search for gold and riches. Spices were of great importance then, for the preservation of foodstuffs and for medical research. The fierce competition in the spice trade was the cause of constant fighting amongst several countries. In addition to authorizing the search for and acquisition of spices, the Company's charter, so graciously approved by Her Majesty, also coyly described the venture as being 'for the honour of this our realm'. It brought the Company – and the Queen of England – great riches: spices and gold and jewels, in measure far beyond the wildest dreams. It also won for her Majesty that jewel which would shine brighter than all the others in her already sparkling crown: before another fifty years would pass, India would be ruled by England.

Though the Company established itself at Madras in the sixteen hundreds, the future relationship of England with India was shaped a hundred miles north of Calcutta. The beginnings of the conquest of India are attributed to the conflict between the Indians and the British in the two small villages of Plassey and Buxar, both in the district of Bengal. This led to the final event that had started with the capture of Kasimbazar and the sack of Calcutta.

There are many people, and certainly the military-minded, who will have heard of Sevastopol, of Waterloo, or Malplaquet, the Somme, or Leningrad or other equally famous battles, yet there are few who have heard of the Battle of Plassey, despite the fact that it won us India. In 1757, in a corner of the world far removed from London, the Nawab of Bengal's private army of fifty thousand men faced three thousand soldiers of the East India Company, commanded by Sir Robert Clive. The Nawab of Bengal's defeat culminated in an agreement letting Clive continue the trading depots established by the Company. This battle also gave rise to the prophecy that the centenary would see the end of British rule in India; though heralded to be true by the sepoys during the Indian Mutiny of 1857, the dominance of India by Britain would endure until 1947.

Chandernagor, from where the British advanced to start the battle, was originally occupied by the French (who had built a very profitable factory there in 1673). In the early hours of the morning, Clive used his artillery to such masterful effect that the Indian soldiers were routed, and many of them deserted. Their forced retreat exposed the French, allied with the Nawab; the Nawab promptly surrendered. The battle, essentially won by the artillery, was an easy victory for the British, whose casualties were less than fifty against the Nawab's two hundred, and it made possible their conquest of Bengal.

Equally important in the winning of Bengal, and ultimately of India, was the more serious conflict at Buxar, where the British Cameronian Highlander Regiment scored a difficult and costly victory against the King, Shah Alam. Before the King surrendered to the British and sought their protection, the British had lost more than eight hundred, killed and wounded.

The Company had arrived in Bengal in 1633; at first their trading requirements were quite modest, only a 'factory', in which to conduct their business, which was established at Balasore at the mouth of the river Hoogly, which emptied into the Bay of Bengal. They then built another at Hoogly itself. There had been a Portuguese trading post at Hoogly in 1537, but the Emperor banned them five years later, attacking their fort, taking them prisoners and forcibly converting them to Islam. Within the next twenty-five years the Company had expanded its operations to include Kazimbazar and Murshidabad, both of which were close to the future site of Calcutta, and Patna, about one hundred and fifty miles to the north-west. By the middle of the century they had twenty-five factories; much of this success was attributed to Job Charnock, who was promoted to Chief at Hoogly.

Over the years, as the business prospered, so did the corruption and demands of the authorities, to the point where the Company felt this was having an unacceptable effect on their revenues. Not wishing to lose the profitable trade they had built up, they informed the Nawab of Murshidabad of their displeasure and of their intention to use force to rectify the matter. In support of this threat the Company sent a very small force of ten ships and six hundred men against the mighty power of the Nawab, hoping to intimidate him. The Nawab, however, was not impressed and ordered the trading posts to be seized, the occupants to be imprisoned and a large force to be dispatched against Hoogly. The Nawab attacked the town and the British, with Job Charnock, burned the Balasore factory and fled to Madras. Eventually, troops arrived, Calcutta was retaken, and the Nawab agreed to the continuance of the factories.

And this was also the time of the infamous Black Hole of Calcutta: to show their wrath, the Nawab of Murshidabad's troops attacked the English settlements, imprisoning a hundred and forty-five of them in the sealed prison of the barracks of Fort William, an area of barely three hundred square feet. The captives were forced in by guards armed with clubs and drawn scimitars; had they known they would die in there, it is recorded, they would have attacked the guards and risked being cut to pieces as the lesser of two evils.

The conditions in that small room were appalling: it was a close, sultry summer's night in Bengal, and the men and women were packed like sardines; the only air was through a small grille in the heavily barred door. They were highly agitated, though their leader, Mr Holwell, entreated them to remain calm. He knew one of the guards, an old Jemadar, and pleaded with him to move the prisoners to a larger area, offering him a thousand rupees, then two thousand rupees; the Jemadar said only by the order of the Suba – the Viceroy of Bengal – could they be freed. In a desperate attempt to alleviate the situation, most stripped off, except for Holwell and the wounded, and lay down on the floor as he suggested. Not all did so, and some of those who did were trampled to death by the boots of the British soldiers. Soon they were gripped with a raging thirst and shouted for water, but when it arrived they had to use a soft hat to try to pass it through the grille. What little didn't spill was fought over violently. Those who failed to get a drop started wailing and in the panic several more people were trampled to death.

Efforts to force the steel door failed, and by midnight the room stank of urine. Most of the occupants were suffocating. Mr Holwell, himself in distress, pleaded further with the guard for mercy, but in vain, nor would the prisoners heed his call for their own fighting to stop. He laid himself down on those who had already died, but chest pains obliged him to regain his feet and struggle to the door for water. He consoled himself that the end was near and his suffering would soon be over. By three o'clock in the morning most were in a state of delirium. The guards watched, doing nothing, though they could see people dying before their very eyes. As dawn came and the door was thrown open, the few who struggled out were almost beyond help; only twenty-three of them lived.

When news of this reached the ears of the white population, the British troops were quick to seek vengeance. Though, later, the Indians claimed it was an unfortunate mistake; the orders had been simply to detain them as prisoners and there had been no intent to punish or to kill. But the British fraternity across the country remained shocked and angered by the cruelty, and the incident further soured their opinion of Indians.

Charnock later received permission to rent three villages, Kalikat, Gobindpur and Chuttannuttee, which stood on the present site of Calcutta, for a new trading post. The new Gobindpur site flourished, and segregated 'white' and 'black' towns developed by 1696. Job Charnock was credited as being the founder of the great city of Calcutta, which would one day become the capital of India. By the mid-nineteenth century it had grown to a population of almost half a million souls. The Company established itself at Madras in 1639, where its business developed around Fort George, but it was not the first European operation to seek trade in India. Vasco de Gama had first arrived in Kalikut in 1498 after a ten-month voyage from Lisbon, and the Portuguese established themselves in Goa, on the west coast, in the year 1510: the first Christian colony in the country, and it remained so for some four hundred years.

A few years later the Portuguese plundered the town of Daman just south of Surat on the Arabian Sea, a hundred and fifty miles north of Bombay, but surrendered it to Akbar in 1573 after a long siege. The Portuguese did not confine their activities to trading in spices; they were very active in the slave trade, with a penchant for high-caste Muslim women and children. This eventually proved their undoing, because the Nawab took strong exception to this practice and ousted them.

When the English arrived in 1612, the Mogul Emperor invited their envoy to his court and opened up trading. Two years later the British fleet of four ships defeated a much larger Portuguese armada of several warships and a host of smaller vessels. Then came the Dutch in 1616, followed by the French in 1668. It was also about that time that the New London Company received its charter and started building in the area. The French also were very active; there was a trading post in Chandernagor, close to the East India Company, and a very substantial business empire in other parts of the country, of which Pondicherry was the capital. The Dutch opened a factory at Chinsurah, between Chandernagor and Hoogly. All these factories and trading posts were well fortified. It was the rivalry in Bengal between these companies and the nations they represented that led to the Battle of Plassey and Britain's eventual domination of India.

By the end of the century the East India Company was well established. It had raised a large and well-equipped standing army of British and native troops, operated its own justice system, and was in the process of forming a wide and comprehensive administrative network for the governing of the country. The local commanders of the Company had the power to raise troops as they wished and to arrange their own courts, at which the native employees of the company could be tried. They could be punished by imprisonment, whipping – in some instances, being whipped to death – or hanging. Europeans were also subject to the local Governor's tribunal, and more than one Englishman was hanged for piracy. The Company could, and did, proclaim martial law. Its powers appeared limitless. The Raj had come to stay, with not a few despots at the helm.

Yet for all their progress and the luxurious life they eventually carved out for themselves, the British paid the supreme penalty of early death: the climate was harsh and merciless, claiming the lives of men, women and children of all ages. Few were able to withstand its rigours; some died within months or even weeks of arriving in India. They died not only from disease and climate, but from the excess of alcohol to which they were driven in order to escape their unbearable life. There are countless English graves across the land, both soldiers and civilians, on the plains and in the hills. Tales of the orgies of the Indian Maharajas were not exclusively an Indian prerogative; there were those British, inclined to drink more than they should and take opium, who indulged their fantasies of Indian women. The President of the Bombay Council demanded a trumpet to be sounded to herald the serving of each course at dinner, followed by soft music playing whilst actually eating.

The history of India is rife with bloodshed and violence; the invasion by England, France, Portugal and others perpetuated the countrywide strife and terror. Britain insisted that whatever measures they implemented were beneficial to the Indians, who required enlightenment – though the natives might not have agreed. They were not slow to use force to achieve their desires. In 1905 the territory of North East Bengal was divided into Hindu and Muslim provinces, despite the widespread riots it caused. In 1919, a General Dyer ordered his troops to open fire on an unarmed and peaceful gathering in a park in Amritsar. Three hundred and seventy-nine people were killed: it was later called the Amritsar Massacre.

Punitive expeditions by the military were not uncommon; there were other major disturbances besides the Great Indian Mutiny of 1857. In 1751, in the Hindu kingdom of Trichinopoly, the British-allied Mohammad Ali was besieged and in danger of losing the battle, and also the Company's factory. In support of the Nawab, Robert Clive suggested a ruse to draw off some of the French soldiers who were supporting the besiegers: he led an attack on the fort at Arcot and the local ruler (and French puppet) Chandra Sahib. Clive's force of two hundred British soldiers and three hundred sepoys, with a few inexperienced officers, left only fifty British soldiers at Madras. Besieging the fort had the desired effect, and the local defenders fled without fighting, though they had twice Clive's numbers. Several thousand native troops were sent from Trichinopoly, so relieving Mohammad Ali, but in spite of this huge force opposing him, Clive continued to pursue the enemy. Though it continued to grow until it was ten times his own strength, yet Clive defeated them in the ensuing battle.

French troops were then sent from 'Trichy', and the conflict grew to enormous proportions – but Clive again prevailed and won the day again, though he had one man to every thirty of the enemy. In the battle of Arcot, several thousand Indians and French were killed. Three hundred British lost their lives.

The Sepoy Mutiny at Vellore took place in 1806 when the Madras Commander in Chief decreed the wearing of beards and sect marks was no longer permissible. On the morning of July 10, the garrison's fifteen hundred sepoys arose and confined the three hundred and eighty British soldiers in their barracks. Help came in the form of a squadron of the 19th Dragoons and a troop of Madras cavalry. Galloper guns blasted the main gates open while men climbed up the ramparts. The mutiny was quelled, the sepoy leaders hanged, and the rest of the mutineers imprisoned. A stone still stands in the cemetery by the entrance to the fort, in memory of the English who died there.

Pondicherry, a few miles from Madras, was in a constant state of turmoil, changing hands as many as ten times between the British and the French between 1634 and 1816, except for a four-year period when it was held by the Dutch. In 1816 it became a permanent French possession until India gained its independence in 1947.

These are but a few of the wars and upheavals during the colourful military history of the East India Company. Yet the English made many worthwhile and much-needed changes. Suttee – the practice of the living widow burning to death on her husband's funeral pyre – was forbidden in 1680, after which a wife could only be immolated with her dead husband by consent. Slavery also was forbidden, in 1683. The decision to make English the official language of the country was not universally popular; even more unpopular was the decision, under the 1856 General Enlistment Act, that all new recruits must agree to cross the oceans in ships if ordered to do so, though sailing across the *kala pawnee* (black water) was forbidden to orthodox Hindus by their religion. The first indication of trouble was the mutiny at Barrackpore in 1824, when the Indian troops in Bengal refused to go to Pegu, where they were needed to deal with civilian unrest, because it necessitated a five-day sea voyage. The incident sparked discontent in other parts of the country; it probably contributed to the Great Indian Mutiny of 1857.

The lust for riches and glory was paramount in the minds of many who sought to rule India; Sir Robert Clive was one who won fame and fortune there, earning himself a royal title and wealth beyond his wildest dreams: hundreds of thousands of pounds, and a very handsome pension of ten thousand pounds a year. In the early days, expeditions to the Spice Islands and the eastern countries made huge profits for the speculators, returning as much as sixty times the cost of financing the voyage. And, strangely, perhaps, there was never a concerted effort by the Indians, either the authorities or the general population, for independence from this foreign rule.

GLOSSARY

arrack fermented juice from the coco tree

atcha OK

babu Indian clerk

badmash rascal

baksheesh money given to beggars or a bribe or tip

bangi wallah sweeper

Banyan tree Indian fig tree

beadies cigarettes

bhistie water carrier

bibi Indian woman

bibikhana women's quarters

buck jow go away

bunduck rifle

burgoo porridge

burrah peg large whisky

bustee slum area

Chandi Chauk 'the richest street in the world' in Delhi

chaplis sandals

char and wads tea and cakes

charpoy string bed

charpoy-bashing sleeping

chaung stream

Chillan wallah an old soldier of the Chillan campaign

choky prison

chota babba young boy

chota hazri small breakfast

chowkidar watchman

chuberao keep quiet

dastar the custom (of bribery)

dhobi wallah laundryman

doab the country between two rivers

dood milk

durzi tailor

estaminet bar

feringhee a European, or foreigner

ghazi fanatic

gonga pouch backside

goojars thieves

gora log lord

grumble and grunt prostitute

havildar sergeant

hozoor master

idderao towards me

idderao jao ('Itherow towards me jow') come here, towards me go

jankers punishment

jao go

jawan soldier

jeldi – ek dum quickly – at once

jeldi duffey a quickie

jemadar Indian officer

jezaill long-barrelled rifle

kala bibi or **bibby** black woman

khabadar be careful

khansama house servant

khitmagar servant

khuds hills

lathi a stick, steel tipped, used by the police and about six feet long

loose wallah thief

maidan exercise ground or parade ground

maro kill

mofussil hinterland, in the sticks

muchli fish

mukkin butter

munshi teacher

muttee mud

naik corporal

napee barber

nullah ravine

OP Ack Observation Post Assistant

pan the leaf of the betel creeper, a mild stimulant

peepul tree great fig tree

pick a chip fall off your horse

pongo soldier

puggled drunk

puggled pawnee alcohol

punkah large overhead cloth fan pulled manually

Raj rule or reign

risaldar native cavalry officer

roti bread

rupee coin worth sixteen annas

sahib lord – to a gentleman

sepoy native soldier

shabash well done

Sirkar the government

sowar native horse soldier

subadar native officer corresponding to a captain

suttee the sacrifice by the faithful widow on her husband's funeral pyre

syce groom

tatty matting a mat shade

tiffin lunch

tonga two-wheeled vehicle towed by a pony

topee Pith or Wolseley helmet

tulwar native sword

tum sewer cabutch you son of a pig

undah egg